Advances in Image Processing, Artificial Intelligence and Intelligent Robotics

Advances in Image Processing, Artificial Intelligence and Intelligent Robotics

Guest Editors

Vladimir Tadić
Peter Odry

Basel • Beijing • Wuhan • Barcelona • Belgrade • Novi Sad • Cluj • Manchester

Guest Editors

Vladimir Tadić
Department of Mechanical Engineering
Technical College of Applied Sciences
Zrenjanin
Serbia

Peter Odry
Department of Control Engineering and Information Technology
University of Dunaujvaros
Dunaujvaros
Hungary

Editorial Office
MDPI AG
Grosspeteranlage 5
4052 Basel, Switzerland

This is a reprint of the Special Issue, published open access by the journal *Electronics* (ISSN 2079-9292), freely accessible at: https://www.mdpi.com/journal/electronics/special_issues/BFT3H4DQ2P.

For citation purposes, cite each article independently as indicated on the article page online and as indicated below:

Lastname, A.A.; Lastname, B.B. Article Title. *Journal Name* **Year**, *Volume Number*, Page Range.

ISBN 978-3-7258-3904-9 (Hbk)
ISBN 978-3-7258-3903-2 (PDF)
https://doi.org/10.3390/books978-3-7258-3903-2

© 2025 by the authors. Articles in this book are Open Access and distributed under the Creative Commons Attribution (CC BY) license. The book as a whole is distributed by MDPI under the terms and conditions of the Creative Commons Attribution-NonCommercial-NoDerivs (CC BY-NC-ND) license (https://creativecommons.org/licenses/by-nc-nd/4.0/).

Contents

About the Editors . . . . **vii**

Bojan Kuljic, Zoltan Vizvari, Nina Gyorfi, Mihaly Klincsik, Zoltan Sari, Florian Kovacs, et al.
An Effective and Robust Parameter Estimation Method in a Self-Developed, Ultra-Low Frequency Impedance Spectroscopy Technique for Large Impedances
Reprinted from: *Electronics* **2024**, *13*, 3300, https://doi.org/10.3390/electronics13163300 . . . . . **1**

Hao Huang and Kai Zhu
Automotive Parts Defect Detection Based on YOLOv7
Reprinted from: *Electronics* **2024**, *13*, 1817, https://doi.org/10.3390/electronics13101817 . . . . . **22**

Gaofan Ji, Yunhan He, Chuanxiang Li, Li Fan, Haibo Wang and Yantong Zhu
A Novel Multi-LiDAR-Based Point Cloud Stitching Method Based on a Constrained Particle Filter
Reprinted from: *Electronics* **2024**, *13*, 1777, https://doi.org/10.3390/electronics13091777 . . . . . **38**

Yingnan Zhang, Zhizhong Kang and Zhen Cao
An Image Retrieval Method for Lunar Complex Craters Integrating Visual and Depth Features
Reprinted from: *Electronics* **2024**, *13*, 1262, https://doi.org/10.3390/electronics13071262 . . . . . **55**

Zoltan Vizvari, Mihaly Klincsik, Peter Odry, Vladimir Tadic, Nina Gyorfi, Attila Toth and Zoltan Sari
Continuous Electrode Models and Application of Exact Schemes in Modeling of Electrical Impedance Measurements
Reprinted from: *Electronics* **2024**, *13*, 66, https://doi.org/10.3390/electronics13010066 . . . . . . **80**

Jin-Ung Ha, Hyun-Woo Kim, Myungjin Cho and Min-Chul Lee
A Method for Visualization of Images by Photon-Counting Imaging Only Object Locations under Photon-Starved Conditions
Reprinted from: *Electronics* **2024**, *13*, 38, https://doi.org/10.3390/electronics13010038 . . . . . . **98**

Chao-Chung Peng, Nai-Jen Cheng and Min-Che Tsai
Application of an Output Filtering Method for an Unstable Wheel-Driven Pendulum System Parameter Identification
Reprinted from: *Electronics* **2023**, *12*, 4569, https://doi.org/10.3390/electronics12224569 . . . . . **115**

Sun-Ho Jang, Woo-Jin Ahn, Yu-Jin Kim, Hyung-Gil Hong, Dong-Sung Pae and Myo-Taeg Lim
Stable and Efficient Reinforcement Learning Method for Avoidance Driving of Unmanned Vehicles
Reprinted from: *Electronics* **2023**, *12*, 3773, https://doi.org/10.3390/electronics12183773 . . . . . **132**

Mingju Chen, Zhengxu Duan, Lan Li, Sihang Yi and Anle Cui
A Two-Stage Image Inpainting Technique for Old Photographs Based on Transfer Learning
Reprinted from: *Electronics* **2023**, *12*, 3221, https://doi.org/10.3390/electronics12153221 . . . . . **151**

Ean-Gyu Han, Tae-Koo Kang and Myo-Taeg Lim
Physiological Signal-Based Real-Time Emotion Recognition Based on Exploiting Mutual Information with Physiologically Common Features
Reprinted from: *Electronics* **2023**, *12*, 2933, https://doi.org/10.3390/electronics12132933 . . . . . **168**

Mingju Chen, Tingting Liu, Xingzhong Xiong, Zhengxu Duan and Anle Cui
A Transformer-Based Cross-Window Aggregated Attentional Image Inpainting Model
Reprinted from: *Electronics* **2023**, *12*, 2726, https://doi.org/10.3390/electronics12122726 . . . . . **188**

Ameen Al-Azzawi and Gábor Lencse
Analysis of the Security Challenges Facing the DS-Lite IPv6 Transition Technology
Reprinted from: *Electronics* **2023**, *12*, 2335, https://doi.org/10.3390/electronics12102335 . . . . . **202**

Vladimir Tadic
Study on Automatic Electric Vehicle Charging Socket Detection Using ZED 2i Depth Sensor
Reprinted from: *Electronics* **2023**, *12*, 912, https://doi.org/10.3390/electronics12040912 . . . . . . **225**

About the Editors

Vladimir Tadić

Vladimir Tadić is an Assistant Professor with the Department of Mechanical Engineering, Electrical Engineering and Computer Science, Technical College of Applied Sciences in Zrenjanin, Serbia. He is a researcher, and he has been an Assistant Professor at the John von Neumann Faculty of Informatics, Obuda University. Additionally, he is a member of the Symbolic Methods in Material Analysis and Tomography Research Group at the Faculty of Engineering and Information Technology, University of Pecs, Hungary. He has held a researcher title at the Institute of Information Technology, University of Dunaujvaros, where he still participates in research work. He received his Graduade Engineer MSc, Magister, and PhD degrees in electrical engineering and computer science from the University of Novi Sad, Faculty of Technical Sciences, in 2004, 2009, and 2018, respectively. His research interests include digital image processing, computer vision, digital signal processing, biomedical image and signal processing, fuzzy logic, soft computing methods, biomatics, telecommunications, measurement methods, sensors, remote sensing, electronics, and robotics.

Peter Odry

Péter Odry is a Professor in the Department of Control Engineering and Information Technology, University of Dunaujvaros, Hungary. Also, he is a member of the Symbolic Methods in Material Analysis and Tomography Research Group at the Faculty of Engineering and Information Technology, University of Pecs. He received his MSc and PhD degrees in electrical engineering from the University of Belgrade in 1986 and 1992, respectively. His research interests include measurement technologies; impedance tomography; inverse problems; image and signal processing; remote sensing, system complete modelling, optimization, and validation; robotics; robust control techniques; and soft computing methods.

Article

An Effective and Robust Parameter Estimation Method in a Self-Developed, Ultra-Low Frequency Impedance Spectroscopy Technique for Large Impedances

Bojan Kuljic [1], Zoltan Vizvari [2,3,4], Nina Gyorfi [4,5], Mihaly Klincsik [3,6], Zoltan Sari [3,4,6], Florian Kovacs [7], Katalin Juhos [7], Tibor Szakall [1], Akos Odry [8,9], Levente Kovacs [10], Vladimir Tadic [3,11,12,13], Mirjana Siljegovic [14], Peter Odry [3,11,*] and Istvan Kecskes [11]

1. Depaertment of Informatics, Subotica Tech College of Applied Sciences, Marka Oreškovića 16, 24000 Subotica, Serbia; bojan@vts.su.ac.rs (B.K.); tibi@vts.su.ac.rs (T.S.)
2. Department of Environmental Engineering, Faculty of Engineering and Information Technology, University of Pecs, Boszorkany Str. 2, H-7624 Pecs, Hungary; vizvari.zoltan@mik.pte.hu
3. Symbolic Methods in Material Analysis and Tomography Research Group, Faculty of Engineering and Information Technology, University of Pecs, Boszorkany Str. 6, H-7624 Pecs, Hungary; klincsik.mihaly@mik.pte.hu (M.K.); sari.zoltan@mik.pte.hu (Z.S.); tadity.laszlo@uni-obuda.hu or vladimir.tadic@vts-zr.edu.rs (V.T.)
4. Multidisciplinary Medical and Engineering Cellular Bioimpedance Research Group, Szentagothai Research Centre, University of Pecs, Ifjusag Str. 20, H-7624 Pecs, Hungary; gyorfi.nina@pte.hu
5. Institute of Physiology, Medical School, University of Pecs, Szigeti Str. 12, H-7624 Pecs, Hungary
6. Department of Technical Informatics, Faculty of Engineering and Information Technology, University of Pecs, Boszorkany Str. 6, H-7624 Pecs, Hungary
7. Department of Agro-Environmental Studies, Hungarian University of Agriculture and Life Sciences, Villányi Str. 29-43, H-1118 Budapest, Hungary; kovacs.florian@phd.uni-mate.hu (F.K.); juhos.katalin@uni-mate.hu (K.J.)
8. Department of Mechatronics and Automation, Faculty of Engineering, University of Szeged, Moszkvai Krt. 9, H-6725 Szeged, Hungary; odrya@mk.u-szeged.hu
9. Department of Control Engineering and Information Technology, University of Dunaújváros, Táncsics Mihály u. 1, H-2400 Dunaújváros, Hungary
10. Physiological Controls Research Center, University Research and Innovation Center, Óbuda University, Becsi Str. 96/b, H-1034 Budapest, Hungary; kovacs@uni-obuda.hu
11. Institute of Information Technology, University of Dunaujvaros, Tancsics M. Str. 1/A, H-2401 Dunaujvaros, Hungary; kecskesi@uniduna.hu
12. John von Neumann Faculty of Informatics, Óbuda University, Becsi Str. 96/B, H-1034 Budapest, Hungary
13. Department of Mechanical Engineering, Electrical Engineering and Computer Science, Technical College of Applied Sciences in Zrenjanin, Đorđa Stratimirovića 23, 23000 Zrenjanin, Serbia
14. Department of Physics, Faculty of Sciences, University of Novi Sad, Trg Dositeja Obradovića 4, 21000 Novi Sad, Serbia; mirjana.siljegovic@df.uns.ac.rs
* Correspondence: podry@uniduna.hu

Abstract: Bioimpedance spectrum (BIS) measurements are highly appreciated in in vivo studies. This non-destructive method, supported by simple and efficient instrumentation, is widely used in clinical applications. The multi-frequency approach allows for the efficient extraction of the most information from the measured data. However, low-frequency implementations are still unexploited in the development of the technique. A self-developed BIS measurement technology is considered the pioneering approach for low (<5 kHz) and ultra-low (<100 Hz) frequency range studies. In this paper, the robustness of ultra-low frequency measurements in the prototypes is examined using specially constructed physical models and a dedicated neural network-based software. The physical models were designed to model the dispersion mainly in the ultra-low frequency range. The first set of models was used in the training of the software environment, while the second set allowed a complete verification of the technology. Further, the Hilbert transformation was employed to adjust the imaginary components of complex signals and for phase determination. The findings showed that the prototypes are capable of efficient and robust data acquisition, regardless of the applied frequency range, minimizing the impact of measurement errors. Consequently, in in vivo applications, these prototypes minimize the variance of the measurement results, allowing the resulting BIS data to provide a maximum representation of biological phenomena.

Keywords: bioimpedance spectrum; in vivo bioimpedance measurement; ultra-low frequency investigation; Hilbert transformation; phase errors

1. Introduction

Bioimpedance (BI) measurement is a well-known and commonly used non-destructive material investigation technique [1,2]. Besides being non-destructive, the method's attractiveness arises from its relatively simple and cost-effective instrumentation requirements, easy mass production, and efficient implementation procedures [2]. BI methods hold the promise of creating a portable, wearable spectrometer capable of performing numerous measurements virtually and invisibly at any time of day, even during physical activity [3]. Consequently, there is great interest in in vivo BI measurements, especially in human studies [4,5].

The method's popularity in this field depends on its ability to determine the in vivo body composition of test subjects using prototypes and commercially available devices that are simple, user-friendly, and highly standardized at the same time [1,2,6–8]. The body composition parameters that can be determined by BI measurements are extracellular fluid, intracellular fluid, total body water, fat mass, fat-free mass, etc. [4]. Monitoring these features provides new perspectives for valuable population studies in the field of public health [4]. For example, monitoring the whole-body content of multi-ethnic groups [9], integration into e-Health programs [10], application in the training of athletes [11], and other clinical applications [12] can be considered.

The implementation of modern BI measurements beyond a single frequency (50 kHz) supports multiple-frequency and BI spectrum-based data collection [4]. In such cases, an AC (alternating current) excitation signal at a very low amplitude is usually applied to dedicated surface electrodes through the biological system under investigation, while the other surface electrodes are used to record the parameters (potential or voltage) of the resulting electric field [4]. In the case of multi-frequency implementations, measurement systems have been developed to simultaneously apply several excitation signals of different frequencies, while others measure the BI spectrum using a swept sine signal [2,4]. BI spectroscopy (BIS) has several advantages over other technologies since it maximizes the amount of useful information extracted from the data to characterize biological structures [4]. The excitation frequency range for BIS equipment is usually systematically shifted between 5 kHz and a few hundred kHz [4]. Typically, the frequency domain below 5 kHz is referred to as the low-frequency range [4].

In this paper, measurements of high impedances are conducted to investigate whether the underlying BIS measurement procedure and the self-developed prototype are capable of detecting model parameters as accurately as possible over the full frequency range. In order to accomplish these tasks, a new neural network-based data processing software is developed. The neural networks have already been used to estimate the parameters of the impedance spectrum in solving the inverse problem [13]. In addition, the Hilbert transformation has been used for parameter estimation involving neural networks [14]; however, it has not been used for spectroscopic inverse problem solutions. When the Hilbert transformation is applied, it ensures that the corresponding real and imaginary components of the impedance spectra are appropriately selected during the optimization process. Selecting the real and imaginary spectra in this manner and then applying the inverse procedure results in a more accurate determination of the R and C values compared to not using the Hilbert transformation. This software extracts the model parameters from the imported BIS data. Based on [15], specific physical models have been developed that include the impedance of the excitation electrodes, as well as the impedance of the material under investigation based on the Cole–Cole model [16] for the realization of this study. Two groups of physical models, called phantoms, have been constructed. The first group is used for neural network training, while the second group is used to verify the accuracy and robustness of the technology through the integration of ultra-precise components. Besides developing BIS technology, application development is also actively in progress, which will lead to the primary use of self-developed prototypes in biotechnological and clinical applications.

2. Related Works

In the following section, a brief review of the relevant literature is presented. State-of-the-art in vivo BI measurement systems incorporate, naturally, multi-frequency operation, and the latest tendency is the development of hardware miniaturization and wearable systems [3]. In the clinical routine, in vivo hemodialysis [17] and, of course, body composition [4,5] monitoring devices have already appeared, which also allow the examination of individual body segments [18]. Wearable BIS devices are increasingly appearing in new areas such as muscle [3], human skin Pelotherapy effects [19], body fat percentage and glucose levels [20], or even smartwatch-based [21] monitoring systems.

An outstanding application for this study is human muscle in vivo studies [22], where BIS systems operating at low (<5 kHz) frequencies are often applied and not only in wearable form [22]. In the low-frequency ranges, where the so-called α-dispersion can be detected, the ionic diffusion of the cell membrane and the counterion effects can be investigated [23]. Pislaru-Danescu et al. [23] recognized the potential of low-frequency measurements and new perspectives, proposing a prototype with gold electrodes for the investigation of different human body segments in their publication. Scaliusi et al. also presented a prototype operating mostly below 50 kHz to monitor edema in the human leg using wearable hardware [24].

However, at the same time, it cannot be ignored that although low-frequency measurements open up a new perspective for BIS applications, it is in many ways a more difficult engineering challenge to create a precise and accurate instrument in this frequency range [24,25]. In addition to explaining the operation of the prototypes, Scaliusi et al. [24,25] provided a passive electrical model of the complete measurement system (electrodes and test material). Similarly, the impedance of the electrodes and the measuring wires are represented by RC components, suggesting that they may cause a significant error in the measurement data at low frequencies [24,25]. These effects are collectively referred to as errors caused by residual impedances.

Consequently, the BI measurements are unique because they detect not only the signal of the unknown material sample but also the impedance of the measuring circuit and even of the components of the instrument [24,25]. A further almost impenetrable problem is that the effect of the measurement artifacts also depends on the unknown impedance [24,25]. In general, however, research on the technology today is still focused on improving the signal-to-noise ratio and minimizing measurement artifacts [1,2]. The pure basic research described in our proposal aims to reverse this trend by placing the technology on a new measurement and mathematical basis [1,2]. Despite the great potential of the technology, BI methods today still have several technological limitations [1,2]. El Khaled et al. [26] described an exponential increase in the number of publications on BI over the last decade. Nevertheless, it can be stated that the technology is stagnating and there is a very strong demand for real basic research on the technology [26,27].

The authors of the current publication have been continuously improving a self-developed BI measurement technique over the last 10 years [28,29]. This special, modified four-electrode technique is designed to generate data with a low measurement using the minimal data processing procedure. This novel measurement technique is a potential comparison technique that can be successfully applied independently from the application of a current or voltage generator. The essence of the method is to obtain the unknown impedance from the measured potentials by comparing it with the reference resistance.

Thus, by taking the difference of the measured potentials, common mode rejection is achieved to minimize measurement errors and to suppress artifacts. The self-developed prototypes use this ground-breaking technique to measure at excitation frequencies between 1 mHz and 100 kHz, primarily to detect dispersion phenomena in the ultra-low (<100 Hz) frequency range of the substances. Nearly a decade of engineering research has resulted in a number of prototypes, which have been used to combine the experience gained with the construction of an ultra-precise digital lock-in amplifier with outstanding features.

The applications being developed by the authors are mainly oriented towards in vivo applications [28,30,31] of BIS measurements in addition to tomographic approaches [32]. For each of these applications, the measurement solutions are based on monitoring the α-dispersion (<100 Hz). In addition to the challenges of accurately realizing ultra-low frequency measurements, the impedance values to be measured usually vary over large ranges with high dynamic ranges (e.g., 100 kOhm–10 MOhm). All this concludes that effective and robust BIS measurements at ultra-low frequencies still remain a challenge for engineers involved in development today due to the residual impedances at low frequencies and the very high impedance values created by the polarization of biological structures [15,31]. In this paper, a technological approach is presented that is able to overcome these problems and provide the possibility of a reliable BIS measurement.

3. Materials and Methods
3.1. BIS Measurement Method

The BIS measurements utilize the modified four-electrode method presented in [15]. This specialized voltage comparison technique can be applied to both current and voltage generators. The core idea behind this implementation is to simultaneously suppress the high impedance (at low frequencies) of the excitation electrodes and the parasitic impedances of the measurement system during the measurement process. Consequently, this BI measurement technology is capable of eliminating the measurement artifacts discussed in Section 2, even at frequencies below 1 Hz, ensuring extremely accurate measurements. The technique achieves common-mode rejection of measurement artifacts by connecting the ground electrode directly to the measured material through a resistor, which raises the potential by a constant value. When calculating the impedance values, dividing the corresponding voltage and current values, along with eliminating the constant shift, results in highly efficient error suppression. Therefore, even at ultra-low frequencies (<10 Hz), the electrical properties of the measured material can be accurately recorded. The technology under investigation is a BI measurement system (Figure 1) developed by Vizvari et al. [15].

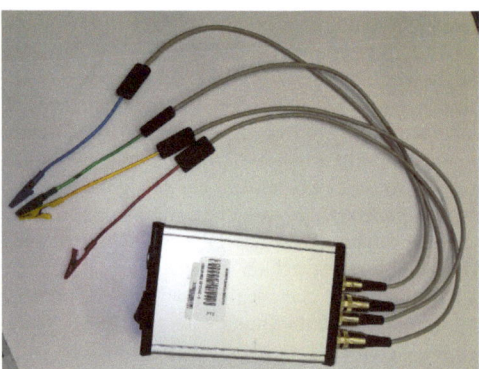

Figure 1. The developed BIS system.

The self-developed digital lock-in algorithm, which was built into the instrument, was developed and improved by further development of the software in [33] (especially with respect to measurement noise) for the four-channel instrument. Lock-in amplifiers detect the measured signal only in the immediate area close to the user-defined reference frequency while suppressing other frequency components very effectively. Hence, lock-in amplifiers can determine the amplitude and phase of the measured signal almost exclusively at the frequency of the excitation signal, even in cases of extremely poor signal-to-noise ratios [33]. However, the use of lock-in amplifiers is routine in the realization of multi-frequency BI measurements [2]. Therefore, the system presented in this paper has outstanding capabilities for ultra-low frequency measurements. The system is designed with the following properties:

- two sampling frequencies are used: in the range 10 kHz–100 kHz, fs = 375 kSample/s, while in the frequency range 1 mHz–10 kHz, the signals are sampled at fs = 37.5 kSample/s. If fs = 375 kSample/s is used, the data management of the real-time calculations is achieved by ping-pong buffering,
- in each decade, the number of excitation frequencies can be selected between three and 100 (the frequency values are selected at equal distances from the logarithmic scale),
- different integration times are used for each frequency, hence the duration of the measurements is different for each frequency decade,
- an excitation signal of the sinusoidal waveform in the frequency range from 1 mHz to 100 kHz with a Total Harmonic Distortion plus Noise (THDN+N) suppression greater than 100 dB,
- the excitation is generated by a voltage generator with a maximum noise of 1.5 = μV_{rms} in the frequency range from 1 mHz to 100 kHz,
- the maximum excitation voltage is 10 V peak-to-peak, which can be reduced by up to 110 dB (i.e., up to about 32 μV peak-to-peak),
- the precision (variance) of the measured data is better than 1 ppm for amplitude and better than $0.01°$ for phase (demonstrated in [29]).

The measuring system's compact dimensions (height: 55 mm, width: 100 mm, length: 170 mm) allow easy manual measurements. The robust construction and battery operation provide precise measurements. The maximum operating time of the measuring system is 6.5 h.

The BI measurement method implemented by the prototype (Figure 1) is the modified four-electrode technique developed by Vizvari et al. [29], which has been successfully applied in a variety of research. A schematic of the modified four-electrode measurement principle is shown in Figure 2.

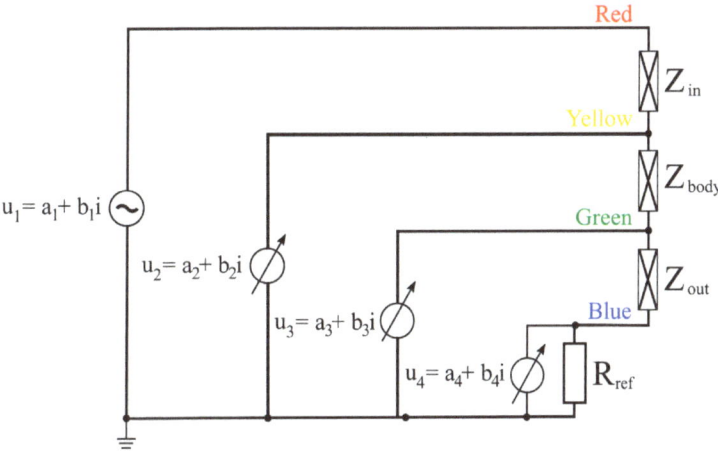

Figure 2. The BI measurement principle.

The purpose of the measurement is to determine the Z_{body} impedance value at several frequency points. The method is based on connecting the ground point (0 V) of the measuring system directly to the measured sample, and then recording the measured data (potential values) to this ground point during the data acquisition process. The efficiency of the method can be increased by incorporating a shunt resistor (R_{ref}). During data processing, the unknown impedance (Z_{body}) is obtained by comparison with the shunt resistor using the following calculation:

$$Z_{body} = \frac{u_2 - u_3}{u_4} \cdot R_{ref} \qquad (1)$$

The excitation of the test sample object is performed using a voltage generator, and the potential values u_2, u_3, and u_4 are measured. The accuracy and efficiency of the method come from the digital subtraction in Equation (1) of these potential data, which allows the method to significantly reduce the various errors in the measured data (using symmetrically balanced hardware).

In a previous study [29], the effectiveness of the measurement principle and its precision is demonstrated. In addition, further information can be found in [15].

3.2. BIS Phantoms

Previously [15], in order to demonstrate the advantageous properties of the technology, a physical model (BIS phantom) was created and applied. The phantoms were designed following the work of Fu et al. [27]. In this case, by evaluating the high-purity data collected during the measurement, the aim is to determine the model parameters of the different phantoms, i.e., the values of the electronic components (resistors and capacitors). By comparing the parameters extracted from the measurements with the values of the components used to make the phantoms, the accuracy and precision of the measurement procedure can be estimated.

The main aim of the phantom's design was to mimic the ultra-low frequency dispersion as accurately as possible, together with the measurement-related artifacts that may result from, for example, the high impedance of the electrodes. The phantom (Figure 3) is a passive electrical circuit that produces a typical ultra-low frequency impedance spectrum. The phantom shown in Figure 3 is built from commercially available resistors and capacitors.

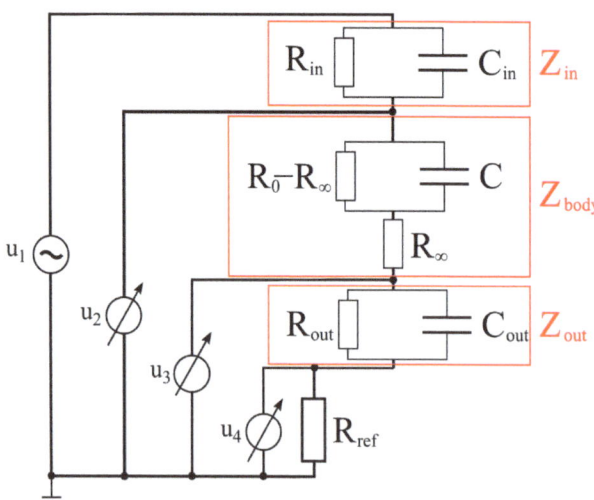

Figure 3. Schematic of the phantom circuit model [15,16].

The objective of this study is to measure the (Z_{body}), which includes resistive (R) and capacitive (C) elements, through single-pole, two-pole, and three-pole approximations. Additionally, the measurement results are influenced by the excitation contacts (Z_{in} and Z_{out}), whose effects are variable and unknown. In order to characterize the model parameters, it is necessary to estimate the R_0, R_∞, and C values from the measurement results.

In order to develop a robust algorithm, the system was simulated using phantom models that employ single-pole and two-pole circuits. Initially, the behavior of the cell culture with a single-pole model is approximated. The phantom includes R-C elements in order to simulate the excitation path. The schematic diagram of the phantom circuit is shown below.

In Figures 2 and 3, the voltages and their phases at points u_2, u_3, and u_4 can be measured with precision impedance measurement instruments. In total, 38 phantoms have been created for the current study. The key aspect in the design of these phantoms was ensuring that the generated pole and zero frequencies spanned nearly the entire frequency range (Table 1) of the measurement system, especially the ultra-low frequencies. This also allows the efficiency of the technology to be investigated over the entire frequency range, even for relatively high impedances.

Table 1. Specification of Measurements Circuits.

Phantom Number	R_{in} [kΩ]	C_{in} [uF]	R_∞ [kΩ]	R_0-R_∞ [kΩ]	R_0 [kΩ]	C [uF]	R_{out} [kΩ]	C_{out} [uF]
01	100	1	1	1	2	0.47	100	1
02	10	10	1	3.7	4.7	2.2	10	10
03	30	1	1	10	11	9.1	30	1
04	50	0.1	1	18	19	56	50	0.1
05	75	1	1	27	28	370	75	1
06	100	1	1	1	2	370	10	10
07	200	0.1	1	2.7	3.7	0.2	75	10
08	5	30	1	4.1	5.1	1	50	1
09	10	0.2	1	6	7	500	30	5
10	30	20	1	9	10	250	20	2
11	50	0.5	1	13	14	3	10	3
12	75	10	1	20	21	6	5	3
13	100	1	1	30	31	150	200	2
14	200	5	1	45	46	90	10	5
15	5	2	1	67	68	12	30	1
16	10	3	1	99	100	20	20	10
17	30	3	1	81	82	0.1	50	0.5
18	50	2	1	55	56	47	75	20
19	75	5	1	25	26	4.7	100	0.2
20	100	1	1	11	12	100	20	30
21	200	10	1	5	6	75	30	0.1
31	100	100	102	210	312	0.0002	100	100
32	100	100	93	402.1	495.1	0.0022	100	100
33	100	100	75	604	679	0.033	100	100
34	100	100	51.1	806	857.1	0.47	100	100

Table 1. Cont.

Phantom Number	R_{in} [kΩ]	C_{in} [uF]	$R_∞$ [kΩ]	$R_0-R_∞$ [kΩ]	R_0 [kΩ]	C [uF]	R_{out} [kΩ]	C_{out} [uF]
35	100	100	30.1	999.9	1030	0.94	100	100
36	100	100	10	1000	1010	0.0002	100	100
37	100	100	30.1	805.9	836	0.0022	100	100
38	100	100	51.1	604	655.1	0.033	100	100
39	100	100	71.5	400.5	472.0	0.48	100	100

The aim was to train a robust system that can accurately estimate the values of C and R_0 from these measured voltages, regardless of the values set for the resistances C_{in}, R_{in}, C_{out}, and R_{out}. The voltage measurements are taken at the following frequencies: fk = $10^{-1.8 + k0.2}$ and k = {0, 1, ..., 33}, which logarithmically span from 0.016 Hz to 63,000 Hz across 34 values (see Table 2), and these are available for all the measurement samples. The angular frequency for each measurement is given as $ω_k = 2πf_k$.

The measurements were taken in the form of a complex number:

$$Z = a + bi$$
$$|Z| = \sqrt{a^2 + b^2}, \; Re(Z) = a, \; Im(Z) = b \quad (2)$$
$$θ = \tan^{-1}\left(\frac{b}{a}\right)$$

where $|Z|$ is the magnitude and $θ$ is the phase.

The impedance measurements were transformed as follows:

Table 2. Measurement points and their transformation (TR—used for training).

Abbreviation	Equation	Description	Unit	Usage
U_1	$U_1 = a_1 + b_1 i$	See Figure 2, complex format	V	
U_2	$U_2 = a_2 + b_2 i$	See Figure 2, complex format	V	
U_3	$U_3 = a_3 + b_3 i$	See Figure 2, complex format	V	
U_4	$U_4 = a_4 + b_4 i$	See Figure 2, complex format	V	
$U_1 p_4 ph$	$= \tan^{-1}\left(\frac{Im(U_1 \cdot U_4^*)}{Re(U_1 \cdot U_4^*)}\right)$	U_1/U_4 phase	Rad	TR
$U_2 p_4 ph$	$= \tan^{-1}\left(\frac{Im(U_2 \cdot U_4^*)}{Re(U_2 \cdot U_4^*)}\right)$	U_2/U_4 phase	Rad	TR
$U_3 p_4 ph$	$= \tan^{-1}\left(\frac{Im(U_3 \cdot U_4^*)}{Re(U_3 \cdot U_4^*)}\right)$	U_3/U_4 phase	Rad	TR
$U_{32} p_4 ph$	$\overline{= \tan^{-1}\left(\frac{Im((U_2-U_3) \cdot U_4^*)}{Re((U_2-U_3) \cdot U_4^*)}\right)}$	$(U_2 - U_3)/U_4$ phase	Rad	TR
$Log10(U_1 p_4 mag)$	$= \log_{10}\left(\frac{|U_1 \cdot U_4^*|}{\sqrt{a_4^2 + b_4^2}}\right)$	Logarithm transform of U_1/U_4 magnitude		TR
$Log10(U_2 p_4 mag)$	$= \log_{10}\left(\frac{|U_2 \cdot U_4^*|}{\sqrt{a_4^2 + b_4^2}}\right)$	Logarithm transform of U_2/U_4 magnitude		TR
$Log10(U_3 p_4 mag)$	$= \log_{10}\left(\frac{|U_3 \cdot U_4^*|}{\sqrt{a_4^2 + b_4^2}}\right)$	Logarithm transform of U_3/U_4 magnitude		TR
$Log10(U_{32} p_4 mag)$	$\overline{= \log_{10}\left(\frac{|(U_2-U_3) \cdot U_4^*|}{\sqrt{a_4^2 + b_4^2}}\right)}$	Logarithm transform of $(U_2 - U_3)/U_4$ magnitude		TR

3.3. Simulation Model

A mathematical model in MATLAB R2023b was developed in order to express the complex impedance using complex numbers, where the real part represents the ohmic resistance and the imaginary part represents the reactance.

The mathematical model of the circuit shown in Figure 3 was implemented in the MATLAB environment. This model served two primary purposes:

1. first, to verify the accuracy of the measurements and the selected R and C values,
2. second, to generate a large training database necessary for training the estimation system.

These aspects are detailed in the following two subsections.

The outputs of the model include the calculated impedance values and the corresponding phase angles at different points in the circuit, providing a comprehensive dataset for both validation and training purposes.

The model relies on operations with complex numbers, a functionality that is well-supported in MATLAB. The inputs to the model are the following:

- input and output impedances: R_{in}, R_{out}, C_{in}, C_{out}
- body model impedance: R_∞, R_0, C
- shunt resistance: $R_s = 96,000\ \Omega$
- supply voltage: $U_1 = 12$ V
- frequency series: $f = [63,000,\ 39,750,\ \ldots,\ 0.016]$ Hz

The equations for the impedances are described in Equation (3), Equation (4) is the current, and Equation (5) represents the voltages and their ratios.

$$Z_{in}(f) = \frac{1}{\frac{1}{R_{in}} + i2\pi f C_{in}}$$
$$Z_{out}(f) = \frac{1}{\frac{1}{R_{out}} + i2\pi f C_{out}} \qquad (3)$$
$$Z_{body}(f) = R_\infty + \frac{1}{\frac{1}{R_0 - R_\infty} + i2\pi f C}$$

$$I = \frac{U_1}{Z_{in} + Z_b + Z_{out}} \qquad (4)$$

$$U_4 = R_s I$$
$$U_3 = (Z_{out} + R_s) I$$
$$U_2 = (Z_b + Z_{out} + R_s) I$$
$$U_{32} = Z_b I \qquad (5)$$
$$U_{1p4} = \frac{U_1}{U_4}$$
$$U_{2p4} = \frac{U_2}{U_4}$$
$$U_{3p4} = \frac{U_3}{U_4}$$
$$U_{32p4} = \frac{U_{32}}{U_4}$$

3.4. Training Database

Using this model, a database is generated that is compatible with the measurements. This means that the same outputs were calculated (U_{1p4}, U_{2p4}, U_{3p4}, and U_{32p4} in polar format, i.e., magnitude + phase form) at the same frequencies (Table 2), using the same supply voltage and shunt resistance ($U1$, Rs). However, the variable electronic components (R_0, C, R_{in}, R_{out}, C_{in}, and C_{out}) differ from those in the measurements and cover a slightly broader range. It was ensured that the training and validation datasets contained different R_0 and C values. This separation is crucial to ensure that the neural network (NN) model's training and validation sets are independent of each other, preventing overfitting.

Table 3 summarizes the statistics of the generated database. The datasets were generated using a combinatorial approach, where every value of R_{in} and C_{in} with every value of

R_0 and C were combined. Consequently, the sizes of the training (TR) and validation (VA) datasets are as follows:

$$n(TR) = n(Rin_{TR}) \cdot n(Cin_{TR}) \cdot n(R0_{TR}) \cdot n(C_{TR}) = 9 \cdot 7 \cdot 36 \cdot 31 = 70308$$
$$n(VA) = n(Rin_{VA}) \cdot n(Cin_{VA}) \cdot n(R0_{VA}) \cdot n(C_{VA}) = 7 \cdot 4 \cdot 22 \cdot 26 = 16016 \quad (6)$$

Table 3. Training database elements.

Element	Set	Size	Value set	Unit	m-Equation
R_{in}, R_{out}	TR	9	5, 10, 20, 30, 50, 100, 200, 300, 500	kΩ	
	VA	7	7, 15, 25, 40, 75, 150, 250	kΩ	
C_{in}, C_{out}	TR	7	0.1, 0.3, 1, 3, 10, 30, 100	μF	
	VA	4	0.2, 2, 20, 200	μF	
R_0	TR	36	1.2, 1.5, 1.8, 2.2, 2.7, 3.3, 4.1, 5.0, 6.0, 7.4, 9.0, 11.0, 13.5, 16.4, 20.1, 24.5, 30.0, 36.6, 44.7, 54.6, 66.7, 81.5, 99.5, 121.5, 148.4, 181.3, 221.4, 270.4, 330.3, 403.4, 492.7, 601.8, 735.1, 897.8 1096.6, 1339.4	kΩ	Roundn (exp(0.2:0.2:7.2),−1) × 10^3
	VA	22	1.2, 1.6, 2.3, 3.2, 4.4, 6.2, 8.6, 12.0, 16.7 23.3, 32.6, 45.5, 63.4, 88.5 123.6, 172.4, 240.6, 335.9, 468.7, 654.1, 912.9 1274.1	kΩ	Roundn (exp(0.15:1/3:7.25),−1) × 10^3
C	TR	31	0.0001, 0.0002, 0.0003, 0.0006, 0.0009 0.0015, 0.0025, 0.0041, 0.0067, 0.0111, 0.0183, 0.0302, 0.0498, 0.0821 0.1353, 0.2231, 0.3679, 0.6065 1, 1.6487, 2.7183, 4.4817, 7.3891 12.182, 20.085, 33.115, 54.598, 90.017 148.41, 244.69, 403.43	μF	Roundn (exp(−9:0.5:6),−4) × 1×10^{-6}
	VA	26	0.0002, 0.0003, 0.0005, 0.0009, 0.0017, 0.0030, 0.0055, 0.0101, 0.0183, 0.0334, 0.0608 0.1108, 0.2019, 0.3679, 0.6703 1.2214, 2.2255, 4.0552, 7.3891 13.464, 24.532, 44.701, 81.451 148.41, 270.43, 492.75	μF	Roundn (exp(−8.8:0.6:6.2),−4) × 1×10^{-6}
R_s	-	1	96	kΩ	
R_∞	TR	11	1, 1.6, 2.7, 4.5, 7.4 12.2, 20.1, 33.1, 54.6, 90, 148.4	kΩ	Roundn (exp(0:0.5:5),−1) × 10^3
	VA	8	1.2, 2.5, 5 10, 20.1, 40.4, 81.5, 164	kΩ	Roundn (exp(0.2:0.7:5.2),−1) × 10^3

The R_∞ was circularly repeated for each combination, but with constrains of $R_0 > R_\infty$. The R_{out} and C_{out} values were not the same as R_{in} and C_{in} since they were chosen randomly from the same set of values. However, this random selection pattern remained consistent across all variations of R_0 and C.

3.5. Neural Network

A small convolutional neural network (CNN) with inputs consisting of various voltage ratios and outputs providing the estimated values of R_0, R_∞, and C was designed. In order to make the neural network's estimation system more linear, the network estimates the logarithm base $log10$ of the output values ($log10(R_0)$, $log10(R_\infty)$, and $log10(C)$).

Two metrics were used in order to measure the performance:

- RMS: The root mean square error of the estimates [34].
- Pearson: The Pearson correlation coefficient of the estimates [35].

These metrics were calculated for either the training set (TR), the validation set (VA), or the test set (TE). The training and validation sets were generated through simulation, while the test set was derived from actual measurements.

A simple 10-layer CNN was designed for the regression task of estimating $log10(R_0)$, $log10(R_\infty)$, and $log10(C)$ (see Figure 4). The input layer accepts two sets of 34 polar numbers, derived from voltage measurements. Following the input layer, there are three convolutional layers with filter sizes of [15 1], [11 1], and [7 1] and corresponding filter counts of 24, 31, and 35, each followed by a Leaky ReLu activation function [36]. These layers are succeeded by two fully connected layers, the first with 126 units and the second with three units, representing the estimated R_0, R_∞, and C values. The training of this CNN is performed using the Adam optimizer [37], which ensures efficient and effective convergence during the learning process.

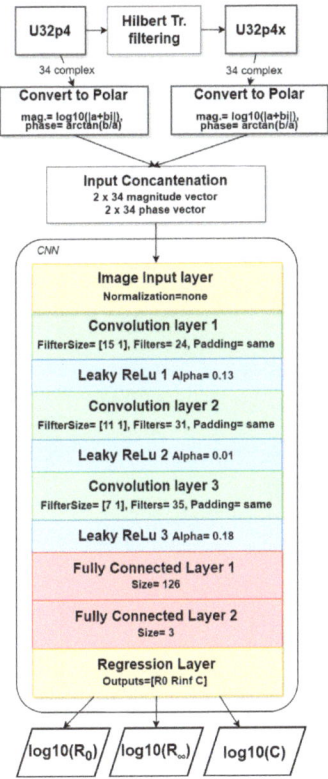

Figure 4. The optimized CNN architecture.

The Leaky ReLu is a parameterized ReLu layer, which works as follows [36]:

$$y = LeakyReLu(x, Alpha) = \begin{cases} x & x > 0 \\ x \cdot Alpha & x \leq 0 \end{cases} \quad (7)$$

The parameters of the CNN are organized in a structure named *param*, which is summarized in Table 4.

Table 4. The CNN configuration.

NN Parameter	Description	Value Range	Initial	Optimum
Hilb	Hilbert Rule Control in complex input signals	0–0.3	0.05	0.1
convSize (1)	Filter size in convolution layer 1	10–25	20	15
convSize (2)	Filter size in convolution layer 2	7–18	14	11
convSize (3)	Filter size in convolution layer 3	3–10	5	7
numFilters (1)	Number of filters in convolution layer 1	10–40	25	24
numFilters (2)	Number of filters in convolution layer 2	10–40	25	31
numFilters (3)	Number of filters in convolution layer 3	10–40	25	35
leakyRelu (1)	Scale of leaky rectified linear unit layer 1	0–0.2	0.1	0.13687
leakyRelu (2)	Scale of leaky rectified linear unit layer 2	0–0.2	0.1	0.01749
leakyRelu (3)	Scale of leaky rectified linear unit layer 3	0–0.2	0.1	0.18037
fullySize (1)	Output size of fully connected layer 1	50–250	64	126
fullySize (2)	Output size of fully connected layer 2	3 (fix)	3	3
initLR	Initial Learn Rate	$1 \times 10^{-4} : 5 \times 10^{-3}$	0.001	0.001
MiniBatchSize	number of samples used in each iteration of the training algorithm	50–400	128	103
LRdropfactor	Learn Rate Drop Factor—factor by which the learning rate is reduced during training at specified drop periods	0.3–0.9	0.6	0.35138
LRdropperiod	Learn Rate Drop Period	1 (fix)	1	1
MaxEpochs	maximum number of training epochs	7 (fix)	7	7

The NN parameters were optimized using a Particle Swarm Optimization (PSO) algorithm [38] in order to achieve the highest possible performance. The algorithm was developed and used in earlier research [39]. The resulting optimized parameters are listed in the last row of Table 3. Later, these parameters were used in training the final NN.

3.6. Hilbert Transformation Filter

The Hilbert transformation allows the generation of an analytic signal, which is valuable in telecommunications for bandpass signal processing, particularly referring to the continuous-time analytic signal [40–42]. An analytic signal is a complex-valued function with non-negative spectral components [41]. The real and imaginary parts of an analytic signal are real-valued functions related by the Hilbert transformation filter.

This technique is used to acquire the minimum-phase response from a spectral analysis, making it convenient for analyzing the signal phase [42]. The Hilbert transformation can estimate the phase and magnitude of an input signal [43–48]. A common method of phase reconstruction, based on the Hilbert transformation, can only reconstruct the interpretable phase from a limited class of signals, such as narrow-band signals [48].

In signal processing, the Hilbert transformation is a linear operator that obtains a function $g(t)$ and creates a function $H(g(t))$ in the same domain [41–45]:

$$H(g(t)) = g(t) * \frac{1}{\pi t} = \frac{1}{\pi}\int_{-\infty}^{\infty} \frac{g(\tau)}{t-\tau} d\tau \qquad (8)$$

In Equation (8), H denotes the Hilbert transformation and * denotes the convolution operation.

In the frequency domain, the Hilbert transformation can be written as follows [41–48]:

$$F(H(g(t))) = G(\omega)F\left(\frac{1}{\pi t}\right) = G(\omega)H(\omega) \qquad (9)$$

where "F" denotes the Fourier transform, and $H(\omega)$ can be calculated with the following expression:

$$F\left(\frac{1}{\pi t}\right) = H(\omega) = -j\,sgn(\omega) = \begin{cases} -j, & \omega > 0 \\ 0, & \omega = 0 \\ j, & \omega < 0 \end{cases} \qquad (10)$$

The Hilbert transformation in the time domain results in a $\frac{\pi}{2}$ phase-shift operator between the input and output signal; therefore, it could be applied as a phase-shifting procedure in a defined bandwidth of interest [46–48].

Further, a standard method for reconstructing the instantaneous phase from a signal is based on the Hilbert transformation [44,46,48]. This method calculates the phase from the analytic signal:

$$\zeta(t) = g(t) + j(H(g(t))) \qquad (11)$$

where $g(t)$ is the observed signal, $H(g(t))$ is its Hilbert transformation, and $\zeta(t)$ is an analytic signal. Hence, for realizable systems, the Hilbert transform links the real and imaginary parts of the signal, with the imaginary part being the Hilbert transformation of the signal's real part [44–48]. This is an important relationship that allows the analysis of the given signal $g(t)$ through the Hilbert transformation. In addition, the Hilbert transformation is also employed to connect the gain and phase characteristics of linear communication channels and minimum-phase filters [45,47].

Thus, the Hilbert transformation reconstructs the instantaneous phase with the argument of the analytic signal (11) as follows:

$$\phi^H = \arg[\zeta(t)] = \tan^{-1}\frac{H(g(t))}{g(t)} \qquad (12)$$

where ϕ^H is the obtained phase using the Hilbert transformation [48].

Further, the instantaneous envelope or magnitude of the analytic signal is given as:

$$|\zeta(t)|^H = \sqrt{(g(t))^2 + (H(g(t)))^2} \qquad (13)$$

where $|\zeta(t)|^H$ represents the obtained magnitude using the Hilbert transformation.

As can be seen in both, the envelope and phase are available as functions of time and if $g(t)$ is known, then $H(g(t))$ can be calculated [44–50]. In certain applications, the instantaneous amplitude and phase often are utilized to measure and detect the local features of the signal, which can result in a correction of the signal itself using its real and imaginary parts [46].

The Hilbert transformation [40] was utilized in order to correct the imaginary parts of complex signals. Essentially, from the real part, the Hilbert transformation creates a quasi-imaginary signal, which is then used to slightly modify (by β = 10%) the original imaginary part. By including this modified complex voltage ratio signal into the neural network, better results can be achieved. If the Hilbert transformation is not used, the real and imaginary parts of the impedance are treated independently by the optimization procedure, without consideration of the physical relationship between them since there is nothing to connect them. Therefore, when the Hilbert transformation is used, it helps to ensure that the corresponding real and imaginary parts of the impedance spectra are selected during the optimization process [44–48]. The real and imaginary spectra selected in this way, when subjected to the inverse procedure, result in a better pair of R and C values than if the Hilbert transformation had not been used. This is also confirmed by the results presented later in Table 5. It is particularly interesting that, even without optimization, the R and C values derived from the real and imaginary spectra linked by the Hilbert transformation are better than those obtained without using the Hilbert transformation. The U_{32p4x} is derived from the U_{32p4} measured complex signal as follows (14):

$$U_{32p4} = a + bi$$
$$U_{32p4x} = a + ((1-\beta)b + \beta H(a))i \tag{14}$$

where the H is the Hilbert transformation, a and b represent the real and imaginary parts of the signal, respectively, and β is the modification factor.

Table 5. RMS Error statistics of the best CNN instances, calculated between nominal values and estimated values in the logarithmic domain. R_0 and R_∞ are expressed as $rms(log10(k\Omega))$ and C is expressed as $rms(log10(\mu F))$.

CNN Instance	Hilbert Filtering	TR			VA			TE		
		R_0	R_∞	C	R_0	R_∞	C	R_0	R_∞	C
Initial CNN architecture (cnn_init_ch_U32p4)	No	0.014	0.047	0.070	0.021	0.039	0.072	0.032	0.024	0.175
Initial CNN architecture (cnn_init_ch_U32p4U32p4x)	Yes	0.012	0.045	0.068	0.018	0.033	0.075	0.033	0.020	0.146
Optimized CNN architecture (cnn_opt_ch_U32p4)	No	0.012	0.046	0.073	0.019	0.037	0.072	0.033	0.020	0.155
Optimized CNN architecture (cnn_opt_ch_U32p4U32p4x)	Yes	0.010	0.042	0.069	0.014	0.038	0.065	0.030	0.017	0.143

Hilbert transformation helps with the accurate phase determination of the signal [44–48]. With the adjustment of the imaginary part of the complex signal using the Hilbert-transformed real part, phase errors can be achieved, leading to more accurate impedance measurements. Moreover, the inherent characteristics of the original signal are maintained by the Hilbert transformation, which slightly modifies the imaginary part (by 10% in this case). The use of the Hilbert transformation in the proposed methodology is not solely for noise reduction, but rather to leverage the relationship between the real and imaginary parts of the signal [49,50]. The Hilbert transformation applies a mathematical rule that inherently links the real and imaginary components, potentially enhancing the signal's interpretability for the neural network. Even in synthetic data, this transformation can serve as a form of regularization, ensuring that the network learns a more generalized model that can handle variations in real-world data more effectively. This approach is based on the hypothesis that the Hilbert transformation helps the network to better understand the underlying phase relationships in the data, which are crucial for accurate impedance measurements [46–48]. By doing so, the essential properties of the original complex signal are retained while the influence of outliers and measurement errors is reduced.

4. Results

4.1. Verification of the Electronics Setup

Additionally, the model was used to perform calculations with the values corresponding to the measurements (Table 1) in order to assess the accuracy of the electronic boards compared to their nominal values. Figure 5 shows the statistical distribution of the RMS error calculated between the measurements and simulation. Figures 4 and 5 represent two types of samples, relatively accurate and typical non-accurate samples.

The distribution shown in Figure 5 is calculated across the available measurements with the actual Phantom circuit.

These comparisons in Figures 6 and 7 revealed that some electronic boards showed significant discrepancies between the measurement and simulation results, specifically phantom boards 4, 5, and 9. This suggests that the components on these electronic phantom boards do not match their nominal values for some reason, with a small likelihood that the measurement instrument itself is faulty. These boards were set aside for further inspection and they were excluded from further testing.

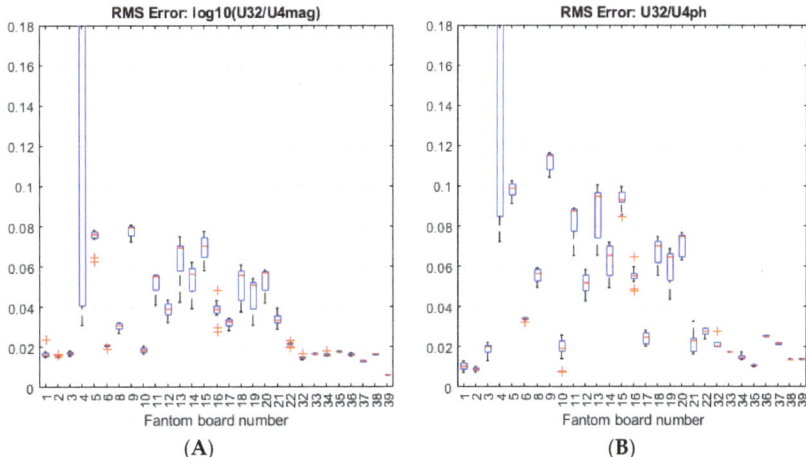

Figure 5. Root mean square (RMS) error statistics between measurements and the simulation along the Phantom circuits: (**A**) the logarithmic magnitude error is on the left side, derived from a log10(U32/U4) signal; (**B**) the phase error is on the right side, derived from U32/U4 signals. The lower error values represent a higher similarity between measurements and the simulation by nominal R_0, R_∞, and C values. The new set of Phantom circuits (32–39) shows consistently low errors compared to the previous set of circuits.

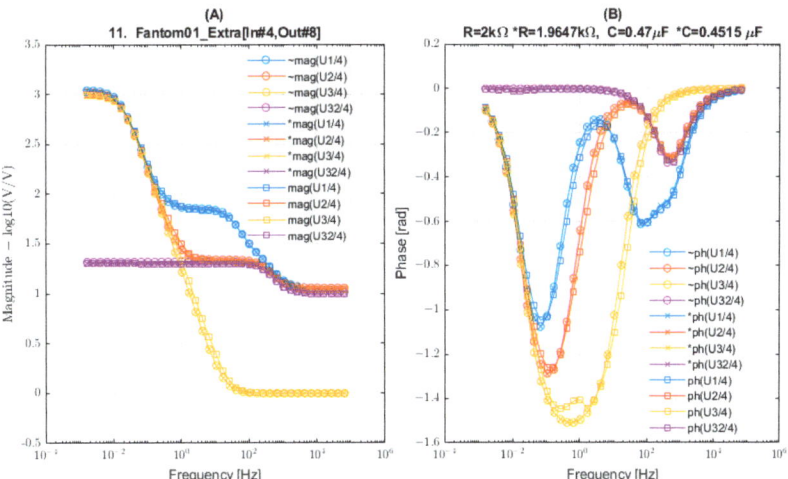

Figure 6. An example of a relatively accurate measurement. Three sets of measurements are compared: ~mag(U) and ~ph(U) represent the simulated results using nominal values (R = 2 kΩ, C = 0.47 µF); *mag(U) and *ph(U) represent the simulated results using values estimated by the NN (*R = 1.9647 kΩ, *C = 0.4515 µF); mag(U) and ph(U) represent the measurements. (**A**) The left graph compares the magnitude signals and (**B**) the right graph compares the phase signals.

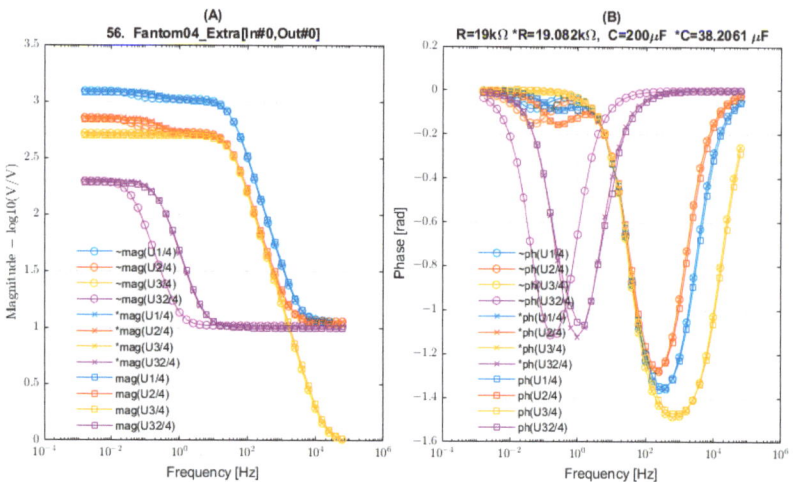

Figure 7. An example of a relatively inaccurate measurement. Three sets of measurements are compared: ~mag(U) and ~ph(U) represent the simulated results using nominal values (R = 19 kΩ, C = 200 µF); *mag(U) and *ph(U) represent the simulated results using values estimated by the NN (*R = 19.082 kΩ, *C = 38.206 µF); mag(U) and ph(U) represent the measurements. (**A**) The left graph compares the magnitude signals and (**B**) the right graph compares the phase signals.

Additionally, new boards were fabricated (phantoms 31–38) and equipped with high-precision components, and such differences were no longer observed. This confirmed that the discrepancies were due to the wide tolerance ranges of the original electronic components.

4.2. Estimation Results with Neural Networks

The neural networks were trained with several input signals (Table 2) in the first round of benchmarks. The network identified the key measurement input corresponding to the Z_{body} impedance voltage, specifically U_{32}, and its normalized form, $U_{32}p4$.

In the second round of the benchmark, the NN architecture and the hyperparameters were optimized, which are listed in Table 4.

The performance was improved when the network included these corrected measurements alongside the enhanced signals processed through the Hilbert filter. This approach ensures that the neural network receives more refined input data, leading to improved accuracy in estimating the resistance and capacitance values.

In Table 5, TR represents the results of the training set, VA represents the results of the validation set, and TE represents the results of the external test set (the real measurements). The measurement unit of resistance error (R_0 and R_∞) is $log10(k\Omega)$ and the measurement unit of capacitor error (C) is $log10(\mu F)$. As shown in Table 5, the real and imaginary spectra selected through the proposed method yield a superior pair of R and C values when subjected to the inverse procedure compared to the results obtained without using the Hilbert transformation.

The best model has been selected as cnn_opt_ch_U32p4U32p4x. This NN model used, as inputs, the U_{32}/U_4 voltages in polar format (U_{32p4}) and their filtered version with Hilbert transformation (U_{32p4x}). The regression analysis is demonstrated in Figure 8. The typical error levels vary along the spectrum and the lower range of R_∞ and C are more difficult to estimate. In contrast, the higher range of R_0 has higher error levels. There are several larger errors in the external test statistics, especially at C, that were due to the Phantom circuits having uncertain values due to high tolerance electronic elements. The explanation of this error is discussed in Section 5.

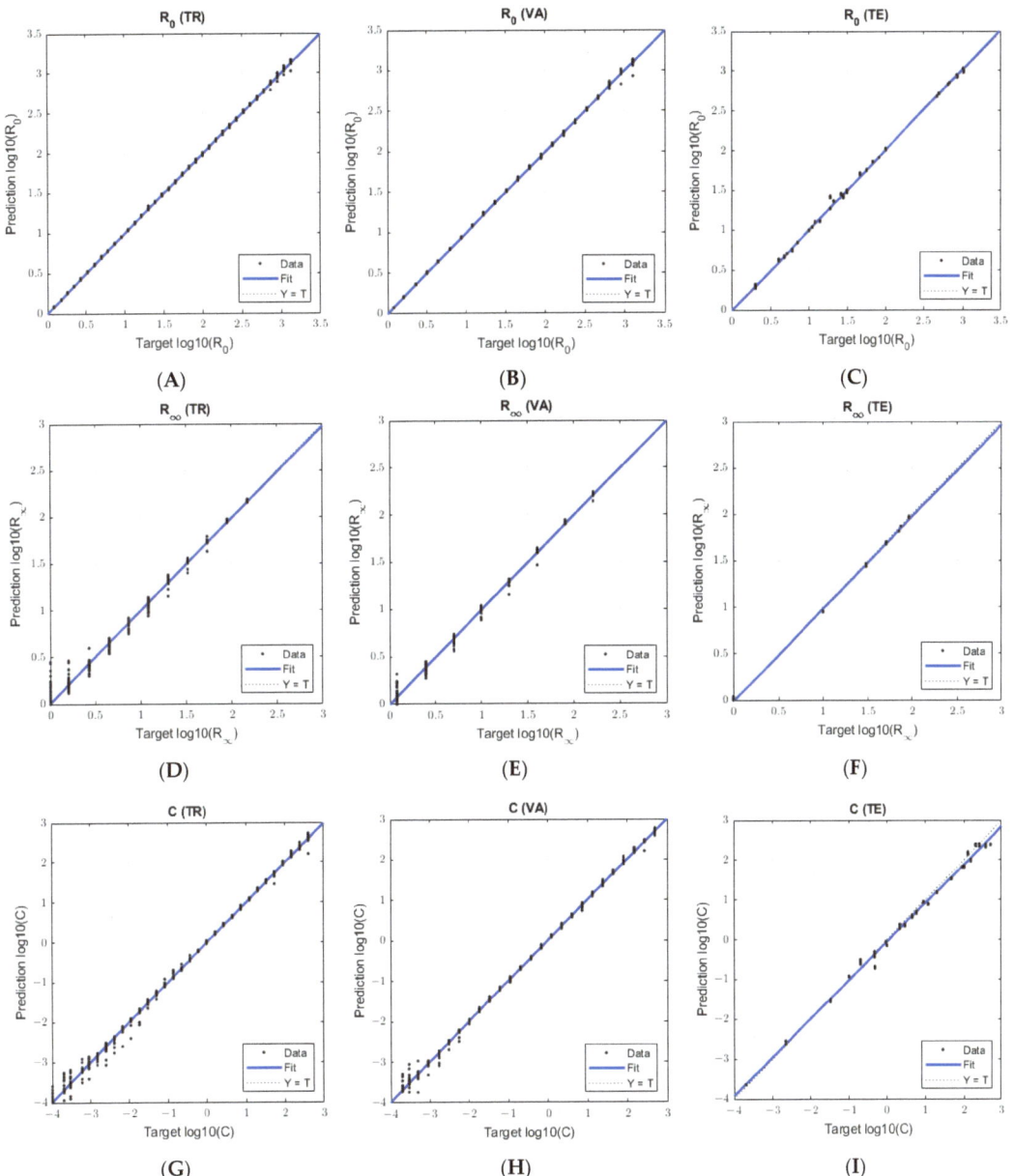

Figure 8. Regression performance analysis of the proposed CNN models: (**A**) R_0 resistor estimation for training set; (**B**) R_0 resistor estimation for validation set; (**C**) R_0 resistor estimation for test set; (**D**) R_∞ resistor estimation for training set; (**E**) R_∞ resistor estimation for validation set; (**F**) R_∞ resistor estimation for test set; (**G**) shows capacitor estimation for training set; (**H**) shows capacitor estimation for validation set; (**I**) shows capacitor estimation for test set—this is where the nominal value differences cause bigger deviations, as discussed in the Discussion section.

Table 6 lists examples from the external set of measurements, showing the estimated or recovered values from the two optimized CNN models identified in Table 5. The variability between different neural network models can be observed in both resistor and capacitor estimations. Capacitor values are commonly estimated to be slightly lower than the nominal values, as seen in a logarithmic format in the graph in Figure 8I. This small bias is observed between the simulation and real measurements.

Table 6. Small group of samples from the test set.

Record Name	R_0 [kΩ]	Estimated R_0 [kΩ]		R_∞ [kΩ]	Estimated R_∞ [kΩ]		C [uF]	Estimated C [uF]	
	Nominal	Cnn_Opt_Ch_U32p4	Cnn_Opt_Ch_U32p4U32p4x	Nominal	Cnn_Opt_Ch_U32p4	Cnn_Opt_Ch_U32p4U32p4x	Nominal	Cnn_Opt_Ch_U32p4	Cnn_Opt_Ch_U32p4U32p4x
Fantom01_Extra00	2.0000	1.9508	1.9624	1.0000	0.9647	0.9674	0.4700	0.4872	0.4324
Fantom03_Extra1,10	11.0000	10.6626	10.8975	1.0000	0.9539	0.9789	9.1000	8.1631	8.8900
Fantom06_Extra10,12	2.0000	1.8970	1.9578	1.0000	0.9860	0.9716	370.0001	223.3616	248.9201
Fantom16_Extra14,10	100.0000	105.1268	107.6225	1.0000	0.9551	0.9880	20.0000	14.5450	17.4282
Fantom19_Extra14,11	26.0000	27.6678	27.6018	1.0000	0.9807	0.9882	4.7000	3.6715	3.9807
Fantom32 (2024-05-02_12-25-31)	495.1000	519.5878	577.8306	93.0000	89.2673	94.4957	0.0022	0.0058	0.0047

5. Discussion

The results presented so far are presented for measurements on BIS phantoms. The phantoms have been created to verify the accuracy of the modified four-electrode measurement procedure and the prototype was developed based on it, over the whole measurement frequency range, even when measuring high-value impedances. Measurement results on phantoms were evaluated using software specially designed for this purpose.

The neural network was trained on a large, simulated database. In the simulated data, there are no tolerance deviations, meaning that each sample is exact and noise-free. However, when running this estimation system on the external test database, the model relies solely on the trends and is likely to show more accurate resistance and capacitance values. This discrepancy arises since the nominal values are not always precise due to the components' higher tolerance ranges. This result was validated using high-precision components on the last eight measurement boards, resulting in no significant deviations.

During the training phase, the minimum and maximum values of resistance and capacity were adjusted in order to match the first set of circuit boards (set 1–22). However, later, the need for a new set of circuit boards with more precise tolerance for the nominal values of resistance and capacity was identified in order to confirm the source of the deviation between simulations, based on nominal values and measurement. Unfortunately, only smaller capacity values were available for the target precision category. Consequently, the new boards (set 32–39) were created with different values compared to the original training dataset, with smaller capacity and higher resistance values in order to maintain the intended frequency range. This new set of circuit boards was added in the last phase of the research, and it was used as an external independent validation. The decision was not to retrain the CNN with the new data since the prediction was robust for the given ranges.

The error level of magnitude and phase curves remained consistently at 0.02 $log10(V/V)$ magnitude error and 0.02 radians phase error (Figure 5). The neural network's error margin aligns with these results: $rms(log10(k\Omega)) = 0.03$ for R_0, $rms(log10(k\Omega)) = 0.017$ for R_0, and $rms(log10(\mu F)) = 0.143$, as shown in Table 5. By adjusting the imaginary part of the complex signal using the Hilbert-transformed real part, phase errors can be reduced, resulting in more accurate impedance estimation, as was shown in the comparison between networks with and without Hilbert filtering, presented in Table 5.

The resistance estimation on external test measurements is two times higher compared to simulation validation ($rms(log10(k\Omega)) = 0.014$ versus 0.030). Similarly, the capacitance estimation error on the external test measurements was significantly higher than simulation validation ($rms(log10(\mu F)) = 0.065$ versus 0.143) due to the circuits having large tolerance ranges.

The study findings suggest that in order to accurately measure performance, components with precisely known values (with 0.1% accuracy) must be chosen. This level of precision is crucial for ensuring that the system's performance is measured correctly and that the resistance and capacitance values can be reliably estimated by the neural network in practical applications.

6. Conclusions

In this paper, self-developed BIS technology has been briefly presented and applied in practice. The investigation examines whether the impressive properties of the new technology are maintained over the entire operating frequency range (1 mHz–100 kHz). To this end, a BIS phantom has been developed and a significant quantity of these phantoms have been completed. Dedicated convolutional neural network-based software was developed in order to evaluate the measurement results. It estimates both the resistors and capacitors in a logarithmic format using the U_{32}/U_4 voltage ratio filtered with Hilbert transformation. The performance of this network reaches a high correlation (>0.99) with the reference values. Some of the phantoms were used to train this software and others were used in testing. The results are very impressive; the most impressive evidence of the cooperation between the measuring system and the measuring software is the fact that very small errors were observed in the extraction of model parameters for the test phantoms. As a result of the impedance spectrum measurement, either the real and imaginary parts of the impedance spectrum or their amplitude and phase characteristics are achieved. These curves are created using the measurement results at discrete frequency points. The fitting of these two curves occurs independently at these measurement points; either in the case of the real-imaginary pair or the amplitude-phase pair characteristics. Each fitting carries its own errors, as inverse procedures are sensitive to the initial data, thus an auxiliary condition that assists the inverse calculation process is beneficial. The auxiliary condition for the inverse procedure presented in this paper is provided by the Hilbert transformation. The Hilbert transformation, for realizable systems, connects the real and imaginary parts of the transfer function since the imaginary part is actually the Hilbert transformation of the real part. The CNN was trained with both real measurement results and numerical examples. The results have clearly presented that the application of the Hilbert transformation supports the inverse procedure. The accuracy of the circuit element values calculated using the inverse method was better even when the CNN was not optimized with the application of the Hilbert transformation, and after optimization, the accuracy became particularly good.

The results showed that the model parameters were successfully recovered over the full range of the measurement frequencies. Consequently, the presented BIS technology is recommended for human body composition and body segment composition studies at ultra-low frequencies, since even high impedances can be measured in this frequency range. Additionally, this technology could also be utilized for the detailed study of apoplastic fluid resistance in plants, providing valuable insights into plant physiology and water transport mechanisms.

Author Contributions: B.K. and I.K. drafted the manuscript and participated in the implementation of the neural network. M.S. and L.K. participated in the design of the neural network. M.K., Z.S. and P.O. designed the BIS phantoms, checked the test results and suggested the corrections. T.S. and A.O. produced the BIS phantoms. Z.V. and N.G. conceived and performed the experiments. V.T. reviewed the article. V.T., F.K. and K.J. supervised the research and contributed to the organization of article. All authors have read and agreed to the published version of the manuscript.

Funding: This research received no external funding.

Data Availability Statement: Data are contained within the article.

Acknowledgments: This research was a part of projects 2020-1.1.2-PIACI-KFI-2020-00173 of the University of Dunaújváros, and GINOP_PLUSZ-2.1.1-21-2022-00249 and 2023-1.1.1-PIACI_FÓKUSZ-2024-00011 of the Óbuda University. The project has been supported by grants 009-2023-PTE-RK/27 and 011-2023-PTE-RK/4 of the University of Pécs.

Conflicts of Interest: The authors declare no conflicts of interest.

References

1. Naranjo-Hernández, D.; Reina-Tosina, J.; Min, M. Fundamentals, recent advances, and future challenges in bioimpedance devices for healthcare applications. *J. Sens.* **2019**, *2019*, 9210258. [CrossRef]
2. Showkat, I.; Khanday, F.A.; Beigh, M.R. A review of bio-impedance devices. *Med. Biol. Eng. Comput.* **2023**, *61*, 927–950. [CrossRef] [PubMed]
3. Kusche, R.; Oltmann, A.; Rostalski, P. A Wearable Dual-Channel Bioimpedance Spectrometer for Real-Time Muscle Contraction Detection. *IEEE Sens. J.* **2024**, *24*, 11316–11327. [CrossRef]
4. Zachariah, V.K.; Priyamvada, P.S. Bioimpedance Analysis: Basic Concepts. *J. Ren. Nutr. Metab.* **2023**, *8*, 30–34. [CrossRef]
5. Aldobali, M.; Pal, K. Bioelectrical Impedance Analysis for Evaluation of Body Composition: A Review. In Proceedings of the 2021 International Congress of Advanced Technology and Engineering (ICOTEN), Taiz, Yemen, 4–5 July 2021; pp. 1–10.
6. Khalil, S.F.; Mohktar, M.S.; Ibrahim, F. The Theory and Fundamentals of Bioimpedance Analysis in Clinical Status Monitoring and Diagnosis of Diseases. *Sensors* **2014**, *14*, 10895–10928. [CrossRef]
7. Mialich, M.S.; Sicchieri, J.F.; Junior, A.J. Analysis of Body Composition: A Critical Review of the Use of Bioelectrical Impedance Analysis. *Int. J. Clin. Nutr.* **2014**, *2*, 1–10.
8. Matthie, J.R. Bioimpedance measurements of human body composition: Critical analysis and outlook. *Expert Rev. Med. Devices* **2008**, *5*, 239–261. [CrossRef]
9. Blue, M.N.M.; Tinsley, G.M.; Hirsch, K.R.; Ryan, E.D.; Ng, B.K.; Smith-Ryan, A.E. Validity of total body water measured by multi-frequency bioelectrical impedance devices in a multi-ethnic sample. *Clin. Nutr. ESPEN* **2023**, *54*, 187–193. [CrossRef]
10. El Dimassi, S.; Gautier, J.; Zalc, V.; Boudaoud, S.; Istrate, D. *Mathematical Issues in Body Water Volume Estimation Using Bio Impedance Analysis in e-Health*; Colloque en TéléSANté et dispositifs biomédicaux, Université Paris 8; CNRS: Paris Saint Denis, France, 2023.
11. Lai, Y.-K.; Ho, C.-Y.; Lai, C.-L.; Taun, C.-Y.; Hsieh, K.-C. Assessment of Standing Multi-Frequency Bioimpedance Analyzer to Measure Body Composition of the Whole Body and Limbs in Elite MaleWrestlers. *Int. J. Environ. Res. Public Health* **2022**, *19*, 15807. [CrossRef]
12. Antipenko, V.V.; Pecherskaya, E.A.; Zinchenko, T.O.; Artamonov, D.V.; Spitsina, K.Y.; Pecherskiy, A.V. Development of an automated bioimpendance analyzer for monitoring the clinical condition and diagnosis of human body diseases. *J. Phys. Conf. Ser.* **2020**, *1515*, 052075. [CrossRef]
13. Doonyapisut, D.; Kannan, P.; Kim, B.; Kim, J.K.; Lee, E.; Chung, C. Analysis of Electrochemical Impedance Data: Use of Deep Neural Networks. *Adv. Intell. Syst.* **2023**, *5*, 2300085. [CrossRef]
14. Guo, M.-F.; Yang, N.-C.; Chen, W.-F. Deep-Learning-Based Fault Classification Using Hilbert–Huang Transform and Convolutional Neural Network in Power Distribution Systems. *IEEE Sens. J.* **2019**, *19*, 6905–6913. [CrossRef]
15. Vizvari, Z.; Gyorfi, N.; Odry, A.; Sari, Z.; Klincsik, M.; Gergics, M.; Kovacs, L.; Kovacs, A.; Pal, J.; Karadi, Z.; et al. Physical Validation of a Residual Impedance Rejection Method during Ultra-Low Frequency Bio-Impedance Spectral Measurements. *Sensors* **2020**, *20*, 4686. [CrossRef] [PubMed]
16. Cole, K.S.; Cole, R.H. Dispersion and absorption in dielectrics, I. Alternating current characteristics. *J. Chem. Phys.* **1941**, *9*, 341–351. [CrossRef]
17. Schoutteten, M.K.; Lindeboom, L.; De Cannière, H.; Pieters, Z.; Bruckers, L.; Brys, A.D.H.; van der Heijden, P.; De Moor, B.; Peeters, J.; Van Hoof, C.; et al. The Feasibility of Semi-Continuous and Multi-Frequency Thoracic Bioimpedance Measurements by a Wearable Device during Fluid Changes in Hemodialysis Patients. *Sensors* **2024**, *24*, 1890. [CrossRef]
18. Campa, F.; Gobbo, L.A.; Stagi, S.; Cyrino, L.T.; Toselli, S.; Marini, E.; Coratella, G. Bioelectrical impedance analysis versus reference methods in the assessment of body composition in athletes. *Eur. J. Appl. Physiol.* **2022**, *122*, 561–589. [CrossRef] [PubMed]
19. Metshein, M.; Tuulik, V.-R.; Tuulik, V.; Kumm, M.; Min, M.; Annus, P. Electrical Bioimpedance Analysis for Evaluating the Effect of Pelotherapy on the Human Skin: Methodology and Experiments. *Sensors* **2023**, *23*, 4251. [CrossRef]
20. Duong Trong, L.; Nguyen Quang, L.; Hoang Anh, D.; Dang Tuan, D.; Nguyen Chi, H.; Nguyen Minh, D. A Portable Band-shaped Bioimpedance System to Monitor the Body Fat and Fasting Glucose Level. *J. Electr. Bioimpedance* **2022**, *13*, 54–65. [CrossRef]
21. Nescolarde, L.; Talluri, A.; Yanguas, J.; Lukaski, H. Phase angle in localized bioimpedance measurements to assess and monitor muscle injury. *Rev. Endocr. Metab Disord.* **2023**, *24*, 415–428. [CrossRef] [PubMed]
22. Wohlgemuth, K.J.; Freeborn, T.J.; Southall, K.E.; Hare, M.M.; Mota, J.A. Can segmental bioelectrical impedance be used as a measure of muscle quality? *Med. Eng. Phys.* **2024**, *124*, 104103. [CrossRef] [PubMed]

23. Pislaru-Danescu, L.; Zarnescu, G.-C.; Telipan, G.; Stoica, V. Design and Manufacturing of Equipment for Investigation of Low Frequency Bioimpedance. *Micromachines* **2022**, *13*, 1858. [CrossRef]
24. Scaliusi, S.F.; Gimenez, L.; Pérez, P.; Martín, D.; Olmo, A.; Huertas, G.; Medrano, F.J.; Yúfera, A. From Bioimpedance to Volume Estimation: A Model for Edema Calculus in Human Legs. *Electronics* **2023**, *12*, 1383. [CrossRef]
25. Scagliusi, S.F.; Delano, M. Characterization and Correction of Low Frequency Artifacts in Segmental Bioimpedance Measurements. In Proceedings of the 2023 45th Annual International Conference of the IEEE Engineering in Medicine & Biology Society (EMBC), Sydney, Australia, 24–27 July 2023.
26. El Khaled, D.; Novas, N.; Gazquez, J.-A.; Manzano-Agugliaro, F. Dielectric and Bioimpedance Research Studies: A Scientometric Approach Using the Scopus Database. *Publications* **2018**, *6*, 6. [CrossRef]
27. Fu, B.; Freeborn, T.J. Residual impedance effect on emulated bioimpedance measurements using Keysight E4990A precision impedance analyzer. *Measurement* **2019**, *134*, 468–479. [CrossRef]
28. Vizvari, Z.; Kiss, T.; Mathe, K.; Odry, P.; Ver, C.; Divos, F. Multi-frequency electrical impedance measurement on a wooden disc sample. *Acta Silv. Lign. Hung.* **2015**, *11*, 153–161. [CrossRef]
29. Vizvari, Z.; Gyorfi, N.; Maczko, G.; Varga, R.; Jakabf-Csepregi, R.; Sari, Z.; Furedi, A.; Bajtai, E.; Vajda, F.; Tadic, V.; et al. Reproducibility analysis of bioimpedance-based self-developed live cell assays. *Sci. Rep.* **2024**, *14*, 16380. [CrossRef] [PubMed]
30. Gyorfi, N.; Odry, A.; Karadi, Z.; Odry, P.; Szakall, T.; Kuljic, B.; Toth, A.; Vizvari, Z. Development of Bioimpedance-based Measuring Systems for Diagnosis of Non-alcoholic Fatty Liver Disease. In Proceedings of the 2021 IEEE 15th International Symposium on Applied Computational Intelligence and Informatics (SACI), Timisoara, Romania, 19–21 May 2021; pp. 135–140.
31. Gyorfi, N.; Gal, A.R.; Fincsur, A.; Kalmar-Nagy, K.; Mintal, K.; Hormay, E.; Miseta, A.; Tornoczky, T.; Nemeth, A.K.; Bogner, P.; et al. Novel Noninvasive Paraclinical Study Method for Investigation of Liver Diseases. *Biomedicines* **2023**, *11*, 2449. [CrossRef]
32. Sari, Z.; Klincsik, M.; Odry, P.; Tadic, V.; Toth, A.; Vizvari, Z. Lumped Element Method Based Conductivity Reconstruction Algorithm for Localization Using Symmetric Discrete Operators on Coarse Meshes. *Symmetry* **2023**, *15*, 1008. [CrossRef]
33. Meade, M.L. Lock-in Amplifiers: Principles and Applications. 1983. Available online: https://archive.org/details/Lock-inAmplifiersPrinciplesAndApplications/page/n1/mode/2up (accessed on 19 August 2020).
34. Hodson, T.O. Root-mean-square error (RMSE) or mean absolute error (MAE): When to use them or not. *Geosci. Model Dev.* **2022**, *15*, 5481–5487. [CrossRef]
35. Ahmed, Z.; Kumar, S. Pearson's correlation coefficient in the theory of networks: A comment. *arXiv* **2018**, arXiv:1803.06937.
36. Qi, X.; Wei, Y.; Mei, X.; Chellali, R.; Yang, S. Comparative Analysis of the Linear Regions in ReLU and LeakyReLU Networks. In *Neural Information Processing. ICONIP 2023*; Luo, B., Cheng, L., Wu, Z.G., Li, H., Li, C., Eds.; Communications in Computer and Information Science; Springer: Singapore, 2023; Volume 1962. [CrossRef]
37. Kingma, D.P.; Adam, B.J. A Method for Stochastic Optimization. *arXiv* **2014**, arXiv:1412.6980.
38. Available online: https://www.mathworks.com/matlabcentral/fileexchange/25986-constrained-particle-swarm-optimization (accessed on 15 May 2024).
39. Available online: https://www.mathworks.com/help/signal/ug/hilbert-transform.html (accessed on 10 April 2024).
40. Zheng, L.; Liu, Z.; Wang, G.; Zhang, Z. *Research on Application of Hilbert Transform in Radar Signal Simulation*; Atlantis Press: Amsterdam, The Netherlands, 2016. [CrossRef]
41. Smith, J.O. Analytic Signals and Hilbert Transform Filters. In *Mathematics of the Discrete Fourier Transform (DFT) with Audio Applications*, 2nd ed.; W3K Publishing: Dordrecht, The Netherlands, 2007. Available online: https://ccrma.stanford.edu/~jos/st/Analytic_Signals_Hilbert_Transform.html (accessed on 20 July 2024).
42. Wang, S.; Xue, L.; Lai, J.; Li, Z. An improved phase retrieval method based on Hilbert transform in interferometric microscopy. *Optik. Int. J. Light Electron Opt.* **2013**, *124*, 1897–1901. [CrossRef]
43. Popović, M.V. *Digitalna Obrada Signala*; Nauka: Beograd, Serbia; Drugo Izdanje: Beograd, Serbia, 1997; ISBN 86-7621-080-1.
44. Matsuki, A.; Kori, H.; Kobayashi, R. An extended Hilbert transform method for reconstructing the phase from an oscillatory signal. *Sci. Rep.* **2023**, *13*, 3535. [CrossRef] [PubMed]
45. Stojanović, I.S. *Osnovi Telekomunikacija*; Naučna Knjiga: Beograd, Serbia; Šesto Izdanje: Beograd, Serbia, 1997; ISBN 8623420071/9788623420078.
46. Simon, M.; Tomlinson, G.R. Use of the Hilbert transform in modal analysis of linear and non-linear structures. *J. Sound Vib.* **1984**, *96*, 421–436. [CrossRef]
47. Oppenheim, A.V.; Willsky, A.S.; Nawab, S.H. *Signals and Systems*, 2nd ed.; Prentice-Hall: Upper Saddle River, NJ, USA, 1996; p. 07458, ISBN 0-13-814757-4.
48. Poularikas, A.D. *The Handbook of Formulas and Tables for Signal Processing*; CRC Press LLC: Boca Raton, FL, USA, 1999; ISBN 0-8493-8579-2.
49. Arcos, E.A.; Castillo, R.E. The Hilbert Transform. *Surv. Math. Its Appl.* **2021**, *16*, 149–192.
50. Rosenblum, M.; Pikovsky, A.; Kühn, A.A.; Busch, J.L. Real-time estimation of phase and amplitude with application to neural data. *Sci. Rep.* **2021**, *11*, 18037. [CrossRef] [PubMed]

Disclaimer/Publisher's Note: The statements, opinions and data contained in all publications are solely those of the individual author(s) and contributor(s) and not of MDPI and/or the editor(s). MDPI and/or the editor(s) disclaim responsibility for any injury to people or property resulting from any ideas, methods, instructions or products referred to in the content.

Article

Automotive Parts Defect Detection Based on YOLOv7

Hao Huang [1] and Kai Zhu [2,*]

[1] School of Mechanical Engineering, Jiangsu University of Technology, Changzhou 213000, China; 2022655079@smail.jsut.edu.cn
[2] School of Automobile and Traffic Engineering, Jiangsu University of Technology, Changzhou 213000, China
* Correspondence: fatkyo@jsut.edu.cn

Abstract: Various complex defects can occur on the surfaces of small automobile parts during manufacturing. Compared with other datasets, the auto parts defect dataset used in this paper has low detection accuracy due to various defects with large size differences, and traditional target detection algorithms have been proven to be ineffective, which often leads to missing detection or wrong identification. To address these issues, this paper introduces a defect detection algorithm based on YOLOv7. To enhance the detection of small objects and streamline the model, we incorporate the ECA attention mechanism into the network structure's backbone. Considering the small sizes of defect targets on automotive parts and the complexity of their backgrounds, we redesign the neck portion of the model. This redesign includes the integration of the BiFPN feature fusion module to enhance feature fusion, with the aim of minimizing missed detections and false alarms. Additionally, we employ the Alpha-IoU loss function in the prediction phase to enhance the model's accuracy, which is crucial for reducing false detection. The IoU loss function also boosts the model's efficiency at converging. The evaluation of this model utilized the Northeastern University steel dataset and a proprietary dataset and demonstrated that the average accuracy (mAP) of the MBEA-YOLOv7 detection network was 76.2% and 94.1%, respectively. These figures represent improvements of 5.7% and 4.7% over the original YOLOv7 network. Moreover, the detection speed for individual images ranges between 1–2 ms. This enhancement in detection accuracy for small targets does not compromise detection speed, fulfilling the requirements for real-time, dynamic inspection of defects.

Keywords: feature attention; automobile parts; YOLOv7

Citation: Huang, H.; Zhu, K. Automotive Parts Defect Detection Based on YOLOv7. *Electronics* **2024**, *13*, 1817. https://doi.org/10.3390/electronics13101817

Academic Editors: Peter Odry and Vladimir László Tadić

Received: 15 April 2024
Revised: 4 May 2024
Accepted: 6 May 2024
Published: 8 May 2024

Copyright: © 2024 by the authors. Licensee MDPI, Basel, Switzerland. This article is an open access article distributed under the terms and conditions of the Creative Commons Attribution (CC BY) license (https://creativecommons.org/licenses/by/4.0/).

1. Introduction

At present, the detection of defects in automobile parts is receiving increasing attention [1], with the quality of these parts having a direct effect on the vehicle's overall quality. Low-quality components can cause significant economic losses and even pose risks to life and safety. The presence of ambiguous information and the rising complexity of defects, including minor ones, complicate the detection process [2]. Despite the fact that object detection methods based on deep learning have demonstrated superior performance in defect detection tasks in recent years [3–6], these methods often fall short when faced with complex and smaller targets. These challenges significantly impair the accuracy of detecting defects in automobile parts.

Addressing one of the challenges, this paper focuses on the issue of background noise [7,8]. The complexity of backgrounds in the detection process can lead to confusion due to the mistaking of noise for relevant information [9]. This confusion can cause missed or incorrect detections, reducing the accuracy when identifying defects. Moreover, defects that blend in with the color of the product present an additional challenge [10] that represents a significant barrier to effective detection.

This paper introduces an innovative approach to detecting defects in automotive parts. The main contributions of this study are outlined as follows:

(1) To enhance the detection accuracy of automobile part defects, we propose a new detection network (MEBA-YOLO). This network utilizes a unique fusion and attention mechanism built on YOLOv7.
(2) To achieve exceptional results for detecting defects in automobile parts, we introduce a model incorporating the AlphaIoU loss function. This function significantly increases accuracy for detecting complex and small defects, marking a significant advancement in the field.
(3) Our proposed method offers real-time defect detection on production lines, which aids with the immediate identification of defects in automobile parts. This contribution is crucial for enhancing vehicle safety.

In addition, we have confirmed the effectiveness of our method through comprehensive testing and benchmarking. The results from these tests are backed by solid evidence that indicates that our method outperforms others in terms of accuracy.

The remainder of this article is organized as follows: In Section 2, we explore our analysis of defect detection and the obstacles encountered when identifying small and complex defects. Section 3 details the method we propose. In Section 4, we share the results of our experiments and our analysis of these results. We conclude with a summary of our findings in Section 5.

2. Related Work

To enhance defect detection in automotive parts, extensive studies have been carried out on various methods for detecting object defects. This section offers an overview of some of the most effective strategies for defect detection. We especially emphasize methods based on deep learning [11–16], which have proven to be highly effective in this area.

2.1. Defect Detection

Networks for detecting surface defects with deep learning typically rely on target localization to fulfill their tasks. This method aligns with traditional approaches to defect detection by aiming to accurately identify the locations and types of defects. Currently, networks for detecting defects can generally be classified into two types based on their architecture:

(1) Two-stage networks, represented by Faster R-CNN (Region-CNN) [17];
(2) One-stage networks, represented by SSD (Single Shot Multibox Detector) [13] or YOLO (You Only Look Once) [12].

The first type, referred to as two-stage detection networks (e.g., Faster R-CNN), starts with generating feature maps from the input image using the backbone network. The region proposal network (RPN) calculates the confidence level of the anchor box and identifies the proposal region. Following ROI pooling, the feature maps from the proposal region are fed into the network for initial detection results, which are then enhanced to determine the accurate location and classification of defects. Cha et al. [18] pioneered the application of Faster R-CNN for the localization of defects on bridge surfaces by substituting the backbone network with ZFnet. They achieved a mean average accuracy (mAP) of 87.8% across five categories of bridge construction defects using a dataset of 2366 images measuring 500 × 375 pixels.

In 2020, Tao et al. [19] developed a two-stage Faster R-CNN framework specifically for identifying insulator defects during UAV power inspections. In the first stage, the framework targets the identification of insulator areas in natural environments. Following this, it focuses on detecting defects in these identified insulator regions. Similarly, He et al. [20] introduced an enhanced defect detection system based on Faster R-CNN for analyzing strip steel surfaces. This enhancement involved integrating multilevel feature maps from the backbone architecture into a comprehensive multiscale feature map. Their approach recorded an mAP of 82.3% on the NEU-DET defect detection dataset when utilizing a ResNet-50 backbone. This detection method, leveraging Faster R-CNN, has also found application across various defect detection areas, including tunnels [21], LCD panel polarizer surfaces [22], thermal imaging for insulator defects [23], aluminum profile surfaces [24], and tire hubs [25].

The second type, single-stage detection networks, is divided into two categories: SSD and YOLO. These methodologies process the entire image as input and directly determine the bounding box's location and category in the output layer. Chen et al. [26] enhanced an SSD network for identifying defects in fasteners on contact network supports: specifically, by employing various feature map layers for detection purposes. Li et al. [27] devised a method based on MobileNetSSD for spotting defects on sealing surfaces of containers on filling production lines. They enhanced the SSD's backbone with MobileNet and streamlined the model's parameters. Zhang et al. [28] adopted the most recent YOLOv3 version for bridge surface defect detection and enhanced the original network with pre-training weights, batch renormalization, and focal loss to increase the detection accuracy.

2.2. Feature Fusion Strategy

The swift progress in computer networks has led to the proposal of several feature fusion methods [29–33]. These methods aim to merge the detailed location information from shallow feature maps with the comprehensive semantic insights from deeper layers. Such integration is designed to enhance the detection of small targets in complex settings.

However, the generation of shallow target features often lacks semantic depth and relies heavily on surrounding context. Li et al. [34] tackled this by incorporating the FPN concept into the SSD framework, thus creating a method for lightweight feature fusion. This approach combines different levels of feature maps to create feature pyramids, enhancing the use of small target feature information.

Shi et al. [35] introduced FFESSD (Single Shot Object Detection with Feature Enhancement and Fusion), which applies a shallow feature enhancement (SFE) module to enhance shallow semantic details and a deep feature enhancement (DFE) module to enrich deep feature mapping with additional input image details.

To advance the improvement of shallow feature details, Pengfei Zhao et al. [36] developed the feature enhancement module (FEM). They combined feature maps from the FEM with those from channel dimensionality reduction. However, this method of combining channels did not consider the interrelationship among channels. To address this oversight, they implemented the efficient channel attention module (ECAM) after merging operations to fully leverage the contextual information of the target features.

2.3. Challenges of Defect Detection in Automotive Parts

The challenge of accurately identifying defects in automotive parts in complex environments remains unresolved and demands further research. To overcome this, several advanced deep learning strategies [37–42] have been employed to enhance the accuracy of defect detection in automotive parts. These strategies include using synthetic automotive part datasets to enlarge training data and enhance method generalization, adjusting the core network or integrating new modules to handle various complex situations, and employing attention mechanisms or post-processing methods to minimize noise and emphasize important features.

The issue of inaccurate localization and categorization is particularly acute in the detection of small targets. When targets are small, image details can become indistinct, complicating the process of identifying object details [43]. This issue is a significant hurdle to the accurate detection of defects in automotive parts.

To achieve accurate identification of defects in automotive parts under complex backgrounds and challenging conditions, we introduce a novel multi-class target detection method named the MBEA-YOLOv7 network. This network incorporates the MBEA structure to enhance accuracy, and we validate its effectiveness specifically for the detection of automotive parts defects. This paper primarily focuses on this method.

3. Method

In the following section, we discuss the details of the MBEA-YOLO method. The rationale behind this method is its ability to outperform traditional classification methods.

Therefore, our proposed method seeks to enhance the accuracy of detection and categorization of defects in automotive parts. In doing so, it confirms the effectiveness and reliability of our approach for boosting the performance of defect detection. The architecture of MBEA-YOLO is illustrated in Figure 1. In the figure, we can see that in the neck part we have added BIFPN and ECA attention mechanisms. In the model, four BIPFN modules are added to improve the feature fusion ability of the model, and an ECA attention mechanism is added to enhance the detection ability for small target defects. Finally, for the loss function part of the model, the original CIoU is replaced with Alpha-IoU, which can improve the robustness of the model. These changes to the model are described in detail later.

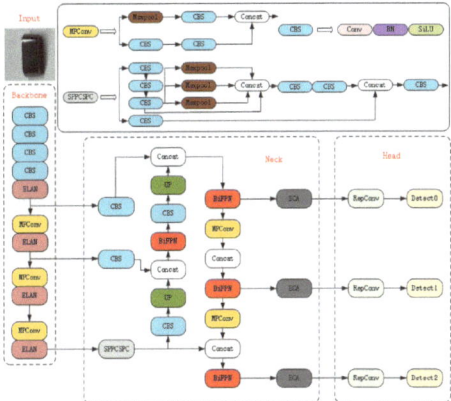

Figure 1. Structure of MBEA-YOLOv7.

3.1. BiFPN-Based Feature Fusion Network

As outlined in Section 2, to tackle the problem of imbalanced feature and semantic information, we use a feature fusion network to enhance our original network. The original version, YOLOv7, employs a PANet feature fusion network for extracting features at various levels. While it is capable of adaptive feature pooling and comprehensive fusion, it faces challenges in efficiently processing images of different resolutions due to its uniform approach to up-sampling and down-sampling in feature fusion.

In this paper, we enhance the bidirectional feature fusion pyramid with a bidirectional feature pyramid network (BiFPN). In the process of feature fusion of auto parts defect detection, different from PANet, PANet adopts a unified feature sampling method, which will lead to deviations of features of different sizes in the process of feature fusion, which will lead to the loss of small defect features. The BiFPN proposed in this paper can effectively solve this problem. According to the different targets of up-sampling and down-sampling, the features of auto parts defects can be effectively fused, combined, and transferred according to the different dimensions of defect features to adapt to the input of different auto parts defect features. Therefore, it can greatly enrich the details of auto parts defects, minimizes the occurrence of missing detection and false positives for small targets, and improves the overall accuracy of the model.

BiFPN enhances feature fusion at a higher level than PANet. It removes nodes with only one input edge (for example, the first node in Figure 2) because removing a node without feature fusion simplifies the network structure. In addition, it introduces additional edges that connect input and output nodes. This change not only simplifies the bidirectional network but also allows other features to be incorporated without significantly increasing computational costs. In BiFPN, each bidirectional path (top-down and bottom-up) is considered to be a layer of the feature network and is replicated multiple times to achieve high-level feature fusion, and BiFPN gives different weights to the features of different inputs so that the fusions of different input features are differentiated.

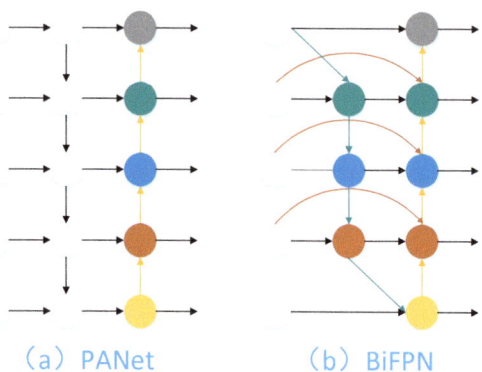

Figure 2. Structures of PANet and BiFPN.

Simultaneously, the integrated feature maps are easily discernible. Depending on the resolution of the input defective feature map, the contribution to the combined feature map also varies. Building upon the BiFPN concept, we have incorporated cross-scale connections into the feature fusion process to enhance model accuracy for anomaly detection. This approach is particularly beneficial for effectively integrating data across various scales and resolutions and thereby improves model detection accuracy.

3.2. Attention Mechanism

The role of the attention mechanism in deep learning models is critical. It isolates a small yet crucial portion of data from a large dataset and concentrates solely on this information. Considering the broad range of defect sizes in automotive parts, which results in inconsistent image defect scales, incorporating the attention mechanism enhances the model's ability to represent data. This adaptation allows the model to pay closer attention to defective areas, thus elevating the accuracy of defect identification. It presents an intelligent solution to the challenge presented due to the varying sizes of defects in automotive components.

The ECA attention mechanism, representing an advancement over SENet, is illustrated in Figure 3. SENet reduces dimensionality to manage nonlinear cross-channel interactions and minimize model complexity. This method, however, affects channel attention prediction and is insufficient in capturing the full spectrum of inter-channel dependencies. In contrast, the ECA attention module circumvents dimensionality reduction and employs one-dimensional convolution to effectively facilitate local cross-channel interactions. This process extracts the dependencies between channels, thereby efficiently capturing their interactions. When a neck module with an ECA attention mechanism is added, the defect features input into this module are convolution in one dimension so as to realize the interdependence of features of different auto parts and to cause effective interaction with context features, which can effectively enhance the recognition ability for objects with different sizes. The simplicity of the ECA mechanism in both concept and execution minimally affects the processing speed of the network, guaranteeing accuracy and efficiency when detecting automotive parts.

$$C = \phi(k) = 2^{(y \neq k - b)} \tag{1}$$

In terms of practical application, ECA first compresses the automotive parts image through global average pooling (GAP). This process averages the feature maps on each channel of the auto parts image to produce a global feature vector through which the overall context information of the auto parts image is captured. The global feature vector is then subjected to a one-dimensional convolution using a kernel of size K. It is possible to connect the cross-channel information of defects of auto parts and understand the relationship between each channel, and the weight coefficient of each channel is determined by the sigmoid activation function. Through these coefficients, the defect characteristics of each channel can be adjusted. Finally, the weight of each channel is applied to the corresponding element of the feature mapping in the original uncompressed auto parts image. Generating a feature map of the final output thereby enhances the ability to extract detailed information about target defects of various sizes in automotive components, which is particularly important for some small defects.

$$k = \varphi(C) = \left| \frac{\log_2(C)}{\gamma} + \frac{b}{\gamma} \right|_{odd} \qquad (2)$$

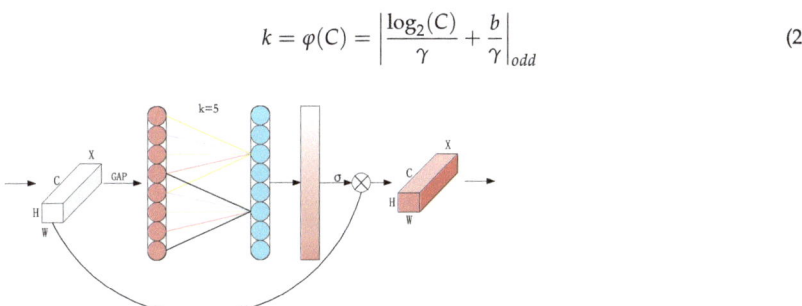

Figure 3. ECA structure diagram.

3.3. Loss Function

The original YOLOv7 algorithm employs the CIoU (complete intersection over union) loss function for prediction box regression calculations. The CIoU algorithm addresses the issue of bounding box aspect ratios. The loss function is an operation function used to measure the degree of difference between the predicted value and the real value of the model. The difference between the predicted value and the real value can be calculated through the loss function. The difference value can be backpropagated to update each parameter so as to make the model closer to the real value to achieve the purpose of learning and to improve the robustness of the model. CIoU operates on the principle illustrated in Figure 4:

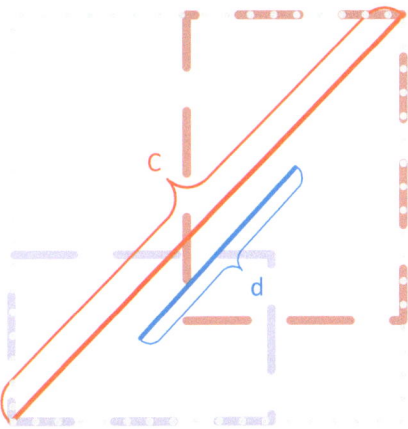

Figure 4. CIoU schematic diagram.

The formula for CIoU is as follows:

$$L_{CIoU} = 1 - IoU + \frac{\rho^2(b, b^{gt})}{c^2} + \alpha v \tag{3}$$

IoU, or the intersection over union, measures the overlap between the predicted bounding box and the actual bounding box relative to their combined area. This metric calculates the ratio of the area of overlap to the total area encompassed by both boxes, providing a quantitative assessment of prediction accuracy. Its formula is:

$$IoU = \frac{|A \cap B|}{|A \cup B|} \tag{4}$$

where α represents the weighting function:

$$\alpha = \frac{v}{(1 - IoU) + v} \tag{5}$$

where v is utilized to indicate the similarity of the aspect ratios.

$$v = \frac{4}{\pi^2} \left(\arctan \frac{w^{gt}}{h^{gt}} - \arctan \frac{w}{h} \right)^2 \tag{6}$$

CIoU considers the overlapping area, the distance between centers of mass, and the aspect ratio of the predicted and actual boxes. However, for the defect features of auto parts, which have large aspect ratio differences, it cannot accurately capture the variance between width and height. This limitation hinders the effectiveness of the model at optimizing the similarity measure, and thus, the ability to improve the robustness of the model is limited. To overcome this challenge, this paper introduces Alpha-CIoU: a method aimed at enhancing the accuracy of bounding box regression and improving target detection.

Alpha-CIoU represents a uniform idempotentization of the existing loss based on IoU. It introduces a novel power IoU loss function that enhances the accuracy of bounding box regression and target detection. This method ensures an accurate representation of the aspect ratio, thus improving the model's performance. The formulation of Alpha-CIoU is as follows:

$$L_{Alpha-CIoU} = 1 - IoU^\alpha + \left(\frac{|C/(B \cup B^{gt})|}{|C|} \right)^\alpha \tag{7}$$

According to this formula, Alpha-CIoU ensures the accurate representation of the aspect ratio, effectively captures the variance between the width and height of the defect of automotive parts, and effectively improves the robustness of the model to improve the accuracy of the model compared with CIoU.

The variable α is selected to enhance the accuracy of bounding box regression through loss and adaptive gradient weighting for the target. In this study, α is set to 3 [44].

4. Experiments and Results

This section details extensive experiments and analyses to confirm the effectiveness of the proposed approach. During these evaluations, datasets from BYD car parts and the Northeastern University steel dataset are utilized to broaden the scope of the experiments. A detailed analysis of the results clearly indicates the superior performance of the proposed method.

4.1. Implementation Details

(1) Training strategy: The experimental environment utilizes PyTorch 1.91+CPU as the software framework, with Python 3.8 as the programming language. The model training hardware environment includes a GPU model NVIDIA GeForce RTX 3070 with 8 GB memory, and CUDA version 11.1 is utilized to accelerate model training.

(2) Evaluation: In this experiment, precision (P), recall (R), average precision (AP), mean average precision (mAP), and frames per second (FPS) are primarily selected as the evaluation indexes. The formulas for P, R, AP, and mAP are as follows:

$$P = \frac{T_P}{T_P + F_P} \tag{8}$$

$$R = \frac{T_P}{T_P + F_N} \tag{9}$$

$$AP = \int_0^1 P(r)dr \tag{10}$$

$$mAP = \frac{1}{c}\sum_{i=1}^{c} AP(i) \tag{11}$$

where T_P denotes the number of positive samples correctly predicted by the model, and F_P denotes the number of positive samples predicted by the model that were actually negative. F_N denotes the number of positive samples predicted by the model that are negative; r denotes the recall of the class, c denotes the number of all classes, and $AP(i)$ denotes the average precision of the ith cumulative iteration. FPS stands for frames per second, which refers to the number of images displayed per second in video or image processing. In practical applications, increasing FPS means being able to capture and process images faster, thereby improving productivity and inspection speed.

4.2. Datasets

The dataset utilized in this study consists of a custom collection focused on the interior button trim rings of BYD vehicles, which are made from PC+ABS material. This dataset comprises several defect types: friction, scratch, particle, black spot, and particle swarm, with 240 images for each category. The details of these defect types and features are illustrated in Figure 5. The dataset is divided into training, validation, and test sets with a ratio of 10:1:1. To assess whether the experimental improvements can be applied to other types of defect detection, we also utilize the NEU-DUT dataset from Northeastern University for comparative analysis.

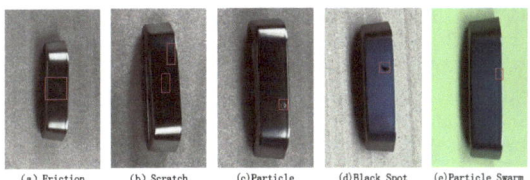

(a) Friction (b) Scratch (c) Particle (d) Black Spot (e) Particle Swarm

Figure 5. Samples of various types of defects in the BYD dataset.

Detecting defects in automotive components often involves dealing with noisy backgrounds. This challenge requires an algorithm with strong generalization capabilities and the ability to process diverse features and background information. In response, this study enhances the original YOLOv7's Mosaic-4 method by introducing a Mosaic-9 enhancement approach. This new method selects nine images at random from the dataset, applies various enhancement methods such as rotation and cropping, and combines them into a single image for input into the network.

The Mosaic-9 method, compared to the Mosaic-4 approach, compiles images that incorporate a richer array of feature and background information as well as targets of varying sizes, as demonstrated in Figure 6. This strategy increases the diversity of the data samples and enlarges the dataset, which significantly boosts the network's ability to generalize and minimizes the risk of model overfitting.

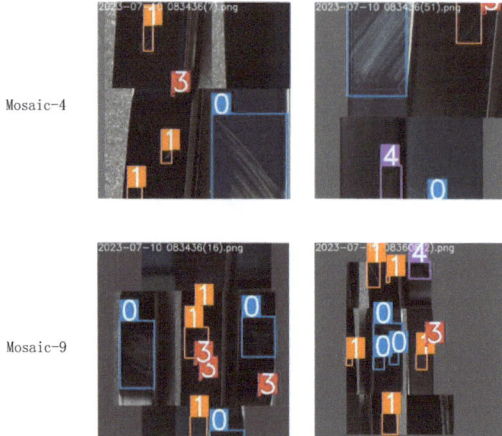

Figure 6. Comparison of different data enhancement methods.

To further verify the enhancement capabilities of our methodology for detecting different defects, we once again reference the NEU-DUT dataset from Northeastern University.

4.3. Ablation Study

4.3.1. Impact of Attention Mechanisms

This paper explores the effect of incorporating attention mechanisms on model accuracy. We integrate SE, SimAM, and ECA attention modules before the prediction layer in the model's multi-scale fusion process. The findings, presented in Table 1, exhibit that the model achieves $mAP50$ scores of 93.1%, 93.3%, and 93.5% after incorporating SE, SimAM, and ECA, respectively. These results indicate that leveraging attention mechanisms significantly boosts the defect detection performance for automotive parts.

Table 1. Performance comparison of different attention mechanisms based on the BYD dataset.

Method	AP_{Sc}	AP_{Bs}	AP_{Pa}	AP_{Ps}	AP_{Fr}	mAP^{50}	FPS	GFLPS	Params
SE	88.2	94.8	88.2	99.5	94.5	93.1	16.7	103.5	36.8
SimAM	90.1	92.3	89.0	98.4	96.5	93.3	38.0	103.2	36.5
ECA	86.9	95.2	90.6	99.6	95.1	93.5	38.6	103.3	36.5

ECA's ability to detect defects in automobile parts outperforms that of SE and SimAM, though it is marginally less effective at identifying Sc and Fr. Despite this, ECA features a faster FPS than both SE and SimAM while maintaining a similar count of parameters and floating-point operations. This indicates ECA's overall excellence in enhancing model detection capabilities without adding complexity.

4.3.2. Effect of Loss Function Hyperparameters

The paper further explores the effect of α in Equation (7) on the accuracy of defect detection in automobile parts. This is achieved through ablation studies with various α values. According to Table 2, the appropriate selection of α can fine-tune the accuracy of bounding box regression. Selecting an α that is either too high or too low can compromise detection accuracy. Adjusting α allows for a focused improvement to achieve a high IoU, leading to better regression accuracy. The findings suggest that setting α to 3 yields the best performance.

Table 2. Comparison of model performance for different α parameters.

α	AP_{Sc}	AP_{BS}	AP_{Pa}	AP_{Ps}	AP_{Fr}	mAP^{50}
1	85.0	94.0	84.2	99.6	95.0	91.6
2	83.5	94.5	85.8	99.6	95.6	91.8
3	88.6	93.5	88.6	99.5	95.5	93.1
4	84.3	94.2	83.8	99.6	95.2	91.6

4.3.3. Ablation Experiments with Different Modules

To verify the detection efficacy of the proposed algorithm and the effect of each enhancement method, the study conducts ablation tests using the YOLOv7 model on a dataset of BYD car parts. The presence of a "✓" in the table signifies the implementation of a particular enhancement strategy, where A stands for Mosaic-9, B stands for BiFPN, C stands for ECA attention, and D stands for Alpha-CIoU. Each experiment utilizes identical hyperparameters and training approaches, and the results are detailed in Table 3.

Table 3. Comparison of ablation experiment results for the MBEA-YOLOv7 model.

Test	Mosaic-9	BiFPN	ECA	Alpha-CIoU	AP_{Sc}	AP_{BS}	AP_{Pa}	AP_{Ps}	AP_{Fr}	mAP^{50}	R	P	FPS
1					84.7	85.2	82.3	99.5	92.1	88.7	89.8	86.1	19
2	✓				85.3	94.4	84.6	99.6	96.3	91.9	92.5	87.5	19
3		✓			87.3	94.9	83.7	99.6	94.3	92.0	93.0	89.0	30
4			✓		86.9	95.2	90.6	99.6	95.1	93.5	89.1	88.8	39
5				✓	88.6	93.5	88.6	99.5	95.5	93.1	90.1	87.8	30
6	✓	✓			90.2	94.8	88.0	99.6	95.1	93.6	91.0	90.3	29
7	✓	✓	✓		91.0	95.2	89.3	99.6	95.0	94.1	94.7	89.5	46
8	✓	✓	✓	✓	91.1	95.5	88.5	99.6	95.4	94.2	95.7	93.0	48

In the experiment, we reflected on the BYD dataset by adding each module. In Experiment 1, the baseline YOLOv7 model was employed. Experiment 2 enhanced the initial Mosaic-4 to Mosaic-9, leading to significant improvements. Specifically, the $mAP50$, recall, and precision increased by 3.2%, 2.7%, and 1.4%, respectively. This demonstrates that Mosaic-9 is capable of capturing a broader range of feature and background information as well as targets with varying scales, thus bolstering the model's robustness.

In Experiments 3 and 4, incorporating the BiFPN module, ECA attention module, and Alpha-IoU loss function resulted in significant enhancements. Specifically, the model's computational speed increased by 11.6/s, 19.9/s, and 10.9/s, respectively. Moreover, the $mAP50$ saw increases of 3.3%, 4.8%, and 4.4%, respectively. The accuracy for identifying various defects also demonstrated improvements. These enhancements mark a significant advancement over the original model. As illustrated in Figure 7, the YOLO-Former model demonstrates rapid convergence and requires shorter training periods. This is beneficial for fine-tuning and optimizing the algorithm. Observations from Figure 8a,b reveal that YOLO-Former performs well across most categories.

In Experiment 5, the adoption of Alpha-CIoU led to a 4.4% increase in $mAP50$ and slight improvements in detection accuracy and recall rates of 0.3% and 1.7%, respectively. In addition, the integration of three bounding box regression methods—DIoU [26], GIoU [27], and EIoU [28]—was introduced. The experiment consisted of 200 iteration rounds, with the mAP50 comparison represented in Figure 9.

The figure evidently demonstrates that the Alpha-CIoU loss function not only converges more swiftly but also achieves a higher $mAP50$ than the competing functions. This superior performance is attributed to the prevalent issue of mismatched anchors due to the anchor presetting mechanism, which results in a scarcity of high-quality anchors. In the regression loss calculation and backpropagation process, the predominance of low-quality frames has a more significant effect than the less frequent high-quality frames.

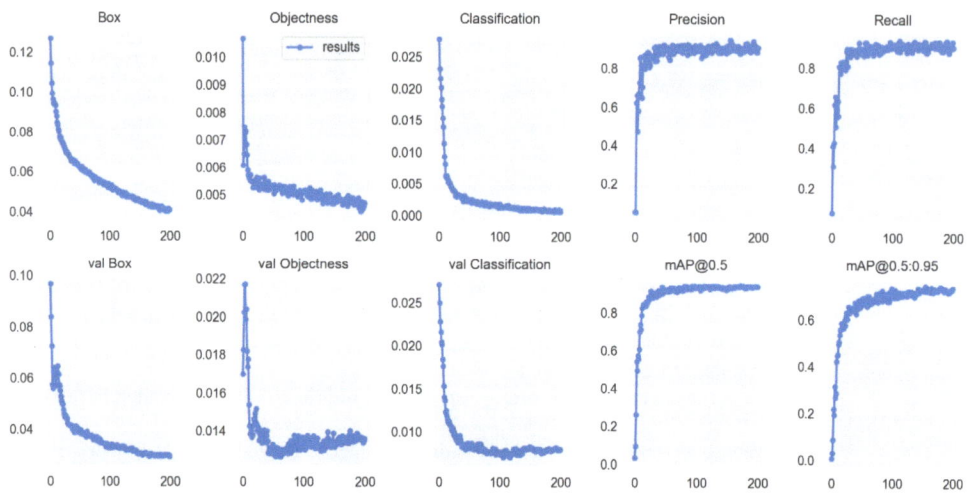

Figure 7. Loss curves of MBEA-YOLO on BYD dataset.

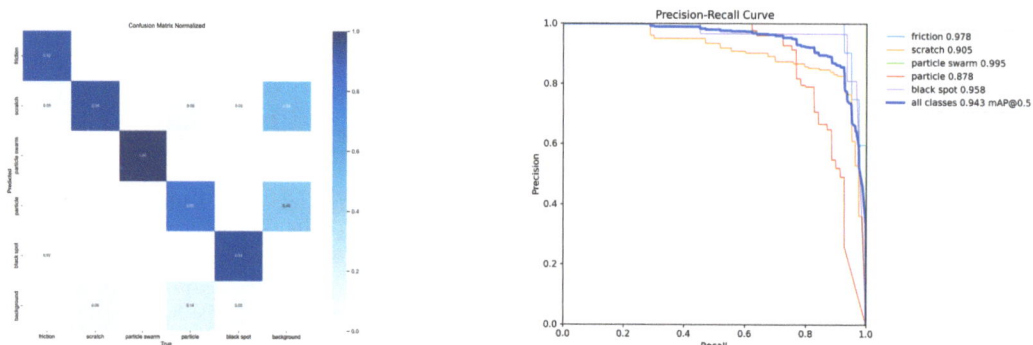

(**a**) Confusion matrix of MBEA-YOLO on BYD dataset. (**b**) Precision–recall curve of MBEA-YOLO on BYD dataset.

Figure 8. (**a**) Confusion matrix and (**b**) precision–recall curve of MBEA-YOLO on BYD dataset.

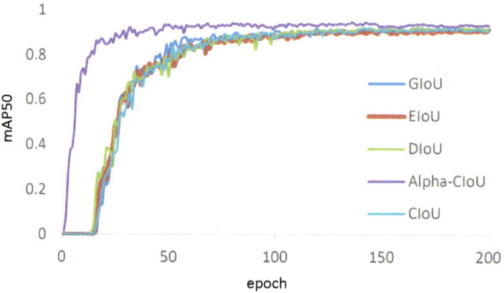

Figure 9. Comparison of different loss functions.

To mitigate this issue, an exponential term (0 < IoU) is added for weighting. When the IoU is larger, indicating a higher quality of the anchor, the weighting value of the exponential term is larger. Conversely, lower IoU scores, indicating poorer anchor quality, receive less weight. Accordingly, the enhanced loss function prioritizes high-quality anchors and minimizes the effect of lower-quality ones. This adjustment effectively counters the challenge of unbalanced training samples in the original bounding box regression model.

4.3.4. Comparison of Detection Effects

To visualize the effect of the enhanced model on defect detection, this study analyzed the test set with both the original and the enhanced models. The comparison between YOLOv7 and the upgraded MBEA-YOLOv7 in some image tests is presented in Figure 10. This comparison aims to clearly demonstrate the enhancements the enhanced model introduces for detecting target defects.

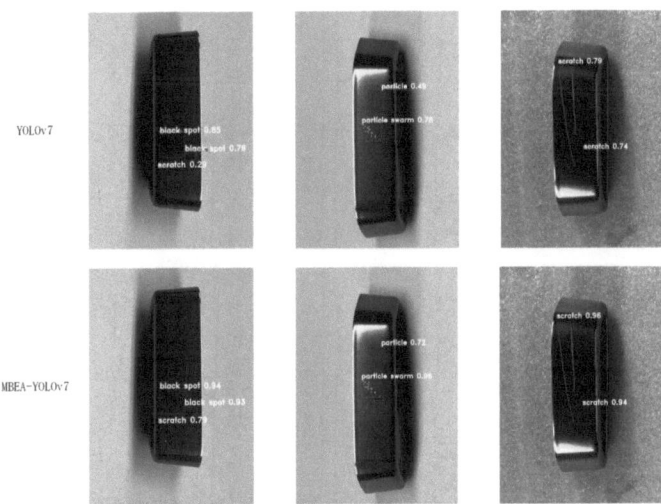

Figure 10. Comparison of detection performance on the BYD dataset.

4.3.5. Comparison and Generalization Experiments

To establish the superiority of the MBEA-YOLOv7 model introduced in this study over existing general target detection algorithms, we conducted comparative experiments on the NEU-DET dataset. These experiments pitted the newly proposed method against mainstream methods such as Faster-RCNN, SSD, YOLOv4, YOLOv5, YOLOv8, and YOLOv7.

The analysis, as illustrated in Table 4, reveals that the $mAP50$ of our proposed method surpasses that of Faster-RCNN, SSD, YOLOv4, YOLOv5, and YOLOv8 by 8.2, 12.9, 13.1, 12.8, and 3.8 percentage points, respectively. It also achieves the highest values in precision, recall, and detection speed. Despite a lower FPS compared to YOLOv8, it manages to detect targets in real time. In summary, the performance of the enhanced MBEA-YOLOv7 model exceeds that of other algorithms.

The exceptional performance of MBEA-YOLOv7 across various datasets confirms the algorithm's consistent detectability and strong ability to generalize across different datasets. The accuracy of MBEA-YOLOv7 reached 94.2% on the self-made BYD dataset and 68.8% on NEU-DUT. Compared with the original YOLOv7 model, the improvement is 5.5% and 7.5%, respectively, and the effect is remarkable.

Indeed, as indicated in the table, MBEA-YOLOv7 enhances the $mAP50$ by 7.5% in comparison to YOLOv7, showcasing enhanced accuracy and recall. The detection results depicted in Figure 11 further demonstrate that the algorithm we propose outperforms the original YOLOv7 model on various defect datasets. This highlights our algorithm's ability to maintain stable detection performance and exhibit a strong generalization capability across diverse datasets.

Table 4. Performance comparison of different algorithms on NEU-DUT.

Method	Precision/%	Recall/%	mAP/%	FPS/s
Faster-RCNN	63.1	65.3	67.3	18
SSD	62.5	60.3	62.6	26
YOLOv4	61.5	61.6	62.4	31
YOLOv5	60.7	64.5	62.7	70
YOLOv7	68.3	65.8	68.0	48
YOLOv8	66.1	68.3	71.7	126
MBEA-YOLOv7	68.8	71.5	75.5	76

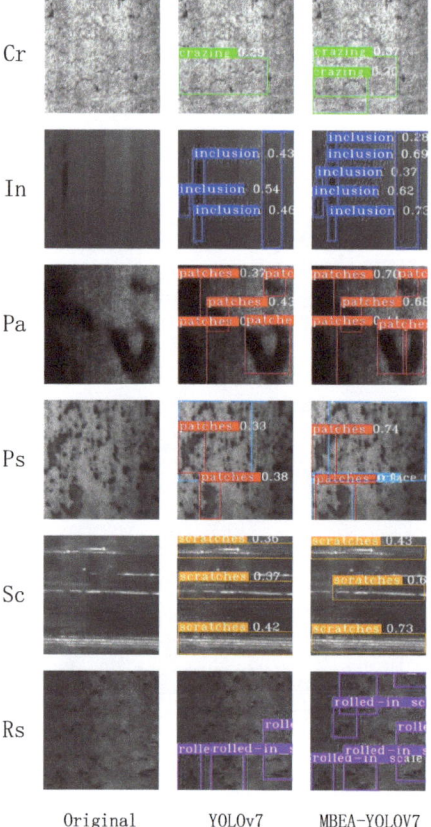

Figure 11. Comparison chart of detection effect.

5. Conclusions

In this paper, we propose a multi-class object detection method, the MBEA-YOLO network, for defect detection in automotive parts. This approach integrates feature extraction and fusion with attention mechanisms. For the self-built BYD data volume, compared with the original YOLOv7, accuracy increased by 3.3% and 4.8%, respectively, and the speed increased by 11.6/s and 19.9/s, respectively. These components enhance the accuracy for detecting small defects while maintaining the speed necessary for real-time, dynamic inspection tasks. Not only has our MBEA-YOLO network proven itself on the BYD dataset that it was trained on, but the Northeastern University steel dataset (NEU-DUT) has also been evaluated, and the effect is equally significant. The accuracy and speed also have significant advantages compared to some popular deep learning methods. Compared to the original model, the accuracy and speed have improved by 7.5% and 28/s, respectively. Even compared to the latest YOLOv8, the accuracy has a 4.8% advantage. This confirms the outstanding efficacy of the method at identifying defects in automotive components. However, it can be seen that MBEA-YOLOv7 is 50/s slower than YOLOv8 for detection speed, and it can be found that YOLOv8 is more lightweight, which is also a goal for the future. The goal is to achieve higher accuracy and faster detection speed with a more lightweight model.

For future studies, we aim to compile extensive datasets from various locations, including a wide array of defect types in automotive parts. This comprehensive data collection is designed to broaden the adaptability of the methods we advocate. We also plan to delve into cutting-edge technologies to forge more powerful and efficient solutions leveraging diverse deep learning architectures. The objective seeks to narrow the divide between theoretical innovation and practical utility, and we aspire to make a significant contribution to the field. We envision our work benefiting traffic survey efforts under demanding conditions; this marks a promising direction for future research. We are eager to witness the progress in this arena.

Author Contributions: Conceptualization, H.H. and K.Z.; Methodology, H.H. and K.Z.; Software, H.H.; Validation, H.H.; Formal analysis, H.H.; Investigation, H.H.; Resources, H.H.; Data curation, H.H.; Writing—original draft, H.H.; Writing—review & editing, K.Z.; Supervision, K.Z.; Funding acquisition, K.Z. All authors have read and agreed to the published version of the manuscript.

Funding: This research was funded by The Natural Science Foundation of the Jiangsu Higher Education Institutions of China (grant number 22KJD440001) and Changzhou Science & Technology Program (grant number CJ20220232).

Data Availability Statement: Data are contained within the article.

Conflicts of Interest: The authors declare no conflict of interest.

References

1. Minaee, S.; Boykov, Y.; Porikli, F.; Plaza, A.; Kehtarnavaz, N.; Terzopoulos, D. Image segmentation using deep learning: A survey. *IEEE Trans. Pattern Anal. Mach. Intell.* **2021**, *44*, 3523–3542. [CrossRef]
2. Yan, H.; Cai, J.-F.; Zhao, Y.; Jiang, Z.; Zhang, Y.; Ren, H.; Zhang, Y.; Li, H.; Long, Y. A lightweight high-resolution algorithm based on deep learning for layer-wise defect detection in laser powder bed fusion. *Meas. Sci. Technol.* **2023**, *35*, 025604. [CrossRef]
3. Li, Z.; Zhang, Y.; Fu, X.; Wang, C. Metal surface defect detection based on improved yolov5. In Proceedings of the 2023 3rd International Symposium on Computer Technology and Information Science (ISCTIS), Chengdu, China, 16–18 June 2023; pp. 1147–1150.
4. Kumar, A. Computer-vision-based fabric defect detection: A survey. *IEEE Trans. Ind. Electron.* **2008**, *55*, 348–363. [CrossRef]
5. Kim, K.J.; Lee, J.-W. Light-weight design and structure analysis of automotive wheel carrier by using finite element analysis. *Int. J. Precis. Eng. Manuf.* **2022**, *23*, 79–85. [CrossRef]
6. Xu, J.; Xi, N.; Zhang, C.; Shi, Q.; Gregory, J. Real-time 3d shape inspection system of automotive parts based on structured light pattern. *Opt. Laser Technol.* **2011**, *43*, 1–8. [CrossRef]
7. Ho, C.-C.; Hernandez, M.A.B.; Chen, Y.-F.; Lin, C.-J.; Chen, C.-S. Deep residual neural network-based defect detection on complex backgrounds. *IEEE Trans. Instrum. Meas.* **2022**, *71*, 5005210. [CrossRef]
8. Yu, X.; Lyu, W.; Wang, C.; Guo, Q.; Zhou, D.; Xu, W. Progressive refined redistribution pyramid network for defect detection in complex scenarios. *Knowl.-Based Syst.* **2023**, *260*, 110176. [CrossRef]
9. Yang, L.; Fan, J.; Huo, B.; Li, E.; Liu, Y. A nondestructive automatic defect detection method with pixelwise segmentation. *Knowl.-Based Syst.* **2022**, *242*, 108338. [CrossRef]
10. Zou, X.; Zhao, J.; Li, Y.; Holmes, M. In-line detection of apple defects using three color cameras system. *Comput. Electron. Agric.* **2010**, *70*, 129–134.
11. Girshick, R.; Donahue, J.; Darrell, T.; Malik, J. Rich feature hierarchies for accurate object detection and semantic segmentation. In Proceedings of the IEEE Conference on Computer Vision and Pattern Recognition, Columbus, OH, USA, 24–27 June 2014; pp. 580–587.
12. Redmon, J.; Divvala, S.; Girshick, R.; Farhadi, A. You only look once: Unified, real-time object detection. In Proceedings of the IEEE Conference on Computer Vision and Pattern Recognition, Las Vegas, NE, USA, 26 June–1 July 2016; pp. 779–788.

13. Liu, W.; Anguelov, D.; Erhan, D.; Szegedy, C.; Reed, S.; Fu, C.-Y.; Berg, A.C. Ssd: Single shot multibox detector. In Proceedings of the Computer Vision–ECCV 2016: 14th European Conference, Amsterdam, The Netherlands, 11–14 October 2016; Proceedings, Part I 14; Springer: Cham, Switzerland, 2016; pp. 21–37.
14. Redmon, J.; Farhadi, A. Yolo9000: Better, faster, stronger. In Proceedings of the IEEE Conference on Computer Vision and Pattern Recognition, Honolulu, HI, USA, 21–26 July 2017; pp. 7263–7271.
15. Redmon, J.; Farhadi, A. Yolov3: An incremental improvement. arXiv 2018, arXiv:1804.02767.
16. Bochkovskiy, A.; Wang, C.-Y.; Liao, H.-Y.M. Yolov4: Optimal speed and accuracy of object detection. arXiv 2020, arXiv:2004.10934.
17. Ren, S.; He, K.; Girshick, R.; Sun, J. Faster r-cnn: Towards real-time object detection with region proposal networks. IEEE Trans. Pattern Anal. Mach. Intell. 2017, 39, 1137–1149. [CrossRef] [PubMed]
18. Cha, Y.-J.; Choi, W.; Suh, G.; Mahmoudkhani, S.; Büyüköztürk, O. Autonomous structural visual inspection using region-based deep learning for detecting multiple damage types. Comput.-Aided Civ. Infrastruct. Eng. 2018, 33, 731–747. [CrossRef]
19. Tao, X.; Zhang, D.; Wang, Z.; Liu, X.; Zhang, H.; Xu, D. Detection of power line insulator defects using aerial images analyzed with convolutional neural networks. IEEE Trans. Syst. Man Cybern. Syst. 2018, 50, 1486–1498. [CrossRef]
20. He, Y.; Song, K.; Meng, Q.; Yan, Y. An end-to-end steel surface defect detection approach via fusing multiple hierarchical features. IEEE Trans. Instrum. Meas. 2019, 69, 1493–1504. [CrossRef]
21. Cheng, J.C.; Wang, M. Automated detection of sewer pipe defects in closed-circuit television images using deep learning techniques. Autom. Constr. 2018, 95, 155–171. [CrossRef]
22. Lei, H.; Wang, B.; Wu, H.; Wang, A. Defect detection for polymeric polarizer based on faster r-cnn. J. Inf. Hiding Multim. Signal Process. 2018, 9, 1414–1420.
23. Zhao, Z.; Zhen, Z.; Zhang, L.; Qi, Y.; Kong, Y.; Zhang, K. Insulator detection method in inspection image based on improved faster r-cnn. Energies 2019, 12, 1204. [CrossRef]
24. Neuhauser, F.M.; Bachmann, G.; Hora, P. Surface defect classification and detection on extruded aluminum profiles using convolutional neural networks. Int. J. Mater. Form. 2020, 13, 591–603. [CrossRef]
25. Sun, X.; Gu, J.; Huang, R.; Zou, R.; Palomares, B.G. Surface defects recognition of wheel hub based on improved faster r-cnn. Electronics 2019, 8, 481. [CrossRef]
26. Chen, J.; Liu, Z.; Wang, H.; Núñez, A.; Han, Z. Automatic defect detection of fasteners on the catenary support device using deep convolutional neural network. IEEE Trans. Instrum. Meas. 2017, 67, 257–269. [CrossRef]
27. Li, Y.; Huang, H.; Xie, Q.; Yao, L.; Chen, Q. Research on a surface defect detection algorithm based on mobilenet-ssd. Appl. Sci. 2018, 8, 1678. [CrossRef]
28. Zhang, C.; Chang, C.-C.; Jamshidi, M. Concrete bridge surface damage detection using a single-stage detector. Comput.-Aided Civ. Infrastruct. Eng. 2020, 35, 389–409. [CrossRef]
29. Zheng, Q.; Wang, L.; Wang, F. Small object detection in traffic scene based on improved convolutional neural network. Comput. Eng. 2020, 46, 26–33.
30. Ju, M.; Luo, J.; Wang, Z.; Luo, H. Multi-scale target detection algorithm based on attention mechanism. Acta Opt. Sin. 2020, 466, 132–140.
31. Cui, Z.; Qin, Y.; Zhong, Y.; Cao, Z.; Yang, H. Target Detection in High-Resolution Sar Image via Iterating Outliers and Recursing Saliency Depth. Remote Sens. 2021, 13, 4315. [CrossRef]
32. Liu, J.; Jia, R.; Li, W.; Ma, F.; Abdullah, H.M.; Ma, H.; Mohamed, M.A. High precision detection algorithm based on improved retinanet for defect recognition of transmission lines. Energy Rep. 2020, 6, 2430–2440. [CrossRef]
33. Liu, J.; Liang, H.; Cui, X.; Zhong, M.; Li, C. SSD visual target detector based on feature integration and feature enhancement. J. Comput. Eng. Appl. 2022, 58, 150-159.. [CrossRef]
34. Li, Z.; Zhou, F. Fssd: Feature fusion single shot multibox detector. arXiv 2017, arXiv:1712.00960.
35. Shi, W.; Bao, S.; Tan, D. Ffessd: An accurate and efficient single-shot detector for target detection. Appl. Sci. 2019, 9, 4276. [CrossRef]
36. Zhao, P.; Xie, L.; Peng, L. Deep small object detection algorithm integrating attention mechanism. J. Front. Comput. Sci. Technol. 2022, 16, 927-937.
37. Ren, J.; Ren, R.; Green, M.; Huang, X. Defect detection from X-ray images using a three-stage deep learning algorithm. In Proceedings of the 2019 IEEE Canadian Conference of Electrical and Computer Engineering (CCECE), Edmonton, AB, Canada, 5–8 May 2019; pp. 1–4.
38. Du, W.; Shen, H.; Fu, J.; Zhang, G.; He, Q. Approaches for improvement of the X-ray image defect detection of automobile casting aluminum parts based on deep learning. NDT E Int. 2019, 107, 102144. [CrossRef]
39. Tsai, D.-M.; Fan, S.-K.S.; Chou, Y.-H. Auto-annotated deep segmentation for surface defect detection. IEEE Trans. Instrum. Meas. 2021, 70, 1–10. [CrossRef]
40. Shin, S.; Jin, C.; Yu, J.; Rhee, S. Real-time detection of weld defects for automated welding process base on deep neural network. Metals 2020, 10, 389. [CrossRef]
41. Block, S.B.; da Silva, R.D.; Dorini, L.B.; Minetto, R. Inspection of imprint defects in stamped metal surfaces using deep learning and tracking. IEEE Trans. Ind. Electron. 2020, 68, 4498–4507. [CrossRef]
42. Chen, X.; Chen, J.; Han, X.; Zhao, C.; Zhang, D.; Zhu, K.; Su, Y. A light-weighted cnn model for wafer structural defect detection. IEEE Access 2020, 8, 24006–24018. [CrossRef]

43. Huang, S.-C.; Le, T.-H.; Jaw, D.-W. Dsnet: Joint semantic learning for object detection in inclement weather conditions. *IEEE Trans. Pattern Anal. Mach. Intell.* **2020**, *43*, 2623–2633. [CrossRef]
44. He, J.; Erfani, S.; Ma, X.; Bailey, J.; Chi, Y.; Hua, X.-S. Alpha-iou: A family of power intersection over union losses for bounding box regression. *Adv. Neural Inf. Process. Syst.* **2021**, *34*, 20230–20242.

Disclaimer/Publisher's Note: The statements, opinions and data contained in all publications are solely those of the individual author(s) and contributor(s) and not of MDPI and/or the editor(s). MDPI and/or the editor(s) disclaim responsibility for any injury to people or property resulting from any ideas, methods, instructions or products referred to in the content.

Article

A Novel Multi-LiDAR-Based Point Cloud Stitching Method Based on a Constrained Particle Filter

Gaofan Ji [1,2], Yunhan He [3,*], Chuanxiang Li [4,*], Li Fan [1,3], Haibo Wang [5] and Yantong Zhu [5]

1. Huzhou Institute of Zhejiang University, Huzhou 313000, China; goafan@163.com (G.J.); fanli77@zju.edu.cn (L.F.)
2. School of Engineering, Huzhou University, Huzhou 313000, China
3. College of Control Science and Engineering, Zhejiang University, Hangzhou 310027, China
4. High-Tech Institution of Xi'an, Xi'an 710025, China
5. Guoneng Lingwu Power Generation Co., Ltd., Lingwu 751400, China; 12895752@ceic.com (H.W.); 12876386@ceic.com (Y.Z.)
* Correspondence: heyunhan@zju.edu.cn (Y.H.); lichuanxiang@zju.edu.cn (C.L.)

Abstract: In coal-fired power plants, coal piles serve as the fundamental management units. Acquiring point clouds of coal piles facilitates the convenient measurement of daily coal consumption and combustion efficiency. When using servo motors to drive Light Detection and Ranging (LiDAR) scanning of large-scale coal piles, the motors are subject to rotational errors due to gravitational effects. As a result, the acquired point clouds often contain significant noise. To address this issue, we proposes a Rapid Point Cloud Stitching–Constrained Particle Filter (RPCS-CPF) method. By introducing random noise to simulate servo motor rotational errors, both local and global point clouds are sequentially subjected to RPCS-CPF operations, resulting in smooth and continuous coal pile point clouds. Moreover, this paper presents a coal pile boundary detection method based on gradient region growing clustering. Experimental results demonstrate that our proposed RPCS-CPF method can generate smooth and continuous coal pile point clouds, even in the presence of servo motor rotational errors.

Keywords: point cloud stitching; edge detection; coal stock pile; 3D reconstruction; lidar scanning

Citation: Ji, G.; He, Y.; Li, C.; Fan, L.; Wang, H.; Zhu, Y. A Novel Multi-LiDAR-Based Point Cloud Stitching Method Based on a Constrained Particle Filter. *Electronics* 2024, 13, 1777. https://doi.org/10.3390/electronics13091777

Academic Editors: Vladimir László Tadić and Peter Odry

Received: 6 April 2024
Revised: 28 April 2024
Accepted: 30 April 2024
Published: 4 May 2024

Copyright: © 2024 by the authors. Licensee MDPI, Basel, Switzerland. This article is an open access article distributed under the terms and conditions of the Creative Commons Attribution (CC BY) license (https://creativecommons.org/licenses/by/4.0/).

1. Introduction

With the rapid growth in demand for electricity supply, the need for coal is also steadily increasing. In the operation of coal-fired power plants, coal piles serve as the fundamental units of management. Obtaining point cloud data of coal piles allows for the easy measurement of various parameters such as volume [1–3], density, and boundaries, which are crucial for ensuring safe operations at coal yards and effectively managing coal combustion efficiency.

1.1. 3D Reconstruction of Coal Piles

Traditional methods for obtaining point clouds of coal piles involve the tedious process of manual scanning using handheld scanners [4]. This approach demands significant time and effort. Recently, researchers have explored more efficient 3D reconstruction techniques [5,6], such as employing GNSS-RTK technology, utilizing multiple fixed LiDARs for scanning coal heaps [7], and deploying drones. Each of these methods offers their own advantages and disadvantages depending on specific circumstances and applications.

Handheld devices, typically employing laser scanners or cameras, are utilized by operators to manually scan coal piles for data collection. However, the scanning efficiency of this method is relatively low, making it unsuitable for rapid scanning and continuous monitoring of large coal piles. Moreover, measuring larger coal piles presents significant challenges for workers.

Drone scanning involves the use of unmanned aerial vehicles (UAVs) equipped with cameras or laser scanners to perform aerial scans of coal piles [8–11]. This system can rapidly capture surface data of extensive coal piles within a short timeframe, thereby offering the advantages of improved resolution and comprehensiveness. However, drone scanning does have certain limitations. A study by Alsayed et al. [9] revealed that drones equipped with LiDAR sensors may have blind spots during data scanning, particularly in enclosed coal yard environments, which pose challenges for optimizing flight trajectories and may require further refinement. Additionally, research by Davis et al. [12] demonstrated that increasing the altitude of drone flights can result in greater errors and reduced reliability.

Mahlberg et al. [13] pioneered a portable LiDAR device mounted on a pole for scanning point clouds in expansive granaries. However, this method relies on complex point cloud registration techniques, leading to considerable evaluation complexity. Farhood et al. [14] proposed using smartphone cameras to extract material point clouds by capturing moving images. However, it is important to note that this approach is restricted to smaller materials and faces challenges in ensuring the accuracy of point cloud reconstruction.

While GNSS-RTK can provide precise location data, it often faces challenges like signal obstruction and multipath interference in indoor enclosed environments. These issues negatively affect its positioning accuracy and reliability, making it unable to provide continuous point cloud data [15]. Raevaa et al. [8] utilized GNSS-RTK for measurements in an open-pit quarry, but they found that the measurement speed was significantly slow, resulting in decreased work efficiency.

In contrast, using laser scanning [16–18] allows for the acquisition of complete point cloud data for coal piles, but, for large-scale coal piles, a single laser scanner operates at a slow speed and produces sparse point clouds [19,20]. Therefore, this study employs a system of multiple fixed LiDARs to construct a coal pile scanning system, which offers several advantages. Firstly, fixed LiDARs exhibit higher scanning precision and stability [21–23]. By adjusting the installation height and angle appropriately, they can adapt to coal piles of varying heights, thus better covering the entire surface of the coal pile and obtaining more comprehensive and accurate point cloud data [12,24]. Secondly, fixed LiDARs enable long-term continuous scanning, allowing for the continuous acquisition of point cloud data for coal piles. This makes them suitable for long-term monitoring of changes in coal pile morphology and real-time volume calculations. Therefore, this study adopts the approach of using multiple laser scanners to obtain coal pile point clouds.

However, employing multiple LiDARs for scanning coal piles does pose certain limitations. Applying pressure to actuators can induce instability, leading to deviations in the generated point clouds. These discrepancies may cause non-smooth surfaces when stitching point clouds using the existing coordinate system. To address this challenge, this study introduces the RPCS-CPF method as a solution for coal pile point cloud stitching.

1.2. Point Cloud Edge Detection

During coal pile operations, vehicles often need to climb to the top of coal piles for tasks such as loading, leveling, or measurement. However, the surface terrain of coal piles is complex and variable. When nearing the edges of the pile or encountering depressed areas, vehicles are susceptible to sliding hazards, resulting in potential casualties. Therefore, detecting boundaries of coal piles and providing early warnings are crucial for ensuring the safety of personnel.

By analyzing and meticulously processing dense point cloud data, it becomes possible to accurately detect the boundaries and depressions on the surface of the coal pile, thus revealing potential safety risks. Chen et al. [25] introduced a 3D boundary identification technique that utilizes DBSCAN clustering. This method demonstrated favorable outcomes when applied to point clouds exhibiting conventional local shapes. However, it was found to be unsuitable for point clouds representing complex coal piles. Furthermore, the controllability of the parameters in this clustering method is limited, posing a challenge in identifying the Pareto optimum. In their study, Mineo et al. [26] introduced a unique algorithm called BPD for boundary point identification, along with a spatial FFT-based filtering approach. This approach is effective in fitting surfaces with polynomials and is particularly suitable for smooth coal pile surfaces. However, its performance is suboptimal when dealing with complex coal heaps that have pits and tunnels. Additionally, Runge's phenomenon arises when the order of the polynomial exceeds 10. In their study, Yang et al. [27] introduced an algorithm that utilizes multi-scale directional curvature to extract and quantify the borders of accumulations from 3D point cloud data. This algorithm is capable of detecting the boundaries of various wave peak materials, but it faces difficulties in detecting pits and trenches. Hu et al. [28] introduced a boundary identification technique that utilizes semantic segmentation. This method demonstrated favorable outcomes when used on the S3DIS and ScanNet datasets. However, it encounters challenges in accurately differentiating the intricate distribution of coal pile surface terrain.

Given these challenges, it is crucial to devise a robust and flexible strategy for surface identification and assessment of coal piles, ensuring the safety and efficiency of coal handling operations. The adoption of such technology holds promise for significantly reducing accident rates and optimizing the performance of coal handling facilities.

The innovations in this work are as follows:

(1) A rapid point cloud stitching algorithm grounded in the Constrained Particle Filter (CPF) is presented, which addresses the stochastic rotational errors of servos through mathematical modeling and has undergone algorithmic validation on a large coal pile. Utilizing multiple LiDAR–servo units, we scanned the coal pile and initially processed the point cloud generated by a single LiDAR scan with the CPF. Following this, we applied the CPF to the point cloud resulting from the stitching of multiple LiDAR scans. Experimental results have confirmed that our stitching algorithm not only ensures a smooth transition at the junction points but also maintains the surface integrity of the coal pile's point cloud.

(2) We propose a complex coal pile surface edge detection algorithm based on gradient region growing clustering. Initially, we estimate the normal vectors and calculate the gradients of the stitched point cloud. Subsequently, clustering is performed using the slope and gradient magnitude of the coal pile. By setting specific slope and magnitude intervals, we extract the boundaries of the coal pile. Experimental results indicate that our method is capable of detecting the boundaries of hazardous terrains such as pits, aisles, and ridges within the coal pile, thereby enhancing the safety of coal pile operations. This approach holds broad application value.

2. Method

When acquiring point cloud data for a large coal pile in an enclosed coal yard, using a handheld scanner is impractical for scanning the entire coal pile, and employing drones requires planning complex scanning routes while avoiding obstacles within the coal yard. Therefore, we opted to use multiple fixed LiDARs to scan the coal pile. Each LiDAR was mounted on a servo, which rotated the LiDAR to scan a local area of the coal pile. Ultimately, the point clouds obtained from the multiple LiDAR scans were stitched together. With the known spatial relationships of the LiDARs' coordinates, we could conveniently merge the coal pile point clouds, thereby circumventing the complex process of point cloud registration.

The point cloud processing workflow employed in this study is illustrated in Figure 1. Initially, a series of LiDAR scans were utilized to acquire point cloud data from various sections of the coal stockpile. To mitigate noise arising from random errors in servo motor rotation angles, the RPCS-CPF algorithm was applied to each cloud data point for refined filtering. Subsequently, coordinate transformations were applied to the filtered point clouds prior to fusion, followed by another round of RPCS-CPF algorithmic treatment to obtain a smooth point cloud representation of the entire coal pile. Building upon this framework, a gradient-based region growing clustering algorithm is proposed for identifying boundaries on the coal pile surface, with the effectiveness of the algorithm corroborated through the meticulous construction of point cloud models.

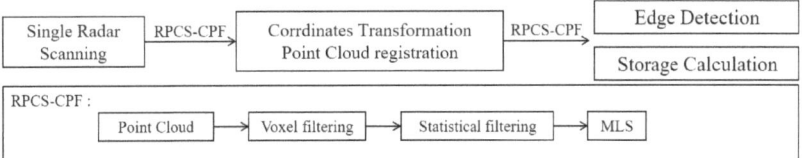

Figure 1. Flowchart of our method. Initially, the point cloud obtained from a single LiDAR scan undergoes CPF processing. Subsequently, the point clouds from various LiDAR sections are subjected to coordinate transformation and then stitched together. Following this, CPF is applied to the concatenated point cloud to obtain an integrated point cloud of the coal pile. This comprehensive point cloud can then be utilized for boundary detection or for the statistical analysis of coal pile reserves.

2.1. Point Cloud Coordinate Transformation

The original point cloud's coordinates are aligned with the three-dimensional coordinate system of the LiDAR. To analyze the 3D point clouds collected by the LiDAR at various angles, it is essential to calculate the coordinate transformation between them. As illustrated in Figure 2, the actuator coordinate system rotates around point O, which is the center of rotation. Assuming the distance from point O to the center of the LiDAR is r, the actuator captures a 3D point cloud of the coal pile with each rotation of $\Delta \varphi$. At each distinct rotational position ($n = 0, 1, \ldots$), the 3D points are expressed in the actuator's coordinate system (X_n^S, Y_n^S, Z_n^S) with coordinates (x_n^s, y_n^s, z_n^s). The actuator's rotation is around the X_n^s-axis.

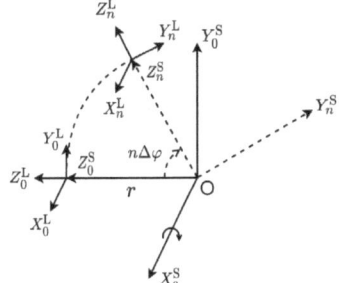

Figure 2. Rotation of the servo motor coordinate system.

Then, the coordinates of point cloud in servo coordinate system can be obtained as follows:

$$P_n^S = \begin{bmatrix} x_n^S \\ y_n^S \\ z_n^S \end{bmatrix} = \begin{bmatrix} x_n^L \\ y_n^L \\ z_n^L + r \end{bmatrix} = P_n^L + \begin{bmatrix} 0 \\ 0 \\ r \end{bmatrix} \quad (1)$$

where P_n^L represents the coordinates of the point in the LiDAR coordinate system (X_n^L, Y_n^L, Z_n^L). During the rotation of the actuator, since the rotation axis is parallel to the X-axis, the x-coordinate of the point remains unchanged. The relationship of transformation between the coordinates of the point after the n-th rotation and the coordinates in the initial state ($n = 0$) can be expressed as follows:

$$P_n^S = \begin{bmatrix} x_n^S \\ y_n^S \\ z_n^S \end{bmatrix} = R_n^S \begin{bmatrix} x_0^S \\ y_0^S \\ z_0^S \end{bmatrix} \quad (2)$$

where the rotation matrix R_n^S is:

$$R_n^S = \begin{bmatrix} 1 & 0 & 0 \\ 0 & \cos(n \cdot \Delta\varphi) & -\sin(n \cdot \Delta\varphi) \\ 0 & \sin(n \cdot \Delta\varphi) & \cos(n \cdot \Delta\varphi) \end{bmatrix} \quad (3)$$

According to Formula (1), Formula (2) can be expressed as follows:

$$P_n^L + \begin{bmatrix} 0 \\ 0 \\ r \end{bmatrix} = P_n^S = \begin{bmatrix} x_n^S \\ y_n^S \\ z_n^S \end{bmatrix} = R_n^S \begin{bmatrix} x_0^S \\ y_0^S \\ z_0^S \end{bmatrix} = R_n^S \left(P_0^L + \begin{bmatrix} 0 \\ 0 \\ r \end{bmatrix} \right) \quad (4)$$

Therefore, we derive the subsequent transformation relation:

$$P_n^L = R_n^S P_0^L + \left(R_n^S - 1 \right) \begin{bmatrix} 0 \\ 0 \\ r \end{bmatrix} \quad (5)$$

$$P_0^L = \left(R_n^S \right)^{-1} P_n^L + \left(\left(R_n^S \right)^{-1} - 1 \right) \begin{bmatrix} 0 \\ 0 \\ r \end{bmatrix} \quad (6)$$

Based on Equation (6), it is feasible to transform the point cloud coordinates from various scanning angles into the initial state within the LiDAR coordinate system. This makes it easier to integrate point clouds from various scanning angles on a single LiDAR. A thorough point cloud of a sizable coal pile can be obtained by using many LiDARs and matching their coordinate systems into a single global coordinate system.

Given the large area of a coal pile, the comprehensive acquisition of its point cloud data generally requires the deployment multiple LiDARs positioned above the pile to facilitate scanning. Following this, it is necessary to integrate the point clouds acquired from several LiDAR scans. Nevertheless, the accuracy of rotation cannot be assured as a result of the gravitational impact exerted by the LiDAR on the actuator. Consequently, following the process of coordinate transformation, the point clouds exhibit an inability to be effectively integrated. Given the aforementioned concern, it is evident that Equation (3) is no longer capable of accurately depicting the rotation matrix of the point clouds. Consequently, it is restructured in the following manner:

$$R_n^{S'} = \begin{bmatrix} 1 & 0 & 0 \\ 0 & \cos(n \cdot \Delta\varphi + \theta_n) & -\sin(n \cdot \Delta\varphi + \theta_n) \\ 0 & \sin(n \cdot \Delta\varphi + \theta_n) & \cos(n \cdot \Delta\varphi + \theta_n) \end{bmatrix} \quad (7)$$

where θ_n denotes the error in the nth rotation of the actuator. The rotation deviation is assumed to follow a uniform distribution with a range of [0, $\triangle_\theta$], where $\triangle_\theta$ represents the range of rotation error from 0 to 5 degrees. Consequently, the new point cloud coordinates can be expressed as follows:

$$P_0^{L'} = \left(R_n^{S'} \right)^{-1} P_n^L + \left(\left(R_n^{S'} \right)^{-1} - 1 \right) \begin{bmatrix} 0 \\ 0 \\ r \end{bmatrix} \quad (8)$$

2.2. RPCS-CPF Method

This study introduces a rapid point cloud registration approach called RPCS-CPF to tackle the problem of inadequate robustness in point cloud stitching caused by LiDAR rotation deviation. The algorithm assumes that the rotation plane remains constant. The formula can be expressed as follows:

$$P_m = \{MLS(G_S(G_v(P_i)))\}_{i=1}^N \quad (9)$$

where P_i represents the original point cloud, P_m denotes the point cloud after undergoing particle filtering, G_V signifies voxel filtering, G_S indicates statistical filtering, and MLS represents the moving least square.

2.2.1. Voxel Filtering

The expanded number of laser emission lines in a 16-line LiDAR system enhances the spatial resolution of the resultant point set, yielding a densely populated point cloud. However, this results in an escalated computational load and a reduction in processing efficiency. To address this, we employed voxel filtering to downsample the point cloud of the coal pile, while preserving its geometric integrity.

Voxel filtering is a method used for downsampling point clouds, wherein the density of the point cloud is reduced by partitioning it into individual cubic cells. This partitioning process ensures that just one representative point is retained within each cell. The process of voxel filtering involves dividing an original point cloud, represented as $P = (x_i, y_i, z_i)_{i=1}^{N}$, into cubic cells of size 0.3 m^3. The centroid of each cell is used to replace the points within that cell. The point cloud obtained following the application of voxel filtering can be expressed as follows:

$$P_v = \{(x_i', y_i', z_i')\} = \left\{ \left(\frac{1}{n} \sum_{j=1}^{n} x_{ij}, \frac{1}{n} \sum_{j=1}^{n} y_{ij}, \frac{1}{n} \sum_{j=1}^{n} z_{ij} \right) \right\}_{i=1}^{M_v} \tag{10}$$

where P_v represents the filtered point cloud after the application of the statistical method, M_v denotes the number of points remaining after the filtering process.

2.2.2. Statistical Filtering

The point cloud obtained from LiDAR scanning displays slight positional discrepancies attributed to imprecisions in the rotation angle of the actuator during each rotation. As a result, the stitched point cloud contains an increased number of outlier points, which adversely affects the reconstruction of the coal pile surface. To alleviate the presence of outlier points and improve the overall smoothness of the point cloud surface, this study employs a statistical filtering technique for point cloud processing.

The process of statistical filtering entails assessing the point cloud by calculating the statistical attributes of individual points and their neighboring points to identify any outliers. The method commences by computing the mean μ_i and standard deviation σ_i for each point, assuming that the set of the nearest 100 points for each point is represented as N_i. Subsequently, it ascertains if a given data point is classified as an outlier. After applying statistical filtration, the resulting point cloud may be expressed as follows:

$$P_s = \{(x_i, y_i, z_i) | |z_i - \mu_i| < k \cdot \sigma_i\}_{i=1}^{M_s} \tag{11}$$

where P_s represents the filtered point cloud after the application of the statistical method, M_s denotes the number of points remaining after the filtering process, and k is the threshold value that controls the criteria for identifying outlier points.

2.2.3. Moving Least Squares

Following voxel and statistical filtering, the point cloud tends to exhibit sparsity and local point cloud voids. Hence, a two-step moving least squares method was employed to upsample the point cloud and fit smooth surfaces, thereby enhancing the continuity and smoothness of the coal pile point cloud surface and achieving a desirable point cloud density. For each point i in the point cloud P_s, a neighbor set N_i^s is selected within a 0.5 m radius, and a plane is fitted using the moving least squares method:

$$z_i = ax_i + by_i + c \tag{12}$$

The projection coordinates on the plane for each point i can be determined as $(\hat{x}_i, \hat{y}_i, \hat{z}_i)$. To fill gaps in the point cloud, we incrementally move 5 cm along the x- and y-axes, using Formula (12) to generate new points for the surface. The resultant point cloud is commonly represented as follows:

$$P_m = \{\hat{x}_i, \hat{y}_i, \hat{z}_i\}_{i=1}^{M_m} \tag{13}$$

where P_m represents the point cloud after being fitted by the least squares method, and M_m denotes the number of points in the fitted P_m.

2.3. Edge Detection Algorithm Based on Gradient Clustering

This study introduces a novel approach to address the complex terrain of coal piles by employing a gradient-based region-expanding clustering algorithm for edge detection. The method begins with the calculation of local normal vectors for the point cloud representing the coal pile surface. Subsequently, the local slope is determined based on these normal vectors.

The initial step involves constructing a KD-tree structure, followed by loading the point cloud data into the KD tree to facilitate nearest neighbor searches. Within a radius of $r = 0.5$ m, the nearest neighbors for point p are determined.

The covariance matrix is then computed using Equation (14). Utilizing Equation (15), the covariance matrix is decomposed, leading to the determination of eigenvalues and eigenvectors. The eigenvector corresponding to the minimum eigenvalue provides an approximation of the normal vector at the given point.

$$C = \frac{1}{k}\sum_{i=1}^{k} \cdot (\mathbf{p}_i - \overline{\mathbf{p}}) \cdot (\mathbf{p}_i - \overline{\mathbf{p}})^T \tag{14}$$

$$C \cdot \vec{\mathbf{v}_j} = \lambda_j \cdot \vec{\mathbf{v}_j}, j \in \{0, 1, 2\} \tag{15}$$

where C denotes the covariance matrix, k represents the size of the set of nearest neighbor points, P_i denotes the i-th nearest neighbor point, $\bar{P}$ denotes the centroid of the set of nearest neighbor points, which is the average of all nearest neighbor points, λ_j represents the j-th eigenvalue, and $\vec{v_j}$ corresponds to the eigenvector associated with λ_j.

In order to maintain consistency in the acquired normal directions, all normals are oriented towards the view vector V_p, as depicted in Figure 3.

$$\vec{n}_i \cdot (v_p - \mathbf{p}_i) > 0 \tag{16}$$

where $\vec{n_i}$ represents the normal vector of the i-th point, V_p denotes the view vector, which is aligned with the positive Z-axis direction in this paper, and P_i indicates the coordinates of the i-th point.

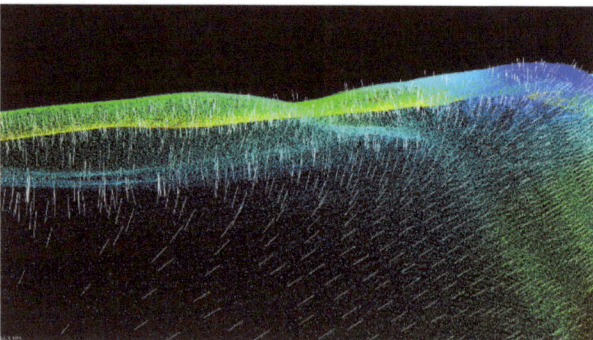

Figure 3. Part of the point cloud normal vector.

After obtaining the normal vectors for each point, the approximate gradient for each point can be calculated using the finite difference method:

$$\nabla f(P_i) = \left(\frac{f(P_i + h\Delta x) - f(P_i)}{h}, \frac{f(P_i + h\Delta y) - f(P_i)}{h}\right) \tag{17}$$

where h is the step size parameter, Δx and Δy are the unit vectors along the x- and y-axes, respectively. $f(P_i + h\Delta x)$ represents the corresponding height at point P_i after moving h along the x-axis direction.

Once the gradient for each point is obtained, we proceed with clustering using a method that relies on the growth of the gradient region. The first step involves establishing a neighborhood connection, where each point is designated as the center and a neighborhood radius r is defined. Points that are located within a distance of less than r from a certain point are regarded as constituents of the neighborhood of that point. The procedure proceeds to cycle through all seed points, denoted as $S_i \in S$, within the set S. For every seed point S_i, it verifies if the points P_j in its vicinity meet the following criteria:

$$\cos(\theta_{ij}) = \frac{G_i \cdot G_j}{\|G_i\| \|G_j\|} > \cos(\theta_{\text{threshold}}) \tag{18}$$

$$\left|\frac{M_i - M_j}{M_i}\right| < \varepsilon, M_i = |G_i| \tag{19}$$

where G_i and G_j represent the gradient direction vectors of points G_i and G_j, respectively, θ_{ij} is the angle between the two direction vectors, $\theta_{\text{threshold}}$ is the maximum allowable angle of gradient direction variation which is set to 15 degrees, M_i and M_j are the magnitudes of the gradients for P_i and P_j, respectively, and ε is the maximum allowable relative change in gradient magnitudes, which is set to 2.

Point P_j is incorporated into the same region as S_i if it meets the stated conditions, allowing for a smooth merging process. By means of consecutive iterations, this methodology utilizes gradient information to efficiently propagate the process of region growth.

3. Experiments

3.1. Hardware System

To validate the efficacy of the RPCS-CPF and the gradient-based region-growing clustering algorithm, experimental validation was conducted at Guoneng Ningxia Lingwu Power Generation Co., Ltd., Yinchuan, China. Four LiDARs were deployed across a significant coal pile measuring 200 m by 50 m, ensuring extensive coverage of the coal pile area, as depicted in Figure 4.

Figure 4. Multiple LiDAR arrangement scheme. Four LiDARs are evenly spaced and fixed above the coal pile.

We employed 16-line 3D LiDARs as our primary sensors. LiDARs are instrumental in acquiring precise three-dimensional positional data, allowing for the determination of an object's position, size, external morphology, and even material composition. The LiDARs chosen for this study possess a horizontal field of view spanning 360° and a vertical field of view of 30°. To facilitate the scanning of large coal piles, we mounted the LiDARs on servo actuators, thereby expanding their vertical scanning range. These actuators rotate the LiDARs to scan the entire coal pile.

The installation setup of the LiDARs is depicted in Figure 5. Initially, the servo actuators were securely affixed beneath the I-beams of the coal storage facility's canopy, while the LiDARs were mounted on the rotating structures of these actuators. With a maximum rotation angle of 180°, the LiDARs could capture a comprehensive point cloud of the coal pile.

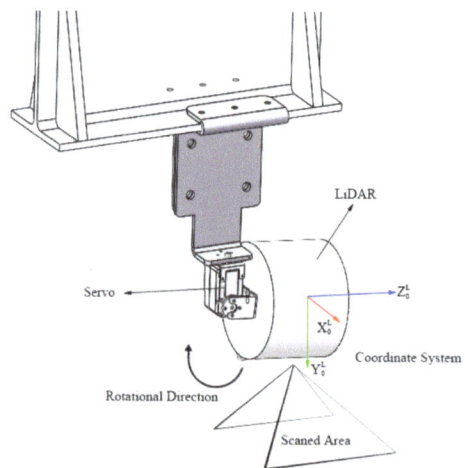

Figure 5. Installation diagram of LiDAR and servo motor.

3.2. Single LiDAR Particle Filter Results

The coal pile under investigation is illustrated in Figure 6. However, owing to the restricted field of view of the camera utilized, the representation is confined to a segment of the entire coal pile.

Figure 6. Coal pile.

The point clouds of the coal pile acquired from the four lidar scans are shown in Figure 7.

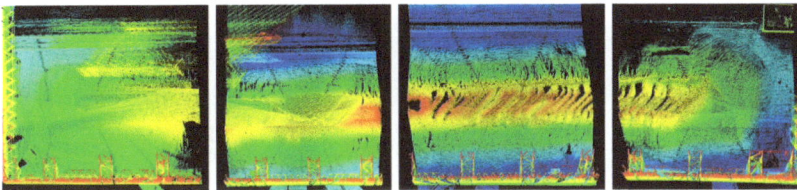

Figure 7. Point clouds obtained from four LiDAR scans. From left to right, the point clouds obtained from the four LiDAR scans are designated as cloud1, cloud2, cloud3, and cloud4.

To achieve seamless and continuous point cloud data, we initially employ the RPCS-CPF algorithm on the point cloud generated from a single LiDAR scan. Subsequently, the same RPCS-CPF algorithm was applied to the point cloud 3 of the coal pile, yielding the point cloud depicted in Figure 8.

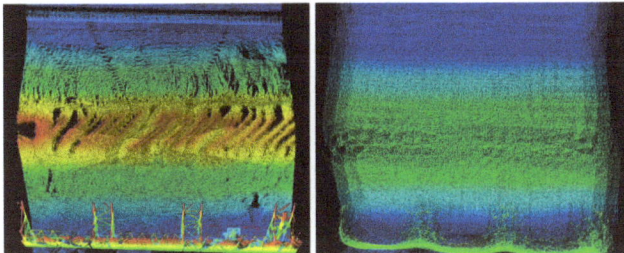

Figure 8. Comparison of point cloud 3 before and after the RPCS-CPF algorithm.

3.3. Point Cloud Registration

We first conducted a coordinate transformation on the point cloud depicted in Figure 7 to align it with the coordinate system of the coal yard. Subsequently, a straightforward stitching operation was performed on the point cloud. Following the stitching process, we filtered the point cloud corresponding to the greenhouse section based on their coordinates. The resulting stitched point cloud is illustrated in Figure 9.

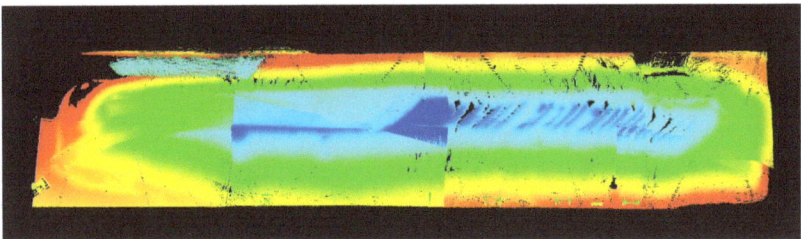

Figure 9. Concatenated point cloud.

Figure 9 indicates that the point cloud of the coal pile obtained from the 16-line LiDAR scan is highly dense, witch leads to a significant computational load for subsequent point cloud processing. The objective of our study is to perform downsampling on the point cloud while maintaining the integrity and smoothness of the surface. To achieve this, we proceeded with voxel filtering. The point cloud after voxel filtering is presented in Figure 10a.

Statistical filtering. Figure 10a reveals that the merged point cloud contains a significant number of outlier points. This is attributed to the overlapping regions scanned by two adjacent LiDARs, where the presence of servo actuator rotation errors prevented the proper alignment of the point clouds within these areas. To mitigate this issue, statistical filtering was implemented to eliminate the outliers, with the post-filtering results displayed in Figure 10b.

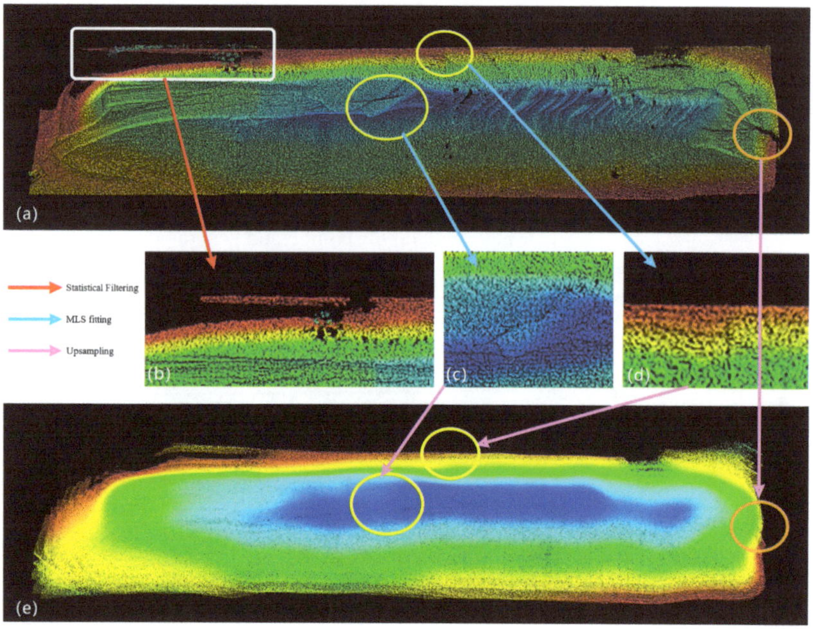

Figure 10. A rendering of the point cloud filtering process, where the red arrow represents statistical filtering, the blue arrows represent least squares surface fitting, and the pink arrows represent upsampling. (**a**) The point cloud; (**b**) the point cloud after statistical filtering; (**c**,**d**) are the point cloud with moving least squares technique; (**e**) the point cloud after iteration of moving least squares upsampling.

Moving least squares. After using voxel and statistical filtering procedures, a significant decrease in point cloud density was observed, resulting in a notably smoother surface characterized by a minimal presence of outlier points. The utilization of a moving least squares technique was employed for surface fitting in order to improve the continuity and smoothness of the resultant point cloud. The results of this fitting procedure are depicted in Figure 10c,d. The point cloud of the coal pile surface obtained after the application of the moving least squares approach demonstrates enhanced smoothness, as there are no observable outliers in the merged sections. Nevertheless, following the process of voxel downsampling and statistical filtering, the point cloud underwent a reduction in density, resulting in the presence of several regions with localized point loss. In order to tackle this issue, an additional iteration of moving least squares upsampling was implemented, and the outcomes are illustrated in Figure 10e.

As depicted in Figure 10, the RPCS-CPF algorithm demonstrated noteworthy outcomes. The combined point cloud preserves the coherence and uniformity while precisely representing the topographic arrangement of the coal pile's surface. In contrast to alternative techniques like point cloud registration, this particular approach exhibits reduced computing complexity, thereby indicating its wide-ranging potential for various applications.

Smoothness comparison. To compare the point cloud stitching effects before and after the application of the particle filtering algorithm, we extracted the point cloud at the stitching areas and voxelized them with a size of 0.5×0.5 along the x- and y-coordinates. The standard deviation of the height values and the maximum height difference were subsequently computed for each point cloud. The mathematical expression used to get the standard deviation is as follows:

$$\sigma = \sqrt{\frac{\sum_{i=1}^{n}(z_i - \mu^2)}{n}} \tag{20}$$

where σ represents the standard deviation of the Z-values within the same voxel, z_i is the height value of the i-th point within the voxel, and μ is the average height value of the points within the same voxel. The average standard deviation and average maximum difference of all voxels near the same stitching boundary are used to measure the smoothness at the stitching site, as shown in Table 1.

Table 1. Comparison of smoothness at the stitching before and after the RPCS-CPF algorithm.

Standard Deviation—Before	Maximum Difference—Before	Standard Deviation—After	Maximum Difference—After
0.47	1.75	0.19	0.82
0.35	1.17	0.20	0.85
0.47	1.48	0.21	0.90

Figure 11 displays the point cloud that was extracted in close proximity to the stitching line. The point cloud's range in the X direction has been extended to enhance clarity. Figure 11a,c depict the point cloud from various viewpoints prior to the implementation of the particle filtering technique. The presence of layering in the up and down regions of the stitching site is evident, indicating a lack of smooth flow. Figure 11b,d depict the point cloud pictures subsequent to the implementation of the particle filtering technique. Based on the presented data, it is apparent that the stitching site exhibits minimal layering and a seamless transition, suggesting that the RPCS-CPF algorithm, as proposed, has yielded satisfactory outcomes.

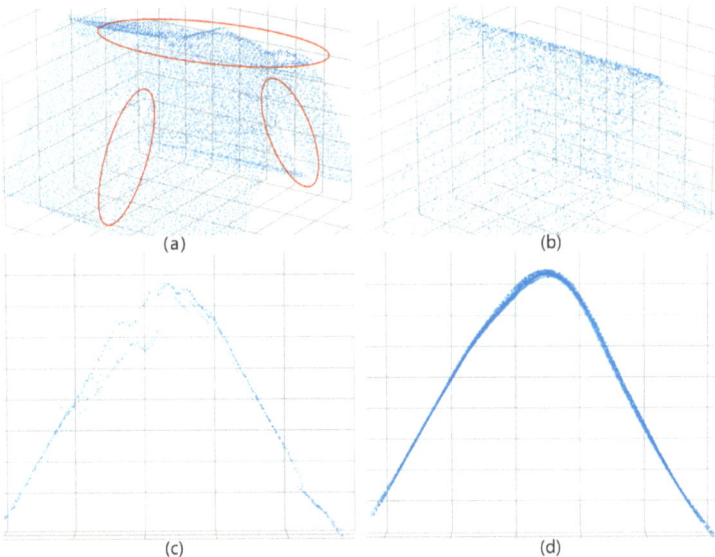

Figure 11. Comparison of point cloud stitching before and after RPCS-CPF algorithm. (**a**,**c**) are the stitched point cloud of different viewpoint without particle filtering; the red cicrle areas in (**a**) are the discontinuous point cloud. (**b**,**d**) are the stitched point cloud of different viewpoint with particle filtering.

3.4. Edge Detection

We conducted algorithm validation within an enclosed coal yard, as depicted in Figure 12. This paper introduces a region-growing clustering algorithm that leverages preliminary edge cues derived from gradient information. The algorithm initiates with seed points exhibiting strong gradient responses and incrementally incorporates neighboring pixels into the same region, adhering to a predetermined consistency in gradient direction, until a specified termination condition is met.

Figure 12. Coal yard vehicle operating environment.

The experimental results affirmed the algorithm's proficiency at defining the boundaries of unique features within the coal pile. The algorithm was first utilized to extract the boundary of the coal pile as shown in Figure 13. Following this, visual inspection revealed that the algorithm could also identify the edges of critical terrain features, including depressions (Figure 14a), corridors (Figure 14b), and ridges (Figure 14c). This observation indicates that, although our algorithm is primarily intended for precise extraction of the coal pile boundary, it effectively captures the boundaries of specific terrain features as well.

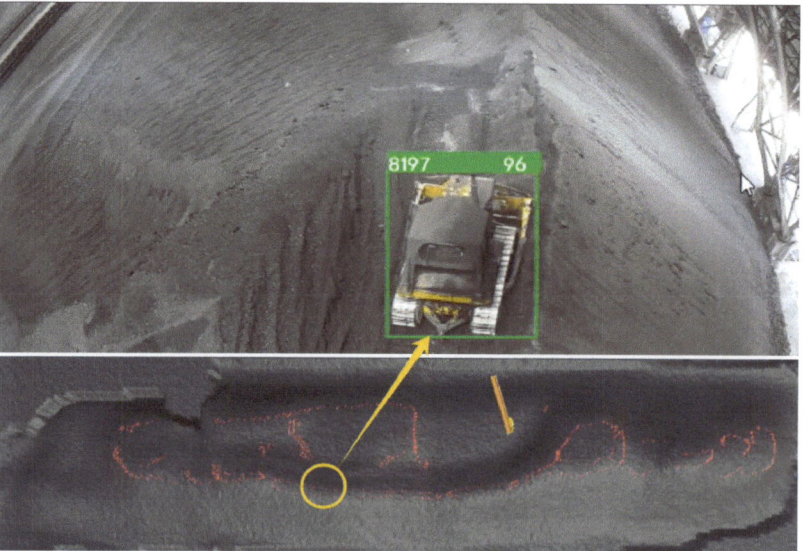

Figure 13. Vehicle approaching the danger boundary.

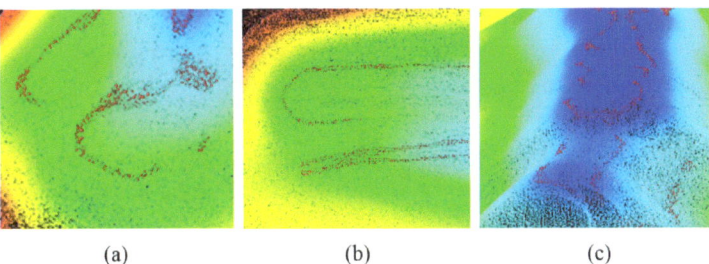

Figure 14. Boundarys of coal pile. (**a**) explanation; (**b**) explanation; (**c**) explanation.

4. Discussion

Coal piles, as fundamental units of management, allow for the convenient measurement of daily coal usage and the efficiency of coal combustion when their point clouds are obtained. The current popular methods for acquiring point clouds of large coal piles involve using drones equipped with LiDARs for scanning or employing movable 2D LiDAR devices. Both methods have certain drawbacks. For example, scanning with drones requires planning complex flight paths, and, if the internal environment of the coal yard changes, the original path may no longer be suitable. Although 2D LiDAR can capture the entire point cloud of a coal pile, the scanning speed is slow, and the resulting point cloud is relatively sparse. Therefore, we propose that using multiple LiDAR devices to scan large coal piles and then stitching together the obtained segments can both increase the scanning speed and ensure the completeness of the point cloud.

In the experimental portion of our study, we deployed four LiDAR devices, each affixed to a servo to allow for scanning across the breadth of the coal pile. However, when the servos operated the LiDAR devices to scan the coal pile, there was a rotational discrepancy due to the effects of gravity, which introduced noise into the scanned point cloud. This generated two primary issues: firstly, the point cloud derived from the LiDAR scan was non-continuous and contained numerous outliers; secondly, the post-stitching point cloud did not merge seamlessly, as illustrated in Figure 9, where a distinct demarcation line is visible at the juncture. This demarcation is a direct consequence of the servo's rotational error. Consequently, the RPCS-CPF method introduced in this paper is of significant importance. In this section, we will be comparing the stitching method predicated on CPF with the original method, which relies on coordinate transformation, from the perspectives of point cloud smoothness and the number of parameters involved.

4.1. Smoothness Comparison

To verify the effectiveness of our CPF (Conditional Point Filtering) filter, we conducted comparative experiments by applying the CPF filter to both individual point clouds and the entire point cloud, as shown in Table 2. We have compiled and presented the mean values of the standard deviation and the maximum difference at three coal pile point cloud stitching locations. It is evident from the table that, prior to the CPF process, the point clouds were merely stitched together through coordinate rotation transformations. However, due to the presence of servo rotational errors, it was nearly impossible to ensure a successful stitch at every junction. After applying our CPF method to filter the individual point clouds followed by the entire point cloud, this approach substantially lessened the influence of servo rotational errors during the stitching process of point clouds. Therefore, it is essential to apply CPF filtering to individual point clouds as well as to the entire point cloud ensemble.

Table 2. Comparison of smoothness between CPF and the original method.

	Standard Deviation	Maximum Difference	SP	EP
Original method	0.43	1.47		
CPF (ours)	0.31	1.22	✓	
CPF (ours)	0.26	1.05		✓
CPF (ours)	0.2	0.85	✓	✓

"SP" denotes the application of CPF to an individual point cloud, whereas "EP" signifies its application to the concatenated point cloud.

4.2. Comparison of Parameters

As can be observed from Figure 9, the point cloud immediately after scanning is extremely dense, containing a significant amount of noise and outliers. To reduce the density of the point cloud and enhance computational speed, downsampling was initially applied to the point cloud. This was followed by upsampling to achieve a better presentation. To facilitate a more comprehensive demonstration, statistics on the quantity and density of the point clouds at each step were compiled, as shown in Table 3. It can be seen from the table that, after downsampling the initial point cloud, the number of parameters was reduced by 90%, and the processing time was also reduced by the same percentage. Upon final upsampling, the density of the point cloud was similar to that before processing, yet the smoothness and integrity of the point cloud were significantly improved, which indicates that our method has yielded satisfactory results.

Table 3. Comparison of density between CPF and the original method.

	Number	Density	Voxel Filtering	Statistical Filtering	MLS-Upsample
Original method	1,057,584	105			
CPF (ours)	100,510	10	✓		
CPF (ours)	99,689	9	✓	✓	
CPF (ours)	797,512	80	✓	✓	✓

4.3. Limitations

This study still has several limitations in the acquisition and processing of coal pile point cloud data. Due to the mechanical structure, it is challenging for multiple LiDAR devices to achieve fully synchronized scanning, which may lead to temporal errors during point cloud stitching. These temporal discrepancies could potentially impact the consistency and accuracy of the point cloud data. Although the CPF proposed in this study has demonstrated satisfactory performance in practical applications, there is scope for improvement in terms of algorithmic precision and the extent of surface detail restoration of the coal pile point cloud. The current approach may not fully recover all the details of the coal pile surface, particularly in instances where significant discontinuities are present on the coal pile surface. We intend to explore more efficient and accurate algorithms in future research to replicate the surface characteristics of the coal pile point cloud as closely as possible.

5. Conclusions

This paper focused on addressing the efficient stitching of coal pile point cloud data and the precise detection of boundaries, with the aim of enhancing safety and efficiency in the coal mining industry. The primary contributions of this study are as follows:

(1) The RPCS-CPF (Rapid Point Cloud Stitching–Constrained Particle Filter) algorithm is proposed, specifically optimized for integrating point cloud data in large-scale coal pile environments. Experimental validations conducted on real large-scale coal piles demonstrated the unique advantages of this algorithm. It not only facilitates smooth

transitions in stitched areas, but also ensures the consistency and integrity of the overall point cloud data while preserving the detailed geometric features of the coal pile surface.

(2) Proposal of an edge detection algorithm based on gradient region expanding clustering to address the complex surface characteristics of coal piles. Experimental results validated the capability of this method to accurately identify boundaries, thereby significantly contributing to safety assessments and guidance in coal mining operations.

In conclusion, this study has not only presented the novel RPCS-CPF algorithm for point cloud stitching and edge detection, but also provided a foundation for future research. The outputs of this research have immediate practical applications in the coal mining industry, improving both the safety and efficiency of operations. For future work, we suggest exploring the integration of these algorithms with real-time monitoring systems and expanding the study to include a wider range of coal pile environments and conditions. Additionally, we will continue to explore more efficient and precise algorithms to replicate the surface characteristics of coal pile point clouds as closely as possible.

Author Contributions: G.J. write the paper and analysis the data. C.L. analyzed the data, wrote the C++ source code and write the paper. Y.H., L.F., H.W. and Y.Z. helped with project. All authors have read and agreed to the published version of the manuscript.

Funding: This research was supported by the Intelligent Aerospace System Leading Innovation Team Program of Zhejiang (Grant No. 2022R01003).

Data Availability Statement: The data used to support the findings of this study are available from the corresponding author upon request.

Acknowledgments: We gratefully acknowledge the generous support provided by the Intelligent Unmanned Systems for Coal Yard Safety Supervision and Intelligent Coal Inventory Project, funded by the China Huadian Corporation, which has significantly contributed to the advancement of this research endeavor.

Conflicts of Interest: Author Mr. Haibo Wang and Mr. Yantong Zhu were employed by the company Guoneng Lingwu Power Generation Co., Ltd. The remaining authors declare that the research was conducted in the absence of any commercial or financial relationships that could be construed as a potential conflict of interest.

References

1. Cao, D.; Zhang, B.; Zhang, X.; Yin, L.; Man, X. Optimization methods on dynamic monitoring of mineral reserves for open pit mine based on UAV oblique photogrammetry. *Measurement* **2023**, *207*, 112364. [CrossRef]
2. Vacca, G. UAV photogrammetry for volume calculations. A case study of an open sand quarry. In Proceedings of the International Conference on Computational Science and Its Applications, Malaga, Spain, 4–7 July 2022; Springer: Cham, Switzerland, 2022; pp. 505–518.
3. Alsayed, A.; Nabawy, M.R.; Yunusa-Kaltungo, A.; Arvin, F.; Quinn, M.K. Enhancing 1D LiDAR scanning for accurate stockpile volume estimation within drone-based mapping systems. In Proceedings of the AIAA Aviation 2021 Forum, Virtual, 2–6 August 2021; p. 3213.
4. Zhang, W.; Yang, D. Lidar-based fast 3d stockpile modeling. In Proceedings of the 2019 International Conference on Intelligent Computing, Automation and Systems (ICICAS), Chongqing, China, 6–8 December 2019; pp. 703–707.
5. Abbaszadeh, S.; Rastiveis, H. A comparison of close-range photogrammetry using a non-professional camera with field surveying for vplume estimation. *Int. Arch. Photogramm. Remote Sens. Spat. Inf. Sci.* **2017**, *42*, 1–4. [CrossRef]
6. Yan, Z.; Liu, R.; Cheng, L.; Zhou, X.; Ruan, X.; Xiao, Y. A concave hull methodology for calculating the crown volume of individual trees based on vehicle-borne LiDAR data. *Remote Sens.* **2019**, *11*, 623. [CrossRef]
7. Chen, J.; Wu, X.; Wang, M.Y.; Li, X. 3D shape modeling using a self-developed hand-held 3D laser scanner and an efficient HT-ICP point cloud registration algorithm. *Opt. Laser Technol.* **2013**, *45*, 414–423. [CrossRef]
8. Raeva, P.; Filipova, S.; Filipov, D. Volume computation of a stockpile–a study case comparing gps and uav measurements in an open pit quarry. *Int. Arch. Photogramm. Remote Sens. Spat. Inf. Sci.* **2016**, *41*, 999–1004. [CrossRef]
9. Alsayed, A.; Nabawy, M.R. Indoor stockpile reconstruction using drone-borne actuated single-point lidars. *Drones* **2022**, *6*, 386. [CrossRef]
10. Gago, R.M.; Pereira, M.Y.; Pereira, G.A. An aerial robotic system for inventory of stockpile warehouses. *Eng. Rep.* **2021**, *3*, e12396. [CrossRef]

11. Dang, T.; Tranzatto, M.; Khattak, S.; Mascarich, F.; Alexis, K.; Hutter, M. Graph-based subterranean exploration path planning using aerial and legged robots. *J. Field Robot.* **2020**, *37*, 1363–1388. [CrossRef]
12. Davis, D.; Guy, N. An Assessment of Point Cloud Data Acquisition Techniques for Aggregate Stockpiles and Volumetric Surveys. *Int. Arch. Photogramm. Remote Sens. Spat. Inf. Sci.* **2023**, *48*, 65–69. [CrossRef]
13. Mahlberg, J.A.; Manish, R.; Koshan, Y.; Joseph, M.; Liu, J.; Wells, T.; McGuffey, J.; Habib, A.; Bullock, D.M. Salt stockpile inventory management using LiDAR volumetric measurements. *Remote Sens.* **2022**, *14*, 4802. [CrossRef]
14. Farhood, H.; Muller, S.; Beheshti, A. Surface Area Estimation Using 3D Point Clouds and Delaunay Triangulation. In Proceedings of the Second International Conference on Innovations in Computing Research (ICR'23), Madrid, Spain, 4–6 September 2023; Springer: Cham, Switzerland, 2023; pp. 28–39.
15. Tucci, G.; Gebbia, A.; Conti, A.; Fiorini, L.; Lubello, C. Monitoring and computation of the volumes of stockpiles of bulk material by means of UAV photogrammetric surveying. *Remote Sens.* **2019**, *11*, 1471. [CrossRef]
16. Zhao, S.; Lu, T.F.; Koch, B.; Hurdsman, A. 3D stockpile modelling and quality calculation for continuous stockpile management. *Int. J. Miner. Process.* **2016**, *140*, 32–42. [CrossRef]
17. Jaboyedoff, M.; Oppikofer, T.; Abellán, A.; Derron, M.H.; Loye, A.; Metzger, R.; Pedrazzini, A. Use of LIDAR in landslide investigations: A review. *Nat. Hazards* **2012**, *61*, 5–28. [CrossRef]
18. Hu, C.; Zhou, Y.H.; Zhao, C.J.; Pan, Z.G. Hydraulic engineering topographic mapping and modeling based on three dimensional laser scanning technology. *Appl. Mech. Mater.* **2015**, *744*, 1695–1700. [CrossRef]
19. Ding, W.; Zhang, K.; Shao, C. A fast volume measurement method for obtaining point cloud data from bulk stockpiles. *Meas. Sci. Technol.* **2023**, *34*, 105204. [CrossRef]
20. Xu, Z.; Lu, X.; Xu, E.; Xia, L. A Sliding System Based on Single-Pulse Scanner and Rangefinder for Pile Inventory. *IEEE Geosci. Remote Sens. Lett.* **2022**, *19*, 7003605. [CrossRef]
21. Lato, M.; Diederichs, M.S.; Hutchinson, D.J.; Harrap, R. Optimization of LiDAR scanning and processing for automated structural evaluation of discontinuities in rockmasses. *Int. J. Rock Mech. Min. Sci.* **2009**, *46*, 194–199. [CrossRef]
22. Riquelme, A.J.; Abellán, A.; Tomás, R.; Jaboyedoff, M. A new approach for semi-automatic rock mass joints recognition from 3D point clouds. *Comput. Geosci.* **2014**, *68*, 38–52. [CrossRef]
23. Kim, M.K.; Cheng, J.C.; Sohn, H.; Chang, C.C. A framework for dimensional and surface quality assessment of precast concrete elements using BIM and 3D laser scanning. *Autom. Constr.* **2015**, *49*, 225–238. [CrossRef]
24. Koshan, Y.; Manish, R.; Joseph, M.; Habib, A. Alternative LIDAR Technologies for Stockpile Monitoring and Reporting. *Int. Arch. Photogramm. Remote Sens. Spat. Inf. Sci.* **2023**, *48*, 649–656. [CrossRef]
25. Chen, H.; Liang, M.; Liu, W.; Wang, W.; Liu, P.X. An approach to boundary detection for 3D point clouds based on DBSCAN clustering. *Pattern Recognit.* **2022**, *124*, 108431. [CrossRef]
26. Mineo, C.; Pierce, S.G.; Summan, R. Novel algorithms for 3D surface point cloud boundary detection and edge reconstruction. *J. Comput. Des. Eng.* **2019**, *6*, 81–91. [CrossRef]
27. Yang, X.; Huang, Y.; Zhang, Q. Automatic stockpile extraction and measurement using 3D point cloud and multi-scale directional curvature. *Remote Sens.* **2020**, *12*, 960. [CrossRef]
28. Hu, Z.; Zhen, M.; Bai, X.; Fu, H.; Tai, C.l. Jsenet: Joint semantic segmentation and edge detection network for 3d point clouds. In Proceedings of the Computer Vision–ECCV 2020: 16th European Conference, Glasgow, UK, 23–28 August 2020; Springer: Cham, Switzerland, 2020; pp. 222–239.

Disclaimer/Publisher's Note: The statements, opinions and data contained in all publications are solely those of the individual author(s) and contributor(s) and not of MDPI and/or the editor(s). MDPI and/or the editor(s) disclaim responsibility for any injury to people or property resulting from any ideas, methods, instructions or products referred to in the content.

Article

An Image Retrieval Method for Lunar Complex Craters Integrating Visual and Depth Features

Yingnan Zhang [1,2], Zhizhong Kang [1,2,*] and Zhen Cao [1,2]

1 School of Land Science and Technology, China University of Geosciences, Beijing 100083, China; zyn@glut.edu.cn (Y.Z.); caozhen@email.cugb.edu.cn (Z.C.)
2 Subcenter of International Cooperation and Research on Lunar and Planetary Exploration, Center of Space Exploration, Ministry of Education of the People's Republic of China, Beijing 100083, China
* Correspondence: zzkang@cugb.edu.cn

Abstract: In the geological research of the Moon and other celestial bodies, the identification and analysis of impact craters are crucial for understanding the geological history of these bodies. With the rapid increase in the volume of high-resolution imagery data returned from exploration missions, traditional image retrieval methods face dual challenges of efficiency and accuracy when processing lunar complex crater image data. Deep learning techniques offer a potential solution. This paper proposes an image retrieval model for lunar complex craters that integrates visual and depth features (LC^2R-Net) to overcome these difficulties. For depth feature extraction, we employ the Swin Transformer as the core architecture for feature extraction and enhance the recognition capability for key crater features by integrating the Convolutional Block Attention Module with Effective Channel Attention (CBAMwithECA). Furthermore, a triplet loss function is introduced to generate highly discriminative image embeddings, further optimizing the embedding space for similarity retrieval. In terms of visual feature extraction, we utilize Local Binary Patterns (LBP) and Hu moments to extract the texture and shape features of crater images. By performing a weighted fusion of these features and utilizing Principal Component Analysis (PCA) for dimensionality reduction, we effectively combine visual and depth features and optimize retrieval efficiency. Finally, cosine similarity is used to calculate the similarity between query images and images in the database, returning the most similar images as retrieval results. Validation experiments conducted on the lunar complex impact crater dataset constructed in this article demonstrate that LC^2R-Net achieves a retrieval precision of 83.75%, showcasing superior efficiency. These experimental results confirm the advantages of LC^2R-Net in handling the task of lunar complex impact crater image retrieval.

Keywords: LC^2R-Net; CBAM; ECA; impact crater; image retrieval; deep learning; triplet loss function

1. Introduction

Impact craters on the lunar surface are significant witnesses to the history of the Solar System. Their size, shape, and distribution provide key insights into understanding the geological history of the Moon and other celestial bodies [1–4]. With the advancement of space exploration technology, we are now able to obtain high-resolution imagery of the lunar surface. Over the past few decades, lunar exploration projects such as NASA's Apollo program, the Lunar Reconnaissance Orbiter, and China's Chang'e program have accumulated a vast amount of lunar data, which have been used for in-depth studies [5–9]. These images contain rich information, such as the morphology, structure, and geological features of impact craters, as well as the distribution of rocks related to impact events. However, this also presents a challenge: how to effectively retrieve and analyze the vast amount of crater imagery data [10]. Content-based image retrieval (CBIR) technology may be an effective solution to this problem.

Content-based image retrieval systems have a wide range of applications in lunar and planetary science research. Traditional CBIR methods typically rely on the visual content of images, such as texture, shape, and color features, to index and retrieve images. These methods depend on handcrafted features such as Speeded Up Robust Features (SURF) [11], Hu moments, and Gabor features [12]. Although these features are effective in certain scenarios, their application is limited in the complex lunar environment, where they struggle to capture detailed information within images effectively. Moreover, these methods often require meticulous feature engineering and parameter tuning, which is not only time-consuming but also limits their generalization ability and scalability. With the rise of deep learning technologies, particularly the successful application of Convolutional Neural Networks (CNNs) in remote sensing image recognition and classification tasks [13–15], researchers have begun to explore the use of deep features to enhance the performance of CBIR systems.

The successful application of deep learning methods in the field of remote sensing image retrieval has demonstrated their significant advantages over traditional manual feature methods [16–18]. Deep learning models are capable of automatically extracting abstract feature representations from images by learning from large-scale datasets. These deep features can better capture the semantic information and contextual relationships within images, thus enhancing the accuracy and robustness of CBIR systems. Given the complexity of remote sensing image description, some scholars have begun to explore strategies for feature fusion. Yan et al. have found through research that CNN features and SIFT features are highly complementary and can significantly improve the performance of image retrieval tasks [19]. Cheng et al. have proposed a distributed retrieval system architecture suitable for high-resolution satellite images by combining deep features with traditional manual features [20]. Their work indicates that the combination of deep features and traditional manual features can provide a more comprehensive image representation method. Although these methods have achieved commendable results, these models generally use the cross-entropy loss function during training, which has certain limitations in image retrieval tasks. In image retrieval tasks, we are more concerned with the similarity between images rather than just the accuracy of categories. This means that models need to be able to not only identify the categories of images but also capture the subtle differences within categories and the significant distinctions between categories. To this end, deep metric learning has become a key technology for addressing such problems.

Deep metric learning integrates the advantages of deep learning and metric learning. This approach automatically extracts image features through deep learning models and optimizes the distances between features through metric learning, making the distances in feature space closer for similar images while expanding the distances between dissimilar images. Deep metric learning has shown significant effectiveness in multiple applications in the field of remote sensing, including image retrieval [21–25], image classification [26,27], and object recognition [28,29], etc. However, the task of image retrieval for lunar impact craters demands more complex and meticulous feature extraction requirements, and these models do not always effectively capture all the key features of the craters. In this context, the Swin Transformer, as a novel deep learning architecture [30], has demonstrated its powerful performance in various visual tasks, which has inspired us to utilize this technology to address the challenges of lunar impact crater image retrieval.

The Swin Transformer is a neural network architecture based on the Transformer, widely applied as an efficient feature extractor in computer vision tasks [31–35]. Compared to traditional CNNs, the Swin Transformer not only effectively models global contextual information but also captures features at different scales through its hierarchical structure, which is crucial for understanding complex scenes and relationships within images. Inspired by this, we propose a lunar complex crater image retrieval model (LC^{2}R-Net) that fuses visual and depth features. We employ the Swin Transformer as the core architecture for depth feature extraction and integrate LBP and Hu moments for visual feature extraction. Moreover, to evaluate the effectiveness of our method, we have constructed a lunar crater image retrieval dataset and conducted extensive experiments. Our main contributions are as follows:

1. The Swin Transformer is utilized as the feature extraction structure, and the CBAM-with-ECA module is integrated into the linear embedding and patch merging modules. Through the attention mechanism, the channel and spatial relevance of features are enhanced, allowing for a comprehensive capture of the details and structural information within images. This enhancement improves the model's capability to recognize and extract image features. It directs the model's focus toward the global context, elevating the perceptibility of key features while concurrently suppressing less important features and noise information.
2. By integrating visual features (texture features, shape features) with deep features, we balance the contribution of different features through a weighted approach, emphasizing important features during the fusion process. Furthermore, we apply PCA to condense the dimensionality of the integrated feature set. This process not only trims down the number of feature dimensions but also amplifies the retrieval process's swiftness and effectiveness.
3. Within the network's training framework, we integrate a triplet loss function coupled with a strategy for mining difficult negative examples. This approach is designed to prompt the network to cultivate features with greater discrimination. By utilizing triplet loss, we optimize the embedded space, ensuring that vectors of akin images are positioned in closer proximity, whereas those of non-akin images are segregated, thereby markedly boosting the precision of our retrieval system.

The structure of this document is laid out in the following manner: Section 2 introduces the work related to content-based image retrieval. Section 3 delineates the method we propose. Section 4 details the dataset used for the retrieval of complex impact crater images on the lunar surface. Section 5 is dedicated to an in-depth presentation of experimental outcomes and their subsequent analysis. Finally, Section 6 summarizes the findings and conclusions of this study.

The related codes are publicly available at https://github.com/ZYNHYF/lunar-complex-crater-image-retrieval (released on 27 March 2024).

2. Related Works

In this section, we provide a detailed overview of prior research work related to content-based image retrieval. We categorize these studies into three groups: methods based on traditional features, methods based on deep features, and methods based on metric learning.

2.1. Methods Based on Traditional Features

Early CBIR systems primarily relied on traditional image processing techniques to extract features, such as color histograms, texture features, and shape descriptors. The advantages of these methods lie in their computational simplicity and intuitive understanding, and they have been extensively studied by scholars. Tekeste et al. conducted a comparative study to explore the impact of different LBP variants on the results of remote sensing image retrieval [36]. Aptoula applied global morphological texture descriptors to remote sensing image retrieval and, despite the shorter length of the extracted feature vectors, achieved high retrieval scores [37]. Xie et al. proposed an image retrieval method that combines a dominant color descriptor with Hu moments, leveraging the advantages of color and shape detection [38]. Chen et al. introduced a feature descriptor based on the relationships between prominent craters on the lunar surface and a composite feature model composed of different features. Based on these characteristics, similarity measurement rules and a retrieval algorithm were proposed and detailed [39]. Hua et al. utilized a general saliency-based landmark detection algorithm to identify regions of interest on the lunar surface, then indexed and retrieved them using feature vectors extracted from the region-of-interest images, evaluating the performance of saliency-based landmark detection [12]. However, these methods also have apparent limitations; they perform well under specific conditions, particularly when the image content structure is simple and changes little. Nevertheless, they often fail to effectively handle high-level semantic information and have limited robustness in complex scenes.

2.2. Methods Based on Deep Features

With the advancement of deep learning technology, methods based on Convolutional Neural Networks have become a research hotspot in the field of Content-Based Image Retrieval. These methods automatically extract deep representations of image content by learning multi-level abstract features. Compared to handcrafted features, deep features are better at capturing the complex patterns and high-level semantic information in images. Wang et al. designed a Multi-Attention Fusion Network with dilated convolution and label smoothing capabilities, using label smoothing to replace the cross-entropy loss function, which yielded competitive retrieval results [40]. Ye et al. proposed a query-adaptive feature fusion method based on a CNN regression model, which can accurately predict the DCG values of the ranked image list to assign weights to each feature, thereby enhancing retrieval precision [41]. Wang et al. introduced a novel Wide Context Attention Network (W-CAN), utilizing two attention modules to adaptively learn relevant local features in spatial and channel dimensions, thus obtaining discriminative features with extensive contextual information [42]. Chaudhuri et al. designed a GCN-based Context Attention Network, including node and edge attention. Beyond highlighting the fundamental features within each node, edge attention enables the network to learn the most critical neighborhood structures from the RAG within each target class image [43]. Furthermore, methods based on deep features can also leverage transfer learning to adapt these pre-trained models to specific domains or datasets [40], further improving retrieval performance.

2.3. Methods Based on Metric Learning

Metric learning methods aim to learn an optimized distance metric such that similar images are closer in the feature space while dissimilar images are farther apart. These methods are often combined with deep learning, adjusting the feature space through the loss function during training. Zhang et al. constructed a Triplet Non-Local Neural Network (T-NLNN) model that combines deep metric learning with non-local operations, significantly improving the performance of high-resolution remote sensing image retrieval [21]. Cao et al. proposed a method based on a triplet deep metric learning network to enhance the retrieval performance of remote sensing images [22]. Zhong et al. introduced an L2-normed attention and multi-scale fusion network (L2AMF-Net) to achieve accurate and robust lunar image patch matching [44]. Additionally, some scholars focus on constructing new loss functions to enhance retrieval performance. Fan et al. proposed a ranking loss result, thereby building a global optimization model based on feature space and retrieval outcomes, which can be optimized in an end-to-end manner [45]. Zhao et al. designed a similarity-preserving loss-based deep metric learning strategy, utilizing the ratio of easy to hard samples within classes to dynamically weigh the selected hard samples in experiments, learning the structural characteristics of intra-class samples [46]. Fan et al. introduced a distribution consistency loss to address the problem of imbalanced sample distribution in remote sensing datasets, constructing an end-to-end fine-tuned network suitable for remote sensing image retrieval, achieving state-of-the-art performance [47]. Compared to methods based on deep features, metric learning-based approaches are particularly suitable for tasks requiring refined retrieval and sensitivity to similarity.

3. Proposed Method

The LC^2R-Net model proposed in this paper achieves the task of lunar complex impact crater image retrieval by fusing low-level visual features with deep features of images. By integrating these two complementary types of features, a more comprehensive image representation is formed, which enhances the model's ability to recognize and differentiate complex impact craters, thereby improving the accuracy of retrieval. Figure 1 outlines the overall process by which LC^2R-Net completes the retrieval task.

As illustrated in Figure 1, the core steps include: (1) extracting deep features of impact crater images using an improved Swin Transformer model, which, by integrating the CBAMwithECA attention module, mines potential information within feature maps across channel and spatial dimensions, achieving comprehensive calibration and meticulous optimization of features, thereby enhancing the model's capability to represent image features; (2) utilizing LBP and Hu moments to extract texture and shape features of impact crater images as low-level visual features; (3) the extracted low-level visual and deep features are weighted and fused, followed by dimensionality reduction to create a more compact and efficient feature representation for retrieval tasks; (4) finally, the model employs the fused feature representation to perform the image retrieval task, matching query images with images in the database, and identifying the most similar images based on the queried features.

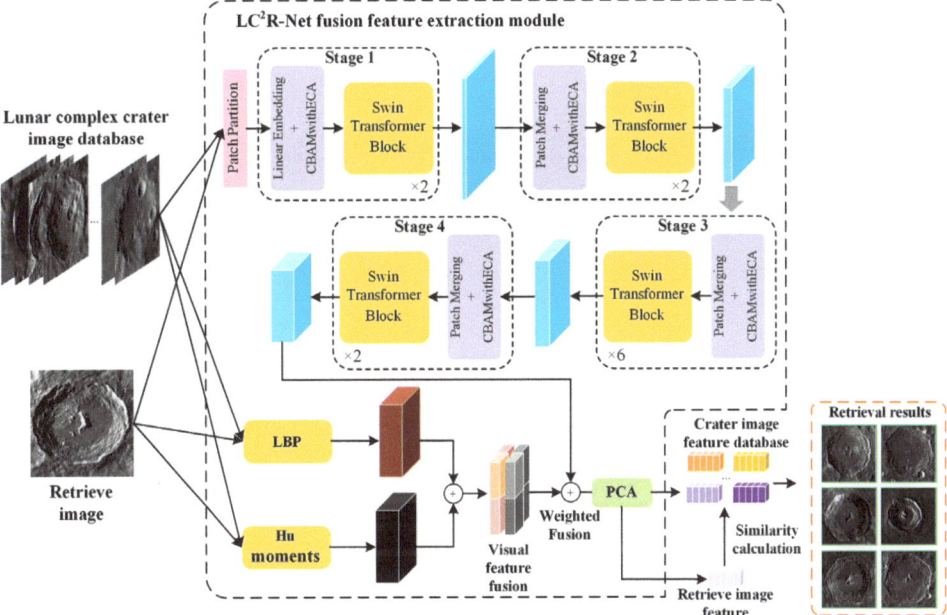

Figure 1. Image retrieval framework for lunar complex crater images based on the LC^{2}R-Net.

3.1. Visual Feature Extraction

In order to effectively capture the distinctive visual attributes of intricate lunar crater images, we utilized two resilient techniques for visual feature extraction: LBP [48] and Hu Moments [49]. LBP serves as a potent texture descriptor, capturing local texture nuances within an image by contrasting the grayscale intensity of a pixel with its neighboring pixels. To elaborate, the LBP value for each pixel is computed by juxtaposing the grayscale intensity of the surrounding pixels with that of the central pixel. This operation can be mathematically represented as follows:

$$LBP(x_c, y_c) = \sum_{i=0}^{P-1} s(I(x_i, y_i) - I(x_c, y_c))2^i \tag{1}$$

where P is the number of pixels in the domain, and $s(z)$ is a sign function defined as:

$$s(z) = \begin{cases} 1, z \geq 0 \\ 0, z < 0 \end{cases} \tag{2}$$

In this way, for each pixel point $I(x_c, y_c)$ is transformed into a P-bit binary number, i.e., the LBP code, which reflects the texture structure of the region around that pixel. By computing the histogram of the LBP code for the entire image, we can obtain the feature vector characterizing the texture of the image.

Hu moments are similarly employed to serve as descriptors of shape features, encapsulating the geometric characteristics of an image through the synthesis of its central moments, which are inherently invariant to transformations such as translation, scaling, and rotation of the image. The initial step in this process involves the calculation of the image's raw moments and central moments. Raw moments are defined by the following equation:

$$m_{pq} = \sum_x \sum_y x^p y^q I(x, y) \tag{3}$$

where $I(x, y)$ is the pixel intensity of the image at coordinate (x, y), and p and q are the orders of the moments. Then, the center of mass of the image is computed using the original moments $(\bar{x}, \bar{y})$:

$$\bar{x} = \frac{m_{10}}{m_{00}}, \bar{y} = \frac{m_{01}}{m_{00}} \tag{4}$$

where m_{00} is the zero-order primitive moment, representing the total luminance of the image, and m_{10} and m_{01} are the first-order primitive moments, related to the position of the center of mass of the image in the x and y directions. Subsequently, the center moments with respect to the center of mass are calculated:

$$\mu_{pq} = \sum_x \sum_y (x - \bar{x})^p (y - \bar{y})^q I(x, y) \tag{5}$$

The central moment describes the shape of the image, and seven Hu moments are calculated from the central moment in the following form:

$$\begin{aligned}
H_1 &= \mu_{20} + \mu_{02} \\
H_2 &= (\mu_{20} - \mu_{02})^2 + 4\mu_{11}^2 \\
H_3 &= (\mu_{30} - 3\mu_{12})^2 + (3\mu_{21} - \mu_{03})^2 \\
H_4 &= (\mu_{30} + \mu_{12})^2 + (\mu_{21} + \mu_{03})^2 \\
H_5 &= (\mu_{30} - 3\mu_{12})(\mu_{30} + \mu_{12})\left[(\mu_{30} + \mu_{12})^2 - 3(\mu_{21} + \mu_{03})^2\right] \\
&+ (3\mu_{21} - \mu_{03})(\mu_{21} + \mu_{03})\left[3(\mu_{30} + \mu_{12})^2 - (\mu_{21} + \mu_{03})^2\right] \\
H_6 &= (\mu_{20} - \mu_{02})\left[(\mu_{30} + \mu_{12})^2 - (\mu_{21} + \mu_{03})^2\right] \\
&+ 4\mu_{11}(\mu_{30} + \mu_{12})(\mu_{21} + \mu_{03}) \\
H_7 &= (3\mu_{21} - \mu_{03})(\mu_{30} + \mu_{12})\left[(\mu_{30} + \mu_{12})^2 - 3(\mu_{21} + \mu_{03})^2\right] \\
&- (\mu_{30} - 3\mu_{12})(\mu_{21} + \mu_{03})\left[3(\mu_{30} + \mu_{12})^2 - (\mu_{21} + \mu_{03})^2\right]
\end{aligned} \tag{6}$$

where μ_{ij} is the central moment with respect to the center of mass, and H_i is the ith Hu moment.

3.2. Deep Feature Extraction

The deep features extracted through neural networks can effectively describe the semantic information of complex lunar impact crater images. The strategy for extracting deep features in this paper is to use the Swin Transformer as the backbone network, removing the classification head from the network to extract deep feature representations. In addition, this paper introduces the CBAMwithECA module at the patch merging layer and the linear embedding layer of the Swin Transformer. The CBAMwithECA module combines the spatial attention mechanism of Effective Channel Attention (ECA) and Convolutional Block

Attention Module (CBAM), mining information in both the channel and spatial dimensions of the feature map. This achieves comprehensive calibration and optimization of features, further enhancing the model's capability to express features.

3.2.1. Backbone: Swin Transformer

The core advantage of the Swin Transformer lies in its unique hierarchical structure, which encodes images via a partitioning strategy, thereby effectively capturing multi-scale features within the image. Specifically, the input image is segmented into patches by the Patch Partition module, followed by the construction of feature maps at varying scales through four stages. Beyond the initial stage, which begins with a Linear Embedding layer, the subsequent three stages each commence with a Patch Merging operation and then proceed with a series of stacked Swin Transformer Blocks to achieve a deep feature representation of the image.

1. Patch Partition

At the outset of the Swin Transformer's processing pipeline, the Patch Partition layer plays a pivotal role in decomposing the incoming image into a sequential array of patches. Given an image with dimensions $H \times W \times 3$, where H and W denote the height and width, and the numeral 3 indicates the RGB color channels, this layer segments the image into a grid of 4×4 patches. These patches are subsequently flattened along the channel dimension and undergo a linear projection into an elevated dimensional space, culminating in a feature map with dimensions of $\frac{H}{4} \times \frac{W}{4} \times 48$. This feature map is then subject to a linear transformation within the Linear Embedding layer, producing an output feature map dimensionally characterized as $\frac{H}{4} \times \frac{W}{4} \times C$. The ensuing feature map is channeled into the initial Swin Transformer Block, referred to as Stage 1, for additional refinement. This mechanism is conceptually analogous to the convolutional operation found in conventional convolutional neural networks, and the intricacies of this process are graphically depicted in Figure 2.

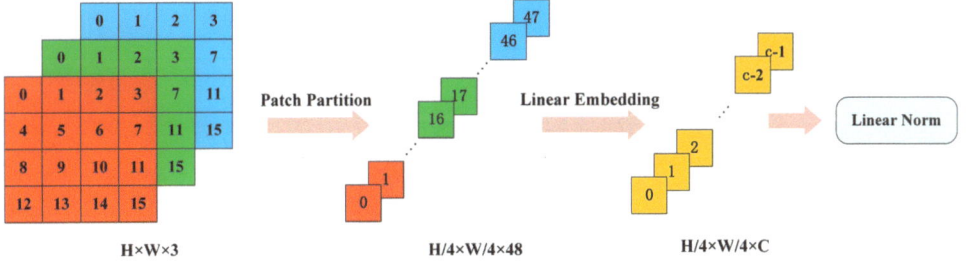

Figure 2. Schematic diagram of the Patch Partition operation.

2. Patch Merging

The Patch Merging technique in the Swin Transformer architecture functions analogously to the pooling layers found in classical convolutional neural networks, effectively generating a pyramidal hierarchy of representations through the downsampling of feature maps. Imagine an input feature map with dimensions $H \times W \times C$. The Patch Merging operation commences with the segmentation of the feature map into distinct 2×2 pixel blocks, treating each as a separate patch. Within these patches, corresponding pixels are extracted and amalgamated, yielding four distinct feature maps, each with a reduced size of $\frac{H}{2} \times \frac{W}{2} \times C$. These quartet of feature maps are then concatenated along the channel axis, resulting in a singular, enhanced feature map with dimensions $\frac{H}{2} \times \frac{W}{2} \times 4C$.

Following the concatenation, the resultant feature map is normalized by a LayerNorm layer, which precedes the final transformation. A fully connected layer then undertakes a linear transformation on the concatenated feature map, specifically targeting its channel depth. This transformation modifies the channel depth from 4C to 2C, effectively halving it. The procedural specifics of this Patch Merging operation are visually detailed in Figure 3.

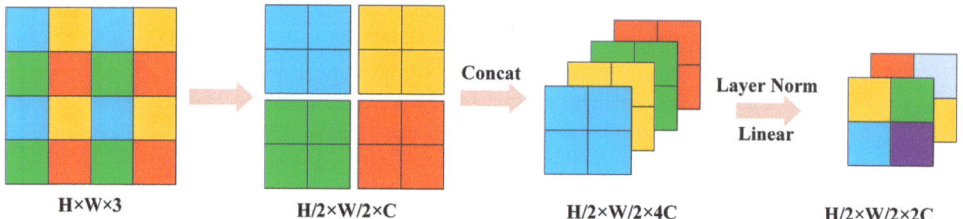

Figure 3. Schematic diagram of the Patch Merging operation.

3. Swin Transformer Block

The Swin Transformer Block represents the fundamental building block of the Swin Transformer architecture. As illustrated in Figure 4, this block is structured as a sequence of two Transformer Blocks. Each Transformer Block is crafted from a series of components: an initial layer normalization (LN), a multi-head self-attention mechanism (MSA), a subsequent layer normalization (LN), and a multilayer perceptron (MLP). To facilitate stable training and mitigate the vanishing gradient issue in deep networks, both the MSA and MLP are equipped with skip connections.

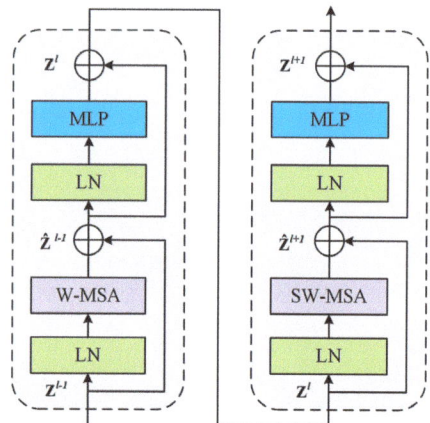

Figure 4. Swin Transformer Block.

The distinguishing feature between the two Transformer Blocks within the Swin Transformer Block is the type of self-attention mechanism employed. The first block integrates a window-based multi-head self-attention (W-MSA), which confines the self-attention process within predetermined window boundaries to lower computational demands and hone in on local feature extraction. Conversely, the second block incorporates shifted window multi-head self-attention (SW-MSA). By offsetting the window alignment, SW-MSA broadens the receptive field of the model, enabling feature interactions across neighboring windows, which in turn amplifies the model's global contextual comprehension. This operation is encapsulated in Equation (7):

$$\begin{aligned}
\hat{Z}^l &= W\text{-}MSA\left[LN\left(Z^{l-1}\right)\right] + Z^{l-1} \\
Z^l &= MLP\left[LN\left(\hat{Z}^l\right)\right] + \hat{Z}^{\wedge l} \\
\hat{Z}^{l+1} &= SW\text{-}MSA\left[E\left(Z^l\right)\right] + Z^l \\
Z^{l+1} &= MLP\left[LN\left(\hat{Z}^{l+l}\right)\right] + \hat{Z}^{l+1}
\end{aligned} \quad (7)$$

where Z^{l-1} and Z^{l+1} represent the input and output of the Swin Transformer Block, respectively, while $W\text{-}MSA$, $SW\text{-}MSA$, and MLP denote the window-based multi-head self-attention, the shifted window multi-head self-attention, and the multilayer perceptron modules, respectively.

3.2.2. CBAMwithECA Attention Module

Due to the high homogeneity and rich detail of lunar complex crater imagery, relying solely on the self-attention mechanism is insufficient to fully capture the prominent features of impact craters. Therefore, we have introduced the CBAMwithECA module [50], which combines the channel attention of ECA [51] and the spatial attention of CBAM [52] to further enhance the representational capability of features. As shown in Figure 5, the core of ECA-Net is the adaptive computation of the size k of the one-dimensional convolutional kernel, which depends on the number of input channels C and the hyperparameters γ and b. The formula is calculated as follows:

$$k = \left| \frac{\log_2(C) + b}{\gamma} \right|_{odd} \quad (8)$$

where $|t|_{odd}$ represents the odd number closest to t, ensuring that the $1D$ convolutional kernel has symmetric padding. In ECA-Net, adaptive average pooling and a $1D$ convolutional layer are used to learn the channel attention weights:

$$M_{channel} = \sigma(Conv1D(AvgPool(x))) \quad (9)$$

where the input feature map is denoted by x and is a four-dimensional tensor within the real number space $\mathbb{R}^{B \times C \times H \times W}$, where B, C, H, and W represent the batch size, number of channels, height, and width, respectively. The channel attention mechanism is encapsulated by $M_{channel}$, which is a tensor of dimensions $\mathbb{R}^{B \times C \times 1 \times 1}$, capturing the importance of each channel. The Sigmoid function, symbolized by σ, is utilized to activate and normalize the elements of $M_{channel}$. Subsequently, the feature map x is modulated by $M_{channel}$ to produce the channel-wise enhanced feature map x_{ca}, which is formulated as follows:

$$x_{ca} = M_{channel} \odot x \quad (10)$$

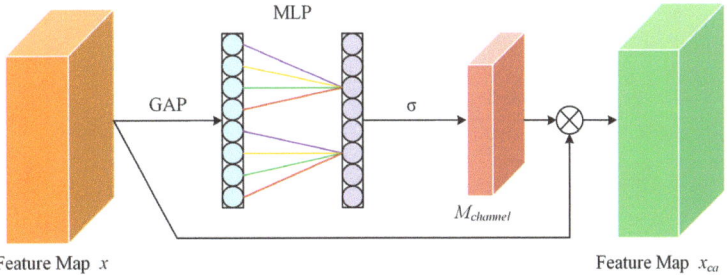

Figure 5. ECA channel attention module.

Concerning the mechanism for spatial attention, illustrated in Figure 6, the process begins by subjecting the feature map x_{ca} to both average pooling and max pooling operations across the channel axis, resulting in a pair of distinct feature descriptors. Subsequently, these descriptors are merged and proceed through a convolutional layer with a kernel size of 7×7, culminating in the formation of the spatial attention map.

$$M_{spatial} = \sigma(Conv2D(Concat(Avgpool(x_{ca}), Maxpool(x_{ca})))) \quad (11)$$

The spatial attention map is then applied to the feature map x_{ca}, resulting in a weighted feature map.

$$x_{sa} = M_{spatial} \odot x_{ca} \quad (12)$$

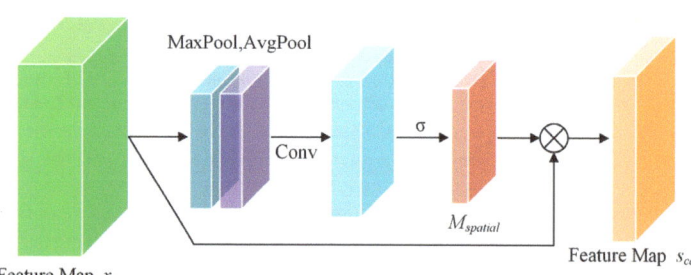

Figure 6. CBAM spatial attention module.

Finally, the feature map weighted by the attention mechanism is added to the original input feature map to realize a residual connection, resulting in the enhanced feature map $x_{enhanced}$:

$$x_{enhanced} = x + x_{sa} \quad (13)$$

The process of inserting the CBAMwithECA module into the linear embedding module is illustrated in Figure 7.

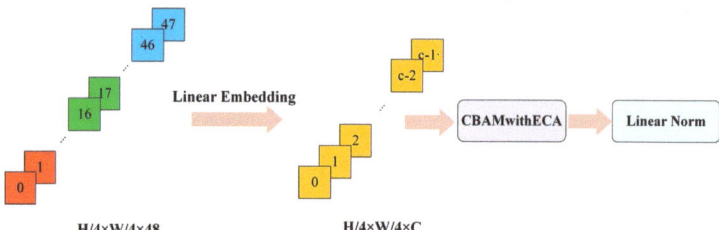

Figure 7. Insertion of the CBAMwithECA module into the linear embedding module.

The process of inserting the CBAMwithECA module into the patch merging module is shown in Figure 8.

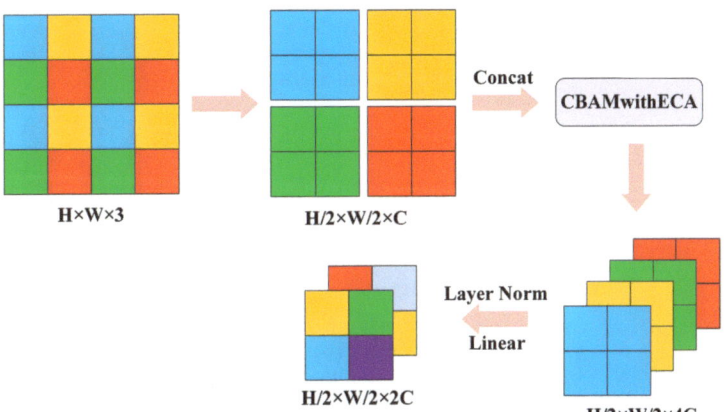

Figure 8. Insertion of the CBAMwithECA module into the patch merging module.

3.2.3. Loss Function

In our research, the training phase utilized a triplet loss function [53] to guide the optimization. This loss function operates on triplets, which include an anchor image, a corresponding positive image, and a contrasting negative image. The primary objective is to amplify the model's ability to discriminate between varying classes. This is achieved by diminishing the distance metric between the anchor and the positive instance while concurrently enlarging the gap between the anchor and the negative instance. The functional form of the triplet loss is delineated below:

$$L_{triplet} = \sum_{i=1}^{N} max\left(0, \|f(a_i) - f(p_i)\|^2 - \|f(a_i) - f(n_i)\|^2 + \alpha\right) \quad (14)$$

where $f(\cdot)$ denotes the output of the feature mapping function derived from the Gempool layer. The terms a_i, p_i, and n_i correspond to the anchor, positive, and negative images within the i-th triplet, respectively. Here, N signifies the aggregate count of triplets, while α represents a predetermined margin parameter that delineates the threshold between the proximities of positive and negative pairs. This loss function is instrumental in clustering akin features of images and concurrently dispersing the features of dissimilar images, an aspect that is crucial in areas where the terrain, such as the lunar surface, exhibits high degrees of similarity.

During training, a hard negative sample mining strategy [53] was employed to enhance the effectiveness of the triplet training. For each anchor image, we select negative samples with lower structural similarity by calculating the Structural Similarity Index $SSIM$ with all negative samples in the dataset. $SSIM$ is used to quantify the visual similarity between two images, and its formula is as follows:

$$SSIM(x,y) = \frac{(2\mu_x\mu_y + c_1)(2\sigma_{xy} + c_2)}{\left(\mu_x^2 + \mu_y^2 + c_1\right)\left(\sigma_x^2 + \sigma_y^2 + c_2\right)} \quad (15)$$

where x and y are utilized to denote two distinct image windows. The terms μ_x and μ_y refer to their respective mean intensity values. Variance for each window is indicated by σ_x^2 and σ_y^2, while σ_{xy} represents the covariance between the two windows. Constants c_1 and c_2 are incorporated within the formulation to prevent the occurrence of division by zero, ensuring numerical stability.

During the hard negative sample mining process, for each anchor image a, we select the negative sample n with the smallest $SSIM$ value from all negative sample images, satisfying the following condition:

$$n = \arg\min_{n'} d(f(a), f(n')) \tag{16}$$

The hard negative mining strategy ensures that the anchor image and the selected negative sample image have significant structural differences, providing more challenging samples for training and enhancing the model's discriminative ability.

3.3. Feature Fusion and Retrieval

Feature fusion is used to concatenate visual features and depth features to get a fused feature vector. Let the visual feature be F_{VC} and the depth feature be F_{DC}. Set the feature weight of F_{VC} to λ and the feature weight of F_{DC} to $1 - \lambda$. Change the importance of the feature by adjusting the size of λ. The fused feature is shown in Equation (17).

$$F = (\lambda F_{VC}, (1-\lambda) F_{DC}) \tag{17}$$

Since the dimensionality of the fused feature vectors is too high, the fused features are downscaled using PCA. The principle is to maximize the variance of the downscaled features, and if the downscaled features are uncorrelated, then it can be expressed as an optimization problem, as shown in Equation (18).

$$\max_{W} tr\left(W^T S_t W\right), s.t., W^T W = I \tag{18}$$

where S_t represents the covariance matrix of the sample features, $tr(W^T S_t W)$ is the variance of the sample features after dimensionality reduction, $w^T w^T = I$ denotes the constraint conditions, and I is the identity matrix.

After the dimensionality reduction in the fused features, cosine similarity is used to calculate the similarity between different impact crater images, as shown in Equation (19).

$$\cos\theta = \frac{\sum_{i=1}^{n}(A_i \times B_i)}{\sqrt{\sum_{i=1}^{n} A_i^2 \times \sum_{i=1}^{n} B_i^2}} \tag{19}$$

where A_i denotes the composite feature vector derived from the query image, whereas B_i signifies the composite feature vector corresponding to the lunar impact crater images within the image repository. The ultimate retrieval outcomes are the k highest-ranked images determined by their respective cosine similarity measures.

4. Lunar Complex Crater Dataset

The lunar surface is home to a multitude of impact craters that cover much of its terrain. To date, a vast number of lunar craters have been identified in images and Digital Elevation Model (DEM) data through expert visual inspection as well as automated detection methods, leading to the establishment of numerous crater databases. This paper selects 3234 craters ranging from 20 to 30 km in diameter from the lunar impact crater database (2015 revision) maintained by the Lunar and Planetary Institute as the research subjects to construct the Lunar Complex Impact Crater Dataset; the data can be obtained from https://www.lpi.usra.edu/lunar/surface/Lunar_Impact_Crater_Database_v08Sep2015.xls (accessed on 1 January 2020). Utilizing 100-m resolution imagery and DEM data provided by the Lunar Reconnaissance Orbiter (LRO), an analysis based on the morphological texture features and profile characteristics of the craters is conducted (when a crater contains two or more types of local structures, the most prominent feature is chosen as the basis for classification). These craters are categorized into six types, including simple craters, floor-fractured craters, central peak craters, multi-impacted floor craters, lunar oceanic remnant impact craters, and impact residual craters. Example images for each category are shown in Figure 9.

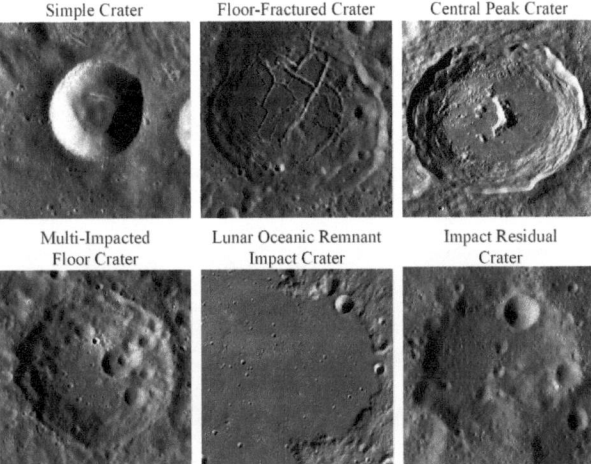

Figure 9. Images of six different types of impact crater samples: simple craters, floor-fractured craters, central peak craters, multi-impacted floor craters, lunar oceanic remnant impact craters, and impact residual craters.

Due to the specificity of impact crater types, the number of different categories of impact craters in the constructed dataset is severely imbalanced. To prevent overfitting during network training, we employed a series of data augmentation techniques to expand the original dataset. These techniques include random rotation, random horizontal flipping, color jittering, random affine transformations, and random Gaussian blur, all aimed at simulating the various conditions that impact craters may encounter during actual imaging processes. Ultimately, we obtained 5597 images, of which 80% were randomly selected to constitute the training data, with the remainder used for model validation.

5. Experiments and Analysis

This section presents a comprehensive evaluation of the performance of the proposed method through a series of extensive experiments and provides a clear and accurate description of the experimental results.

5.1. Implementation Details

5.1.1. Experimental Setup

All experiments in this study were conducted on a deep learning server equipped with an Intel(R) Xeon(R) Platinum 8255C CPU and an RTX 3090 (24GB) GPU. The software environment consisted of Pytorch 1.10.0 and Python 3.8, with the operating system being Ubuntu 20.04. During the model training phase, weights trained on the ImageNet dataset were used as the initial parameters. The model was optimized using the Adam optimizer, and a cosine annealing algorithm was employed to dynamically adjust the learning rate. Parameters were updated every 4 batches, with each batch containing 16 samples. The detailed parameters are shown in Table 1. The experiments returned the top 20 images in the retrieval results to evaluate the model's retrieval accuracy.

Table 1. Experimental parameter configuration.

Parameter Name	Parameter Configuration
Initial learning rate	5×10^{-6}
Weight decay	1×10^{-5}
Margin α	2
Training epochs	25

5.1.2. Evaluation Metrics

During the experimental phase of this research, we employed three principal metrics to assess the efficacy of the lunar complex crater image retrieval system: mean average precision mAP, average normalized modified retrieval rank $ANMRR$, and the time taken for retrieval.

1. Mean Average Precision (mAP)

When performing image retrieval for lunar complex craters, for a given query image and an image database with a total of N images, the Average Precision (AP) is defined as follows:

$$AP = \frac{1}{n} \sum_{k=1}^{N} P(k) \cdot rel(k) \tag{20}$$

where n is indicative of the aggregate count of images in the repository which are categorized under the identical impact crater classification as the query image. The index k refers to the ordinal position within the ranked retrieval outcomes. The function $P(k)$ quantifies the precision attained at the juncture of the k-th result in the retrieval sequence. The function $rel(k)$ operates as a binary indicator, assigning a value of 1 when the k-th result in the retrieval sequence is of the same impact crater category as the query image, and 0 in all other instances. The mAP, is derived by computing the mean of precision values across all query instances, which is elucidated in Equation (21).

$$mAP = \frac{1}{Q} \sum_{q=1}^{Q} AP(q) \tag{21}$$

where Q stands for the cumulative quantity of all the queries processed, while $AP(q)$ signifies the Average Precision AP computed for each distinct query. The mAP value, which falls within the interval $[0, 1]$, serves as a performance indicator for the retrieval system; a value approaching 1 denotes the superior performance of the system.

2. Average Normalized Modified Retrieval Rank ($ANMRR$)

In the dataset of images, every image is allocated a ranking $Rank(i)$, with i denoting the image's sequence in the outcome set. Given a query's reference image S_K, the count of analogous images within the dataset is denoted as $G(S_K)$. Within the uppermost K images of the search outcomes, should the $Rank(i)$ of an image surpass K, the $Rank(i)$ is recalibrated as per the subsequent expression:

$$Rank(i) = \begin{cases} Rank(i) & Rank(i) \leq K \\ 1.25 \times K & Rank(i) > K \end{cases} \tag{22}$$

For each query S_K, its average rank $AvgRank(S_K)$ is calculated as follows:

$$AvgRank(S_K) = \frac{1}{G(S_K)} \sum_{i=1}^{G(S_K)} Rank(i) \tag{23}$$

The normalized and corrected retrieval rank is defined as $NMRR(S_K)$:

$$NMRR(S_K) = \frac{AvgRank(S_K) - 0.5 \times (K+1)}{1.25 \times K - 0.5 \times (K+1)} \quad (24)$$

In assessing the efficacy of image retrieval approaches within a collection of images, suppose that M queries have been executed. To compute the aggregate mean normalized modified retrieval rank, denoted as $ANMRR$, the following procedure is adopted:

$$ANMRR = \frac{1}{M} \sum_{j=1}^{M} NMRR\left(S_{K_j}\right) \quad (25)$$

The value of $ANMRR$ is within the range $[0, 1]$. It should be noted that the lower the value of $ANMRR$, the higher the retrieval precision.

3. Retrieval Time

The retrieval duration stands as a crucial metric for gauging the performance of an image retrieval system. It spans from the moment the query image is submitted to the point when a full set of search outcomes is obtained. The efficiency of the system is inversely proportional to the retrieval time; the less time it takes to complete the search, the more efficient the system is considered to be.

5.2. Comparison of LC^2R-Net with Other Methods

To verify the effectiveness of the LC^2R-Net model and its advantages over traditional methods in the task of complex lunar crater image retrieval, we selected several widely used convolutional neural network models and Transformer models for comparative analysis. These included VGG16 [54], ResNet101 [55], DenseNet121 [56], EfficientnetV2-S [57], and Vision Transformer (ViT) [58]. The dataset, optimization algorithms, loss functions, and hyperparameters during training were consistent with those used for LC^2R-Net. In LC^2R-Net, λ was set to 0.2, and features were reduced to 128 dimensions using the PCA method. The augmented dataset was used for training, while the original, unmodified dataset was used for testing. The retrieval precision of each model was compared by calculating the mAP for each category. Table 2 presents a detailed comparison of the performance between LC^2R-Net and the aforementioned models. The results indicate that LC^2R-Net achieves better retrieval precision, with the mAP of 83.75%. Compared to VGG16, ResNet101, DenseNet121, EfficientnetV2-S, and Vision Transformer, the mAP of LC^2R-Net is higher by 32.31%, 39.85%, 30.65%, 26.58%, and 21.52%, respectively. These results further demonstrate the significant advantage of LC^2R-Net in integrating low-level visual features and deep features for lunar image retrieval, achieving more precise retrieval results compared to methods relying on the deep features of traditional CNN models.

Table 2. Mean average precision by category on the lunar complex crater dataset for different methods.

Category	Methods					
	VGG16	ResNet101	DenseNet121	EfficientnetV2-S	ViT	LC^2R-Net
Simple Crater	55.33%	54.99%	58.73%	63.77%	61.91%	80.82%
Floor-Fractured Crater	31.32%	24.05%	53.51%	42.08%	55.33%	99.77%
Central Peak Crater	50.80%	43.83%	47.06%	58.33%	52.87%	70.52%
Multi-Impacted Floor Crater	43.50%	38.99%	41.88%	45.44%	46.08%	64.32%
Lunar Oceanic Remnant Impact Crater	80.62%	59.98%	73.61%	81.40%	89.78%	98.22%
Impact Residual Crater	47.09%	41.56%	43.81%	52.03%	52.23%	68.44%
Average	51.44%	43.90%	53.10%	57.17%	62.23%	83.75%

In Table 2, the retrieval accuracy for Multi-Impacted Floor Craters and Impact Residual Craters is significantly lower compared to other categories. The reason is that the features of the crater images in these categories bear a high visual similarity to those of other categories, making it difficult to distinguish between them even with the use of fused features. Nonetheless, in the face of such challenges of feature similarity, the LC^2R-Net model still demonstrates superior performance compared to traditional convolutional neural network models that rely solely on deep features. This indicates the effectiveness of LC^2R-Net in integrating multi-level features, particularly in dealing with image categories with high feature similarity, significantly enhancing the accuracy of retrieval. It is noteworthy that among the mentioned convolutional neural networks, EfficientNetV2-S significantly outperforms VGG16, ResNet-101, and DenseNet121. The reason lies in EfficientNetV2-S's effective balancing of model depth, width, and resolution through scaling methods and the introduction of several novel architectures, thereby preserving more image detail information, which is crucial for retrieval tasks. Furthermore, the Vision Transformer surpasses traditional convolutional neural network models in performance, indicating that models based on self-attention mechanisms can more effectively capture global dependencies, thereby enhancing the model's generalization capability.

To more visually demonstrate the effectiveness of LC^2R-Net, Figures 10–12 present some retrieval examples. Taking the top 10 returned images as an example, the retrieval results of LC^2R-Net are shown in Figure 10, and the comparative retrieval results of LC^2R-Net and other methods are shown in Figures 11 and 12.

5.3. Ablation Study

To evaluate the performance of the LC^2R-Net model in the task of image retrieval for complex lunar craters, this section conducts ablation experiments on the feature fusion and attention mechanisms within the LC^2R-Net network. The experiments are carried out on the complex lunar crater dataset constructed for this paper, utilizing *mAP* and *ANMRR* as metrics to assess retrieval performance. Table 3 presents the ablation study for the attention mechanism.

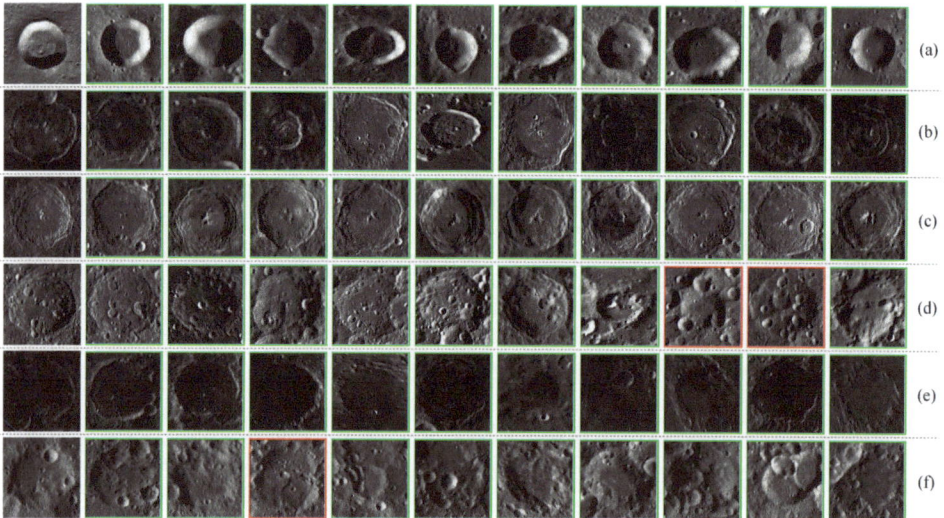

Figure 10. Retrieval results of LC^2R-Net for various crater categories (the first image in each row is the query image, green borders indicate correct retrieval results, and red borders indicate incorrect retrieval results): (**a**) Simple crater. (**b**) Floor-fractured crater. (**c**) Central peak crater. (**d**) Multi-impacted floor crater. (**e**) Lunar oceanic remnant impact crater. (**f**) Impact residual crater.

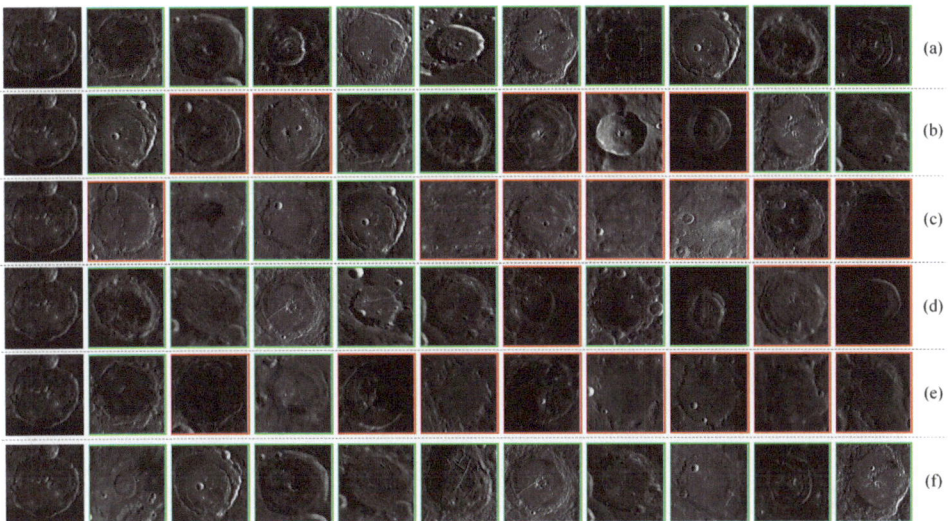

Figure 11. Examples of retrieving central peak craters using different methods (the first image in each row is the query image, green borders indicate correct retrieval results, and red borders indicate incorrect retrieval results): (**a**) LC^{2}R-Net. (**b**) VGG-16. (**c**) ResNet-101. (**d**) DenseNet-121. (**e**) EfficientNetV2-S. (**f**) ViT.

Figure 12. Examples of retrieving Lunar Oceanic Remnant Impact Craters using different methods (the first image in each row is the query image, green borders indicate correct retrieval results, and red borders indicate incorrect retrieval results): (**a**) LC^{2}R-Net. (**b**) VGG-16. (**c**) ResNet-101. (**d**) DenseNet-121. (**e**) EfficientNetV2-S. (**f**) ViT.

Table 3. Ablation study on the attention mechanism.

Methods	mAP/%	ANMRR
Swin-T	83.01	0.0755
Swin-T + CBAMwithECA	83.65	0.0725
LC^{2}R-Net	83.75	0.0721

As shown in Table 3, the features extracted using the Swin-T network achieve mAP and $ANMRR$ of 83.08% and 0.0755, respectively, on the dataset. By integrating the CBAMwithECA attention module, the model's mAP is improved by 0.64%, and the $ANMRR$ is reduced by 0.003. These results confirm that the introduction of attention mechanisms can more effectively highlight key features in images, enhance the discrimination ability for images of different categories, and thereby improve the accuracy of lunar complex crater image retrieval tasks.

Ablation studies were conducted on the feature fusion module with the value of λ set to 0.2. The results are shown in Table 4, where LBP represents texture features, and Hu denotes shape features.

Table 4. Feature fusion ablation study.

Methods	mAP/%	ANMRR
LBP	39.85	0.3717
Hu	29.81	0.4064
LBP + Hu	41.37	0.3616
LC^{2}R-Net	83.75	0.0721

The data in Table 4 reveal the limitations of relying solely on visual features for retrieving complex images such as lunar impact craters, resulting in lower image retrieval accuracy. Furthermore, although combining texture (LBP) and shape (Hu) features (LBP + Hu) can improve retrieval performance to some extent, the retrieval accuracy on the complex lunar crater dataset only increased by 1.52% and 11.56%, respectively, when using these features in isolation. However, when deep features were fused, the mAP increased by 43.9% and 53.94%, and the $ANMRR$ decreased by 0.2996 and 0.3343, respectively. It is noteworthy that the contribution of texture features to retrieval performance was greater than that of shape features, which may be due to the high visual similarity of lunar crater images. These results fully demonstrate the effectiveness of fusing deep and visual features in improving image retrieval accuracy.

5.4. Parametric Analyses

In the LC^{2}R-Net model, the fusion of visual and deep features involves a key parameter λ, which is used to adjust the weight between different features. The specific calculation method is detailed in Section 3.3. This section designs a series of experiments to illustrate the impact of the value of λ on the performance of LC^{2}R-Net by adjusting its value (ranging from 0 to 1, with an interval of 0.1). The features are reduced to 128 dimensions using the PCA method, and the results are shown in Table 5.

From Table 5, it is evident that when the value of λ is set to 0.2, the mAP of the LC^{2}R-Net in the lunar complex crater dataset reaches 83.75%, with the $ANMRR$ of 0.0721. The retrieval accuracy of the fused features is higher than that of using depth features alone when the value of λ ranges from 0 to 0.3. However, when the value of λ exceeds 0.4, the retrieval accuracy using fused features or visual features alone is lower than that of using depth features alone. This indicates that the depth features extracted by the Swin Transformer are more effective than traditional visual features in performing image retrieval tasks for lunar complex craters.

Table 5. Impact of different a values on the retrieval performance of LC²R-Net.

Method	λ	mAP/%	ANMRR
LC²R-Net	0	83.65	0.0725
	0.1	83.67	0.0716
	0.2	83.75	0.0721
	0.3	83.71	0.0728
	0.4	83.29	0.0756
	0.5	83.19	0.0769
	0.6	82.91	0.0752
	0.7	82.46	0.0798
	0.8	81.73	0.0811
	0.9	78.79	0.0934
	1.0	37.99	0.3943

5.5. Comparison of Retrieval Time

In addition to accuracy, retrieval efficiency is also extremely important in practical applications. To evaluate the performance of different models, we conducted tests on the retrieval time for each model using the lunar complex crater dataset. Each model was subjected to 20 retrieval trials, and the average retrieval time was calculated. The retrieval time consumed by each model is shown in Table 6.

The data in Table 6 indicate that as the dimensionality of deep features is reduced, there is a downward trend in model retrieval time. The incorporation of the CBAMwithECA module results in a slight increase in the retrieval time for the Swin-T model. Among all the models compared, the LC²R-Net model, which employs PCA for dimensionality reduction, achieves the shortest retrieval time of only 0.1041 seconds, performing the best among all models. This result demonstrates that the LC²R-Net model successfully reduces the dimensionality and complexity of features while maintaining retrieval efficiency. Additionally, the retrieval time for traditional visual features is also short, which is due to the fact that deep features are denser; even with lower dimensions, they incur greater computational and storage costs compared to sparse visual features. These results highlight the efficiency advantages of the LC²R-Net model in the task of lunar crater image retrieval.

Table 6. Comparison of retrieval time by different methods on the lunar complex drater dataset.

Methods	Feature Vector Length	Retrieval Times/s
VGG-16	4096	0.2134
ResNet101	2048	0.2046
DenseNet121	1024	0.1922
EfficientNetV2-S	1280	0.1942
ViT	768	0.1878
Swin-T	768	0.1884
Swin-T + CBAMwithECA	768	0.1907
LBP + Hu	2367	0.1630
LC²R-Net	128	0.1041

5.6. Impact of PCA Dimensionality Reduction on Retrieval Accuracy

The LC²R-Net model proposed in this paper initially integrates the low-level visual features with the deep features of lunar crater images to generate a feature vector with 3135 dimensions. Subsequently, to enhance the efficiency of retrieval, PCA is employed for feature dimensionality reduction, enabling more efficient retrieval. Therefore, experiments were conducted with different feature dimensions (16, 32, 64, 128, 256, and the original 3135 dimensions) to observe the impact on retrieval accuracy and retrieval time, with the value of λ set to 0.2. The results are shown in Figure 13.

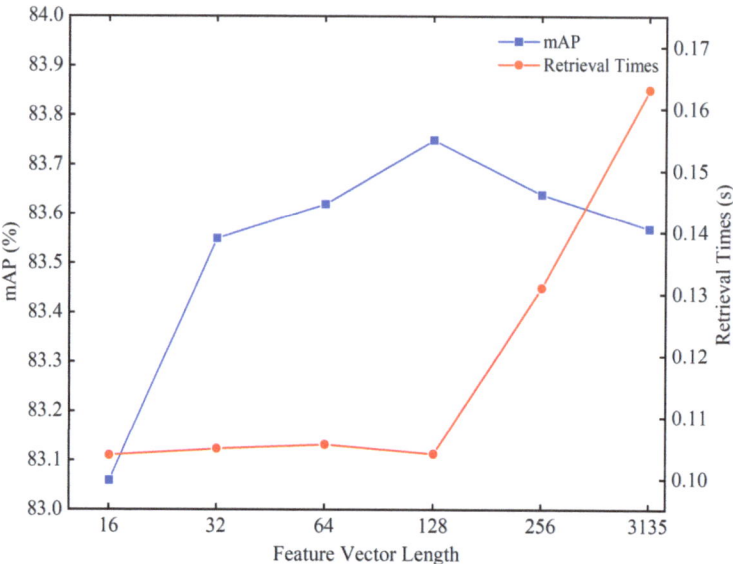

Figure 13. The impact of feature dimensions on the retrieval of lunar complex crater images.

In Figure 13, the retrieval accuracy peaks at a feature vector dimensionality of 128, with the mAP reaching 83.75%. Within the range of increasing feature dimensions from 16 to 128, the retrieval accuracy consistently improves. This phenomenon indicates that within this range of dimensions, as the richness of feature information increases, the system is able to more accurately distinguish and retrieve lunar crater images. However, when the feature vector dimensionality exceeds 128, the retrieval accuracy begins to decline. This decrease is due to the excessive expansion of the feature space, which introduces redundant information or increases noise, thereby negatively impacting the model's discriminative ability. When the feature dimensionality is below 128, the retrieval time remains relatively stable, suggesting that at this level of dimensionality, the system's computational efficiency is less affected by the number of features. In contrast, retrieval time significantly increases when the dimensionality exceeds 128, reflecting the computational burden brought about by higher dimensions. These results demonstrate that the PCA dimensionality reduction technique plays a significant role in enhancing the accuracy and efficiency of lunar crater image retrieval.

5.7. The Impact of Data Augmentation on Retrieval Accuracy

In this study, we address the challenge of imbalanced class distribution within our dataset of lunar impact craters, a factor that may lead to overfitting of certain classes by the neural network during the training process. To mitigate this issue, we have employed data augmentation algorithms to expand our dataset and enhance the model's generalization capabilities. To assess the specific impact of data augmentation on the performance of lunar impact crater image retrieval, we conducted model training on both the original dataset and the augmented dataset. Throughout the training process, to ensure comparability of results, we maintained consistency in our algorithmic optimization strategies, loss function, and hyperparameter settings. For LC^{2}R-Net, the λ was set to 0.2, and feature dimensionality was reduced to 128 dimensions using the PCA method. The experimental results are presented in Figure 14.

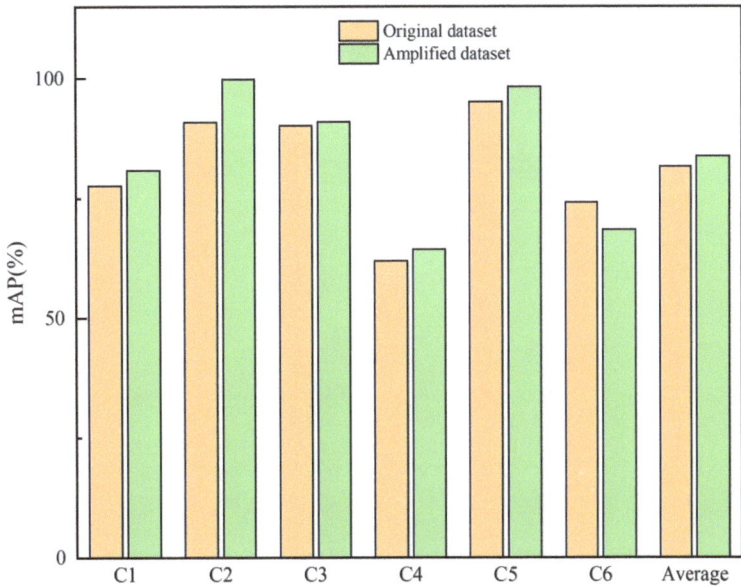

Figure 14. The impact of image augmentation algorithms on the retrieval of lunar complex craters. C1: Simple crater. C2: Floor-fractured crater. C3: Central peak crater. C4: Multi-impacted floor crater. C5: Lunar oceanic remnant impact crater. C6: Impact residual crater.

In Figure 14, it is observed that when the model is trained on the augmented dataset, its performance on the retrieval task is significantly superior to that of the model trained directly on the original dataset. Specifically, the mAP saw a notable increase, improving from 81.63% on the original dataset to 83.75%. This enhancement is reflected not only at a global average level but also across the majority of individual classes, indicating the universality of data augmentation in boosting model performance. However, it is important to note that for the specific category of impact residual crater, the mAP of the model trained on the augmented dataset was actually lower than that of the model trained on the original dataset. This phenomenon suggests that data augmentation does not invariably lead to positive effects. The performance decline in this particular category is attributed to the failure to consider its unique characteristics during augmentation, which hindered the model's ability to effectively discern the differences between impact residual craters and other categories. Therefore, when implementing data augmentation, it is crucial to adopt targeted strategies for different categories to ensure that data augmentation effectively enhances the model's learning and recognition of the distinctions between categories rather than merely increasing the quantity of data.

5.8. Further Discussion

In this study, in order to enhance the model's capability to capture and represent the features of lunar complex crater images, we utilized the CBAMwithECA attention mechanism module during deep feature extraction. To discuss the impact of different attention modules on feature extraction and image retrieval tasks, we conducted comparative experiments by introducing the SE attention mechanism module and the CBAM attention mechanism module at the same position, respectively. The experimental results are shown in Table 7.

Table 7. The impact of different attention mechanisms on lunar complex crater image retrieval tasks.

Methods	mAP/%	ANMRR
Swin-T	83.01	0.0755
Swin-T + SE	82.16	0.0795
Swin-T + CBAM	78.23	0.1038
Swin-T + CBAMwithECA	83.65	0.0725
LC^{2}R-Net	83.75	0.0721

As shown in Table 7, the introduction of the SE module and the CBAM module into the Swin-T model did not enhance the model's performance. On the contrary, the addition of these attention mechanisms had a negative impact on the performance of the original Swin-T model. However, upon integrating the CBAMwithECA attention module, the model's performance saw a significant improvement, with the mAP increasing by 0.64% and the $ANMRR$ decreased by 0.003. It is noteworthy that, in comparison to the attention modules, the SE module outperformed the CBAM module because the SE module provided a more effective feature weighting strategy in channel recalibration. These results indicate that the CBAMwithECA attention module outperforms both the SE and CBAM attention modules in the task of lunar crater image retrieval.

The experimental results adequately substantiate the efficacy of the method we proposed. By integrating the CBAMwithECA module into both the patch embedding and merging modules, LC^{2}R-Net is enabled to capture image details with greater finesse, markedly boosting the model's capability in feature recognition and extraction when dealing with complex crater imagery. Furthermore, we employed a weighted strategy to merge visual and depth features, which not only facilitated an effective complementarity between the two but also accentuated their individual significance. Concurrently, the introduction of a triplet loss function and a hard negative sample mining strategy further encouraged the network to learn more distinctive feature representations, thereby realizing a significant improvement in precision for image retrieval tasks. These results demonstrate that our approach can substantially enhance the model's ability to learn and extract features, significantly improving the accuracy of image retrieval for complex lunar crater imagery.

6. Conclusions

In this paper, we propose the LC^{2}R-Net model, which achieves lunar complex crater image retrieval by fusing the underlying visual features with deep features of images. During the model training phase, we employed a triplet loss function and a hard negative sample mining strategy to generate more distinctive features. In the deep feature extraction stage, we integrated the CBAMwithECA module into the Swin Transformer, successfully capturing the rich details and significant information in lunar crater images, thus enabling better differentiation between different types of lunar complex crater images. In the visual feature extraction stage, we extracted texture and shape features, which effectively complement the deep features. During the feature fusion stage, we introduced feature fusion weights to highlight the importance of different features in retrieval and performed PCA dimensionality reduction after feature fusion, significantly improving the model's retrieval efficiency. We conducted extensive experiments on the lunar complex crater dataset generated in this paper, and the results show that compared to traditional deep learning methods, LC^{2}R-Net achieved the highest retrieval accuracy of 83.75% when the feature fusion weight was set to 0.2 and PCA dimensionality was reduced to 128 while maintaining a fast retrieval speed. Through ablation experiments, we detailed the key role of the CBAMwithECA module and the feature fusion strategy in improving retrieval performance. We explored the impact of different dimensionality reductions on retrieval performance and found that the setting of 128 dimensions offered the best retrieval performance. In addition, we compared the effects of different attention mechanisms on retrieval results, and the experiments proved that the CBAMwithECA attention module performed the best in this study. The LC^{2}R-Net model not only advances the technology of lunar crater image retrieval but also provides a new perspective for the application of deep learning in the analysis of complex geological images.

In future work, we will consider adopting deep hashing techniques to replace PCA dimensionality reduction to further optimize the precision and efficiency of image retrieval. Secondly, we will explore the feasibility of applying our method to video stream processing. Although current research focuses on single image frames, our proposed network architecture and algorithms can be extended through time series analysis to handle consecutive frames within video streams. This will involve additional training of the network to adapt to dynamic changes. Lastly, we plan to combine object detection methods with image retrieval techniques to explore the detection of different types of impact craters within single image frames to address more realistic application scenarios.

Author Contributions: Y.Z. analyzed the data and wrote the Python source code. Z.K. and Z.C. helped with project and study design, paper writing, and data analysis. All authors have read and agreed to the published version of the manuscript.

Funding: This research received no external funding.

Data Availability Statement: The data used to support the findings of this study are available from the corresponding author upon request.

Conflicts of Interest: The authors declare no conflicts of interest.

References

1. Hartmann, W.K. Lunar cratering chronology. *Icarus* **1970**, *13*, 299–301. [CrossRef]
2. Ryder, G. Mass flux in the ancient Earth-Moon system and benign implications for the origin of life on Earth. *J. Geophys. Res. Planets* **2002**, *107*, 6–11. [CrossRef]
3. Chapman, C.R.; Cohen, B.A.; Grinspoon, D.H. What are the real constraints on the existence and magnitude of the late heavy bombardment? *Icarus* **2007**, *189*, 233–245. [CrossRef]
4. Bottke, W.F.; Norman, M.D. The late heavy bombardment. *Annu. Rev. Earth Planet. Sci.* **2017**, *45*, 619–647. [CrossRef]
5. Chen, M.; Lin, H.; Wen, Y.; He, L.; Hu, M. Sino-VirtualMoon: A 3D web platform using Chang'e-1 data for collaborative research. *Planet. Space Sci.* **2012**, *65*, 130–136. [CrossRef]
6. Di, K.; Li, W.; Yue, Z.; Sun, Y.; Liu, Y. A machine learning approach to crater detection from topographic data. *Adv. Space Res.* **2014**, *54*, 2419–2429. [CrossRef]
7. Sawabe, Y.; Matsunaga, T.; Rokugawa, S. Automated detection and classification of lunar craters using multiple approaches. *Adv. Space Res.* **2006**, *37*, 21–27. [CrossRef]
8. Vijayan, S.; Vani, K.; Sanjeevi, S. Crater detection, classification and contextual information extraction in lunar images using a novel algorithm. *Icarus* **2013**, *226*, 798–815. [CrossRef]
9. Yang, C.; Zhao, H.; Bruzzone, L.; Benediktsson, J.A.; Liang, Y.; Liu, B.; Zeng, X.; Guan, R.; Li, C.; Ouyang, Z. Lunar impact crater identification and age estimation with Chang'E data by deep and transfer learning. *Nat. Commun.* **2020**, *11*, 6358. [CrossRef]
10. Meyer, C.; Deans, M. Content based retrieval of images for planetary exploration. In Proceedings of the 2007 IEEE/RSJ International Conference on Intelligent Robots and Systems, San Diego, CA, USA, 29 October–2 November 2007; pp. 1377–1382.
11. Chen, H.Z.; Jing, N.; Wang, J.; Chen, Y.G.; Chen, L. A novel saliency detection method for lunar remote sensing images. *IEEE Geosci. Remote Sens. Lett.* **2013**, *11*, 24–28. [CrossRef]
12. Hua, K.A.; Shaykhian, G.A.; Beil, R.J.; Akpinar, K.; Martin, K.A. Saliency-based CBIR system for exploring lunar surface imagery. In Proceedings of the 2014 ASEE Annual Conference & Exposition, Indianapolis, Indiana, USA, 15–18 June 2014; pp. 24–1065.
13. Tombe, R.; Viriri, S. Adaptive deep co-occurrence feature learning based on classifier-fusion for remote sensing scene classification. *IEEE J. Sel. Top. Appl. Earth Obs. Remote Sens.* **2020**, *14*, 155–164. [CrossRef]
14. Zhang, Z.; Jiang, T.; Liu, C.; Zhang, L. An effective classification method for hyperspectral image with very high resolution based on encoder–decoder architecture. *IEEE J. Sel. Top. Appl. Earth Obs. Remote Sens.* **2020**, *14*, 1509–1519. [CrossRef]
15. Zhang, Y.; Zheng, X.; Yuan, Y.; Lu, X. Attribute-cooperated convolutional neural network for remote sensing image classification. *IEEE Trans. Geosci. Remote Sens.* **2020**, *58*, 8358–8371. [CrossRef]
16. Li, Y.; Zhang, Y.; Huang, X.; Zhu, H.; Ma, J. Large-scale remote sensing image retrieval by deep hashing neural networks. *IEEE Trans. Geosci. Remote Sens.* **2017**, *56*, 950–965. [CrossRef]
17. Napoletano, P. Visual descriptors for content-based retrieval of remote-sensing images. *Int. J. Remote Sens.* **2018**, *39*, 1343–1376. [CrossRef]
18. Ye, F.; Xiao, H.; Zhao, X.; Dong, M.; Luo, W.; Min, W. Remote sensing image retrieval using convolutional neural network features and weighted distance. *IEEE Geosci. Remote Sens. Lett.* **2018**, *15*, 1535–1539. [CrossRef]

19. Yan, K.; Wang, Y.; Liang, D.; Huang, T.; Tian, Y. Cnn vs. sift for image retrieval: Alternative or complementary? In Proceedings of the 24th ACM international conference on Multimedia, Amsterdam, The Netherlands, 15–19 October 2016; pp. 407–411.
20. Cheng, Q.; Shao, K.; Li, C.; Li, S.; Li, J.; Shao, Z. A distributed system architecture for high-resolution remote sensing image retrieval by combining deep and traditional features. In Proceedings of the Image and Signal Processing for Remote Sensing XXIV, Berlin, Germany, 10–13 September 2018; Volume 10789, pp. 413–432.
21. Zhang, M.; Cheng, Q.; Luo, F.; Ye, L. A triplet nonlocal neural network with dual-anchor triplet loss for high-resolution remote sensing image retrieval. *IEEE J. Sel. Top. Appl. Earth Obs. Remote Sens.* **2021**, *14*, 2711–2723. [CrossRef]
22. Cao, R.; Zhang, Q.; Zhu, J.; Li, Q.; Li, Q.; Liu, B.; Qiu, G. Enhancing remote sensing image retrieval using a triplet deep metric learning network. *Int. J. Remote Sens.* **2020**, *41*, 740–751. [CrossRef]
23. Liu, Y.; Ding, L.; Chen, C.; Liu, Y. Similarity-based unsupervised deep transfer learning for remote sensing image retrieval. *IEEE Trans. Geosci. Remote Sens.* **2020**, *58*, 7872–7889. [CrossRef]
24. Zhang, Y.; Zheng, X.; Lu, X. Remote Sensing Image Retrieval by Deep Attention Hashing With Distance-Adaptive Ranking. *IEEE J. Sel. Top. Appl. Earth Obs. Remote Sens.* **2023**, *16*, 4301–4311. [CrossRef]
25. Ding, C.; Wang, M.; Zhou, Z.; Huang, T.; Wang, X.; Li, J. Siamese transformer network-based similarity metric learning for cross-source remote sensing image retrieval. *Neural Comput. Appl.* **2023**, *35*, 8125–8142. [CrossRef]
26. Cheng, G.; Li, Z.; Han, J.; Yao, X.; Guo, L. Exploring hierarchical convolutional features for hyperspectral image classification. *IEEE Trans. Geosci. Remote Sens.* **2018**, *56*, 6712–6722. [CrossRef]
27. Chaudhuri, U.; Dey, S.; Datcu, M.; Banerjee, B.; Bhattacharya, A. Interband retrieval and classification using the multilabeled sentinel-2 bigearthnet archive. *IEEE J. Sel. Top. Appl. Earth Obs. Remote Sens.* **2021**, *14*, 9884–9898. [CrossRef]
28. Li, Y.; Zhang, Y.; Huang, X.; Yuille, A.L. Deep networks under scene-level supervision for multi-class geospatial object detection from remote sensing images. *ISPRS J. Photogramm. Remote Sens.* **2018**, *146*, 182–196. [CrossRef]
29. Cheng, G.; Li, Q.; Wang, G.; Xie, X.; Min, L.; Han, J. SFRNet: Fine-Grained Oriented Object Recognition via Separate Feature Refinement. *IEEE Trans. Geosci. Remote Sens.* **2023**, *61*, 5610510. [CrossRef]
30. Liu, Z.; Lin, Y.; Cao, Y.; Hu, H.; Wei, Y.; Zhang, Z.; Lin, S.; Guo, B. Swin transformer: Hierarchical vision transformer using shifted windows. In Proceedings of the IEEE/CVF International Conference on Computer Vision, Montreal, BC, Canada, 11–17 October 2021; pp. 10012–10022.
31. Lin, A.; Chen, B.; Xu, J.; Zhang, Z.; Lu, G.; Zhang, D. Ds-transunet: Dual swin transformer u-net for medical image segmentation. *IEEE Trans. Instrum. Meas.* **2022**, *71*, 4005615. [CrossRef]
32. Ma, J.; Tang, L.; Fan, F.; Huang, J.; Mei, X.; Ma, Y. SwinFusion: Cross-domain long-range learning for general image fusion via swin transformer. *IEEE/CAA J. Autom. Sin.* **2022**, *9*, 1200–1217. [CrossRef]
33. He, X.; Zhou, Y.; Zhao, J.; Zhang, D.; Yao, R.; Xue, Y. Swin transformer embedding UNet for remote sensing image semantic segmentation. *IEEE Trans. Geosci. Remote Sens.* **2022**, *60*, 4408715. [CrossRef]
34. Gao, L.; Liu, H.; Yang, M.; Chen, L.; Wan, Y.; Xiao, Z.; Qian, Y. STransFuse: Fusing swin transformer and convolutional neural network for remote sensing image semantic segmentation. *IEEE J. Sel. Top. Appl. Earth Obs. Remote Sens.* **2021**, *14*, 10990–11003. [CrossRef]
35. Liu, Z.; Tan, Y.; He, Q.; Xiao, Y. SwinNet: Swin transformer drives edge-aware RGB-D and RGB-T salient object detection. *IEEE Trans. Circuits Syst. Video Technol.* **2021**, *32*, 4486–4497. [CrossRef]
36. Tekeste, I.; Demir, B. Advanced local binary patterns for remote sensing image retrieval. In Proceedings of the IGARSS 2018-2018 IEEE International Geoscience and Remote Sensing Symposium, Valencia, Spain, 22–27 July 2018; pp. 6855–6858.
37. Aptoula, E. Remote sensing image retrieval with global morphological texture descriptors. *IEEE Trans. Geosci. Remote Sens.* **2013**, *52*, 3023–3034. [CrossRef]
38. Xie, G.; Guo, B.; Huang, Z.; Zheng, Y.; Yan, Y. Combination of dominant color descriptor and Hu moments in consistent zone for content based image retrieval. *IEEE Access* **2020**, *8*, 146284–146299. [CrossRef]
39. Chen, H.Z.; Jing, N.; Wang, J.; Chen, Y.G.; Chen, L. Content Based Retrieval for Lunar Exploration Image Databases. In Proceedings of the Database Systems for Advanced Applications: 18th International Conference, DASFAA 2013, Wuhan, China, 22–25 April 2013; Proceedings, Part II 18; Springer: Berlin/Heidelberg, Germany, 2013; pp. 259–266.
40. Wang, S.; Hou, D.; Xing, H. A novel multi-attention fusion network with dilated convolution and label smoothing for remote sensing image retrieval. *Int. J. Remote Sens.* **2022**, *43*, 1306–1322. [CrossRef]
41. Ye, F.; Chen, S.; Meng, X.; Xin, J. Query-adaptive feature fusion base on convolutional neural networks for remote sensing image retrieval. In Proceedings of the 2021 International Conference on Digital Society and Intelligent Systems (DSInS), Chengdu, China, 3–4 December 2021; pp. 148–151.
42. Wang, H.; Zhou, Z.; Zong, H.; Miao, L. Wide-context attention network for remote sensing image retrieval. *IEEE Geosci. Remote Sens. Lett.* **2020**, *18*, 2082–2086. [CrossRef]
43. Chaudhuri, U.; Banerjee, B.; Bhattacharya, A.; Datcu, M. Attention-driven graph convolution network for remote sensing image retrieval. *IEEE Geosci. Remote Sens. Lett.* **2021**, *19*, 8019705. [CrossRef]
44. Zhong, W.; Jiang, J.; Ma, Y. L2AMF-Net: An L2-Normed Attention and Multi-Scale Fusion Network for Lunar Image Patch Matching. *Remote Sens.* **2022**, *14*, 5156. [CrossRef]
45. Fan, L.; Zhao, H.; Zhao, H. Global optimization: Combining local loss with result ranking loss in remote sensing image retrieval. *IEEE Trans. Geosci. Remote Sens.* **2020**, *59*, 7011–7026. [CrossRef]

46. Zhao, H.; Yuan, L.; Zhao, H. Similarity retention loss (SRL) based on deep metric learning for remote sensing image retrieval. *ISPRS Int. J. Geo-Inf.* **2020**, *9*, 61. [CrossRef]
47. Fan, L.; Zhao, H.; Zhao, H. Distribution consistency loss for large-scale remote sensing image retrieval. *Remote Sens.* **2020**, *12*, 175. [CrossRef]
48. Ojala, T.; Pietikäinen, M.; Harwood, D. A comparative study of texture measures with classification based on featured distributions. *Pattern Recognit.* **1996**, *29*, 51–59. [CrossRef]
49. Hu, M.K. Visual pattern recognition by moment invariants. *IRE Trans. Inf. Theory* **1962**, *8*, 179–187.
50. Zhu, L.; Geng, X.; Li, Z.; Liu, C. Improving YOLOv5 with attention mechanism for detecting boulders from planetary images. *Remote Sens.* **2021**, *13*, 3776. [CrossRef]
51. Wang, Q.; Wu, B.; Zhu, P.; Li, P.; Zuo, W.; Hu, Q. ECA-Net: Efficient channel attention for deep convolutional neural networks. In Proceedings of the IEEE/CVF Conference on Computer Vision and Pattern Recognition, Seattle, WA, USA, 13–19 June 2020; pp. 11534–11542.
52. Woo, S.; Park, J.; Lee, J.Y.; Kweon, I.S. Cbam: Convolutional block attention module. In Proceedings of the European conference on computer vision (ECCV), Munich, Germany, 8–14 September 2018; pp. 3–19.
53. Balntas, V.; Riba, E.; Ponsa, D.; Mikolajczyk, K. Learning local feature descriptors with triplets and shallow convolutional neural networks. *Bmvc* **2016**, *1*, 3.
54. Simonyan, K.; Zisserman, A. Very deep convolutional networks for large-scale image recognition. *arXiv* **2014**, arXiv:1409.1556.
55. He, K.; Zhang, X.; Ren, S.; Sun, J. Deep residual learning for image recognition. In Proceedings of the IEEE Conference on Computer Vision and Pattern Recognition, Las Vegas, NV, USA, 27–30 June 2016; pp. 770–778.
56. Huang, G.; Liu, Z.; Van Der Maaten, L.; Weinberger, K.Q. Densely connected convolutional networks. In Proceedings of the IEEE Conference on Computer Vision and Pattern Recognition, Honolulu, HI, USA, 21–26 July 2017; pp. 4700–4708.
57. Tan, M.; Le, Q. Efficientnetv2: Smaller models and faster training. In Proceedings of the International Conference on Machine Learning, Virtual, 18–24 July 2021; pp. 10096–10106.
58. Dosovitskiy, A.; Beyer, L.; Kolesnikov, A.; Weissenborn, D.; Zhai, X.; Unterthiner, T.; Dehghani, M.; Minderer, M.; Heigold, G.; Gelly, S.; et al. An image is worth 16x16 words: Transformers for image recognition at scale. *arXiv* **2020**, arXiv:2010.11929.

Disclaimer/Publisher's Note: The statements, opinions and data contained in all publications are solely those of the individual author(s) and contributor(s) and not of MDPI and/or the editor(s). MDPI and/or the editor(s) disclaim responsibility for any injury to people or property resulting from any ideas, methods, instructions or products referred to in the content.

Article

Continuous Electrode Models and Application of Exact Schemes in Modeling of Electrical Impedance Measurements

Zoltan Vizvari [1,2,3,*], Mihaly Klincsik [2,3,4], Peter Odry [2,5], Vladimir Tadic [2,5,6], Nina Gyorfi [3,7], Attila Toth [2,3,7] and Zoltan Sari [2,3,4]

[1] Department of Environmental Engineering, Faculty of Engineering and Information Technology, University of Pecs, Boszorkany Str. 2, H-7624 Pecs, Hungary
[2] Symbolic Methods in Material Analysis and Tomography Research Group, Faculty of Engineering and Information Technology, University of Pecs, Boszorkany Str. 6, H-7624 Pecs, Hungary; klincsik.mihaly@mik.pte.hu (M.K.); tadityv@uniduna.hu (V.T.)
[3] Multidisciplinary Medical and Engineering Cellular Bioimpedance Research Group, Szentagothai Research Centre, University of Pecs, Ifjusag Str. 20, H-7624 Pecs, Hungary; gyorfi.nina@pte.hu
[4] Department of Technical Informatics, Faculty of Engineering and Information Technology, University of Pecs, Boszorkany Str. 6, H-7624 Pecs, Hungary
[5] Institute of Information Technology, University of Dunaujvaros, Tancsics M. Str. 1/A, H-2401 Dunaujvaros, Hungary
[6] John von Neumann Faculty of Informatics, University of Obuda, Becsi Str. 96/B, H-1034 Budapest, Hungary
[7] Institute of Physiology, Medical School, University of Pecs, Szigeti Str. 12, H-7624 Pecs, Hungary
* Correspondence: vizvari.zoltan@mik.pte.hu

Citation: Vizvari, Z.; Klincsik, M.; Odry, P.; Tadic, V.; Gyorfi, N.; Toth, A.; Sari, Z. Continuous Electrode Models and Application of Exact Schemes in Modeling of Electrical Impedance Measurements. *Electronics* **2024**, *13*, 66. https://doi.org/10.3390/electronics13010066

Academic Editor: Sergio Colangeli

Received: 28 November 2023
Revised: 15 December 2023
Accepted: 20 December 2023
Published: 22 December 2023

Copyright: © 2023 by the authors. Licensee MDPI, Basel, Switzerland. This article is an open access article distributed under the terms and conditions of the Creative Commons Attribution (CC BY) license (https://creativecommons.org/licenses/by/4.0/).

Abstract: The crucial issue in electrical impedance (EI) measurements lies in the galvanic interaction between the electrodes and the investigated material. This paper brings together the basic and applied research experience and combines their results with excellent properties. Consequently, innovative precise methodologies have emerged, enabling the direct modeling of EI measurements, free from the inaccuracies often associated with numerical approaches. As an outcome of the efficiency and robustness of the applied method, the conductivity of the material and the electrodes are represented by a common piecewise function, which is used to solve the differential equation modeling of the EI measurement. Moreover, this allows the possibility for modeling the conductivity of electrodes with continuous functions, providing an important generalization of the Complete Electrode Model (CEM), which has been widely used so far. The effectiveness of the novel approach was showcased through two distinct case studies. In the first case study, potential functions within both the material and the electrodes were computed using the CEM. In the second case study, calculations were performed utilizing the newly introduced continuous electrode model. The simulation results suggest that the new method is a powerful tool for biological research, from in vitro experiments to animal studies and human applications.

Keywords: electrical impedance measurement; exact schemes; electrode artifacts; measurement modeling

1. Introduction

The main goal of this paper is to combine the measurement and theoretical research results in a joint study in order to introduce a completely new electrical impedance (EI) modeling approach. This new modeling method is now able to entirely represent the measurement circuit, including electrodes and electrode–material interactions, constructed during the EI measurements. Moreover, due to the use of a unique mathematical method, the resulting procedure is able to calculate the potentials in the electrodes and in the material without the errors that are common in numerical computation methods. This provides a completely unique and new basis for EI measurement modeling, both for understanding the behavior of electrodes and for reconstructing the impedance of the material.

The relevance of EI measurements is increasing [1,2]. This non-destructive technique detects the physicochemical properties of the measured material and its variations [3,4]. Several approaches for the implementation of EI measurements are currently being developed: discrete frequency EI, EI spectrum (EIS) measurement, and EI tomography (EIT) [3]. The combination of all these methods offers interesting and useful implementation possibilities. For example, combining EIS and EIT can contribute to overcoming difficulties in the image reconstruction with the EIT method [4,5]. An example of such a technology is the multi-frequency EIT (mfEIT), where the application-specific prototypes have been developed beyond the basic research [5,6]. The motivation of this research is to develop a completely new mathematical method in order to implement the mfEIT. Since this is a strongly ill-conditioned, non-linear, and unstable inverse problem, even very small perturbations of the voltage and/or potential values used in the model can cause significant variations in the results [3,4]. Therefore, it is important to apply models that accurately describe the physics of the measurement method. Thus, errors caused by model inaccuracies in the reconstructed impedance images can be minimized.

Regardless of which type of EI measurement is used, the implementation is always based on similar principles [3,4]. Electrodes are placed on the surface of the investigated material and an excitation signal is applied to the selected electrodes. The parameters of the generated electric field are measured and, based on the obtained values of the measured parameters, conclusions are drawn about the complex electrical impedance of the material. Further, based on the results, the physicochemical properties of the material can be analyzed [2,3]. The generator used in the measurement may be either a current generator or a voltage generator [3]. The most commonly used signal type for multi-frequency approaches is the monochromatic sine signal [7,8].

Based on these considerations, it is evident that the interaction between the electrode and the investigated material is crucial for the reliability of the analysis, since the galvanic contact between the electrode and the surface of the material is required to close the circuit utilized for the measurement [3]. The role of the electrode is also essential from another point of view, since electrodes are made of a conductive material and, due to the presence of galvanic connections, they significantly influence the electric field in the material [9]. Incorrect recognition and modeling of the electrodes (and the interaction between electrode and material) significantly reduces the reliability of the EI measurement since the resulting distortions and artifacts are propagated into the result generation, causing errors [10,11]. The state-of-the-art electrode modeling technique is the Complete Electrode Model (CEM), which is the basis for various EIT imaging algorithms [12–14].

The basic idea behind the CEM is that the electrical properties of the electrode, as a function of its material, are considered as an impedance in a series connection with the material under measurement [11]. Consequently, the voltage measured on an electrode is modeled as the sum of two components—the voltages across the electrode and the measured material. Naturally, this effect is significant if the current passing through the electrode is not zero [11]. The CEM is a convenient model for the implementation of EIT numerical methods; however, the CEM approach can be easily applied to EIS and more general EI methods [4]. The implementation of the CEM can be described as follows. First, the elliptic differential equation modeling of the electric field is discretized with the finite element method over the given domain, and then the potential values representing the boundary conditions are substituted with the values expressed from the voltages across the electrodes [11]. In this way, the system of linear equations obtained with the domain discretization under the consideration directly represents the electrode impedance (in the form of a concentrated parameter) and the measured potential value. The potential value arises from the electrode–material interaction and thus it is eliminated from the model [3,4,11].

In contrast, the approach presented in this paper, beyond the possibilities exploited in the case of the CEM, is able to model the electrodes and the complete measurement circuit used in EI measurements without any errors caused by the numerical modeling.

This is explained by the possibility that the method presented in this paper applies the same differential equation not only to the material, but also to the electrodes and even to the material–electrode interaction. This raises the possibility that not only the material, but also the electrodes are represented by continuous functions in the model. As a consequence, the values of the analytical solution of the differential equation, which is the physical representation of the measurement, are calculated at any point in the measurement assembly, regardless of whether the electrode, material, or interaction between these two is being investigated. Therefore, the main contribution of this research is the improvement of the efficacy and robustness of EI measurements—from spectroscopy to tomography—or even in hybrid technologies.

This publication is structured as follows. The Section 1 contains the introduction, the Section 2 describes the related works, the Section 3 introduces a completely new modeling approach, the continuous electrode model. The Section 4 describes the case studies comparing the results obtained using the CEM and the continuous model, while conclusions are drawn in the Section 5.

2. Related Works

The behavior of a wide variety of electrodes used to perform EI measurements often cannot be represented by simple RC elements. Electrodes may also have properties that change over time; therefore, special techniques are needed to compensate for this behavior [15]. Considering the relevant literature, it can be concluded that, in general, the multi-frequency approach is the one that represents the most electrode artefacts, and therefore most studies are related to this issue [16]. The most common application of multifrequency measurements is in the field of human body composition [4,17]. In this context, a large number of studies have been published on electrode–skin interaction properties and their potential errors [18,19]. Since in EI measurements, electrodes with large surfaces are usually used, electrode contact effects were investigated in a separate study. Significant work on understanding the failures has been undertaken by Hwang et al. [20], who investigated the effects of temperature variation, changes in oxygen partial pressure, and other mechanical effects on the contact impedance of the electrode. The failure effects of imperfect contact on solid electrolytes have also been investigated by Fleig et al. [21]. In addition, studies have been carried out to understand and eliminate the error phenomena caused by electrode mismatches in EI measurements [22,23]. The detection and elimination of these errors is crucial for the success of EIS measurements [24].

In the previous study, Vizvari et al. [8] presented a new EI prototype and a specific data collection procedure on simple RC elements, which provided impressive results even at an early stage. In order to implement the technology in praxis, further research is needed on the degree of uncertainty, and additional steps may be required to create a technology suited for practical utilization. In the next step of the development, the use of electrodes complicates the implementation of the method. The electrodes naturally involve the previously described risk of errors; therefore, it is essential to describe and model the electrode–matter interaction in detail.

Moreover, great attention is paid to the application of the most efficient computational procedures for modeling EI measurements. Vizvari et al. [5,25] have established a completely new basis for the mathematical modeling procedures required for their interpretation. One of the achievements is the absolutely new mathematical approach, where Vizvari et al. [25] introduced the exact scheme for second-order ordinary differential equations (ODEs) using arbitrary spatial discretization. Exact schemes were also first introduced by Vizvari et al. [25] for second-order ODEs with a self-adjoint differential operator. The exact schemes are characterized by the property that they always provide the values of the analytic solution of the ODEs in the grid points, independently of the spatial discretization. The efficiency and robustness of this outstanding ability and the mathematical structures have been demonstrated in detail by Vizvari et al. [25].

Moreover, the previous studies have also introduced a specific property of exact schemes. Since they are based on Local Green's functions defined by solutions to the homogeneous ODE of the original problem, the exact schemes are perfectly suitable for difficult mathematical problems where the functions in the ODE have discontinuities [25]. All these outstanding properties are exploited in this study, where a completely new modeling aspect of EIS measurements is presented, based on the improvement of the CEM and on the use of exact schemes. In this completely new approach, the electrodes and the material under investigation are modeled using a piecewise conductivity function, which has the advantage that the electrode–material interaction can be modeled more directly and accurately. Moreover, the electrical behavior of the electrodes may be modeled using continuous functions in addition to RC elements. Utilizing all this, it is possible to model and visualize the frequency-dependent potential profiles in the material under investigation and in the electrodes with the least possible error.

3. The Continuous Electrode Model Using the Exact Schemes

The basic equation for the physical modeling of EI measurements is the ODE with the following self-adjoint operator [3]:

$$Du(x) = \frac{d}{dx}\left(\kappa(x)\frac{d}{dx}u(x)\right) = f(x) \qquad x \in [0, L], \tag{1}$$

where

- D denotes the second order, self-adjoint differential operator;
- $\kappa(x) \geq \kappa_0 > 0$ denotes a positive, isotropic conductivity function (S/m);
- $u(x)$ denotes the electric potential function (V);
- $f(x)$ denotes the source function (A/m^2).

It is assumed that the classical solution $u(x)$ exists on $[0, L]$ with the appropriate boundary conditions.

Vizvari et al. have implemented EI measurements by specifying the following mixed boundary conditions [8]:

$$\mathcal{B}_{DN} = \{\kappa(0)u(0) = i, u(L) = 0\}. \tag{2}$$

The exact scheme for Equation (1) is defined by the following result, specifying the boundary conditions in Equation (2).

Theorem 1 (Exact scheme for Dirichlet and Neumann boundaries). *Let*

$$x_0 = 0 < x_1 < \cdots < x_{i-1} < x_i < x_{i+1} < \cdots < x_{n-1} < x_n < x_{n+1} = L \tag{3}$$

be an arbitrary discretization of the interval $[0, L]$ into $(n+1)$ subintervals. Let $\psi_{i-1}(x) = \int_{x_{i-1}}^{x} \frac{1}{\kappa(s)}\,ds$ and $\varphi_i(x) = \int_{x}^{x_{i+1}} \frac{1}{\kappa(s)}\,ds$ be the test functions obtained from the following initial value problems:

$$\begin{cases} D\psi_{i-1}(x) = 0, & \text{(4a)} \\ \psi_{i-1}(x_{i-1}) = 0, & \text{(4b)} \\ \kappa(x_{i-1})\dfrac{d}{dx}\psi_{i-1}(x_{i-1}) = 1, & \text{(4c)} \end{cases}$$

$$\begin{cases} D\varphi_i(x) = 0, & \text{(5a)} \\ \varphi_i(x_{i+1}) = 0, & \text{(5b)} \\ \kappa(x_{i+1})\dfrac{d}{dx}\varphi_i(x_{i+1}) = -1, & \text{(5c)} \end{cases}$$

where $i = 1, 2, \cdots, n$. By using these structures and considerations, the following system of $n \geq 3$ linear equations is constructed:

$$\begin{cases} (a_0 + a_1)u_1 - a_1 u_2 & = a_0 u(0) + a_0 G_0 + a_1 H_1, \\ -a_{i-1} u_{i-1} + (a_{i-1} + a_i) u_i - a_i u_{i+1} & = a_{i-1} G_{i-1} + a_i H_i, \\ -a_{n-1} u_{n-1} + (a_{n-1} + a_n) u_n & = a_n u(L) + a_{n-1} G_{n-1} + a_n H_n, \end{cases} \quad (6)$$

with indexes $i = 2, 3, \cdots, (n-1)$. The coefficients in Equation (6) are defined as

$$a_{i-1} = \frac{1}{\psi_{i-1}(x_i)} = \frac{1}{\varphi_i(x_{i-1})}, \quad (7)$$

$$G_{i-1} = \int_{x_{i-1}}^{x_i} f(t) \psi_{i-1}(t) dt, \quad (8)$$

$$H_i = \int_{x_i}^{x_{i+1}} f(t) \varphi_i(t) dt, \quad (9)$$

where $i = 1, 2, 3, \cdots, n$. The $u(L)$ value can be substituted directly from Equation (2), while the $u(0)$ value is calculated using the Neumann-to-Dirichlet transformation:

$$u(0) = u(L) + \varphi_n(0) \kappa(0) u(0) + \int_0^L f(t) \varphi_n(t) dt. \quad (10)$$

The solution vector of Equation (6) $U = [u_1, u_2, \ldots, u_n]^T$ leads to the same values as the solution $u(x)$ of the second-order ODE (1) with boundary conditions (Equation (2)) at the interior grid points (Equation (3)) without any error; that is, $u(x_i) = u_i$.

A detailed proof of Theorem 1 can be found in Vizvari et al. [25] for further reading.

Theorem 1 is applied in cases where the material sample and the measurement assemblies are represented by a one-dimensional model. This is correct in all cases where the electric current density propagates in such geometry, where the perpendicular cross-section is constant along the entire length of the sample. Then, the electrodes are fixed to the two sides of the sample, where the surface area is equal to the whole perpendicular cross-section. In metrology practice, because of easier adaptation to sampling methods, the cylindrical geometry is preferred, for example in geophysical [26,27] or medical applications [28] of EIS. Based on this, a schematic illustration of the cylindrical geometry material sample and the associated measurement setup is shown in Figure 1.

The one-dimensional nature of the model problem depicted in Figure 1 arises from the specific geometry of the electrodes and the material, which possess a constant cross-sectional area denoted with A. As can be seen in Figure 1, the current generator (i) is connected to Electrode 1 with width a, the ground point ($u_{n+1} = 0$) of the generator is connected to Electrode 2 with width b. As a consequence, it is easy to see from Theorem 1 that the integral functions, defined by Equations (4) and (5), represent the concentrated parameter derived from the impedance of the material. The potential values ($[u_0, u_1, u_2, u_3, \ldots, u_i, \ldots, u_n]$), which can be calculated using Theorem 1, are consequently the values of u_i pertaining exclusively to the cross-sectional position x_i:

$$u(x_i) = u_i, \quad i = 1, 2, \ldots, n. \quad (11)$$

Based on Figure 1, the measurement method is modeled using the following statements defined in Equation (2). The application of these constraints, and the substitution of

Equation (10), simplifies the corresponding system of linear equations in Equation (6) in the following, easily applicable, form:

$$\begin{cases} (a_0 + a_1)u_1 - a_1 u_2 & = a_0 \varphi_n(0)i, \\ -a_{i-1} u_{i-1} + (a_{i-1} + a_i)u_i - a_i u_{i+1} & = 0, \\ -a_{n-1} u_{n-1} + (a_{n-1} + a_n)u_n & = 0, \end{cases} \qquad (12)$$

with indexes $i = 2, 3, \cdots, (n-1)$. The matrix in Equation (12) is symmetric and tridiagonal, and the sum of row elements is equal to zero, except the first and last rows. As a consequence of these advantageous properties, this reduced Laplacian matrix [5] is always invertible and Equation (12) has a unique $U = [u_1, u_2, u_3, \ldots, u_n]^T$ solution vector.

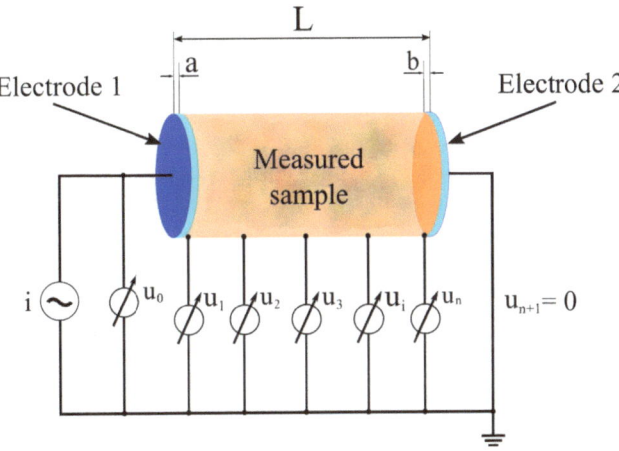

Figure 1. The schematic illustration of the modeled measuring setup extended with electrodes (a and b are the electrode widths and L is the total width including the measured sample).

Corresponding to the model concept, since the domain is extended with the electrode lengths a and b, the $\kappa(x)$ function now describes the conductivity function on the whole $[0, L]$ interval.

$$\kappa(j\omega, x) = \begin{cases} \kappa_{el,1}(j\omega, x), & \text{if } x < a, \\ \kappa_m(j\omega, x), & \text{if } a \leq x \leq (L-b), \\ \kappa_{el,2}(j\omega, x), & \text{if } (L-b) < x, \end{cases} \qquad (13)$$

where

$\kappa(j\omega, x)$ is the complex admittance of the complete measured setup;
$\kappa_{el,1}(j\omega, x)$ is the complex admittance of the electrode placed on the left side of the investigated material sample;
$\kappa_m(j\omega, x)$ is the complex admittance of the investigated material sample;
$\kappa_{el,2}(j\omega, x)$ is the complex admittance of the electrode placed on the right side of the investigated material sample;
ω is the angular frequency, $\omega = 2\pi \cdot f$;
f is the frequency; and
$j = \sqrt{-1}$.

The impedance of the investigated material and the electrodes is defined in the model as the function $\kappa(j\omega, x)$ in Equation (13). The functions $\kappa_{el,1}(j\omega, x)$ and $\kappa_{el,2}(j\omega, x)$, interpreted on $[0, a)$ and $((L-b), L]$, respectively, represent the impedance of the electrodes applied to the measurement and they are placed on the surface of the material.

The handling of piecewise functions defined in Equation (13) is highly efficient when using the exact scheme defined in Theorem 1. In a related result by Vizvari et al. [25], it is demonstrated that, even for the piecewise function $\kappa(x)$, the values of the analytic solution in the mesh points can be calculated (if the function $\kappa(x)$ is integrable on the interval $[0, L]$). Moreover, the application of the exact scheme allows for the calculation of potential values at the discontinuities of the $\kappa(x)$ function. In a case study by Vizvari et al. [25], it has already been shown that the exact scheme can provide the analytical solution (in addition to the values recorded in the mesh points) in the simple case. The resulting analytic solution ($u(x)$) is continuous, but is not derivable at the discontinuity points of $\kappa(x)$ [25]. Naturally, if the differential operator D is applied to $u(x)$, the resulting discontinuities are eliminated, since $u(x)$ satisfies Equation (1). Therefore, for the piecewise conductivity function $\kappa(x)$, defined in Equation (13), these properties are expected using the exact scheme; however, in the case studies presented in Section 4, the symbolic construction of the analytical solution is omitted.

4. Brief Case Studies

The aim of the case studies is to investigate how the composition of the test material and the electrodes applied for the measurement is applicable to the modeling of the EIS measurement using the exact scheme described in Theorem 1. In this brief case study, two electrode modeling approaches are described:

1. The electrodes are modeled with concentrated parameters, as is usual for the CEM;
2. Modeling the impedance of electrodes with functions using continuous electrode models to include anomalies in the model more accurately.

For each of these case studies (based on Figure 1), the spatial discretization parameters are

$$x_{el,1} = [0, 0.5, 0.625, 0.75, 0.875, 1], \tag{14}$$

$$x_m = [1, 2, 3, 4, 5, 6, 7, 8, 9, 10], \tag{15}$$

$$x_{el,2} = [10, 10.125, 10.25, 10.375, 10.5, 11], \tag{16}$$

which implies

$$a = 1, b = 1, L = 11. \tag{17}$$

The parameters of the EIS measurement model are as follows:

$$f = [0.1, 10, 25.119, 63.096, 158.49, 398.107, 10^3, 10^5], \tag{18}$$

and

$$\kappa(0)u(0) = i = 10^{-3} \text{ A}, \quad \text{and} \quad u(L) = 0 \text{ V}. \tag{19}$$

Now consider the mathematical method used to model the electrical behavior of the material under investigation.

4.1. The Model of Measured Sample

The basic and well-known method for electrical modeling of the measured sample, the Cole–Cole model, can be used to describe the frequency-dependent behavior of the material [29]. The flexibility of the Cole–Cole model lies in describing the relaxation of the materials under investigation, whether it is described in terms of concentrated parameters or material properties (conductivity, resistivity, or dielectric constant) [28,29]. In the case studies, however, in addition to the frequency domain behavior of the sample under study, inhomogeneities along the x coordinate were considered in the model, since the resistivity of the material sample is used to build the model. Thus, the Cole–Cole parameters represent the physical properties of the material with continuous functions, which leads to the longitudinal behavior of the model. These functions are substituted into the Cole–Cole equation, whose variable is, by definition, the angular frequency. Finally, all these together yield a common model to represent the spatial and frequency domain properties of the material's impedance. The extended mathematical model can be represented as follows:

$$\rho_m(j\omega, x) = \frac{1}{\kappa_m(j\omega, x)} = \rho_\infty(x) + \frac{\rho_0(x) - \rho_\infty(x)}{1 + (j\omega\tau(x))^{\alpha(x)}}, \quad (20)$$

where

$\rho_m(j\omega, x) = \frac{1}{\kappa_m(j\omega,x)}$ is the complex impedance of the material sample (Ωm);
$\rho_\infty(x) = R_\infty(x) \cdot \frac{A}{L}$ is the resistivity corresponding to the ∞ frequency (Ωm);
$\rho_0(x) = R_0(x) \cdot \frac{A}{L}$ is the resistivity corresponding to 0 Hz frequency (Ω m);
$\tau(x)$ is the time constant (s);
$\alpha(x)$ is the exponent parameter ($0 < \alpha(x) \leq 1$).

In the case of the location-dependent model parameters, inhomogeneities are modeled with the following functions:

$$\rho_\infty(x) = 10 + 10 \cdot e^{-(x-2.5)^2}, \quad (21)$$

$$\rho_0(x) = 110 + 10 \cdot e^{-\frac{(x-7.5)^2}{4}}, \quad (22)$$

$$\tau(x) = 10^{-3} + 10^{-3} \cdot e^{-\frac{(x-4.5)^2}{8}}, \quad (23)$$

$$\alpha(x) = 0.75 + 5 \cdot 10^{-2} \cdot e^{-\frac{(x-7.5)^2}{8}}. \quad (24)$$

Graphs of the Cole–Cole parameters defined in this way are illustrated in Figure 2.

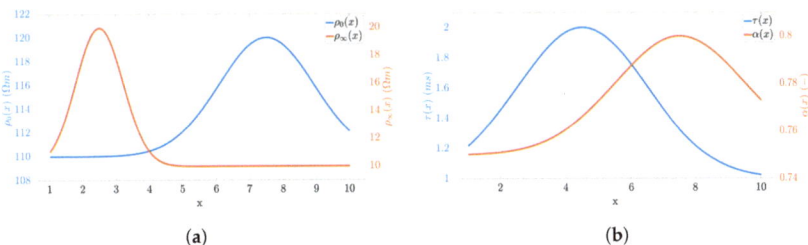

(a)   (b)

Figure 2. The graphs of the space-dependent Cole–Cole parameters ($\rho_0(x)$ and $\rho_\infty(x)$ (in (**a**)), while $\tau(x)$ and $\alpha(x)$ (in (**b**)) are modeled using Equations (21), (22), (23) and (24), respectively).

In EIS measurements, the material sample cannot be accessed directly, hence the electrical behavior of the electrodes used to perform the measurements must be added to the mathematical model. Using the modeling approach provided by Equation (13), the reciprocal of the function in Equation (20) appears in the middle term of the piecewise function, i.e.,

$$\kappa_m(x) = \frac{1}{\rho_m(j\omega, x)} \quad x \in [1, 10]. \quad (25)$$

The functions $\kappa_{el,1}(x)$ and $\kappa_{el,2}(x)$ are defined in the case of the complete and continuous electrode models in the next two subsections separately. The use of two different electrode modeling techniques leads to two different mathematical problems, which can be solved uniformly by applying Theorem 1 and Equation (12) respectively.

4.2. Complete Electrode Model Approach

The CEM considers the electrodes used for EIS measurement concentrated parameters. These concentrated parameters are included in the mathematical model in the form of resistance and capacitance, from which RC components can be obtained. Therefore, in case of the CEM approach, the electrodes in Figure 1 can be modeled by RC circuits. Figure 3 shows the changed electrodes in parallel RC circuits.

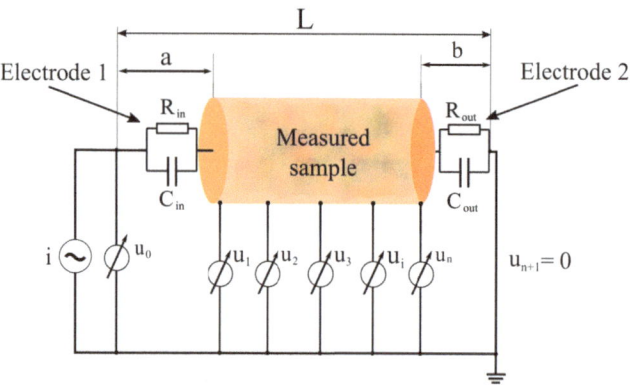

Figure 3. The modeled measuring setup extended with electrodes modeled with RC circuits (Electrode 1 is replaced with R_{in} and C_{in}, while Electrode 2 is replaced with R_{out} and C_{out}).

Figure 3 shows that the electrodes from Figure 1 are replaced by RC elements where the admittance of the new circuits can be obtained as follows:

$$\kappa_{el,1}(j\omega, x) = \frac{1}{R_{in}} + j\omega \cdot C_{in} = 10^{-2} + j\omega \cdot 10^{-4} \quad x \in [0,1], \tag{26}$$

and

$$\kappa_{el,2}(j\omega, x) = \frac{1}{R_{out}} + j\omega \cdot C_{out} = 1.25 \times 10^{-2} + j\omega \cdot 1.2 \times 10^{-4} \quad x \in [10,11], \tag{27}$$

where

R_{in} is the resistance of the electrode on the input in Figure 3;
C_{in} is the capacitance of the electrode on the input in Figure 3;
R_{out} is the resistance of the electrode on the output in Figure 3;
C_{out} is the capacitance of the electrode on the output in Figure 3.

It is easy to observe from Equations (26) and (27) that, in the case of the CEM, the admittance of the electrodes depends only on the frequency, while the concentrated parameter values are constant along the whole length of the electrode.

In this case, the function $\kappa(j\omega, x)$ is constructed using Equations (26) and (27). The reciprocal of the constructed piecewise function (impedance function) is defined in Equation (28) and is shown in Figure 4.

$$\rho_{CEM}(j\omega, x) = \frac{1}{\kappa_{CEM}(j\omega, x)} = \begin{cases} \frac{1}{\kappa_{el,1}(j\omega,x)}, & \text{if } 0 < x < 1, \\ \frac{1}{\kappa_m(j\omega,x)}, & \text{if } 1 \leq x \leq 10, \\ \frac{1}{\kappa_{el,2}(j\omega,x)}, & \text{if } 10 < x < 11. \end{cases} \tag{28}$$

Naturally, the main properties of the impedance function $\rho_{CEM}(j\omega, x)$ (Equation (28)) can be deduced from Equations (26) and (27); however, the graphical representation of the most important aspects that influence the measurement is even more illustrative in

Figure 4. Figure 4 clearly shows that, based on the impedance values of the same color and considered at the same frequency, the electrodes always produce different values to the material under investigation. Further, it can be observed that, while the impedance of the material is strongly spatially dependent, the electrodes are represented as a constant function. Focusing on the frequency dependence, it is noticed that the impedance of the electrodes decreases significantly as the frequency increases, hence the influence of the electrodes is relevant only at low frequencies. It is also remarkable that the difference between the electrodes placed on the input and the output is also highlighted.

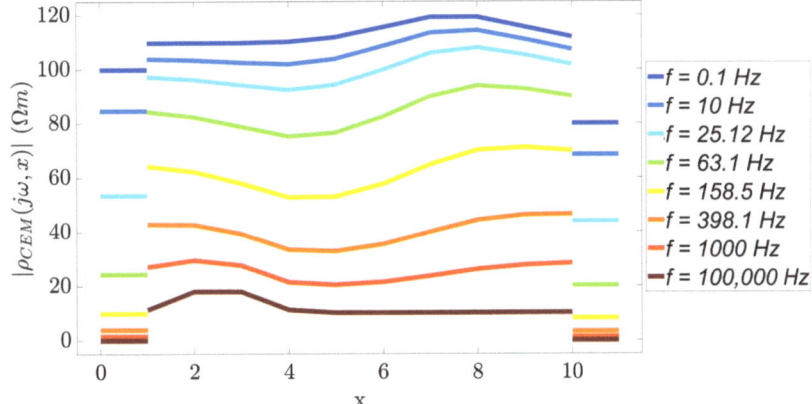

Figure 4. Piecewise impedance function plotted along the length for different frequency values in case of the CEM (the $\frac{1}{\kappa_{el,1}(j\omega,x)}$ on the interval $[0,1]$, the $\frac{1}{\kappa_m(j\omega,x)}$ on the interval $[1,10]$ and the $\frac{1}{\kappa_{el,2}(j\omega,x)}$ on the interval $[10,11]$ functions are calculated using Equations (26), (25) and (27)), respectively.

The next step in solving the case study using the CEM is to calculate the potentials based on Theorem 1 and on the derived system of the linear equation in Equation (12). The first step is to calculate the values of a_{i-1} (based on Equation (7)), which is easily carried out using the discretization (Equations (14)–(16)) and the function ρ_{CEM} (Equation (28)). Therefore, the matrix in Equation (12) can be constructed from the values a_{i-1}, while the right-hand side can be constructed using the measurement properties defined in Equation (19). The solution of the resulting system of linear equations provides the potential values in each x obtained in the spatial discretization and at each frequency. The calculated potential values are depicted in Figure 5.

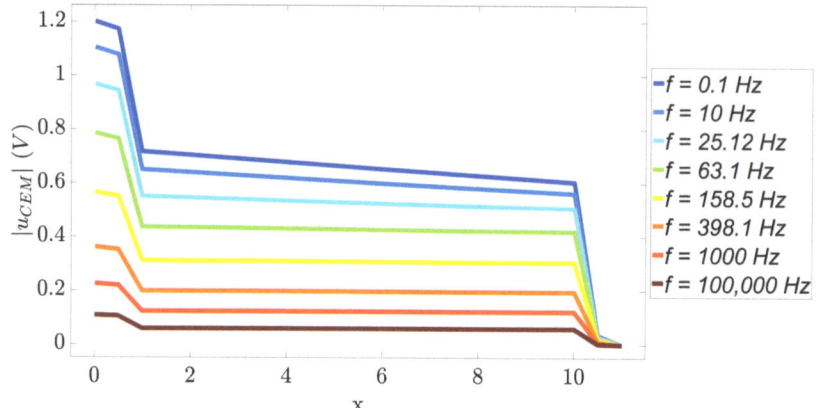

Figure 5. Potential values calculated by the exact scheme along the length of the measurement setup shown in Figure 3.

Figure 5 clearly shows that the sharp potential changes are in the electrodes; in fact, they are the most important factor that determines the change in potential values. It is especially noticeable, that although the electrodes are now modeled with constant functions (Equations (26) and (27)), the steepest changes in potential values occur at the electrode–matter transition, since the length distribution of the impedance is described by a discontinuity function (Figure 4) and the potential functions are continuous (but not differentiable at the discontinuity points). It is interesting to observe that, as a consequence of the spectral behavior of the electrodes (Equations (26) and (27)), at low frequencies, there is a high potential difference between the electrodes and the material under investigation, which decreases significantly with the increasing frequency.

To allow for an easier comparison of the results obtained using the CEM with the continuous case, the magnitude of the potential values is not only presented graphically (Figure 5), but also in tabular form. Table 1 summarizes the functions shown in Figure 5 with a representation of the most typical values of the analytical solution of Equation (1), calculated with mixed boundary conditions in Equation (19) using Theorem 1.

Table 1. Typical values of the potential functions $u(x)$ calculated with the CEM (shown in Figure 5) at mesh points $x = 0$, $x = 1$, $x = 5$, $x = 10$, and $x = 11$.

$u(x)$ (V)	0.1 Hz	10 Hz	25 Hz	63 Hz	158 Hz	398 Hz	1 kHz	10 kHz
$x = 0$	1.2026	1.1065	0.9691	0.7878	0.5692	0.3635	0.2269	0.1091
$x = 1$	0.7183	0.6516	0.5524	0.4382	0.3138	0.1996	0.1243	0.0595
$x = 5$	0.6666	0.6103	0.5308	0.4300	0.3105	0.1984	0.1238	0.0595
$x = 10$	0.6054	0.5632	0.5073	0.4211	0.3067	0.1967	0.1232	0.0595
$x = 11$	0	0	0	0	0	0	0	0

The potential values shown in Table 1, based on the spatial discretization defined in Equations (14)–(16) were chosen at the following grid points: the Neumann boundary condition ($x = 0$), the input electrode and material boundary ($x = 1$), the midpoint of the material length ($x = 5$), the output electrode and material boundary ($x = 10$), and the Dirichlet boundary condition ($x = 11$). In Table 1, essentially the same trend is observed as in Figure 5 and, in addition, it is noted that, with increasing frequency, the individual potential profiles are better described with constant functions.

From the modeling of the measurement setup, these main properties can be concluded; however, it is also clear from Figure 5 that the modeling of the electrode–material interface is a sensitive area in the field of EIS. Now, let us consider an extended version of the case study presented so far.

4.3. Continuous Electrode Approach

In the following, consider a case where the measurement setup (in Figure 1) is modeled with the Cole–Cole model defined in Equation (20) and the electrodes are modeled with continuous functions. These functions are able to consider the properties of the electrodes that the CEM is not capable of. This study details the case where the conductivity at the electrode–material contact points is degraded, for example, due to erroneous electrode contact setup.

Now, let the complex conductivity of the electrodes be defined with the following functions:

$$\kappa^*_{el,1}(j\omega, x) = \left(1 - e^{10(x-1.01)}\right)\kappa_{el,1}(j\omega, x) \quad x \in [0,1], \tag{29}$$

and

$$\kappa^*_{el,2}(j\omega, x) = \left(1 - e^{-10(x-9.99)}\right)\kappa_{el,1}(j\omega, x) \quad x \in [10,11]. \tag{30}$$

From Equations (29) and (30), it can be seen that the functions $\kappa^*_{el,1}(j\omega, x)$ and $\kappa^*_{el,2}(j\omega, x)$ are generated from $\kappa_{el,1}(j\omega, x)$ and $\kappa_{el,2}(j\omega, x)$ such that, respectively, by multiplying them with a special space-dependent function, it results in a significant decrease in conductivity in the electrode's material as it approaches the material under investigation. The piecewise impedance function now takes the following form:

$$\rho^*(j\omega, x) = \frac{1}{\kappa^*(j\omega, x)} = \begin{cases} \frac{1}{\kappa^*_{el,1}(j\omega,x)}, & \text{if } 0 < x < 1, \\ \frac{1}{\kappa_m(j\omega,x)}, & \text{if } 1 \le x \le 10, \\ \frac{1}{\kappa^*_{el,2}(j\omega,x)}, & \text{if } 10 < x < 11. \end{cases} \tag{31}$$

Figure 6 shows the function $\kappa^*(j\omega, x)$ at only one frequency, 0.1 Hz, due to the high dynamics of the frequency dependence.

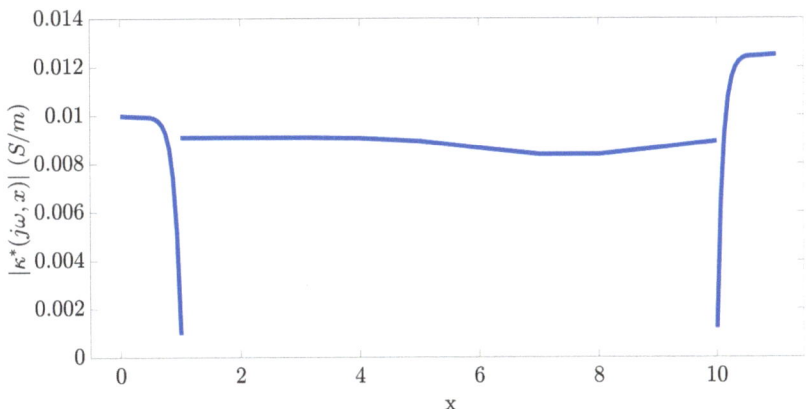

Figure 6. Piecewise $\kappa^*(j\omega, x)$ function plotted along the length for 0.1 Hz frequency value in case of the continuous electrode approach (the $\kappa^*_{el,1}(j\omega, x)$ on the interval $[0, 1]$, the $\kappa_m(j\omega, x)$ on the interval $[1, 10]$, and the $\kappa^*_{el,2}(j\omega, x)$ on the interval $[10, 11]$ functions are calculated using Equations (29), (25) and (30)), respectively.

Figure 6 clearly shows that the electrodes represented by Equations (29) and (30) model an extreme measurement artefact. Compared to the previous case in Figure 4, where the electrodes were represented by the concentrated parameter used by the CEM, in the case of Figure 6, the electrodes near the points $x = 0$ and $x = L$ also behave as concentrated parameters, since their conductivity is constant. However, now, approaching the investigated material, i.e., $x \to 1^-$ and $x \to 10^+$, the conductivity starts to decrease very drastically, hence the applicability of the electrode for EI measurements is seriously reduced. (Naturally, the piecewise function used to model conductivity is always positive on the interval $[0, 11]$.) A further remarkable feature of the piecewise functions shown in Figure 6 is that there is a discontinuity at $x = 1$ and $x = 10$, since the impedance of the electrodes is drastically degraded at the boundary of the material, but this property of the electrodes does not affect the conductivity of the material, hence the conductivity function defined in Section 4.1 is still obtained. Figure 6 shows the piecewise function defined in Equation (31) at a single frequency (0.1 Hz) for clarity. Obviously, varying the frequency generates different functions; however, from Equations (29) and (30), regardless of the frequency at which the electrode conductivity function is considered, a very drastic decrease at the material–electrode interface is always apparent.

The impedance functions $\frac{1}{\kappa_{el,1}^*}$ and $\frac{1}{\kappa_{el,2}^*}$ are illustrated in Figure 7.

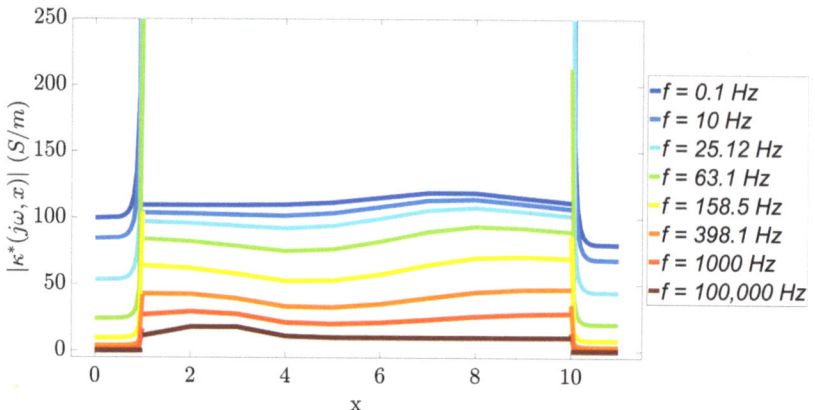

Figure 7. Piecewise impedance function plotted along the length for different frequency values in case of the continuous electrode approach (the $\frac{1}{\kappa_{el,1}^*(j\omega,x)}$ on the interval $[0, 1]$, the $\frac{1}{\kappa_m^*(j\omega,x)}$ on the interval $[1, 10]$, and the $\frac{1}{\kappa_{el,2}^*(j\omega,x)}$ on the interval $[10, 11]$ functions are calculated using Equations (29), (25) and (30)), respectively.

Compared to Figure 4, while most of the findings are still valid, Figure 7 clearly shows the most important difference: the impedance of the electrodes starts to increase significantly as they approach the material under investigation. This tendency remains true regardless of frequency; however, at lower frequencies, where the electrode impedance becomes dominant, the impedance of the electrodes increases more drastically. Importantly, the curves with the same color in Figure 7 are still the piecewise impedance functions for the same frequency.

Based on Theorem 1, using the exact scheme adapted specifically for the measurement (Equation (12)) and the measurement parameters in Equation (19), the potential values along the length of the material under investigation can still be calculated. The absolute values of the potentials are shown in Figure 8 as a function of the frequency and the x coordinate.

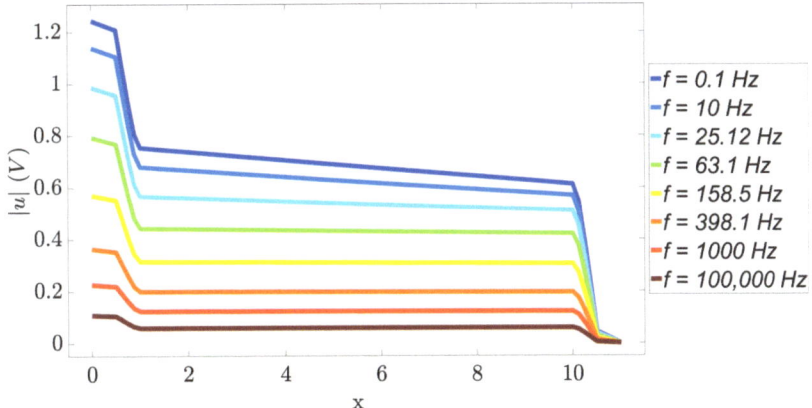

Figure 8. Potential values calculated by the exact scheme along the length of the measurement setup shown in Figure 1 (the electrodes were modeled with continuous functions defined using Equations (29) and (30)).

Typical $u(x)$ potential values in this case can also be presented in tabular form, similar to Table 1. Table 2 summarizes the functions shown in Figure 8 with a representation of the $u(0)$, $u(1)$, $u(5)$, $u(10)$, and $u(11)$ values of the analytical solution calculated using the continuous electrode approach defined in Equation (31).

Table 2. Typical values of the potential functions $u(x)$ calculated with continuous electrode approach defined in Equation (31) (shown in Figure 8) at mesh points $x = 0$, $x = 1$, $x = 5$, $x = 10$, and $x = 11$.

$u(x)$ (V)	0.1 Hz	10 Hz	25 Hz	63 Hz	158 Hz	398 Hz	1 kHz	10 kHz
$x = 0$	1.2449	1.1402	0.9869	0.7947	0.5720	0.3647	0.2273	0.1091
$x = 1$	0.7547	0.6806	0.5677	0.4440	0.3162	0.2006	0.1246	0.0595
$x = 5$	0.6897	0.6286	0.5404	0.4336	0.3120	0.1990	0.1241	0.0595
$x = 10$	0.6128	0.5694	0.5109	0.4225	0.3073	0.1970	0.1233	0.0595
$x = 11$	0	0	0	0	0	0	0	0

Table 2 illustrates clearly (in addition to the properties shown in Figure 8) that, when the frequency increases, the resulting potential profiles are increasingly represented by constant functions. The modeling of the electrodes with a continuous function have provided interesting results; as can be seen in Figure 8, the decrease in conductivity considered for the continuous model visibly modified the potential values measured in the measurement setup. The properties of the functions shown in Figure 8 are almost identical to those in Figure 5; however, the shape of the curves is visibly different from the results calculated using the CEM. The differences between the results are further highlighted in the following discussion by summarizing the results.

4.4. Discussion

The case studies developed in this study present the mathematical modeling of EIS measurements using two different approaches to analyze the modeling of electrodes used in measurements. The investigated material is represented by a location- and frequency-dependent Cole–Cole model, while the electrodes are modeled with two approaches. In the first case study, the well-known and widely used CEM approach is utilized, while in the second, a continuous electrode approach was formulated to exploit exact schemes. The same material was analyzed in all case studies. While for the CEM approach, a location-independent function with constant concentrated parameters was applied, the behavior of the functions used for the continuous electrode approach modelled the conductivity loss of the electrodes.

The calculated potential values show that different potential profiles were obtained for the two electrode approaches. Figure 9 compares the potentials calculated at 0.1 Hz (Figure 9a) and 1 kHz (Figure 9b), respectively.

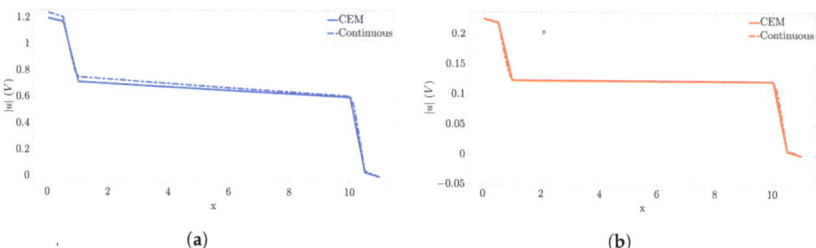

(a) (b)

Figure 9. Comparison of potentials obtained by using exact schemes combined with the CEM and the continuous electrode approach (the calculations are performed at 0.1 Hz (in (**a**)) and 1 kHz (in (**b**))).

Figure 8 shows, systematically, that, despite a minimal mathematical change in the applied functions (Equations (26) and (27) vs. Equations (29) and (30)), where the conductivity of the electrodes decreases in the direction of the material, the calculated potential values differ significantly at 0.1 Hz (Figure 9a). The potential profile indicated by the dashed line takes higher values as it approaches the left endpoint. It is interesting to note that, at higher frequencies (1 kHz, Figure 9b), the difference disappears as the electrode impedance becomes insignificant.

Comparing Table 1 and Table 2, it can be seen that the continuous modeling of the electrodes (although only the impedance of the electrode–matter interface was modified) affected the calculated potential values. As a consequence of the properties of the functions used to model the electrodes, the largest difference between the electrode models is observed at the lowest frequency (0.1 Hz). This difference disappears when the frequency increases. This suggests that the differences arising from electrode modeling are significant at frequencies where the electrode properties dominate over the material properties. As a consequence, the inappropriate modeling of the electrodes causes errors in the calculated potential values, which distort the reconstructed impedance profiles in the case of possible impedance measurements.

These results certainly bring a new perspective to the completed research for developing increasingly effective EI measurement and data evaluation procedures. Namely, the methods presented in this paper can be easily implemented in curricular EI-based biological research such as the study of non-alcoholic fatty liver disease [30], the rapid detection of breast cancer in mouse models [31,32], and the development of a new method for in vitro biological studies [33,34].

5. Conclusions

This paper presents a more complete and extended version of combined EI measurements modeling and its advantages. To achieve this, the introduced exact schemes were applied by combining the conductivity functions of the material under investigation and the electrodes into a general piecewise conductivity function. Consequently, the exact scheme of the ODE, defined in this way, produces the values of its analytical solution in the grid points independently of the spatial discretization. Accordingly, a general modeling procedure has been developed, which is capable of implementing a conventional CEM approach; however, it can be efficiently applied to modeling electrodes with continuous functions.

The longitudinal change in the electrode conductivity is dominant in the frequency range where the electrode impedance is comparable with the impedance of the tested material. This justifies the use of continuous functions to model the electrodes used for measurements in terms of space and frequency. The accuracy of the electrode modeling affects the potential values obtained since, in both case studies, the same material is modeled; however, the resulting potentials are different (obviously due to differences in the electrode models). Consequently, when the purpose of the measurement is to reconstruct the impedance profile of the material, two different reconstructed impedance profiles may be obtained for the same material, which is a significant discrepancy. This emphasizes the need for correct and accurate consideration of the electrode artifacts, which minimizes the detailed error effects.

6. Future Works

Consequently, the intention is to apply the results presented in this study to the modeling of EI measurement solutions that have been developed, and to identify several directions for further development.

The first, and perhaps the most important, task is to transfer the findings presented in this paper into practical applications, whether in in vitro or human EI measurements, tomography, or spectroscopy, for each developed prototype. Additionally, the modeling of electrode anomalies is also a major research topic, where the aim is to investigate how these phenomena can be represented as continuous functions and how they can be incorporated into the presented method. Moreover, the aim is to generalize the obtained results to two- and/or three-dimensional cases, in order to extend the relevance of the method to the whole range of EI measurements. Further, research on exact schemes for solving model equations used to describe non-stationary cases for electric field modeling and charge distribution during electrode–material interaction will play a prominent role in future work.

Author Contributions: Z.V. drafted the manuscript and conceived and performed the experiments. M.K., N.G. and Z.S. checked the test results and suggested the corrections. P.O., V.T. and A.T. supervised the research and contributed to the organization of article. All authors have read and agreed to the published version of the manuscript.

Funding: This research is a part of projects GINOP PLUSZ-2.1.1-21-2022-00249 of the University of Obuda and 2020-1.1.2-PIACI-KFI-2020-00173 of the University of Dunaujavaros, co-financed by the Hungarian State. The project has also been supported by grants 009-2023-PTE-RK/27 and 011-2023-PTE-RK/4 of the University of Pécs.

Institutional Review Board Statement: Not applicable.

Informed Consent Statement: Not applicable.

Data Availability Statement: Data are contained within the article.

Conflicts of Interest: The authors declare no conflicts of interest.

References

1. Stupin, D.D.; Kuzina, E.A.; Abelit, A.A.; Emelyanov, A.K.; Nikolaev, D.M.; Ryazantsev, M.N.; Koniakhin, S.V.; Dubina, M.V. Bioimpedance Spectroscopy: Basics and Applications. *ACS Biomater. Sci. Eng.* **2021**, *7*, 1962–1986. [CrossRef] [PubMed]
2. Showkat, I.; Khanday, F.A.; Beigh, M.R. A review of bio-impedance devices. *Med. Biol. Eng. Comput.* **2023**, *61*, 927–950. [CrossRef] [PubMed]
3. Holder, D. *Electrical Impedance Tomography: Methods, History, and Applications*; Institute of Physics Pub: Bristol, PA, USA, 2005; ISBN 9780750309523.
4. Adler, A.; Holder, D. *Electrical Impedance Tomography: Methods, History and Applications*, 2nd ed.; CRC Press: Boca Raton, FL, USA, 2021.
5. Sari, Z.; Klincsik, M.; Odry, P.; Tadic, V.; Toth, A.; Vizvari, Z. Lumped Element Method Based Conductivity Reconstruction Algorithm for Localization Using Symmetric Discrete Operators on Coarse Meshes. *Symmetry* **2023**, *15*, 1008. [CrossRef]
6. Ma, J.; Guo, J.; Li, Y.; Wang, Z.; Dong, Y.; Ma, J.; Zhu, Y.; Wu, G.; Yi, L.; Shi, X. Exploratory study of a multifrequency EIT-based method for detecting intracranial abnormalities. *Front. Neurol.* **2023**, *14*, 1210991. [CrossRef] [PubMed]
7. Naranjo-Hernández, D.; Reina-Tosina, J.; Min, M. Fundamentals, recent advances, and future challenges in bioimpedance devices for healthcare applications. *J. Sens.* **2019**, *2019*, 9210258. [CrossRef]

8. Vizvari, Z.; Gyorfi, N.; Odry, A.; Sari, Z.; Klincsik, M.; Gergics, M.; Kovacs, L.; Kovacs, A.; Pal, J.; Karadi, Z.; et al. Physical Validation of a Residual Impedance Rejection Method during Ultra-Low Frequency Bio-Impedance Spectral Measurements. *Sensors* **2020**, *20*, 4686. [CrossRef]
9. Yorkey, T.J.; Webster, J.G.; Tompkins, W.J. Errors caused by contact impedance in impedance imaging. *Proc. IEEE/Seventh Ann. Conf. Eng. Med. Biol. Soc.* **1985**, *32*, 632–637.
10. Cassar, M.G.; Sebu, C.; Pidcock, M.; Chandak, S.; Andrews, B. Optimal design of electrodes for functional electrical stimulation applications to single layer isotropic tissues. *COMPEL Int. J. Comput. Math. Electr. Electron. Eng.* **2023**, *42*, 695–707. [CrossRef]
11. Cheng, K.S.; Isaacson, D.; Newell, J.C.; Gisser, D.G. Electrode models for electric current computed tomography. *IEEE Trans Biomed Eng.* **1989**, *36*, 918–924. [CrossRef]
12. Tyni, T.; Stinchcombe, A.R.; Alexakis, S. A boundary integral equation method for the complete electrode model in electrical impedance tomography with tests on real-world data. *arXiv* **2023**, arXiv:2305.17294.
13. Darde, J.; Nasr, N.; Weynans, L. Immersed boundary method for the complete electrode model in electrical impedance tomography. *J. Comput. Phys.* **2023**, *487*, 112150. [CrossRef]
14. Park, J.; Jung, B.G.; Kang, J.W. Nonlinear Electrical Impedance Tomography Method Using a Complete Electrode Model for the Characterization of Heterogeneous Domains. *CMES* **2023**, *134*, 1707–1735. [CrossRef]
15. Boverman, G.; Isaacson, D.; Newell, J.C.; Saulnier, G.J.; Kao, T.J.; Amm, B.C.; Wang, X.; Davenport, D.M.; Chong, D.H.; Sahni, R.; et al. Efficient Simultaneous Reconstruction of Time-Varying Images and Electrode Contact Impedances in Electrical Impedance Tomography. *IEEE Trans. Biomed. Eng.* **2017**, *64*, 795–806. [CrossRef] [PubMed]
16. Lazanas, A.C.; Prodromidis, M.I. Electrochemical Impedance Spectroscopy—A Tutorial. *ACS Meas. Sci.* **2023**, *3*, 162–193. [CrossRef]
17. Acar, G.; Ozturk, O.; Golparvar, A.J.; Elboshra, T.A.; Böhringer, K.; Yapici, M.K. Wearable and Flexible Textile Electrodes for Biopotential Signal Monitoring: A review. *Electronics* **2019**, *8*, 479. [CrossRef]
18. McEwan, A.; Cusick, G.; Holder, D.S. A review of errors in multi-frequency EIT instrumentation. *Physiol. Meas.* **2007**, *28*, S197. [CrossRef]
19. Buendia, R.; Seoane, F.; Bosaeus, I.; Gil-Pita, R.; Johannsson, G.; Ellegard, L.; Lindecrantz, K. Robustness study of the different immittance spectra and frequency ranges in bioimpedance spectroscopy analysis for assessment of total body composition. *Physiol. Meas.* **2014**, *35*, 1373. [CrossRef]
20. Hwang, J.H.; Kirkpatrick, K.S.; Mason, T.O.; Garboczi, E.J. Experimental limitations in impedance spectroscopy: Part IV. Electrode contact effects. *Solid State Ionics* **1997**, *98*, 93–104. [CrossRef]
21. Fleig, J.; Maier, J. The impedance of imperfect electrode contacts on solid electrolytes. *Solid State Ionics* **1996**, *85*, 17–24. [CrossRef]
22. Buendia, R.; Bogonez-Franco, P.; Nescolarde, L.; Seoane, F. Influence of electrode mismatch on Cole parameter estimation from Total Right Side Electrical Bioimpedance Spectroscopy measurements. *Med. Eng. Phys.* **2012**, *34*, 1024–1028. [CrossRef]
23. Montalibet, A.; McAdams, E. A Practical Method to Reduce Electrode Mismatch Artefacts during 4-electrode BioImpedance Spectroscopy Measurements. In Proceedings of the 2018 40th Annual International Conference of the IEEE Engineering in Medicine and Biology Society (EMBC), Honolulu, HI, USA, 18–21 July 2018; pp. 5775–5779.
24. Ayllon, D.; Gil-Pita, R.; Seoane, F. Detection and Classification of Measurement Errors in Bioimpedance Spectroscopy. *PLoS ONE* **2016**, *11*, e0156522. [CrossRef]
25. Vizvari, Z.; Klincsik, M.; Odry, P.; Tadic, V.; Sari, Z. General Exact Schemes for Second-Order Linear Differential Equations Using the Concept of Local Green Functions. *Axioms* **2023**, *12*, 633. [CrossRef]
26. Tarasov, A.; Titov, K. On the use of the Cole–Cole equations in spectral induced polarization. *Geophys. J. Int.* **2013**, *195*, 352–356. [CrossRef]
27. Li, J.; Ke, S.; Yin, C.; Kang, Z.; Jia, J.; Ma, X. A laboratory study of complex resistivity spectra for predictions of reservoir properties in clear sands and shaly sands. *J. Pet. Sci. Eng.* **2019**, *177*, 983–994. [CrossRef]
28. Dodde, R.E.; Kruger, G.H.; Shih, A.J. Design of Bioimpedance Spectroscopy Instrument With Compensation Techniques for Soft Tissue Characterization. *J. Med. Device* **2015**, *9*, 210011–210018. [CrossRef]
29. Cole, K.S.; Cole, R.H. Dispersion and absorption in dielectrics, I. Alternating current characteristics. *J. Chem. Phys.* **1941**, *9*, 341–351. [CrossRef]
30. Gyorfi, N.; Gal, A.R.; Fincsur, A.; Kalmar-Nagy, K.; Mintal, K.; Hormay, E.; Miseta, A.; Tornoczky, T.; Nemeth, A.K.; Bogner, P.; et al. Novel Noninvasive Paraclinical Study Method for Investigation of Liver Diseases. *Biomedicines* **2023**, *11*, 2449. [CrossRef]
31. Meani, F.; Barbalace, G.; Meroni, D.; Pagani, O.; Perriard, U.; Pagnamenta, A.; Aliverti, A.; Meroni, E. Electrical Impedance Spectroscopy for Ex-Vivo Breast Cancer Tissues Analysis. *Ann. Biomed. Eng.* **2023**, *51*, 1535–1546. [CrossRef]
32. Szebenyi, K.; Furedi, A.; Bajtai, E.; Sama, S.N.; Csiszar, A.; Gombos, B.; Szabo, P.; Grusch, M.; Szakacs, G. Effective targeting of breast cancer by the inhibition of P-glycoprotein mediated removal of toxic lipid peroxidation byproducts from drug tolerant persister cells. *Drug Resist. Updat.* **2023**, *71*, 101007. [CrossRef]
33. Gheorghiu, M. A short review on cell-based biosensing: challenges and breakthroughs in biomedical analysis. *J. Biomed. Res.* **2020**, *35*, 255–263. [CrossRef]
34. Wang, H.; Shi, X.; Cao, X.; Dong, X.; Yang, L. Discrimination between human normal renal tissue and renal cell carcinoma by dielectric properties using in-vitro BIA. *Front. Physiol.* **2023**, *14*, 1121599. [CrossRef] [PubMed]

Disclaimer/Publisher's Note: The statements, opinions and data contained in all publications are solely those of the individual author(s) and contributor(s) and not of MDPI and/or the editor(s). MDPI and/or the editor(s) disclaim responsibility for any injury to people or property resulting from any ideas, methods, instructions or products referred to in the content.

Article

A Method for Visualization of Images by Photon-Counting Imaging Only Object Locations under Photon-Starved Conditions

Jin-Ung Ha [1], Hyun-Woo Kim [1], Myungjin Cho [2,*,†] and Min-Chul Lee [1,*,†]

[1] Department of Computer Science and Networks, Kyushu Institute of Technology, 680-4 Kawazu, Iizuka-shi 820-8502, Fukuoka, Japan; ha.jinung663@mail.kyutech.jp (J.-U.H.); kim@ois3d.cse.kyutech.ac.jp (H.-W.K.)
[2] School of ICT, Robotics, and Mechanical Engineering, Hankyong National University, IITC, 327 Chungang-ro, Anseong 17579, Kyonggi-do, Republic of Korea
* Correspondence: mjcho@hknu.ac.kr (M.C.); lee@csn.kyutech.ac.jp (M.-C.L.)
† These authors contributed equally to this work.

Abstract: Recently, many researchers have been studying the visualization of images and the recognition of objects by estimating photons under photon-starved conditions. Conventional photon-counting imaging techniques estimate photons by way of a statistical method using Poisson distribution in all image areas. However, Poisson distribution is temporally and spatially independent, and the reconstructed image has a random noise in the background. Random noise in the background may degrade the quality of the image and make it difficult to accurately recognize objects. Therefore, in this paper, we apply photon-counting imaging technology only to the area where the object is located to eliminate the noise in the background. As a result, it can be seen that the image quality using the proposed method is better than that of the conventional method and the object recognition rate is also higher. Optical experiments were conducted to prove the denoising performance of the proposed method. In addition, we used the structure similarity index measure (SSIM) as a performance metric. To check the recognition rate of the object, we applied the YOLOv5 model. Finally, the proposed method is expected to accelerate the development of astrophotography and medical imaging technologies.

Keywords: photon-counting imaging; digital image processing; computational imaging; object recognition

1. Introduction

Recently, research on estimating and visualizing photons under photon-starved conditions has been conducted in various fields such as aerospace optics, medical optics, etc. Furthermore, there is a new field of research using photon-counting detectors (PCDs), which detect photon energy to visualize images [1–19]. The Hubble Space Telescope (HST), launched from Earth in 1990, is a space telescope developed by the National Aeronautics and Space Administration (NASA) and the European Space Agency (ESA) that is used for observational astronomy from space [2]. The HST is equipped with a variety of cameras, spectrographs, and optical instruments, including a spectrograph optimized for ultraviolet observation, which uses PCDs with photon-counting technology that perform better than a CCD (Charge-Coupled Device) at estimating and visualizing ultraviolet photons even under photon-starved conditions such as in space [2–5]. As a result, the HST has enabled the observation of the expanding universe as well as the Hubble constant measurement project, which has provided us with a deeper understanding of the universe and its structure [6,7].

Hounsfield was awarded the 1979 Nobel Prize in Physiology or Medicine for developing and first introducing the medical imaging technology computed tomography (CT) into

medicine [8,9]. X-ray CT is a medical imaging technique that non-destructively reconstructs three-dimensional (3D) images of human internal structures. More recently, advances in X-ray CT imaging technology have led to the development of photon-counting computed tomography (PCCT), which uses PCDs to estimate individual incoming X-ray photons and measure their energy levels [10–12]. PCDs can significantly reduce image noise and increase spatial resolution, and k-edge imaging can be used to measure the concentration of specific elements for material discrimination. Moreover, these technological advances will reduce radiation dose by at least 30–40% compared to traditional X-ray CT imaging techniques [10]. Techniques, such as using PCDs to estimate individual incoming X-ray photons and measure their energy levels, have been developed by many researchers in recent years [2–14]. However, PCDs may have some imperfections. First, charge sharing occurs when an X-ray photon arrives near the boundary between two pixels. This causes the X-ray photon to be detected both times at the wrong energy, reducing spatial resolution. Second, two independent photons may arrive at the same pixel at very high speeds, causing the signal to "pile up" and be interpreted by the electronic processing unit as a single photon. Finally, PCDs can be susceptible to electron noise, similar to CCDs, and suffer from the problem that measurements become uncertain when low-energy photons are detected [15]. Many researchers have studied these problems [20], and research is ongoing to accurately estimate photons to visualize images.

In general, photon-counting imaging techniques use a specialized sensor such as an EM-CCD camera, rather than a general camera, to acquire images. However, these specialized sensors require high prices and are difficult to commercialize. To overcome this problem, in this paper, we use a computational algorithm with a general camera to implement a photon-counting imaging technique [18,21–26]. Photon-counting imaging techniques, which estimate photons in a statistical way, may be an alternative to the conventional PCD problem. The computational photon-counting imaging method is an image processing technique that solves the hardware problems of photon-counting imaging by using software methods similar to the physical photon-counting imaging method. Photon-counting imaging techniques can visualize images by estimating photons that rarely occur in a unit of time and space based on Poisson distribution [16–19,21–26]. However, it also has a problem of random noise, and photons can be detected from objects as well as from the background, which degrade the visual quality of the image. Several studies have applied filters to remove the random noise in this background, most notably the median filter or the Kalman filter [21,22]. Using these filters can reduce the quality of the image because they remove not only background noise, but also information about the object. To solve these problems, in this paper, we propose a novel photon-counting imaging method to classify object location and the number of photons by section (COLaNoPS). Since the conventional photon-counting imaging technique applies a Poisson random process to all of the image, we can recognize the random noise from both the object and the background. Therefore, we need to remove noise from the background by applying Poisson distribution only to the area where the object exists. To estimate the location of an object, we assume that the photon energy at the location of the object is higher than that of the background. A threshold for the presence of an object is defined by measuring the photon energy as a section of a certain size moves throughout it. This algorithm reduces noise in the background by applying Poisson distribution only to the area in which the object is present, based on the threshold. As the section moves throughout the image, it applies spatial overlap to the area where the photons overlap each other to improve the photon energy of the object. As a result, we can estimate the photon energy of the object, improving the visual quality of the image.

This paper is organized as follows. In Section 2, we describe conventional photon-counting imaging techniques and the proposed method that estimates the photon energy of the object to reduce background noise. Then, we perform the optical experiment and show the results in Section 3. Finally, in Section 4, we present our conclusions and future works.

2. Reducing Background Noise by Estimating Photons Only in the Object Area

2.1. Photon-Counting Imaging

The human eye can see objects by converting the properties of light reflected from them into electrical signals through the rod and cone cells of the retinal cells. The image sensor (CCD or complementary metal-oxide semiconductor (CMOS) sensor) in the camera is a device similar to the human eye, which uses the photoelectric effect to detect the nature of reflected light and can visualize objects. Therefore, the image sensor in the camera suffers from the inability to visualize objects under photon-starved conditions. To solve this problem, photon-counting imaging techniques [16–19,21–23] can be one of the alternatives to visualizing images under photon-starved conditions. Photon-counting imaging technology estimates photons for an object by applying a statistical process of Poisson distribution to each image pixel under photon-starved conditions. Furthermore, the accuracy of the estimated photons can be improved by applying the maximum likelihood estimation (MLE) and a Bayesian approach such as the maximum a posteriori (MAP). MLE and MAP are the main methods for solving the classification problems using probability. MLE is the method of selecting the class with the maximum likelihood, and MAP is the method of selecting the class with the maximum posterior probability [16,19]. We apply a Poisson distribution to probabilistically estimate the photons of an object under photon-starved conditions. We apply MLE and MAP to the estimated photons for solving the classification problem of determining whether a photon occurs or not. Since photons rarely occur in unit time and space under photon-starved conditions, we can assume that they follow a Poisson distribution, and the Poisson distribution is defined by the following equations:

$$\lambda_E(x,y) = \frac{I_E(x,y)}{\sum_{x=1}^{N_x} \sum_{y=1}^{N_y} I_E(x,y)} \tag{1}$$

$$C_E(x,y) \mid N_p \lambda_E(x,y) \sim \text{Poisson}\left[N_p \lambda_E(x,y)\right], \tag{2}$$

where $\lambda_E(x,y)$ is the normalized intensity of the image at position (x,y) of each elemental image in the array, I_E is the intensity of the elemental image, N_x and N_y are the total number of image pixels, and x and y are the pixel positions of each elemental image, respectively. In addition, C_E is the estimated photons in the elemental image, and N_p is the expected number of photons for each elemental image. The likelihood function and log-likelihood function of the λ_E normalized elemental images are defined as follows [16–19,21–23]:

$$P(C_{kl}|N_p\lambda_{kl}) = \prod_{k=0}^{k-1}\prod_{l=0}^{L-1} \frac{e^{-N_p\lambda_{kl}}(N_p\lambda_{kl})^{C_{kl}}}{C_{kl}!}, \tag{3}$$

$$L(N_p\lambda_{kl}|C_{kl}) \propto \sum_{k=0}^{K-1}\sum_{l=0}^{L-1}\left\{C_{kl}\log[N_p\lambda_{kl}]\right\} - \sum_{k=0}^{K-1}\sum_{l=0}^{L-1} N_p\lambda_{kl}, \tag{4}$$

where λ_{kl} is assumed to be a matrix of k rows and l columns all extracted independently from the elemental images. $P(C_{kl}|N_p\lambda_{kl})$ is the likelihood function, $L(N_p\lambda_{kl}|C_{kl})$ is the log-likelihood function. The MLE for estimating by maximizing the likelihood function is defined as follows:

$$\frac{\partial L(N_p\lambda_{kl}|C_{kl})}{\partial \lambda_{kl}} = \frac{C_{kl}}{\lambda_{kl}} - N_p = 0, \tag{5}$$

$$\therefore \lambda_{kl}^{MLE} = \frac{C_{kl}}{N_p}. \tag{6}$$

In Equations (5) and (6), we can define the MLE for the normalized elemental image λ_{kl} as λ_{kl}^{MLE} by taking a partial derivative of $L(N_p\lambda_{kl}|C_{kl})$ to λ_{kl}. As a result, we can derive the MLE of each elemental image as shown in Figure 1 [16–18].

Figure 1. Computational photon-counting imaging by MLE.

Figure 1 shows the process of the photon-counting imaging by MLE. However, in MLE, the estimation accuracy may be low because it uses uniform distribution as the prior information, which means that the occurrence of photons for each pixel has the same probability. Therefore, more specific prior information is required to obtain better estimation accuracy. A Bayesian approach such as MAP uses the specific statistical distribution as the prior information. In this paper, we assume that the normalized elemental image with the expected number of photons $N_p\lambda_{kl}$ follows a Gamma (Γ) distribution because a general image has a [0 255] pixel range. The MAP method uses the statistical parameters α and β of the image's prior probability distribution, which is defined as a Γ distribution. To estimate λ_{kl}, a posterior distribution is calculated and maximized by multiplying the likelihood function for each elemental image using prior information [19,21–23].

$$\pi(N_p\lambda_{kl}) = \frac{\beta^\alpha}{\Gamma(\alpha)}(N_p\lambda_{kl})^{\alpha-1}e^{-\beta N_p\lambda_{kl}}, \ N_p\lambda_{kl} > 0 \tag{7}$$

$$\mu = \frac{\alpha}{\beta}, \ \sigma^2 = \frac{\alpha}{\beta^2} \rightarrow \alpha^2 = \frac{\mu^2}{\sigma^2}, \ \beta = \frac{\mu}{\sigma^2}, \tag{8}$$

$$\pi(N_p\lambda_{kl}|C_{kl}) \sim Gamma(C_{kl}+\alpha, (1+\beta)), \tag{9}$$

where $\pi(N_p\lambda_{kl})$ is a Γ distribution of the normalized elemental image with the expected number of photons, which is a prior probability distribution and a conjugate prior of Poisson distribution; α and β are the statistical parameters of the Γ distribution and they are both positive; μ, σ^2 are the mean and variance of $N_p\lambda_{kl}$; $\pi(N_p\lambda_{kl}|C_{kl})$ is modeled as a conjugate family of distributions for ease of calculating the *Gamma* distribution, respectively [22,23].

$$\therefore \lambda_{kl}^{MAP} = \frac{C_{kl}+\alpha}{N_p(1+\beta)}, \ C_{kl} > 0. \tag{10}$$

By using Equations (7)–(9), we can calculate the posterior distribution and the estimator of elemental images as written in Equation (10). The original image is reconstructed using the mean of the posterior distribution from each elemental image. That is, λ_{kl}^{MAP} can be defined as the mean of a posterior distribution by MAP [23].

Figure 2 shows the reconstructed images by MLE and MAP under photon-starved conditions. The MAP method can reconstruct the image by estimating the photons more accurately than the MLE method under these conditions with the same number of photons.

Figure 3 shows a noisy image from the background when the image is reconstructed by estimating photons with MAP. To visualize the noise, we increased the brightness by 40% and decreased the contrast by 40%. As shown in Figure 3, the MAP method can estimate photons more accurately than the MLE method to visualize the image under photon-starved conditions. However, since the MAP method applies a Poisson distribution to all areas, random noise occurs in the background. In this case, the noise in the background degrades the image quality of the object and makes it difficult to recognize the object accurately. In the next subsection, we propose a new photon-counting imaging technique to solve these problems.

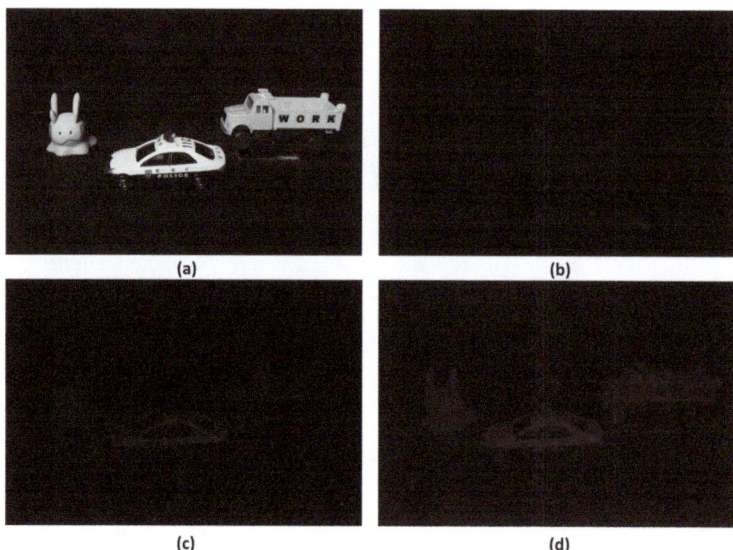

Figure 2. Reconstructed images by photon-counting imaging system under photon-starved conditions. (**a**) Reference image, (**b**) image obtained under photon-starved conditions, (**c**) image reconstructed by MLE, and (**d**) image reconstructed by MAP, where N_p is 400,000.

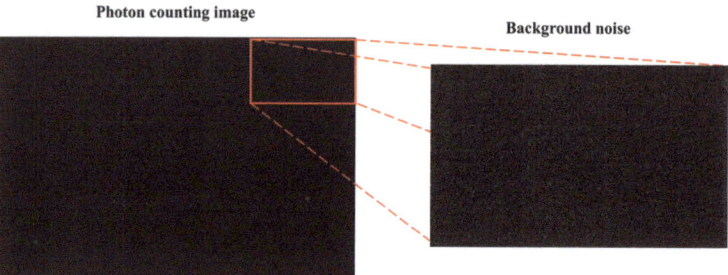

Figure 3. Problem with the background noise of photon-counting imaging.

2.2. Proposed Method

To remove background noise from conventional photon-counting imaging techniques, we propose a novel photon-counting method to classify object location and the number of photons by section (COLaNoPS). The proposed method, COLaNoPS, estimates photons in the section where an object is located by calculating the overall intensity of the section rather than applying Poisson random distribution in all areas, and visualizes it by applying a Poisson distribution only where the object is located to prevent generating noise in the background. Furthermore, spatial overlap is used in areas where photons overlap as the section moves, improving the image quality of objects and the recognition rate of objects. The proposed method assumes that the overall intensity value of the section in the presence of the object is higher than in the absence of the object. The method for estimating the location of an object calculates the overall intensity of the section and the overall intensity of the image as a section of a certain size is moved. By comparing the background pixel intensity to the object pixel intensity, we define the threshold for the presence of the object using the median value. The thresholds for determining the presence of an object are as follows.

$$I_{inten}(x,y) = \sum_{k=0}^{k-1}\sum_{l=0}^{L-1} I_{kl} \text{ and } K_{inten}(x,y) = \sum_{k=0}^{k-1}\sum_{l=0}^{L-1} K_{kl} \qquad (11)$$

$$\gamma_m(x,y) = \text{Med}\left\{\frac{K_{inten}(x,y)}{I_{inten}(x,y)} \times 100\right\} \qquad (12)$$

$$\mu_p = \begin{cases} N_p, & K_{inten}(x,y) > \gamma_m(x,y) \\ 0, & K_{inten}(x,y) \leq \gamma_m(x,y), \end{cases} \qquad (13)$$

where $I_{inten}(x,y)$ is the overall pixel intensity of the original image and $K_{inten}(x,y)$ is the overall pixel intensity of the section. γ_m is the threshold to determine the presence of the object, μ_p is the estimated number of photons in the object based on the threshold, and N_p is the expected number of photons in each elemental image. The presence of an object is determined based on a defined threshold to estimate photons in the object.

$$\hat{\lambda}_{kl}^{MAP} = \frac{\hat{C}_{kl} + \alpha}{\mu_p(1+\beta)}, \; \mu_p \geq 0 \qquad (14)$$

$$\tilde{C}_{kl} \mid \mu_p \hat{\lambda}_{kl}^{MAP} \sim \text{Poisson}\left(\mu_p \hat{\lambda}_{kl}^{MAP}\right). \qquad (15)$$

Using Equations (14) and (15), we can calculate the posterior distribution and estimator of the area in which the object exists. $\hat{\lambda}_{kl}^{MAP}$ is the posterior mean of the photons estimated in the object by the Bayesian approach MAP method, and $\tilde{C}_{kl}$ is the photon estimated from the object of each elemental image. The area in which the object exists is modeled using an estimated posterior mean. As a result, we can define a posterior mean from the MAP method of the photons estimated in the area where the object exists.

$$R(x,y) = \frac{1}{O_{spatial}(x,y)} \sum_{i=0}^{N_x-1}\sum_{j=0}^{N_y-1} \hat{\lambda}_{ij}^{MAP}\{x - S_i, y - S_j\}, \; N_{ij} > S_{ij}, \qquad (16)$$

where R is the elemental image reconstructed by the COLaNoPS method; $O_{spatial}$ is the matrix of spatial overlaps of photons in the object as the section moves; and S_i and S_j is the section's x and y-axis shifting pixel, respectively. Finally, the photon-counting imaging technique is applied only to the areas that are estimated to be objects; where photons overlap, the image can be reconstructed by applying the spatial overlapping.

Figure 4 illustrates a flowchart of the COLaNoPS method. We use the median value to define a threshold for the presence of an object, and we calculate the spatial overlap in the space where photons overlap due to section movement. Finally, we visualize the image by estimating the photons for the object under photon-starved conditions.

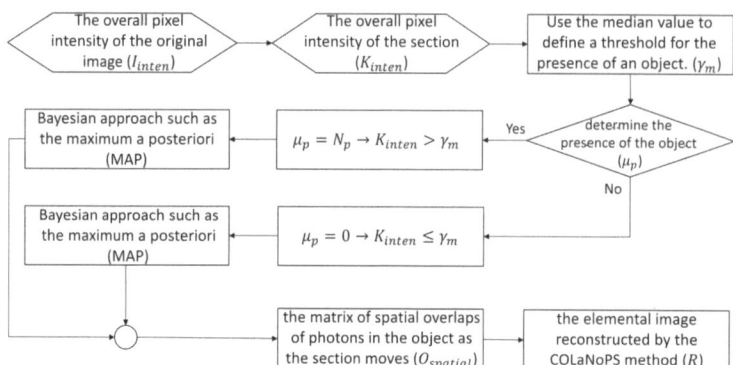

Figure 4. Flow chart of COLaNoPS.

Figure 5 shows the results of the conventional photon-counting imaging technique and the proposed COLaNoPS method under photon-starved conditions, and shows that the COLaNoPS method improves the image quality of objects more than the conventional photon-counting imaging technique.

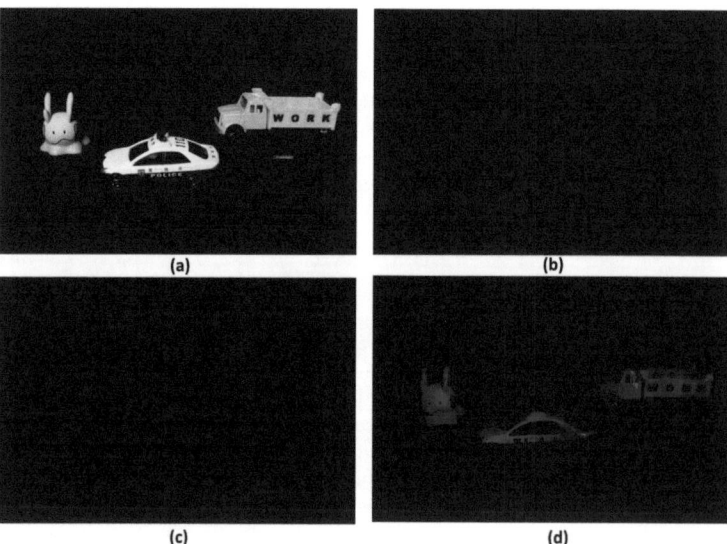

Figure 5. COLaNoPS method results. (**a**) Reference image, (**b**) image obtained under photon-starved conditions, (**c**) conventional photon-counting image with Bayesian approach, and (**d**) reconstructed image by COLaNoPS, where N_p is 400,000.

3. Experimental Setup and Results

3.1. Experimental Setup

In this subsection, we describe the experimental setup to compare the conventional photon-counting imaging technique with the COLaNoPS method. Figure 6a shows the experimental setup in this paper. Figure 6b is the image obtained by the experimental setup. Photon-starved conditions are set by controlling the amount of light in this experiment. In this experiment, we use a Nikon D5300 to take experimental scenes because our proposed method is the computational algorithm with a general camera to implement photon-counting imaging technique as we mentioned earlier in the first section. All three objects are metal objects, and they are located at different distances from the camera. The distances from the camera to the objects are 400 mm, 430 mm, and 460 mm, with a distance difference of 30 mm for each object.

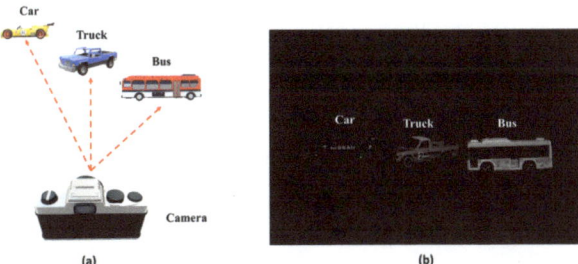

Figure 6. (**a**) Experimental setup and (**b**) the image obtained by the experimental setup.

Table 1 shows the specifications and setup of the camera used in this experiment. The number of photons is gradually increased from 100,000 to 1,100,000 based on images obtained under photon-starved conditions.

Table 1. Camera specifications and setup.

Setup		Nikon D5300
Resolution		2992 × 2000
Sensor size		23.5 mm × 15.7 mm
Section size		400 × 400
Section shifting pixel		50
Focal length		5 mm
ISO		160
Shutter speed	Normal	5 s
	Extremely low-light	180 s

3.2. Results

In this subsection, we show the results of the conventional method and the proposed method. Figure 7a is the image obtained under normal light conditions, and Figure 7b is the image obtained under photon-starved conditions. As shown in Figure 7b, the object cannot be visualized because it is too dark. Figure 7c is the reconstruction result by applying conventional photon-counting imaging techniques to the image in Figure 7b, which is not visible to the human eye. Figure 7d shows the reconstruction result by applying the COLaNoPS technique to the image in Figure 7b. For fair comparison, the number of photons applied to the images in Figure 7c and Figure 7d is 100,000. As a result, the reconstructed result by the conventional photon-counting imaging technique as shown in Figure 7c can visualize the object better than the image in Figure 7b, but it cannot accurately recognize the object due to the insufficient number of estimated photons. In contrast, the reconstruction result obtained using the COLaNoPS method as shown in Figure 7d can visualize the object better than the reconstruction result in Figure 7c, and the object can be visualized more clearly than the conventional photon-counting imaging technology when the same number of photons is estimated.

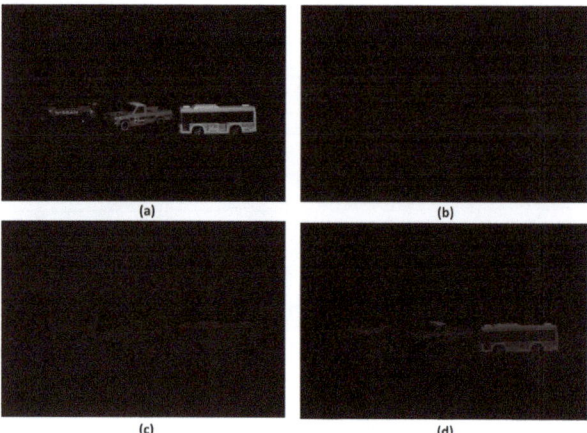

Figure 7. Reconstruction results. (**a**) Reference image, (**b**) image obtained under photon-starved conditions, (**c**) image reconstructed by the conventional photon-counting imaging with Bayesian, and (**d**) image reconstructed by COLaNoPS method, where N_p is 100,000.

Figure 8 shows the background noise generated by the conventional photon-counting imaging method and the proposed method, and shows the improvement in the quality of the objects. In this experiment, we increase the brightness by 40% and decrease the contrast by 40% to visualize the background noise and object noise. Figure 8a is the result of the conventional photon-counting imaging technique. It shows the random noise in the background as the Poisson distribution is applied in all areas. Furthermore, objects cannot be accurately recognized when the number of estimated photons is insufficient. Figure 8b is the result of the COLaNoPS method. It shows that the background noise is also removed by applying the Poisson distribution only to the area where the object exists. Furthermore, by applying spatial overlap to the areas where photons overlap as the section moves, the object can be visualized more clearly and accurately than the result obtained using the conventional photon-counting imaging technique as shown in Figure 8a.

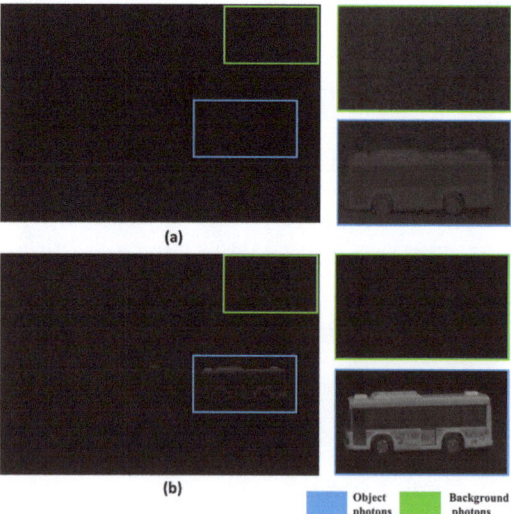

Figure 8. Comparison of the noise of the background and the object. (**a**) Conventional photon-counting image and (**b**) COLaNoPS method image, where N_p is 100,000.

Figure 9 shows the images reconstructed for each object by the conventional photon-counting imaging technique and the COLaNoPS method, where the number of photons is 100,000. Figure 9a,d,g show reference images obtained under normal light conditions. The objects are listed in the order of car, truck, and bus. All of them are identifiable. Figure 9b,e,h show the results of applying the conventional photon-counting imaging technology. The insufficient photon count estimation makes it difficult to identify the object. Figure 9c,f,i is the result of applying the COLaNoPS method. As shown in Figure 9, in the conventional method, the numbers or letters cannot be recognized accurately due to random noise. On the other hand, we can recognize numbers or letters accurately using the proposed method.

Figure 10 shows the result of increasing the number of photons by 1,100,000. Figure 10a,d,g show the reference image obtained under normal light conditions. The objects are listed in the order of car, truck, and bus, and all of them are identifiable. Figure 10b,e,h show the result of applying the conventional photon-counting imaging technology. The objects are listed in the order of car, truck, and bus, and it is difficult to identify them due to the lack of estimated photons, similar to Figure 9. Figure 10c,f,i show the result of applying the COLaNoPS method. The objects are listed in the same order and the objects can be recognized. As shown in the results of Figures 9 and 10, we can see that, as the number of assumed photons increases, the photons for the object are more accurately estimated. As a result, our proposed method can reduce the background noise and visualize the letters or numbers on the surface of the object more accurately than the conventional photon-counting imaging technique.

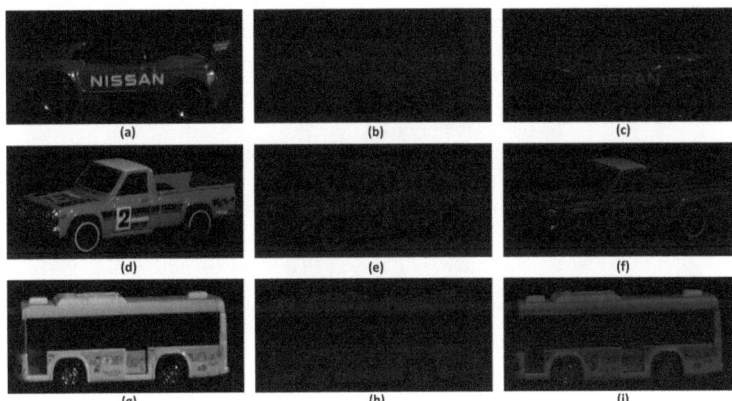

Figure 9. Cropped object images, where objects are car, truck, and bus. (**a,d,g**) are the reference images obtained under normal light conditions; (**b,e,h**) are images obtained using the conventional photon-counting imaging technique; and (**c,f,i**) are images obtained using our proposed method, where N_p is 100,000.

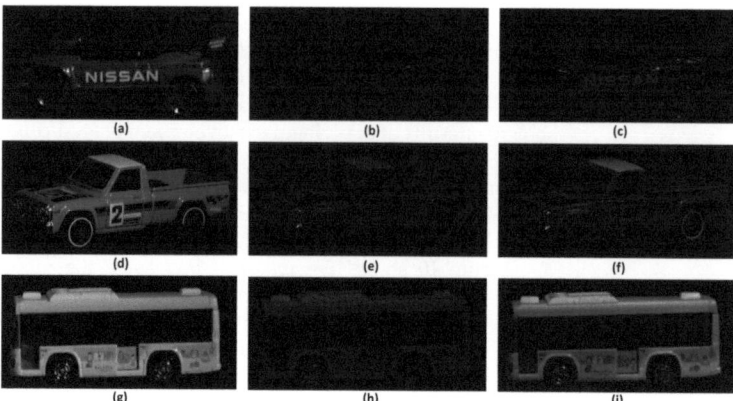

Figure 10. Cropped object images, where objects are car, truck, and bus. (**a**,**d**,**g**) are reference images obtained under normal light conditions; (**b**,**e**,**h**) are images obtained using the conventional photon-counting imaging technique; and (**c**,**f**,**i**) are images obtained using our proposed method, N_p is 1,100,000.

Although it is noticed that the proposed method can reconstruct the image under photon-starved conditions more accurately than the conventional method, the numerical comparison analysis may be required to verify our proposed method. In this paper, we use the structural similarity index measure (SSIM) metric for numerical comparison [27]. In SSIM analysis, we measured the change in SSIM as we incremented the photons from 100,000 to 1,100,000. Figure 11 shows the SSIM results for the conventional photon-counting imaging technique and the COLaNoPS method via various numbers of photons. Figure 11a shows the performance metrics of SSIM on car images. The average SSIM of the proposed method is 0.6917, while that of the conventional method is 0.4987, and there is a difference of about 1.387 times. Figure 11b shows the performance metrics of SSIM on truck images, where the average SSIM of the proposed method is 0.6363 and that of the existing method is 0.4336, and a difference of about 1.467 times. Figure 11c shows the performance metrics of SSIM for bus images, and the average SSIM of the proposed method is 0.6697, while that of the existing method is 0.3801, a difference of about 1.761 times. It can be seen that the SSIM value increases with the position of the object, because the closer the object is, the more photons can be estimated, so the image can be reconstructed clearly. However, photon-counting imaging cannot accurately estimate photons for dark objects, and dark objects are subject to frequent random noise. As a result, dark objects such as cars and trucks have a lower SSIM. As shown in Figure 11, the proposed method in this paper shows better SSIM results than the conventional method.

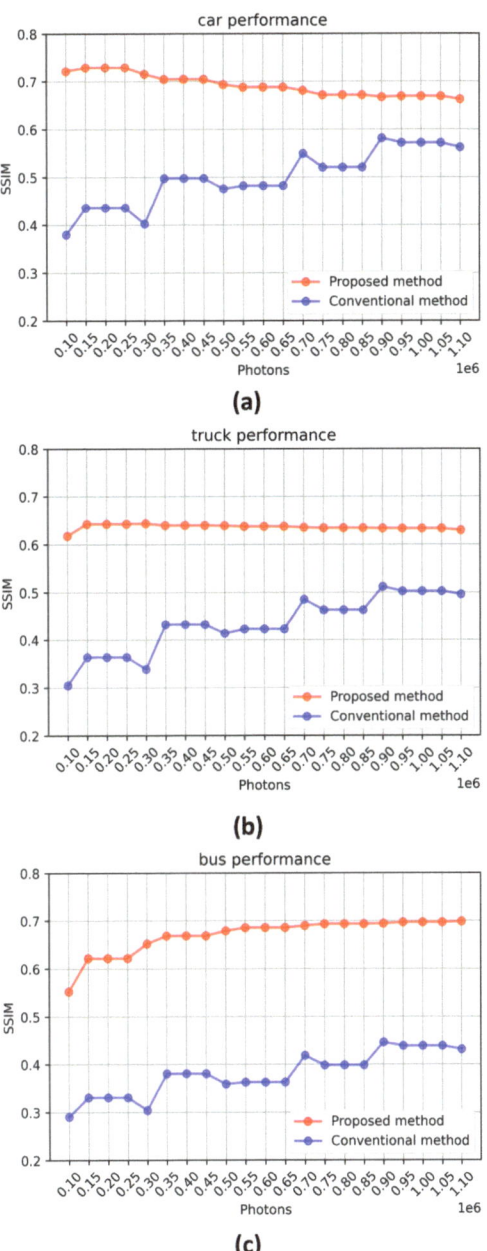

Figure 11. SSIM comparison for (**a**) car, (**b**) truck, and (**c**) bus images.

Figure 12 shows the reconstructed images for each object using the conventional photon-counting imaging technique and the COLaNoPS method with 100,000 photons. Figure 12a,d,g show the reference images obtained under normal lighting conditions and show a magnified image of the numbers or letters on objects. Figure 12 b,e,h show the results of applying the conventional photon-counting imaging technique. It is difficult to identify the numbers or letters on objects due to insufficient photons. Figure 12c,f,i present the results of applying the COLaNoPS technique. As shown in Figure 12, the numbers or letters cannot be recognized accurately with the conventional method due to random noise, while they can be recognized accurately with the proposed method.

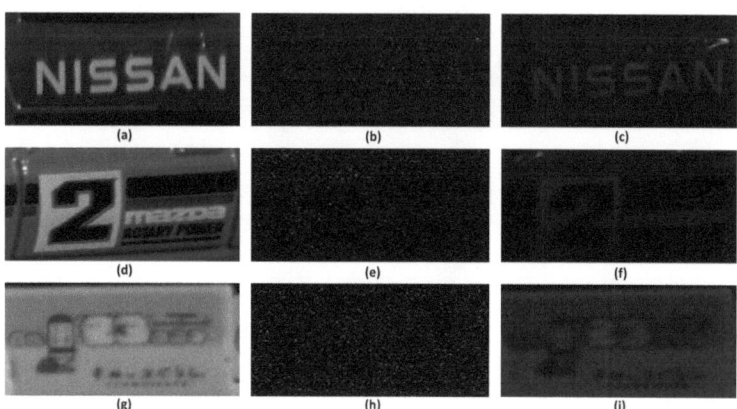

Figure 12. Magnified image of the number or character on the object. (**a,d,g**) are reference images obtained under normal light conditions; (**b,e,h**) are images obtained using the conventional photon-counting imaging technique; and (**c,f,i**) are images obtained using our proposed method, where N_p is 100,000.

Figure 13 uses the peak signal-to-noise ratio (PSNR) [28] metric to compare numbers and letters on objects. In the PSNR analysis, we measured the change in PSNR when the number of photons increased from 100,000 to 1,100,000. Figure 13 shows the PSNR results of the conventional photon-counting imaging technique and the COLaNoPS method for different numbers of photons. Figure 13a shows the performance metric of PSNR for the image of letters on the car. The average PSNR of the proposed method is 15.94 and that of the conventional method is 14.85. Their difference is about 1.073 times. Figure 13b shows the performance metrics of PSNR for numbers or letters on the truck, where the average PSNR of the proposed method is 11.78 and that of the conventional method is 11.31. Their difference is about 1.041 times. Figure 13c shows the performance metrics of PSNR for characters on the bus, where the average PSNR of the proposed method is 11.44 and that of the traditional method is 7.647. Their difference is about 1.497 times. As shown in Figure 13, the proposed method in this paper shows better PSNR results than the traditional method.

Figure 14 shows the object recognition rate by applying the YOLOv5 model [29] to the results of the conventional photon-counting imaging technology and the COLaNoPS method. Figure 14a shows the recognition rate of objects for the image obtained under normal light conditions, where all objects are correctly recognized with a high recognition rate. Figure 14b shows the object recognition rates for images obtained under photon-starved conditions. Only the bus object is correctly recognized, and the truck is incorrectly recognized as a car. Figure 14c shows the recognition rate of objects for the reconstructed image using the conventional photon-counting imaging technology. Only the truck and bus objects are recognized, and it shows that the recognition rate of the two objects is low. Figure 14d shows the recognition rate of objects for the image reconstructed using COLaNoPS technology. It can be seen that all objects, such as car, truck, and bus, are recognized more accurately, and the recognition rate is higher than that of the conventional photon-counting imaging technique.

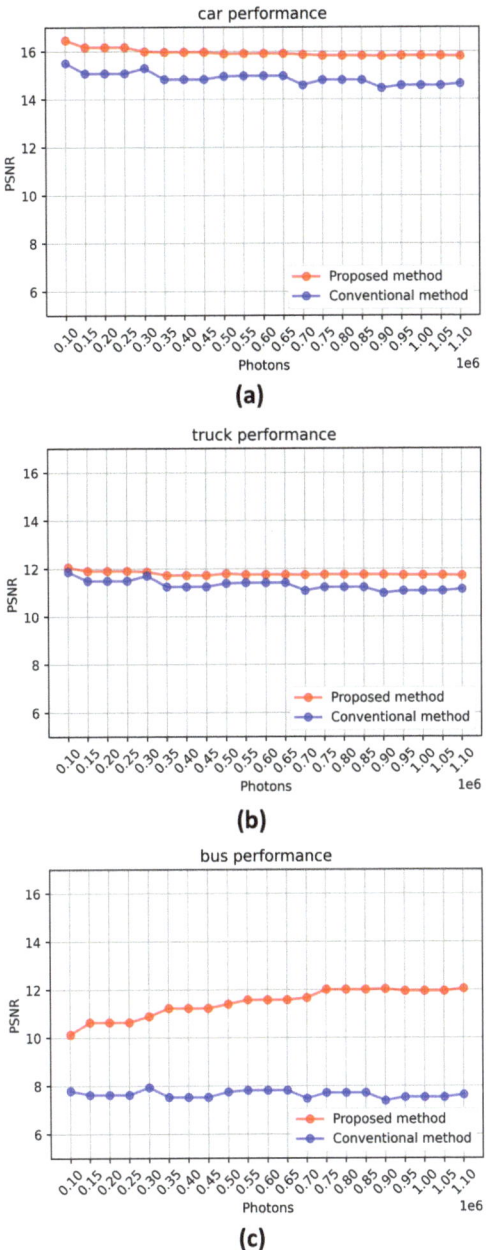

Figure 13. PSNR comparison for (**a**) car, (**b**) truck, and (**c**) bus images.

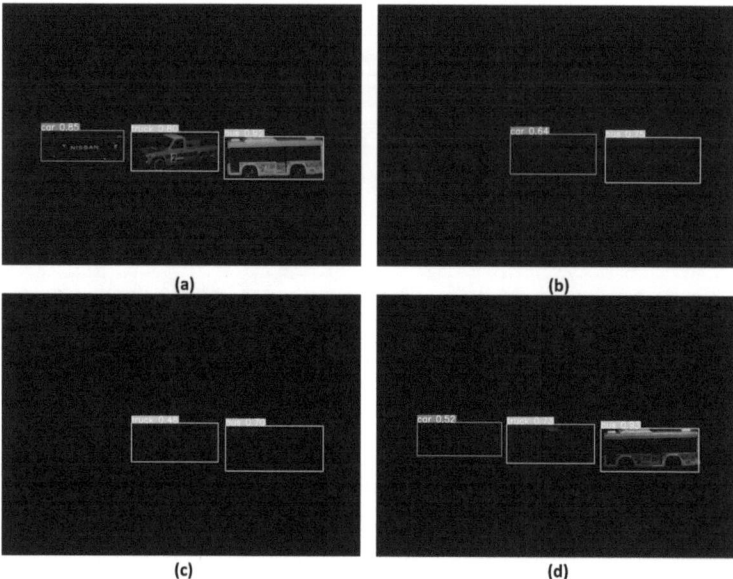

Figure 14. Object recognition result by YOLOv5. (**a**) Reference image, (**b**) image obtained under photon-starved conditions, (**c**) image reconstructed using conventional photon-counting imaging, and (**d**) image reconstructed using the COLaNoPS method, where N_p is 5,984,000.

Finally, the proposed method removes background noise by applying a Poisson distribution only to the areas where objects exist under photon-starved conditions, and improves image quality by applying spatial overlap. As a result, the object can be visualized by estimating only the photons for the object, and the recognition rate of the object can be improved.

4. Conclusions

In this paper, we have proposed the COLaNoPS method to remove random noise from the background by estimating only photons for an object under photon-starved conditions. The proposed method has solved the background noise problem by calculating the total intensity of the background and the total intensity of the object as the section moves to estimate where the object exists, and applying spatial overlap to the areas where photons overlap. In addition, to verify the effect of the proposed method, we have compared the numerical analysis of the proposed method using SSIM performance metrics and the YOLOv5 model. As a result, the proposed method has been able to accurately estimate photons only for an object better than the conventional method, and improves the image quality of the object and can improve the object recognition rate of deep learning techniques.

In this experiment, we have applied the median, mean value, and the average of the maximum and minimum values to define the threshold for determining the presence of an object, and found that the median value can accurately classify the object. Figure 15 shows the difference in SSIM among median, mean, and min-max average. The median and mean values can classify the objects correctly, and we can see that the SSIM for the median value is slightly higher than that for the mean value. The min-max average does not classify correctly, so only the bus is visualized. Furthermore, we can see that the min-max average has the lowest SSIM.

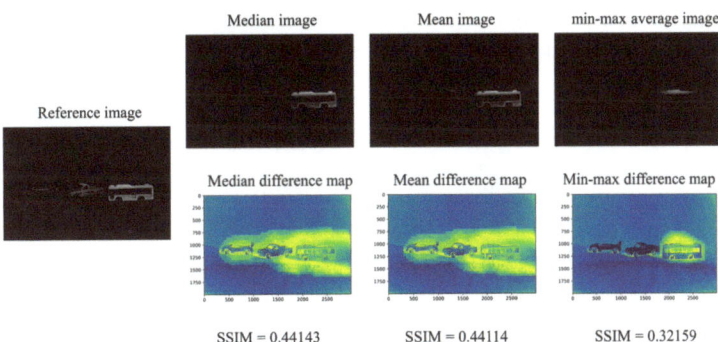

Figure 15. Result of the SSIM for the median, mean, and min-max average.

The proposed method is expected to contribute to the overall development of technologies utilizing photon energy, including astrophotography, medical imaging, photon encryption, autonomous driving, and AR/VR technologies.

The method proposed in this paper is a technology that visualizes 2D images in a situation where the number of photons is insufficient, but it can be visualized as a 3D image, and it is judged that the distance information of the object and the image quality of the object can be improved when reconstructed as a 3D image [30–32].

Author Contributions: Writing—original draft preparation, J.-U.H.; Data curation, H.-W.K.; Conceptualization, J.-U.H. and M.C.; Writing—review and editing, M.C.; Supervision, M.-C.L. All authors have read and agreed to the published version of the manuscript.

Funding: This work was supported under the framework of international cooperation program managed by the National Research Foundation of Korea (NRF-2022K2A9A2A08000152, FY2022) and this work was supported by Kyushu Institute of Technology, On-campus Support Program 2023.

Data Availability Statement: All data underlying the results are available as part of the article and no additional source data are required.

Conflicts of Interest: The authors declare no conflicts of interest.

References

1. Morton, G. Photon counting. *Appl. Opt.* **1968**, *7*, 1–10.
2. Kröger, H.; Schmidt, G.; Pailer, N. Faint object camera: European contribution to the Hubble Space Telescope. *Acta Astronaut.* **1992**, *26*, 827–834.
3. Brandt, J.; Heap, S.; Beaver, E.; Boggess, A.; Carpenter, K.; Ebbets, D.; Hutchings, J.; Jura, M.; Leckrone, D.; Linsky, J.; et al. The Goddard high resolution spectrograph: Instrument, goals, and science results. *Publ. Astron. Soc. Pac.* **1994**, *106*, 890.
4. Adorf, H.M. Hubble space telescope image restoration in its fourth year. *Inverse Probl.* **1995**, *11*, 639.
5. Sirianni, M.; Jee, M.; Benítez, N.; Blakeslee, J.; Martel, A.; Meurer, G.; Clampin, M.; De Marchi, G.; Ford, H.; Gilliland, R.; et al. The photometric performance and calibration of the Hubble Space Telescope Advanced Camera for Surveys. *Publ. Astron. Soc. Pac.* **2005**, *117*, 1049.
6. Freedman, W.L.; Madore, B.F.; Gibson, B.K.; Ferrarese, L.; Kelson, D.D.; Sakai, S.; Mould, J.R.; Kennicutt Jr, R.C.; Ford, H.C.; Graham, J.A.; et al. Final results from the Hubble Space Telescope key project to measure the Hubble constant. *Astrophys. J.* **2001**, *553*, 47.
7. Riess, A.G.; Yuan, W.; Macri, L.M.; Scolnic, D.; Brout, D.; Casertano, S.; Jones, D.O.; Murakami, Y.; Anand, G.S.; Breuval, L.; et al. A comprehensive measurement of the local value of the Hubble constant with 1 km s- 1 Mpc- 1 uncertainty from the Hubble Space Telescope and the SH0ES team. *Astrophys. J. Lett.* **2022**, *934*, L7.
8. Richmond, C. Sir Godfrey Hounsfield. *BMJ Brit. Med. J.* **2004**, *329*, 687.
9. Buzug, T.M. Computed tomography. In *Springer Handbook of Medical Technology*; Springer: Titisee, Germany, 2011; pp. 311–342.
10. Willemink, M.J.; Persson, M.; Pourmorteza, A.; Pelc, N.J.; Fleischmann, D. Photon-counting CT: Technical principles and clinical prospects. *Radiology* **2018**, *289*, 293–312.
11. Flohr, T.; Petersilka, M.; Henning, A.; Ulzheimer, S.; Ferda, J.; Schmidt, B. Photon-counting CT review. *Physica Med.* **2020**, *79*, 126–136.

12. Tortora, M.; Gemini, L.; D'Iglio, I.; Ugga, L.; Spadarella, G.; Cuocolo, R. Spectral photon-counting computed tomography: A review on technical principles and clinical applications. *J. Imaging* **2022**, *8*, 112.
13. Leng, S.; Bruesewitz, M.; Tao, S.; Rajendran, K.; Halaweish, A.F.; Campeau, N.G.; Fletcher, J.G.; McCollough, C.H. Photon-counting detector CT: system design and clinical applications of an emerging technology. *Radiographics* **2019**, *39*, 729–743.
14. Kreisler, B. Photon counting Detectors: Concept, technical Challenges, and clinical outlook. *Eur. J. Radiol.* **2022**, *149*, 110229.
15. Hsieh, S.S.; Leng, S.; Rajendran, K.; Tao, S.; McCollough, C.H. Photon counting CT: Clinical applications and future developments. *IEEE Trans. Radiat. Plasma Med. Sci.* **2020**, *5*, 441–452.
16. Myung, I.J. Tutorial on maximum likelihood estimation. *J. Math. Psychol.* **2003**, *47*, 90–100.
17. Guillaume, M.; Melon, P.; Réfrégier, P.; Llebaria, A. Maximum-likelihood estimation of an astronomical image from a sequence at low photon levels. *J. Opt. Soc. Am. A* **1998**, *15*, 2841–2848.
18. Aloni, D.; Stern, A.; Javidi, B. Three-dimensional photon counting integral imaging reconstruction using penalized maximum likelihood expectation maximization. *Opt. Express* **2011**, *19*, 19681–19687.
19. Bassett, R.; Deride, J. Maximum a posteriori estimators as a limit of Bayes estimators. *Math. Program.* **2019**, *174*, 129–144.
20. Kuin, N.; Rosen, S. The measurement errors in the Swift-UVOT and XMM-OM. *Mon. Not. R. Astron. Soc.* **2008**, *383*, 383–386.
21. Lee, J.; Kurosaki, M.; Cho, M.; Lee, M.C. Noise Reduction for Photon Counting Imaging Using Discrete Wavelet Transform. *J. Inf. Commun. Converg. Eng.* **2021**, *19*, 276–283.
22. Kim, H.W.; Cho, M.; Lee, M.C. Three-Dimensional (3D) Visualization under Extremely Low Light Conditions Using Kalman Filter. *Sensors* **2023**, *23*, 7571.
23. Lee, J.; Cho, M. Enhancement of three-dimensional image visualization under photon-starved conditions. *Appl. Opt.* **2022**, *61*, 6374–6382.
24. Tavakoli, B.; Javidi, B.; Watson, E. Three dimensional visualization by photon counting computational integral imaging. *Optics Express* **2008**, *16*, 4426–4436.
25. Markman, A.; Javidi, B.; Tehranipoor, M. Photon-counting security tagging and verification using optically encoded QR codes. *IEEE Photonics J.* **2013**, *6*, 1–9.
26. Markman, A.; Javidi, B. Full-phase photon-counting double-random-phase encryption. *JOSA A* **2014**, *31*, 394–403.
27. Wang, Z.; Bovik, A.C.; Sheikh, H.R.; Simoncelli, E.P. Image quality assessment: From error visibility to structural similarity. *IEEE Trans. Image Process* **2004**, *13*, 600–612.
28. Gonzalez, R.C.; Woods, R.E. *Digital Image Processing*, 4th ed.; Pearson: New York, NY, USA, 2018.
29. Jiang, P.; Ergu, D.; Liu, F.; Cai, Y.; Ma, B. A Review of Yolo algorithm developments. *Procedia Comput. Sci.* **2022**, *199*, 1066–1073.
30. Lee, J.; Cho, M.; Lee, M.C. 3D Visualization of Objects in Heavy Scattering Media by Using Wavelet Peplography. *IEEE Access* **2022**, *10*, 134052–134060.
31. Hong, S.H.; Jang, J.S.; Javidi, B. Three-dimensional volumetric object reconstruction using computational integral imaging. *Opt. Express* **2004**, *12*, 483–491.
32. Schulein, R.; DaneshPanah, M.; Javidi, B. 3D imaging with axially distributed sensing. *Opt. Lett.* **2009**, *34*, 2012–2014.

Disclaimer/Publisher's Note: The statements, opinions and data contained in all publications are solely those of the individual author(s) and contributor(s) and not of MDPI and/or the editor(s). MDPI and/or the editor(s) disclaim responsibility for any injury to people or property resulting from any ideas, methods, instructions or products referred to in the content.

Article

Application of an Output Filtering Method for an Unstable Wheel-Driven Pendulum System Parameter Identification

Chao-Chung Peng *, Nai-Jen Cheng and Min-Che Tsai

Department of Aeronautics and Astronautics, National Cheng Kung University, Tainan 701, Taiwan; p46114298@gs.ncku.edu.tw (N.-J.C.); p48104029@gs.ncku.edu.tw (M.-C.T.)
* Correspondence: ccpeng@mail.ncku.edu.tw; Tel.: +886-6-2757575 (ext. 63633)

Abstract: This research aims to apply an output filtering method to conduct the system parameter identification of an unstable wheel-driven pendulum system. First, the nonlinear dynamic model of the system is established by utilizing the Lagrangian dynamic theorem. Next, the Least-Square (LS) is introduced for system parameter identification formulation. Nevertheless, considering the real scenario, the wheel displacement is acquired from encoders subject to quantization errors. The pitch angle of the pendulum cart is also accompanied by Gaussian noise. Therefore, using numerical differentiation for angular acceleration in the LS estimations directly would induce incorrect state information seriously. To address this practical issue, an output filtering method is considered. The developed parameter identification algorithm could attenuate the influence of the quantization effect as well as noisy data and thus obtain much more accurate parameter identification results. Comparative simulation reveals that the output filtering method has a superior parameter estimation performance than the direct numerical difference method.

Keywords: pendulum; parameter identification; least square; noise filtering; quantization error

Citation: Peng, C.-C.; Cheng, N.-J.; Tsai, M.-C. Application of an Output Filtering Method for an Unstable Wheel-Driven Pendulum System Parameter Identification. *Electronics* 2023, 12, 4569. https://doi.org/10.3390/electronics12224569

Academic Editors: Vladimir László Tadić and Peter Odry

Received: 25 September 2023
Revised: 2 November 2023
Accepted: 5 November 2023
Published: 8 November 2023

Copyright: © 2023 by the authors. Licensee MDPI, Basel, Switzerland. This article is an open access article distributed under the terms and conditions of the Creative Commons Attribution (CC BY) license (https://creativecommons.org/licenses/by/4.0/).

1. Introduction

System parameter identification (SPI) uses the input and output histories to establish to describe its dynamic behavior [1–4]. Several data-driven identification methods for a nonlinear mechanical system can be found in [5,6]. The reason why SPI is important is that system parameters coupling with states would have a great effect on the system's dynamic response. Namely, those parameters represent the system's features. If those parameters can be identified accurately, it is without a doubt that the procedure of designing a control law will become more time-saving, efficient, and robust.

Nevertheless, without an accurate dynamic model, all attempts at parameter identification and rule-based controller designs are inefficient or even futile. Thus, establishing an accurate system model becomes the primary step. In the past decade, significant progress has been made in the research on self-stabilizing two-wheeled robots. Various models and controllers have been employed to interpret and control the dynamics of two-wheeled robots. Further research on the dynamic modeling of two-wheeled robots is also reviewed in [7]. There are several ways to derive the wheel-driven pendulum's dynamics equation, such as the Newton methods [8] and the Lagrangian dynamic theorem [9]. Among different approaches, this paper adopts the Lagrangian dynamic theorem owing to its systematic formulation procedures. Moreover, due to the unstable nature of an inverted pendulum, a simple PID controller must be applied firstly to stabilize the system's attitude when conducting the SPI processes.

Secondly, based on the derived model, it can be found that the SPI can be formulated as a standard LS solution. The LS method is widely applied in parameter identifications [10,11]. According to the LS, an over-determined normal equation $\mathbf{Y}(t) = \mathbf{\Phi}(t)\mathbf{X}$ is formulated, where the output vector $\mathbf{Y}(t)$ and the observation matrix $\mathbf{\Phi}(t)$ are the key measurements to determine the parameter vector **X** accurately. To fulfill the observation matrix $\mathbf{\Phi}(t)$, some states need to be estimated through numerical differentiation [12,13]. Nonetheless, from the practical realization point of view, the wheel angle data measured from encoders are subjected to quantization effect. Meanwhile, the measured pitch angle and angular velocity from an orientation sensor, such as the inertial measurement unit (IMU), would accompanied by inevitable Gaussian noise. As pointed out in [14], the measurement noise will be amplified if $\mathbf{Y}(t)$ and $\mathbf{\Phi}(t)$ contain serious noise, which further gives rise to a negative influence on parameter identification.

To address the potential issue discussed above, the filter regression model is applied to the identification methodology for robot manipulators and industrial robots, eliminating the need for either the measurement or off-line calculation of the linear and angular accelerations [15–19]. Inspired by the works [20,21], an output filtering method is considered to tackle this problem and is applied to the unstable wheel-driven pendulum system. The advantage of the presented method is that the observation matrix of the filtering method does not contain the raw noise corrupted measurements, the filtered ones are adopted instead. Moreover, there is no need to involve the acceleration information, which is not directly available from sensors. Refer to the associated studies [22,23]; they present an energy-based regression model that only involves position and velocity. This approach avoids using numerical differentiation for acceleration estimations and applies integration on the joint/motor velocities. However, there is no extra degree of freedom to adjust the pure integration, which can be taken as a special case of a low-pass filter. Therefore, the command trajectories should be properly designed. Recent research [24] has emphasized the significance of coarse encoder quantization errors in angular measurements, which introduce noise affecting the estimation of velocity and acceleration. Consequently, the article addresses this issue by applying the filter-based method. Notably, in comparison to the differentiation-based method found in the existing literature, the filter-based primary feature is its avoidance of direct differentiation for velocity information acquisition. Moreover, the filter-based approach offers a more efficient approach to mitigate the influence of quantization noise. Experimental results presented in [24] affirm that filter-based SPI surpasses differentiation-based SPI in terms of parameter estimation accuracy. However, a simple stable motor system was presented [24]. To exploration the potential capability of the filter-based method, this work applied it to highly nonlinear unstable wheel-driven pendulum system.

Note that the selection of a filtering operator is highly important. A great integral operator should preserve the system's dominant frequencies and filter out the unwanted noises. Otherwise, the integral operator might distort the dominant frequencies or could not remove the redundant noises. In summary, the importance of SPI mainly includes two parts: first, SPI allows control engineers to develop a robust control law more easily; second, dynamics modeling together with SPI can be used as a digital twin to monitor the system behavior online [25].

The main contributions of the paper are summarized as follows: (1) extending the filter-based SPI to a nonlinear unstable wheel-driven pendulum system; (2) presenting an output filtering method which can suppress the Gaussian noise and quantization noise effects; (3) conducting a performance comparison study between the proposed output filtering method and the direct numerical differentiation method; and (4) demonstrating the use of aggressive command input citation can enhance the precision of the parameter estimations.

2. System Description

The description of the wheel-driven pendulum dynamics model can be found in [26]. Figure 1 shows the position of the system, where θ_w and θ_p are the wheel's rotational angle, and the inclined angle of the body, respectively. M represents the mass of the body and m denotes the mass of the wheels. J_w and J_p are the moment of inertia with respect to the wheel's axles of the wheel and the body, respectively. R is the wheel radius. W and L are the distance between two wheels and the distance between the wheel and the center of mass, respectively. The positions of the left and right wheels, and the center of mass are represented by the coordinates (x_i, y_i, z_i), where i corresponds to l, r, or b.

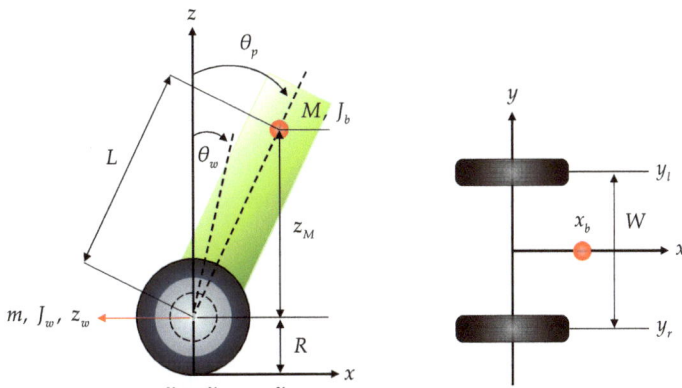

Figure 1. Cartesian coordinate of the wheel-driven cart schematic diagram, where red dot represents the center of mass of the cart.

2.1. Modeling of a Wheel-Driven Pendulum Cart

According to the Lagrangian dynamics, it is composed of the kinetic energy T and the potential energy U, which can be described as $L = T - U$, in which

$$L = mR^2\dot{\theta}_w^2 + \tfrac{1}{2}MR^2\dot{\theta}_w^2 + MR\dot{\theta}_w\dot{\theta}_p L\cos(\theta_p) + \tfrac{1}{2}M\dot{\theta}_p^2 L^2 + J_w\dot{\theta}_w^2 + \tfrac{1}{2}J_b\dot{\theta}_p^2 + \varepsilon^2 J_m\dot{\theta}_w^2 \\ - 2\varepsilon^2 J_m\dot{\theta}_w\dot{\theta}_p + \varepsilon^2 J_m\dot{\theta}_p^2 - MgR - MgL\cos\theta_p \quad (1)$$

Based on the definition of the Lagrangian dynamics, one has

$$\frac{d}{dt}\left(\frac{\partial L}{\partial \dot{\theta}_q}\right) - \frac{\partial L}{\partial \theta_q} = F_q \quad (2)$$

where q denotes the general coordinate, and F_q represents the general force with respect to the general coordinate. Hence, the dynamics equation of a wheel-driven pendulum cart can be written as

$$F_{\theta_w} = \left((2m+M)R^2 + 2J_W + 2\varepsilon^2 J_m\right)\ddot{\theta}_w + \left(MLR\cos(\theta_p) - 2\varepsilon^2 J_m\right)\ddot{\theta}_p - MLR\dot{\theta}_p^2\sin(\theta_p) \quad (3)$$

and

$$F_{\theta_p} = \left(MLR\cos(\theta_p) - 2\varepsilon^2 J_m\right)\ddot{\theta}_w + \left(ML^2 + J_b + 2\varepsilon^2 J_m\right)\ddot{\theta}_p - MgL\sin(\theta_p) \quad (4)$$

where F_{θ_w}, F_{θ_p} denotes the generalized force with respect to the general coordinate $\begin{bmatrix}\theta_w & \theta_p\end{bmatrix}$, respectively.

2.2. Model Description of a Motor

The governing equations of the electrical driving circuit and the motor mechanism can be expressed by

$$L\frac{di}{dt} + iR_m + K_e w = V_{in} \quad (5)$$

and

$$J_m\frac{dw}{dt} = K_t i - B_m w - T_L \quad (6)$$

respectively, in Equation (5), L is the inductance, R_m is the resistance, K_e is the back emf constant, V_{in} is the applied voltage, i is the armature current, and w is the motor's angular velocity which is equivalent to the wheel's angular velocity $\dot{\theta}_w$. Moreover, in (6), J_m is the motor's moment of inertia, K_t is the torque constant, B_m is the viscous coefficient, and T_L represents the external load.

According to the property that electric power is equivalent to mechanical power, it follows that $(K_e w)i = (K_t i)w$. Therefore, one has $K_e = K_t := K$. Since the mechanical dynamics of a wheel-driven pendulum cart are much slower than electrical dynamics, (5) reduces to

$$V_{in} \approx iR_m + Kw \tag{7}$$

Based on (4)–(7), the actuator dynamics can be simplified by

$$J_m \frac{dw}{dt} = \frac{K}{R_m} V_{in} - \left(\frac{K^2}{R_m} + B_m\right) w - T_L \tag{8}$$

The external loads are mainly caused by the friction between the cart's body and wheels, and also between the wheels and the ground. Moreover, the influence of the motor's viscosity can be neglected. Thus, T_L can be modeled by

$$T_L = f_m\left(\dot{\theta}_p - \dot{\theta}_w\right) \tag{9}$$

Substituting (9) into (8) yields

$$J_m \frac{dw}{dt} = F_{\theta_w} \tag{10}$$

in which

$$F_{\theta_w} = \alpha V_{in} - 2(\beta + f_w)\dot{\theta}_w + 2\beta\dot{\theta}_p \tag{11}$$

and the equivalent coefficients α and β are

$$\begin{aligned} \alpha &= \frac{2\varepsilon K_t}{R_m}, \\ \beta &= \frac{\varepsilon K_t K_b}{R_m} + f_m \end{aligned} \tag{12}$$

Furthermore, because of the inverted pendulum's physical behavior, it is obvious that $F_{\theta_w} = -F_{\theta_p}$. Therefore, one has

$$F_{\theta_p} = -\alpha V_{in} + 2(\beta + f_w)\dot{\theta}_w - 2\beta\dot{\theta}_p \tag{13}$$

2.3. Integrate the Model of a Pendulum Cart and Motors

Based on (4), (11) and (13), the complete dynamics equations of the wheel-driven pendulum cart can be represented by

$$\begin{aligned} \alpha V_{in} &= 2(\beta + f_w)\dot{\theta}_w - 2\beta\dot{\theta}_p - MLR\dot{\theta}_p^2 \sin(\theta_p) + \left((2m + M)R^2 + 2J_W + 2\varepsilon^2 J_m\right)\ddot{\theta}_w \\ &\quad + \left(MLR\cos(\theta_p) - 2\varepsilon^2 J_m\right)\ddot{\theta}_p \end{aligned} \tag{14}$$

and

$$\begin{aligned} \alpha V_{in} &= 2(\beta + f_w)\dot{\theta}_w - 2\beta\dot{\theta}_p - \left(ML^2 + J_b + 2\varepsilon^2 J_m\right)\ddot{\theta}_p + MgL\sin(\theta_p) \\ &\quad - \left(MLR\cos(\theta_p) - 2\varepsilon^2 J_m\right)\ddot{\theta}_w \end{aligned} \tag{15}$$

Apparently, the dynamics of the wheel-driven pendulum are highly nonlinear and unstable. In order to estimate the parameters, the equivalent parameter representation should be further considered. Moreover, since the system is unstable, a stabilizing control law must be applied for the collection of input/output excitation signals.

3. System Parameter Identification

3.1. Least-Square Algorithm

The LS algorithm has been widely used to identify a system's parameters since this approach enables the provision of a globally optimal solution to minimize the residual error. As a result, the LS algorithm plays an important role in this paper to perform the system parameter identification.

Consider the regression model as $\mathbf{y}(t) = \varphi(t)\mathbf{X}$, in which $\mathbf{y}(t) \in \mathbb{R}^p$ is the output of the regression model, $\varphi(t) \in \mathbb{R}^{p \times n}$ is the regressor, and $\mathbf{X} = \begin{bmatrix} X_1 & \cdots & X_n \end{bmatrix}^T \in \mathbb{R}^n$ is the unknown parameter vector to be identified.

Based on a sufficiently long period of observation for $t = T, 2T, \cdots, NT$, where T is the sampling interval, it gives the following over-determined equation $\mathbf{Y} = \mathbf{\Phi}\mathbf{X}$, where

$$\mathbf{Y} = \begin{bmatrix} \mathbf{y}(T) \\ \mathbf{y}(2T) \\ \vdots \\ \mathbf{y}(NT) \end{bmatrix}_{m \times 1}, \quad \mathbf{\Phi} = \begin{bmatrix} \varphi(T) \\ \varphi(2T) \\ \vdots \\ \varphi(NT) \end{bmatrix}_{m \times n} \tag{16}$$

and $m = pN > n$. The LS algorithm aims to determine the estimated parameter $\hat{\mathbf{X}} = \begin{bmatrix} \hat{X}_1 & \cdots & \hat{X}_n \end{bmatrix}^T \in \mathbb{R}^n$ to minimize the residual error $\mathbf{E}$, which equals to $\min_{\hat{\mathbf{X}}} \|\mathbf{E}\|^2 \triangleq \|\mathbf{Y} - \mathbf{\Phi}\mathbf{X}\|^2$. For the residual error $\mathbf{E}$, the optimal solution is

$$\hat{\mathbf{X}} = \left(\mathbf{\Phi}^T \mathbf{\Phi}\right)^{-1} \mathbf{\Phi}^T \mathbf{Y} \triangleq \mathbf{\Phi}^\dagger \mathbf{Y} \tag{17}$$

in which $\mathbf{\Phi}^\dagger = \left(\mathbf{\Phi}^T \mathbf{\Phi}\right)^{-1} \mathbf{\Phi}^T$ is the pseudo-inverse of the observation matrix $\mathbf{\Phi}$, and the matrix $\mathbf{\Phi}^T \mathbf{\Phi}$ must be invertible. Moreover, it is worth to note that the identified parameters $\hat{\mathbf{X}}$ will deviate from their references significantly if obvious noise appears in (16).

3.2. Regression Model of a Wheel-Driven Pendulum System

To facilitate the system identification, according to (14) and (15), define $\mathbf{X} = [X_1, X_2, X_3, X_4, X_5, X_6, X_7]^T$ as follows,

$$\begin{aligned} X_1 &= \tfrac{(2m+M)R^2 + 2J_w}{\alpha}, \quad X_2 = \tfrac{2\varepsilon J_m}{\alpha}, \quad X_3 = \tfrac{MLR}{\alpha}, \\ X_4 &= \tfrac{ML^2 + J_b}{\alpha}, \quad X_5 = \tfrac{MgL}{\alpha}, \quad X_6 = \tfrac{2(\beta + f_w)}{\alpha}, \quad X_7 = \tfrac{2\beta}{\alpha} \end{aligned} \tag{18}$$

Based on the equivalent parameter representation (18), Equations (14) and (15) become

$$V_{in} = (X_1 + X_2)\ddot{\theta}_w + (X_3 \cos(\theta_p) - X_2)\ddot{\theta}_p - X_3 \dot{\theta}_p^2 \sin(\theta_p) + X_6 \dot{\theta}_w - X_7 \dot{\theta}_p \tag{19}$$

and

$$V_{in} = -(X_3 \cos(\theta_p) - X_2)\ddot{\theta}_w - (X_4 + X_2)\ddot{\theta}_p - X_5 \sin(\theta_p) + X_6 \dot{\theta}_w - X_7 \dot{\theta}_p \tag{20}$$

respectively. Next, to apply the LS algorithm, it is necessary to express the unknown system parameters in terms of a linear regression form

$$\tau(t) = \varphi(t)\mathbf{X} \tag{21}$$

in which $\tau(t) = [V_{in}(t), V_{in}(t)]^T$ and

$$\varphi(t) = \begin{bmatrix} \ddot{\theta}_w & \ddot{\theta}_w - \ddot{\theta}_p & \varphi_{13} & 0 & 0 & \dot{\theta}_w & -\dot{\theta}_p \\ 0 & \ddot{\theta}_w - \ddot{\theta}_p & \varphi_{23} & -\ddot{\theta}_p & \varphi_{25} & \dot{\theta}_w & -\dot{\theta}_p \end{bmatrix} \tag{22}$$

where

$$\varphi_{13} = \cos(\theta_p)\ddot{\theta}_p - \sin(\theta_p)\dot{\theta}_p^2,$$
$$\varphi_{23} = -\cos(\theta_p)\ddot{\theta}_w,$$
$$\varphi_{25} = \sin(\theta_p)$$
(23)

Given the sampled data for $t = T, 2T, \cdots, NT$, the LS equation can be constructed by $Y = \Phi X$, where

$$Y = \begin{bmatrix} \tau(T) \\ \tau(2T) \\ \vdots \\ \tau(NT) \end{bmatrix}_{2N \times 1}, \quad \Phi = \begin{bmatrix} \varphi(T) \\ \varphi(2T) \\ \vdots \\ \varphi(NT) \end{bmatrix}_{2N \times 7}$$
(24)

Theoretically, the optimal parameters can be obtained by applying the LS solution $\hat{X} = \Phi^{\dagger} Y$ to minimize the residual error.

However, an examination of the observation matrix Φ reveals that it involves not only the wheel rotation angle and the cart's pitch angle and angular velocity but also the wheel's angular velocity, acceleration, and the cart's pitch angular acceleration. From a practical realization scenario, the wheel rotation angle can be directly measured through an encoder. Nevertheless, the angle measurement is subject to the quantization effect. Simultaneously, the pitch angle and the pitch angular velocity are also measurable by an IMU but are prone to measurement noise. Additionally, the regression matrix (22) includes unmeasurable variables such as the cart's pitch angular acceleration, wheel angular velocity, and wheel angular acceleration, which must be obtained through numerical differencing. It is well known that the numerical differencing method can significantly amplify the noise. This amplification of measurement noise leads to the problem formulation of the ideal LS from $Y = \Phi X$ to $Y + \Delta Y = (\Phi + \Delta \Phi) X$, which causes parameter identification bias even using the optimal solution $\hat{X} = \Phi^{\dagger} Y$. In other words, the reduction in ΔY and $\Delta \Phi$ would effectively contribute to the improvement of parameter identification accuracy. This issue is going to be addressed by applying a filtering based regression model, introduced in the following section.

3.3. Filtering-Based Regression Model

It is well known that the measurement encoder quantization effect as well as the Gaussian noise may be amplified by taking the numerical differentiation. To avoid this potential weakness, the filtering-based regression model is considered. In other words, (21) should be rewritten as

$$\tau(t) = \left[\frac{d^2}{dt^2} \varphi_2(t) + \frac{d}{dt} \varphi_1(t) + \varphi_0(t) \right] X$$
(25)

in which

$$\varphi_2(t) = \begin{bmatrix} \theta_w & \theta_w - \theta_p & 0 & 0 & 0 & 0 & 0 \\ 0 & \theta_w - \theta_p & 0 & -\theta_p & 0 & 0 & 0 \end{bmatrix},$$
$$\varphi_1(t) = \begin{bmatrix} 0 & 0 & \cos(\theta_p)\dot{\theta}_p & 0 & 0 & \theta_w & -\theta_p \\ 0 & 0 & -\cos(\theta_p)\dot{\theta}_w & 0 & 0 & \theta_w & -\theta_p \end{bmatrix},$$
$$\varphi_0(t) = \begin{bmatrix} 0 & 0 & 0 & 0 & 0 & 0 & 0 \\ 0 & 0 & -\sin(\theta_p)\dot{\theta}_p\dot{\theta}_w & 0 & \sin(\theta_p) & 0 & 0 \end{bmatrix}$$
(26)

Taking the Laplace transform of (25) yields

$$\tau(s) = \varphi(s) X$$
(27)

in which s represents the Laplace operator; $\tau(s)$ and $\varphi(s)$ are defined as

$$\tau(s) = \mathcal{L}\{\tau(t)\},$$
$$\varphi(s) = \varphi_a(s) + \varphi_b(s) + \varphi_c(s)$$
(28)

and
$$\begin{aligned}\varphi_a(s) &= \mathcal{L}\{\ddot{\varphi}_2(t)\} = s^2\varphi_2(s) - s\varphi_2(0) - \dot{\varphi}_2(0),\\ \varphi_b(s) &= \mathcal{L}\{\dot{\varphi}_1(t)\} = s\varphi_1(s) - \varphi_1(0),\\ \varphi_c(s) &= \mathcal{L}\{\varphi_0(t)\} = \varphi_0(s)\end{aligned} \quad (29)$$

Introduce a double filtering operator

$$I_o(s) = \frac{1}{(\tau_1 s + 1)(\tau_2 s + 1)} \quad (30)$$

where the time constants $\tau_1 \geq 0$ and $\tau_2 \geq 0$ are to be determined. As highlighted in the recent work [21], the selection of the time constants is supposed to consider the excitation frequency of the input as well as the dynamic nature of the control system. An inadequate selection of the time constant may result in an obvious deviation of the identified parameters. Applying (30) to the Laplace transform (27) gives

$$\tau^{2f}(s) = \varphi^{2f}(s)X \quad (31)$$

where

$$\begin{aligned}\tau^{2f}(s) &= I_o(s)\tau(s),\\ \varphi^{2f}(s) &= \varphi_2^{2f}(s) + \varphi_1^{2f}(s) + \varphi_0^{2f}(s)\end{aligned} \quad (32)$$

and

$$\begin{aligned}\varphi_2^{2f}(s) &= I_o(s)(s^2\varphi_2(s) - s\varphi_2(0) - \dot{\varphi}_2(0)),\\ \varphi_1^{2f}(s) &= I_o(s)(s\varphi_1(s) - \varphi_1(0)),\\ \varphi_0^{2f}(s) &= I_o(s)\varphi_0(s)\end{aligned} \quad (33)$$

To avoid the use of $s^2\varphi_2(s)$, reformulate $\varphi_2^{2f}(s)$ as follows

$$\begin{aligned}\varphi_2^{2f}(s) &= \frac{1}{\tau_1\tau_2}\frac{1}{v_1}\left(s^2\varphi_2(s) - s\varphi_2(0) - \dot{\varphi}_2(0)\right)\\ &= \frac{1}{\tau_1\tau_2}\varphi_2(s) + \frac{1}{\tau_1\tau_2 v_1}\left[-v_2\varphi_2(s) - \left(s+\frac{1}{\tau_1}\right)\varphi_2(0)\right]\\ &\quad + \frac{1}{\tau_1\tau_2 v_1}\left[\left(v_2\frac{1}{\tau_1} - \frac{1}{\tau_1\tau_2}\right)\varphi_2(s) + \frac{1}{\tau_1}\varphi_2(0) - \dot{\varphi}_2(0)\right]\\ &= \varphi'_2(s) + Y_{2,1}(s) + Y_{2,2}(s)\end{aligned} \quad (34)$$

where

$$\begin{aligned}\varphi'_2(s) &= \frac{1}{\tau_1\tau_2}\varphi_2(s),\\ Y_{2,1}(s) &= \frac{1}{\tau_1\tau_2}\frac{\tau_2}{\tau_2 s+1}[-v_2\varphi_2(s) - \varphi_2(0)],\\ Y_{2,2}(s) &= \frac{1}{\tau_1\tau_2}\frac{1}{v_1}\left[\frac{1}{\tau_1^2}\varphi_2(s) + \frac{1}{\tau_1}\varphi_2(0) - \dot{\varphi}_2(0)\right]\end{aligned} \quad (35)$$

and

$$\begin{aligned}v_1 &= (s+1/\tau_1)(s+1/\tau_2),\\ v_2 &= (1/\tau_1 + 1/\tau_2)\end{aligned} \quad (36)$$

In the same manner, removing $s\varphi_1(s)$ in $\varphi_1^{2f}(s)$ is followed by

$$\begin{aligned}\varphi_1^{2f}(s) &= \frac{1}{(\tau_1 s+1)(\tau_2 s+1)}(s\varphi_1(s) - \varphi_1(0))\\ &= \frac{1}{\tau_1\tau_2}\frac{\tau_1 s+1}{v_1 \tau_1}\varphi_1(s) + \frac{1}{\tau_1\tau_2}\frac{1}{v_1}\left[-\frac{1}{\tau_1}\varphi_1(s) - \varphi_1(0)\right]\\ &= Y_{1,1}(s) + Y_{1,2}(s)\end{aligned} \quad (37)$$

where

$$\begin{aligned}Y_{1,1}(s) &= \frac{1}{\tau_1\tau_2}\frac{\tau_2}{\tau_2 s+1}\varphi_1(s),\\ Y_{1,2}(s) &= \frac{1}{\tau_1\tau_2}\frac{1}{v_1}\left[-\frac{1}{\tau_1}\varphi_1(s) - \varphi_1(0)\right]\end{aligned} \quad (38)$$

Taking the inverse Laplace transformation of $\tau^{2f}(s) = \varphi^{2f}(s)\mathbf{X}$ yields the filtering-based regression model as

$$\tau^{2f}(t) = \varphi^{2f}(t)\mathbf{X} \tag{39}$$

in which

$$\begin{aligned}
\tau^{2f}(t) &= \mathcal{L}^{-1}\left\{\tau^{2f}(s)\right\}, \\
\varphi^{2f}(t) &= \mathcal{L}^{-1}\left\{\varphi^{2f}(s)\right\} \\
&= \varphi_2^{2f}(t) + \varphi_1^{2f}(t) + \varphi_0^{2f}(t) \\
&= \varphi'_2(t) + \mathbf{Y}_{2,1}(t) + \mathbf{Y}_{2,2}(t) + \mathbf{Y}_{1,1}(t) + \mathbf{Y}_{1,2}(t) + \varphi_0^{2f}(t)
\end{aligned} \tag{40}$$

where $\varphi'_2(t) = \varphi_2(t)/\tau_1\tau_2$. The filtering quantities $\tau^{2f}(t)$, $\mathbf{Y}_{2,1}(t)$, $\mathbf{Y}_{2,2}(t)$, $\mathbf{Y}_{1,1}(t)$, $\mathbf{Y}_{1,2}(t)$ and $\varphi_0^{2f}(t)$ can be estimated by numerically integrating the following matrix differential equations:

$$\begin{aligned}
\ddot{\tau}^{2f}(t) &= -\nu_3\dot{\tau}^{2f}(t) - \tfrac{1}{\tau_1\tau_2}\tau^{2f}(t) + \tfrac{1}{\tau_1\tau_2}\tau(t), \\
\dot{\mathbf{Y}}_{2,1}(t) &= -\tfrac{1}{\tau_2}\mathbf{Y}_{2,1}(t) - \tfrac{\nu_2}{\tau_1\tau_2}\varphi_2(t), \\
\ddot{\mathbf{Y}}_{2,2}(t) &= -\nu_3\dot{\mathbf{Y}}_{2,2}(t) - \tfrac{1}{\tau_1\tau_2}\mathbf{Y}_{2,2}(t) + \tfrac{1}{\tau_1\tau_2\tau_1^2}\varphi_2(t), \\
\dot{\mathbf{Y}}_{1,1}(t) &= -\tfrac{1}{\tau_2}\mathbf{Y}_{1,1}(t) + \tfrac{1}{\tau_1\tau_2}\varphi_1(t), \\
\ddot{\mathbf{Y}}_{1,2}(t) &= -\nu_3\dot{\mathbf{Y}}_{1,2}(t) - \tfrac{1}{\tau_1\tau_2}\mathbf{Y}_{1,2}(t) - \tfrac{1}{\tau_1\tau_2\tau_1}\varphi_1(t), \\
\ddot{\varphi}_0^{2f}(t) &= -\nu_3\dot{\varphi}_0^{2f}(t) - \tfrac{1}{\tau_1\tau_2}\varphi_0^{2f}(t) + \tfrac{1}{\tau_1\tau_2}\varphi_0(t)
\end{aligned} \tag{41}$$

Among (41), $\nu_3 = 1/\tau_1 + 1/\tau_2$ and the initial conditions are

$$\begin{aligned}
\tau^{2f}(0) &= \dot{\tau}^{2f}(0) = 0, \\
\mathbf{Y}_{2,1}(0) &= -\tfrac{1}{\tau_1\tau_2}\varphi_2(0), \\
\mathbf{Y}_{2,2}(0) &= 0, \\
\dot{\mathbf{Y}}_{2,2}(0) &= \tfrac{1}{\tau_1\tau_2}\left(\tfrac{1}{\tau_1}\varphi_2(0) - \dot{\varphi}_2(0)\right), \\
\mathbf{Y}_{1,1}(0) &= 0, \\
\mathbf{Y}_{1,2}(0) &= 0, \\
\dot{\mathbf{Y}}_{1,2}(0) &= -\tfrac{1}{\tau_1\tau_2}\varphi_1(0), \\
\varphi_0^{2f}(0) &= \dot{\varphi}_0^{2f}(0) = 0
\end{aligned} \tag{42}$$

Similar to (16) and (24), and considering the regression model (39), the LS equation can now be modified by the filtered normal equation $\mathbf{Y}_{2f} = \mathbf{\Phi}_{2f}\mathbf{X}$, where

$$\mathbf{Y}_{2f} = \begin{bmatrix} \tau^{2f}(T) \\ \tau^{2f}(2T) \\ \vdots \\ \tau^{2f}(NT) \end{bmatrix}_{2N\times 1}, \quad \mathbf{\Phi}_{2f} = \begin{bmatrix} \varphi^{2f}(T) \\ \varphi^{2f}(2T) \\ \vdots \\ \varphi^{2f}(NT) \end{bmatrix}_{2N\times 7} \tag{43}$$

Hence, the least-square solution to minimize the residual error is given by $\hat{\mathbf{X}} = \mathbf{\Phi}_{2f}^{\dagger}\mathbf{Y}_{2f}$, where $\mathbf{\Phi}_{2f}^{\dagger}$ is the pseudo-inverse of the filtering operator-based observation matrix. Compared to the original LS method, the proposed filtering method only contains the output measurable position and filtered velocity measurements. In short, the filtering method avoids the direct use of noisy acceleration measurements through numerical differentiation estimation and thereby provides a more accurate parameter estimation.

Further, owing to the introduction of the filtering factors τ_1 and τ_2, the regression model can suppress the influence of initial condition and the measurement quantization and Gaussian errors. A guidance of the selection of the filtering factors, which plays a

122

significant role in enhancing the accuracy of parameter identification results, has been addressed and proven in [21].

Regarding the realization of the filtering method presented in this section, firstly, the output filtering method is built upon the output filtering-based regression model (39) and involves arranging the time histories to formulate the least squares equation for optimal parameter estimation. The computational process of the entire method is not overly complex. The filtering quantities at each time point, $t = T, 2T, \ldots, NT$, as indicated in (39), can be estimated through numerical integration of the matrix differential equation provided in (41). We have transformed (41) under the assumption of zero-order hold to a discrete equation for numerical iteration. Further details regarding the numerical integration can be found in the Appendix A of reference [24]. Moreover, for the computation of the optimal solution using the least-squares method, a significant amount of memory may be required to allocate measurement matrices Φ_{2f}. Considering the constraints of memory in embedded systems, it is not feasible to store all time data within the microprocessor. Therefore, to achieve real-time parameter identification, an iterative approach is necessary for the solution of the least squares method. The relevant methodology can be found in reference [21].

4. Numerical Simulation of the Filtering Method

The following simulation is performed in MATLAB/Simulink with the solver Runge-Kutta 4, where the time-step $T = 0.001$ s is applied. Since the wheel-driven pendulum cart is unstable, to meet the real situation when conducting SPI, a simple proportional–integral–derivative (PID) controller is implemented based on the linearized model applied to stabilize the cart's attitude. The control gains are adjusted as follows: the proportional (P) gain, the integral (I) gain and the derivative (D) gain are set to be -168, -800, and -8.8, respectively. Note that the negative sign of the PID gains is from the definition of the tracking error.

The exact parameters are listed as follows: $m = 4.6$ kg, $L = 1.8$ m, $M = 110$ kg, $R = 0.2413$ m, $\varepsilon = 14$, $f_m = 0.3$, $K_b = 0.722$ Vs/rad, $K_t = 0.833$ Nm/A, $R_m = 0.141\ \Omega$, $J_w = 0.1339$ kgm^2, and $J_b = 87.89$ kgm^2. The nominal parameters which are used for the PID control design are set to be around 90% of the exact parameters. The corresponding reference equivalent parameters are displayed in Table 1.

Table 1. Simple command based on differentiation versus filtering.

Reference Parameter.	Differentiation-Based		Filter-Based	
	Est. Para.	Error (%)	Est. Para.	Error (%)
$X_1 = 0.0436$	0.004628	89.38	0.02921	33.04
$X_2 = 0.0178$	-0.006094	134.24	0.03071	72.52
$X_3 = 0.1149$	-0.003984	103.47	0.06709	41.60
$X_4 = 0.8719$	0.008320	99.05	0.51477	40.96
$X_5 = 4.6701$	3.43352	26.48	2.85297	38.91
$X_6 = 0.7268$	0.75595	4.012	0.72685	0.0073
$X_7 = 0.7256$	-2.12978	393.52	0.72526	0.0474

In regard to wheel encoder quantization, the resolution 60,000 counts per revolution is made. Thus, the resulting measurement quantization error is $2\pi/60,000$ rad/count. On the other hand, the standard deviation of the noise for pitch angle and its angular velocity are 0.5 degrees and 0.5 degrees/s, respectively.

The following are the comparison of simulation results between the true parameters and the identified parameters under the condition: time constants $\tau_1 = 2.25$ and $\tau_2 = 6.5$, the initial conditions $\begin{bmatrix} \theta_w = 0 & \theta_p = 0 & \dot{\theta}_w = 0 & \dot{\theta}_p = 0 \end{bmatrix}$ are applied for all the following simulations.

Table 1 summarizes the performance comparison of the SPI between the direct numerical differentiation method and the proposed output filtering method. The results clearly illustrate that the proposed SPI method is able to provide a better accuracy as expected.

Moreover, as analyzed in [21], different excitation of the input commands has a significant impact on the observation matrix $\Phi_{2f}^{-1}\Phi_{2f}$. The simpler the command is, the more likely that the condition number of $\Phi_{2f}^{-1}\Phi_{2f}$ would become bigger. In other words, $\Phi_{2f}^{-1}\Phi_{2f}$ is likely to be ill-conditioned. On the contrary, the more active the input command is, the more probable that the matrix $\Phi_{2f}^{-1}\Phi_{2f}$ is well-conditioned. Therefore, in this paper, a simple as well as an aggressive command are applied. To note, the simple command input is a sinewave while the aggressive command is the combination of several sine and cosine waves with different frequencies and amplitude. To put it clearly, the simple command is designed as $R_{simple}(t) = 20\sin(t)$, and the aggressive command is designed as $R_{aggressive}(t) = 3\sin(7t) + 6(\cos(4t) - \sin(t)) + 10\cos(3t)\sin^2(5t)$.

For the system identification of unstable systems, it is it is essential to begin by designing a controller and performing preliminary parameter tuning to ensure the stability of the closed-loop system. However, overly simplistic reference commands may not fully excite all aspects of the system's behavior. By employing an aggressive command as a reference command to excite the system's response, the controlled loop generates a control input signal to achieve the desired dynamic response of the system as close as possible. Subsequently, system parameter identification is conducted utilizing the closed-loop control input signal and historical data of system outputs. Figure 2 illustrates the input signals used for closed-loop parameter identification under aggressive command excitation, while Figure 3 displays the corresponding system output responses. Apparently, due to the imperfection of the sensors, the input/output signals are contaminated by measurement noise. Therefore, the filter-based method becomes very important for noise suppression during the SPI, which has been highlighted in Table 1.

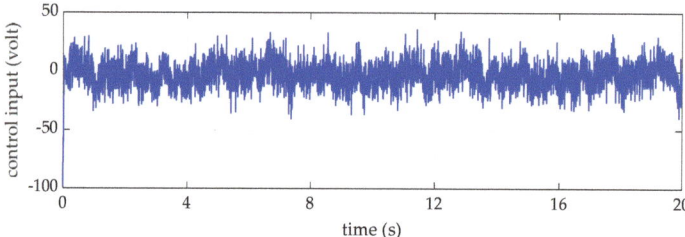

Figure 2. Input data for system identification.

According to Table 2, it is obvious that the parameters identified through the aggressive command are more accurate than the simple command. The results verify the assumption as mentioned before. In other words, an active command can excite wheel-driven pendulum cart's dynamic response more obviously than just a simple command. Note that the selection of the filter time constants should not filter out the original system's dynamic response, but should be able to suppress the measurement noise.

Table 2. Parameter identification results with different excitation command input.

Reference Parameter	Simple Command		Aggressive Command	
	Est. Para.	Error (%)	Est. Para.	Error (%)
$X_1 = 0.0436$	0.02921	33.04	0.04991	14.46
$X_2 = 0.0178$	0.03071	72.52	0.01276	28.26
$X_3 = 0.1149$	0.06709	41.60	0.10695	6.914
$X_4 = 0.8719$	0.51477	40.96	0.83680	4.027
$X_5 = 4.6701$	2.85297	38.91	4.67882	0.1025
$X_6 = 0.7268$	0.72685	0.0073	0.72695	0.0212
$X_7 = 0.7256$	0.72526	0.0474	0.70581	2.7282

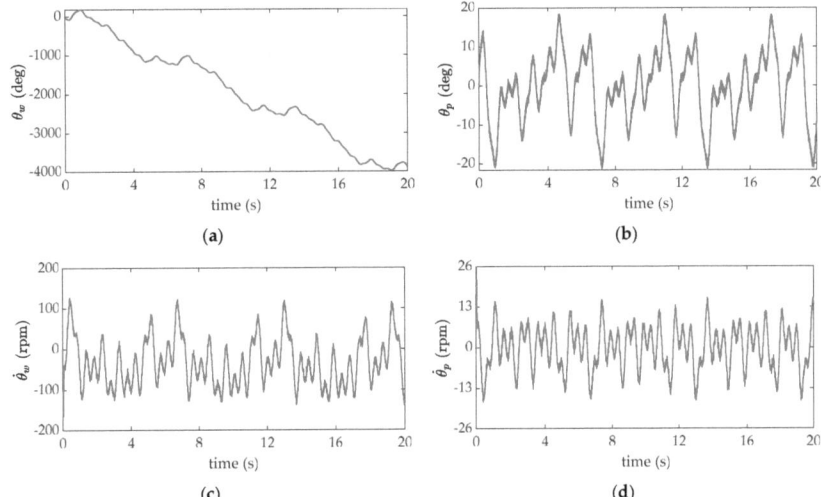

Figure 3. Output data for system identification. (a) Wheel angle. (b) Pitch angle. (c) Wheel angular speed. (d) Pitch angular speed.

Based on the identified parameters, Figure 4 demonstrate the association output predictions. The red line represents the exact output response from true parameters. As for the blue and green line, the former stands for the prediction of parameters identified through simple command, while the latter is the prediction of parameters identified through aggressive command. One can observe that, from Figure 5, the RMSE (Root Mean Square Error) of the output prediction based on applying the identified parameters is very small. According to the simulation results, the RMSE for wheel angle output prediction is 0.3260 for the aggressive command and 0.2423 for the simple command, respectively. Besides, the RMSE for pitch angle output prediction is 6.8181e-04 for the aggressive command and 0.0016 for the simple command. Also, the RMSE for wheel angular rate output prediction is 0.1585 for the aggressive command and 0.1267 for the simple command. Lastly, the RMSE for pitch angular rate output prediction is 0.0064 for the aggressive command and 0.0201 for the simple command.

It is evident that states related to pitch, including pitch angle and pitch angular rate, exhibit lower output prediction errors when excited through an aggressive command compared to those excited by a simple command. In contrast, states associated with the wheel, although not showing significantly lower output prediction errors when excited through an aggressive command than when excited through a simple command, display very similar errors between the two cases.

This phenomenon can be attributed to the fact that the response of parameters identified through an aggressive command is superior to that of parameters identified through a simple command. The rationale behind this lies in the active command input's capability to reduce the condition number of the observation matrix for the wheel-driven pendulum system. This reduction prevents the system from becoming ill-conditioned and thereby enhances the accuracy of parameter identification.

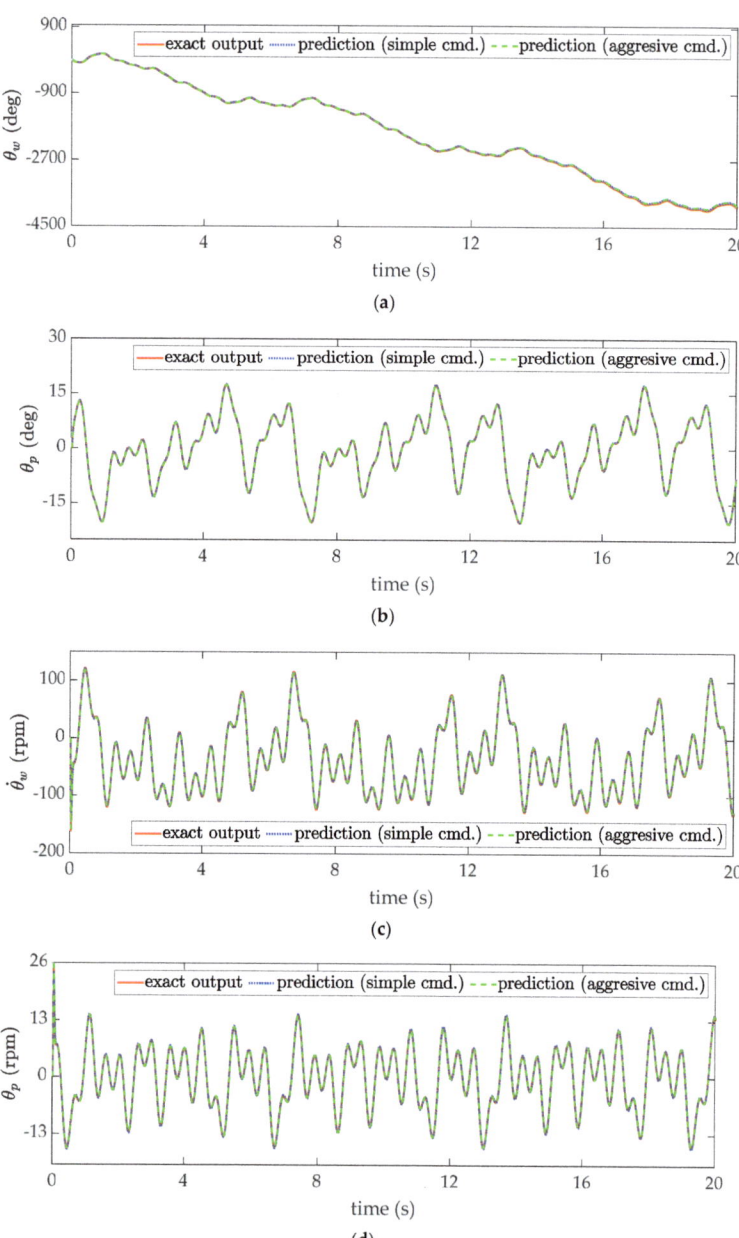

Figure 4. Outputs response predictions of the closed-loop model for the wheel-driven pendulum system. (**a**) Wheel angle. (**b**) Pitch angle. (**c**) Wheel angular speed. (**d**) Pitch angular speed.

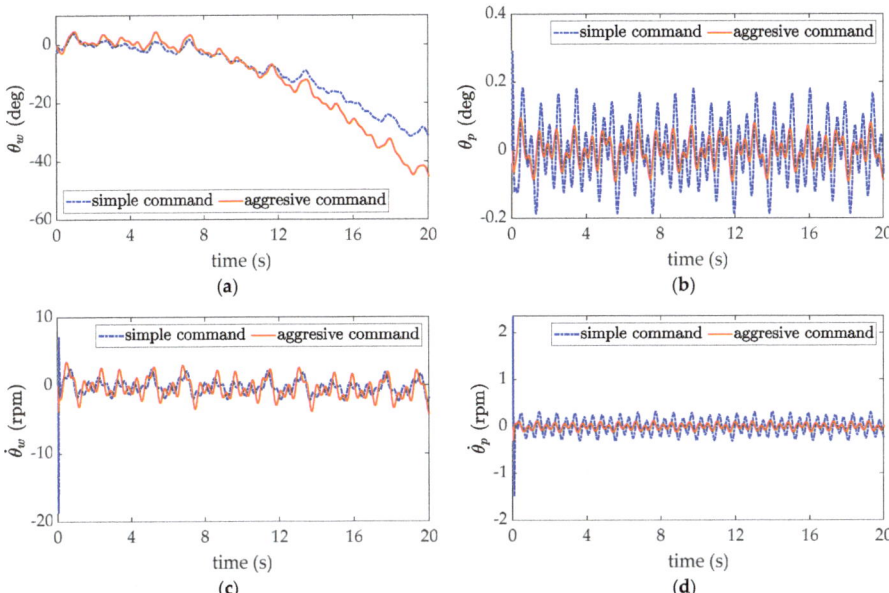

Figure 5. Outputs prediction errors of the closed-loop model. (**a**) Wheel angle. (**b**) Pitch angle. (**c**) Wheel angular speed. (**d**) Pitch angular speed.

In the context of closed-loop system identification, the performance of system identification can be evaluated not only through the prediction of output responses but also by calculating the corresponding control inputs using the controller, thereby enabling control input predictions. Based on the results of closed-loop system identification, Figure 6 presents predictions of control inputs, comparing these predictions with both the measured and exact control inputs.

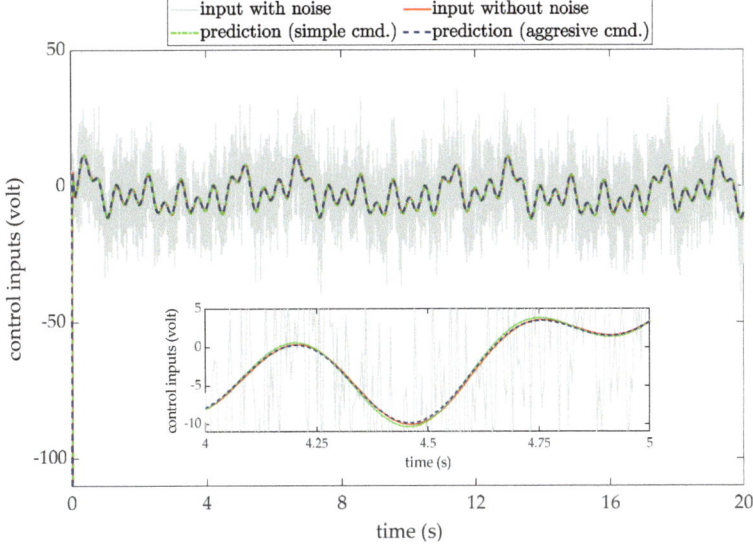

Figure 6. Control input prediction for closed-loop system.

In Figure 6, the gray line represents the control input signal of the actual system with output measurement noise, the red line corresponds to the exact control input signal, while the green and blue lines represent the predicted control inputs obtained through the excitation of an simple command and an aggressive command, respectively. It is evident from the graph that the accuracy of control input prediction is influenced by the accuracy of pitch angle prediction, as control inputs are derived from the error between the reference command and the pitch angle. Consequently, the predictions generated through aggressive command excitation exhibit higher accuracy compared to those obtained through simple command excitation when compared to the exact control inputs.

When applying an output filtering method, it is necessary to perform numerical integration for specific system states as shown in (41), where the associated initial values for the integration is provided by (42). Consequently, any uncertainty in the initial value leading to bias results in the accumulation of errors in the system state over time, affecting the accuracy of the system state integration solution and, consequently, reducing the precision of parameter identification. Based on (42), it is evident that increasing the values of the filter parameters τ_1 and τ_2 can mitigate the impact of initial value uncertainty on numerical integration. To validate this statement, extra simulations are conducted to evaluate the accuracy of parameter identification under different cases. In order to clearly point out how the selection of the parameters τ_1 and τ_2 can affect the precision of the SPI, the following numerical cases are applied in the absence of output measurement noise. The results are summarized in Table 3.

Table 3. The impact of various filter parameters on parameter identification results with initial value deviation.

Ref. Para.	Correct Initial Value		Initial Value with Uncertainty (θ_p Deviation Is +0.5 Degrees)					
	Case A. $\tau_1 = \tau_2 = 0.014$		Case B. $\tau_1 = \tau_2 = 0.014$		Case C. $\tau_1 = \tau_2 = 0.14$		Case D. $\tau_1 = \tau_2 = 4.2$	
	Est. Para.	Error (%)	Est. Para.	Error (%)	Est. Para.	Error (%)	Est. Para.	Error (%)
$X_1 = 0.0436$	0.04355	0.1074	0.00590	86.458	0.04033	7.4825	0.05016	15.053
$X_2 = 0.0178$	0.01781	0.0764	0.03485	95.787	0.01959	10.059	0.01248	29.844
$X_3 = 0.1149$	0.11475	0.1239	-0.00727	1.0633	0.10586	7.8629	0.12766	11.106
$X_4 = 0.8719$	0.87128	0.0707	-0.01024	1.0117	0.80374	7.8169	0.97554	11.886
$X_5 = 4.6701$	4.66554	0.0974	0.65966	85.874	4.34846	6.8870	5.24997	12.416
$X_6 = 0.7268$	0.72684	0.0061	0.72719	0.0546	0.72684	0.0064	0.72686	0.0084
$X_7 = 0.7256$	0.72516	0.0600	0.72203	0.4914	0.72592	0.0442	0.71614	1.3031

In this simulation comparison study, the controller parameters and initial system settings remain consistent with the previous simulations. As mentioned previously, the maximum system frequency of unstable systems is typically challenging to estimate beforehand. Therefore, the easiest way for the design of the filter parameters (τ_1, τ_2) is based on the system's reference commands, see [10,11,18]. In Case A, serving as the ground truth, there is no initial value bias. Considering a cutoff frequency of the output filter that is 10 times the maximum reference command frequency, the filter parameters are designed with $\tau_1 = \tau_2 = 0.014$. In Case B, using the same filter parameters, the initial value uncertainty introduced by the IMU-based estimation of pitch angle is accounted for. Here, the initial value of the pitch angle bias is set to be with positive 0.5 degrees. Furthermore, to mitigate the effects of initial value uncertainty and assess the impact of increased filter parameters, we further conduct Case C, where filter parameters are adjusted to $\tau_1 = \tau_2 = 0.14$. To further discuss an inadequate selection of the parameters degrade the SPI precision, the Case D, where filter parameters are increased to $\tau_1 = \tau_2 = 4.2$, is demonstrated while keeping the same level of initial value uncertainty bias.

From Table 3, it can be observed that, as the ground truth in Case A, since there is no noise interference or initial value uncertainty, the filter-based SPI results in very low parameter estimation errors. However, under the influence of initial value bias in Case B, the accuracy of parameter identification is indeed affected, with some parameter estimation errors reaching up to 95%. To address the SPI error caused by initial value uncertainty, as shown in Case C, appropriately increasing the filter parameter values can effectively mitigate the impact of initial value uncertainty and reduce parameter estimation errors. Nevertheless, it should be emphasized that the filter parameter values cannot be infinitely increased, as previously discussed in the article. The concept of output filtering is based on the removal of noise from output data, and the physical significance of filter parameters is the cutoff frequency of the filter. Therefore, excessive increases in filter parameters may suppress the system's dominant frequency response, making the original system behavior unobservable, which in turn decreases the accuracy of parameter estimation, as demonstrated in Case D.

In summary, when using the output filtering methods, the selection of the filter parameters carries significant implications. For unstable systems, under the condition of meeting basic tracking requirements, filter parameter design can be based on the maximum frequency of reference commands in the closed-loop control. The adjustment of filter parameters should not solely focus on noise removal, but should also consider the suppression of uncertainties in system initial value measurements.

Based on the above simulations, we can firmly conclude that the use of filtering-based system parameter identification can be applied to the nonlinear and unstable wheel-driven pendulum system successfully; the second-order output filtering method does not require the use of noisy acceleration signals, thus enabling more accurate parameter estimation; the filtering method is able to suppress the effects of Gaussian noise and quantization noise effectively; incorporation of aggressive command input can enhance the precision of parameter estimation.

Remark 1. *In the process of system identification, unstable systems may lead to adverse experimental outcomes or even pose safety hazards. Therefore, utilizing closed-loop system identification not only ensures the stability during the SPI but also effectively estimates the parameters of unstable systems, subsequently reducing system uncertainties in later stages of control design. Furthermore, employing unstable systems for closed-loop model estimation as an application of digital twins holds significant value. Given the unique physical characteristics of unstable systems, arbitrary adjustments to system controller parameters may result in system divergence, or even more severe consequences such as system damage. Leveraging the concept of a digital twin, designers can perform preliminary assessments of physical systems within a virtual model and proceed with controller design. Through simulations, they can evaluate the expected performance of the controller, thus verifying the feasibility and effectiveness of the controller design. Ultimately, these designs can be applied to real-world systems, ensuring a safer and more reliable development of controllers prior to implementation and optimization.*

5. Conclusions

This paper introduces an output filtering method to identify the system parameters of a nonlinear unstable wheel-driven pendulum cart. The detailed equations of motions and the associated measurement equations for the parameter identification are derived. Considering the real scenario, the measurement quantization as well as the Gaussian noises, which have a considerable impact on parameter estimations, are both taken into account. According to the presented filtering method, it cannot only suppress noisy acceleration, but preserve the dominant frequencies of the system's response as well. Simulations firmly demonstrate that the presented output filtering method is superior to the direct numerical differentiation method. Furthermore, to excite the special dynamic response of the pendulum cart, a simple command and an aggressive command are applied to the system, respectively. Associated results show that the more active the reference command is, the more accurate the estimation results could be. In conclusion, precise system parameters can be obtained by applying the presented output filtering algorithm even in the presence of the measurement quantization effect as well as the measurement noise. Simulations are carried out to verify the feasibility of the purposed method.

Author Contributions: Conceptualization, C.-C.P. and M.-C.T.; methodology, C.-C.P. and N.-J.C.; software, M.-C.T. and N.-J.C.; validation, C.-C.P., N.-J.C. and M.-C.T.; formal analysis, C.-C.P.; investigation, M.-C.T. and N.-J.C.; resources, C.-C.P.; writing—original draft preparation, N.-J.C.; writing—review and editing, C.-C.P. and M.-C.T.; visualization, N.-J.C. and M.-C.T.; supervision, C.-C.P.; project administration, C.-C.P.; funding acquisition, C.-C.P. All authors have read and agreed to the published version of the manuscript.

Funding: The work is supported by the Ministry of Science and Technology under the grant number: MOST 111-2221-E-006-170.

Data Availability Statement: The data that used in this study are available from the corresponding author, upon reasonable request.

Conflicts of Interest: The authors declare no conflict of interest.

References

1. Juang, J.-N.; Pappa, R.S. An eigensystem realization algorithm for modal parameter identification and model reduction. *J. Guid. Control Dyn.* **1985**, *8*, 620–627. [CrossRef]
2. Juang, J.-N. *Applied System Identification*; Prentice-Hall, Inc.: Hoboken, NJ, USA, 1994.
3. Juang, J.-N. Continuous-time bilinear system identification. *Nonlinear Dyn.* **2005**, *39*, 79–94. [CrossRef]
4. Juang, J.-N.; Phan, M.Q. *Identification and Control of Mechanical Systems*; Cambridge University Press: Cambridge, UK, 2001.
5. Jin, H.; Liu, Z.; Zhang, H.; Liu, Y.; Zhao, J. A dynamic parameter identification method for flexible joints based on adaptive control. *IEEE/ASME Trans. Mechatron.* **2018**, *23*, 2896–2908. [CrossRef]
6. Vicente, B.A.H.; James, S.S.; Anderson, S.R. Linear System Identification Versus Physical Modeling of Lateral–Longitudinal Vehicle Dynamics. *IEEE Trans. Control Syst. Technol.* **2021**, *29*, 1380–1387. [CrossRef]
7. Chan, R.P.M.; Stol, K.A.; Halkyard, C.R. Review of modelling and control of two-wheeled robots. *Annu. Rev. Control* **2013**, *37*, 89–103. [CrossRef]
8. Grasser, F.; D'arrigo, A.; Colombi, S.; Rufer, A.C. JOE: A mobile, inverted pendulum. *IEEE Trans. Ind. Electron.* **2002**, *49*, 107–114. [CrossRef]
9. Kim, H.; Jung, S. Control of a two-wheel robotic vehicle for personal transportation. *Robotica* **2016**, *34*, 1186–1208. [CrossRef]
10. Moreno-Valenzuela, J.; Miranda-Colorado, R.; Aguilar-Avelar, C. A matlab-based identification procedure applied to a two-degrees-of-freedom robot manipulator for engineering students. *Int. J. Electr. Eng. Educ.* **2017**, *54*, 319–340. [CrossRef]
11. Lopez-Sanchez, I.; Montoya-Cháirez, J.; Pérez-Alcocer, R.; Moreno-Valenzuela, J. Experimental Parameter Identifications of a Quadrotor by Using an Optimized Trajectory. *IEEE Access* **2020**, *8*, 167355–167370. [CrossRef]
12. Calanca, A.; Capisani, L.M.; Ferrara, A.; Magnani, L. MIMO Closed Loop Identification of an Industrial Robot. *IEEE Trans. Control Syst. Technol.* **2011**, *19*, 1214–1224. [CrossRef]
13. Jin, J.; Gans, N. Parameter identification for industrial robots with a fast and robust trajectory design approach. *Robot. Comput.-Integr. Manuf.* **2015**, *31*, 21–29. [CrossRef]
14. Peng, C.C.; Su, C.Y. Modeling and Parameter Identification of a Cooling Fan for Online Monitoring. *IEEE Trans. Instrum. Meas.* **2021**, *70*, 1–14. [CrossRef]
15. Moreno-Valenzuela, J.; Aguilar-Avelar, C. *Motion Control of Underactuated Mechanical Systems*; Springer: Berlin/Heidelberg, Germany, 2018; Volume 1.
16. Khalil, W.; Dombre, E. *Modeling Identification and Control of Robots*; CRC Press: Boca Raton, FL, USA, 2002.
17. Miranda-Colorado, R.; Moreno-Valenzuela, J. Experimental parameter identification of flexible joint robot manipulators. *Robotica* **2018**, *36*, 313–332. [CrossRef]
18. Chávez-Olivares, C.; Reyes-Cortés, F.; González-Galván, E.; Mendoza-Gutierrez, M.; Bonilla-Gutierrez, I. Experimental evaluation of parameter identification schemes on an anthropomorphic direct drive robot. *Int. J. Adv. Robot. Syst.* **2012**, *9*, 203. [CrossRef]
19. Guangjun, L.; Iagnemma, K.; Dubowsky, S.; Morel, G. A base force/torque sensor approach to robot manipulator inertial parameter estimation. In Proceedings of the 1998 IEEE International Conference on Robotics and Automation (Cat. No.98CH36146), Leuven, Belgium, 20–20 May 1998.
20. Guého, D.; Singla, P.; Majji, M.; Melton, R.G. Filtered Integral Formulation of the Sparse Model Identification Problem. *J. Guid. Control Dyn.* **2022**, *45*, 232–247. [CrossRef]
21. Peng, C.-C.; Chen, T.-Y. A recursive low-pass filtering method for a commercial cooling fan tray parameter online estimation with measurement noise. *Measurement* **2022**, *205*, 112193. [CrossRef]
22. Gautier, M.; Khalil, W.; Restrepo, P. Identification of the dynamic parameters of a closed loop robot. In Proceedings of the 1995 IEEE International Conference on Robotics and Automation, Nagoya, Japan, 21–27 May 1995.
23. Gautier, M. Dynamic identification of robots with power model. In Proceedings of the International Conference on Robotics and Automation, Albuquerque, NM, USA, 25 April 1997.

24. Li, Y.-R.; Peng, C.-C. Encoder position feedback based indirect integral method for motor parameter identification subject to asymmetric friction. *Int. J. Non-Linear Mech.* **2023**, *152*, 104386. [CrossRef]
25. Peng, C.-C.; Chen, Y.-H. A Hybrid Neural Ordinary Differential Equation Based Digital Twin Modeling and Online Diagnosis for an Industrial Cooling Fan. *Future Internet* **2023**, *15*, 302. [CrossRef]
26. Arvidsson, M.; Karlsson, J. Design, Construction and Verification of a Self-Balancing Vehicle. 2012. Available online: http://publications.lib.chalmers.se/records/fulltext/163640.pdf (accessed on 24 September 2023).

Disclaimer/Publisher's Note: The statements, opinions and data contained in all publications are solely those of the individual author(s) and contributor(s) and not of MDPI and/or the editor(s). MDPI and/or the editor(s) disclaim responsibility for any injury to people or property resulting from any ideas, methods, instructions or products referred to in the content.

Article

Stable and Efficient Reinforcement Learning Method for Avoidance Driving of Unmanned Vehicles

Sun-Ho Jang [1,2], Woo-Jin Ahn [2], Yu-Jin Kim [2], Hyung-Gil Hong [1], Dong-Sung Pae [3,*] and Myo-Taeg Lim [2,*]

[1] Korea Institute of Robotics Technology Convergence, Andong 36728, Republic of Korea; jang1229@kiro.re.kr (S.-H.J.); honghg@kiro.re.kr (H.-G.H.)
[2] School of Electrical Engineering, Korea University, Seoul 02841, Republic of Korea; wjahn@korea.ac.kr (W.-J.A.); sally1004k@korea.ac.kr (Y.-J.K.)
[3] Department of Software, Sangmyung University, Cheonan 31066, Republic of Korea
* Correspondence: paeds915@smu.ac.kr (D.-S.P.); mlim@korea.ac.kr (M.-T.L.)

Abstract: Reinforcement learning (RL) has demonstrated considerable potential in solving challenges across various domains, notably in autonomous driving. Nevertheless, implementing RL in autonomous driving comes with its own set of difficulties, such as the overestimation phenomenon, extensive learning time, and sparse reward problems. Although solutions like hindsight experience replay (HER) have been proposed to alleviate these issues, the direct utilization of RL in autonomous vehicles remains constrained due to the intricate fusion of information and the possibility of system failures during the learning process. In this paper, we present a novel RL-based autonomous driving system technology that combines obstacle-dependent Gaussian (ODG) RL, soft actor-critic (SAC), and meta-learning algorithms. Our approach addresses key issues in RL, including the overestimation phenomenon and sparse reward problems, by incorporating prior knowledge derived from the ODG algorithm. With these solutions in place, the ultimate aim of this work is to improve the performance of reinforcement learning and develop a swift, stable, and robust learning method for implementing autonomous driving systems that can effectively adapt to various environments and overcome the constraints of direct RL utilization in autonomous vehicles. We evaluated our proposed algorithm on official F1 circuits, using high-fidelity racing simulations with complex dynamics. The results demonstrate exceptional performance, with our method achieving up to 89% faster learning speed compared to existing algorithms in these environments.

Keywords: reinforcement learning; meta learning; deep reinforcement learning; autonomous driving; robot operating system

1. Introduction

Reinforcement learning (RL) has recently gained notable attention in various fields, including autonomous driving, due to its capability to address unanticipated challenges in real-world scenarios. Autonomous driving software defects can pose potential risks, thus developing safe and efficient methods when using AI technologies for autonomous driving systems is important [1]. Autonomous driving systems, by employing RL algorithms, are able to accrue experience and refine their decision-making procedures within dynamic environments [2–4]. This can be largely attributed to RL's inherent ability to adapt and learn from complex and fluctuating situations, demonstrating its aptitude for these applications. The basic concept of RL lies in the structure of Markov decision processes (MDP), a system where algorithms learn via a trial-and-error approach, striving to reach predetermined objectives by learning from mistakes and rewards. The aim of RL is to optimize future cumulative rewards and formulate the most efficient policy for distinct problems [5]. Recent integration of deep learning with RL has demonstrated promising outcomes across various domains. This involves the employment of advanced neural networks such as convolutional neural networks (CNNs), multi-layer perceptrons, restricted Boltzmann machines, and recurrent neural networks [6,7]. By fusing reinforcement learning with deep learning, the system's learning capabilities are significantly enhanced, allowing it to process complex data such as sensor feedback and environmental observations, thus facilitating more informed and effective driving decisions [8]. However, the application of RL to autonomous driving presents a unique array of challenges, particularly when it comes to deploying RL in real-world environments. The uncertainties inherent in these environments can make the effective execution of RL quite challenging. As a result, researchers often struggle to achieve optimal RL performance directly within the actual driving context, highlighting the various obstacles encountered when applying RL to autonomous driving [9]. Several challenges plague the application of RL to autonomous driving: overestimation phenomenon, learning time, and sparse reward problems [10,11].

Firstly, the overestimation phenomenon is prevalent in model-free RL methods, such as Q-learning [12] and its variants like the double deep Q network (DDQN) [13,14] and dueling DQN [15]. These methods are susceptible to overestimation and incorrect learning, primarily due to the combination of insufficiently flexible function approximation and the presence of noise, which lead to inaccuracies in action values. Secondly, the significant amount of learning time required is another hurdle. When RL is fused with neural networks, it generates policies directly from interactions with the environment, bypassing the need for a basic dynamics model. However, even simple tasks necessitate extensive trials and a massive number of data for learning. This makes high-performance RL both time-consuming and data-intensive [16]. Lastly, the issue of sparse reward arises during RL training. This presents challenges in scenarios where not all conditions receive immediate compensation. Although techniques like hindsight experience replay (HER) [17,18] have been proposed to mitigate this issue, the direct application of RL to autonomous vehicles is still limited due to the complex fusion of information and potential system failures during the learning process. This paper addresses the challenges of RL in autonomous driving and reduces the reliance on extensive real-world learning by introducing a set of innovative techniques to enhance the efficiency and effectiveness of RL: data preprocessing through obstacle-dependent Gaussian (ODG) [19,20] DQN, prior knowledge through Guide ODG DQN, and meta-learning-based guided ODG DDQN.

The data preprocessing method employs the ODG algorithm to combat the overestimation phenomenon. By preprocessing distance information through ODG DQN, it allows for more accurate action values, fostering stable and efficient learning [21]. The prior knowledge method draws on human learning mechanisms, incorporating knowledge derived from the ODG algorithm. This strategy mitigates the issue of sparse rewards and boosts the learning speed [22], facilitating more effective convergence. Lastly, the meta-learning-based guide rollout method uses ODG DQN to address complex driving decisions and sparse rewards in real-world situations. By enriching prior knowledge using a rollout approach, this method aims to create efficient and successful autonomous driving policies.

Our main contributions can be summarized as follows:

- Efficiency and speed of learning: The newly proposed RL algorithm utilizes ODG DQN on preprocessed information, enabling the agent to make optimal action choices, which significantly enhances the learning speed and efficiency.
- Improvement of learning stability: With the use of prior knowledge, the guide-ODG-DQN helps mitigate the issue of sparse rewards, thus increasing the learning stability and overall efficiency.
- Adaptability to various environments: The meta-learning-based ODG DDQN leverages model similarities and differences to increase learning efficiency. This allows for the reliable training of a universal model across diverse environments, with its performance demonstrated in environments like Gazebo and Real-Environment.

In this context, the purpose and objectives of this study are to propose a stable and efficient reinforcement learning method to effectively address the overestimation phenomenon, learning time, and sparse reward problems faced in the field of autonomous driving. By doing so, we aim to improve the performance of reinforcement learning, overcome the obstacles for implementing autonomous driving systems in real environments, and provide more stable and efficient vehicle control strategies.

The remainder of this paper is organized as follows: in the stable and efficient method section, we mainly introduce the proposed reinforcement learning algorithm. To verify the effectiveness of our work, the experimental evaluations and necessary analysis are presented in the experiment. Finally, we summarize our work in the Conclusions section.

2. Stable and Efficient Reinforcement Learning Method

LiDAR (light detection and ranging) information serves as an invaluable perspective for autonomous driving systems, functioning much like a driver's sense by identifying obstacles through environmental analysis. LiDAR-based RL methods have found extensive application in research focused on judgement and control within autonomous driving systems such as the partially observable Markov decision process (POMDP) [23]. However, learning methodologies based on Q-learning, such as DDQN, encounter persistent overestimation issues, posing obstacles to the enhancement of learning efficiency and convergence speed.

To mitigate these issues, we propose a method that preprocesses and transforms the LiDAR value into valuable information attuned to the operating environment, implementing it as the ODG technique [24]. This approach, as depicted by the ODG module (in yellow) of Figure 1, is designed to reduce learning convergence time and boost efficiency by preprocessing RL input data, thus remedying scenarios with inaccurate action values. Furthermore, we introduce the concept of prior knowledge to address the sparse rewards issue that impedes RL's learning stability [25]. By integrating prior knowledge information from sparse reward sections, as demonstrated in the guide-ODG-DQN framework shown in the guide module (in blue) of Figure 1, we can enhance learning stability.

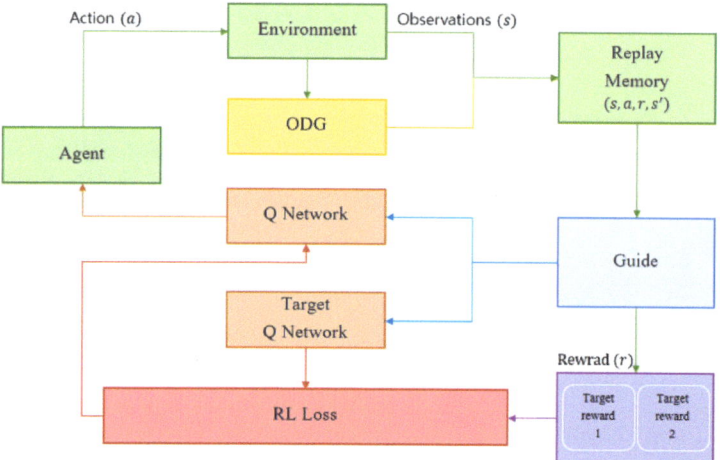

Figure 1. Process flow of stable and efficient reinforcement learning using proposed method.

It is noted that in RL, model performance can decline when the learning environment changes. Thus, we propose the meta-Guide ODG-DDQN method, represented in the target reward module (in purple) in Figure 1, to devise a more robust and adaptable RL algorithm. After training the model according to an initial goal, we modify the reward function to attain subsequent objectives. This approach effectively communicates the action value to the agent in diverse obstacle environments with reliability and swiftness. The proposed methodology consists of three progressively developed algorithms.

2.1. ODG DQN

Overestimation, a consequence of inaccurate action values, is underscored as a critical issue in the DDQN literature [13,26–28]. Traditional LiDAR information incorporates an infinite range, which represents all information at the maximum distance or the value of obstacle-free spaces. This arrangement leads to an overlap of LiDAR information within the system, causing overestimation and impeding the model's ability to select these infinite values. In Q-learning, this predicament can be defined by $Q(s,a) = V_*(s)$ for a given state s, as detailed in Equation (1). When environmental noise triggers an error, it is defined per Equation (2). If the max function is applied at the moment of peak value in Q-learning for action selection, the expression aligns with Equation (3). The bias, symbolized by $\sqrt{C/m-1}$, causes the model to overestimate the bias relative to the optimal value with Q-learning [12,13].

$$\sum_a (Q_t(s,a) - V_*(s)) = 0, \tag{1}$$

$$\frac{1}{m}\sum_a (Q_t(s,a) - V_*(s))^2 = C, \tag{2}$$

$$max_a Q_t(s,a) \geq V_*(s) + \sqrt{\frac{C}{m-1}}, \tag{3}$$

where m is the number of actions and C is a constant.

To address this overestimation, our algorithm utilizes the ODG module to preprocess state values. Illustrated in Figure 2, this module, based on Equation (4) with DQN [6], is engineered to establish an optimized steering angle model for the agent via Q-learning-based RL. This paves the way for the development of an optimized path plan built on the steering angle generated by the agent.

$$Q(s_t, a_t) = \mathbb{E}[r_t + \gamma max_a Q(s_{t+1}, a)]. \tag{4}$$

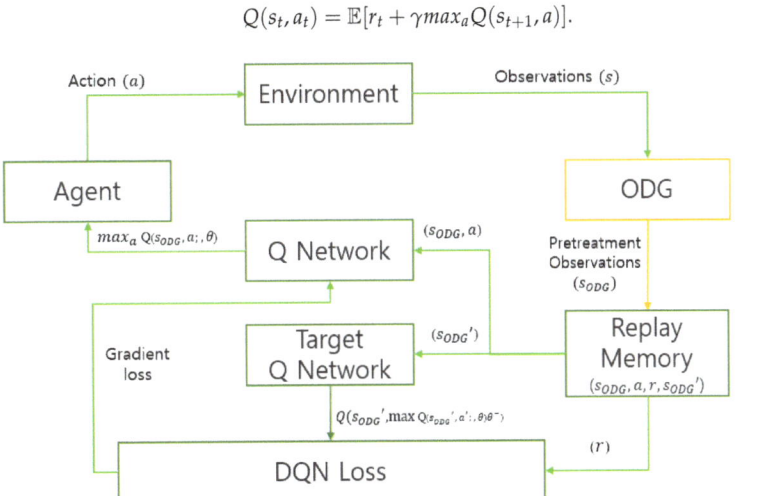

Figure 2. ODG DQN structure.

LiDAR information, a principal component in autonomous driving systems, is preprocessed via the ODG module, subsequently offering the processed data to the RL approach as the state value. Through the use of a Gaussian distribution, the ODG module converts LiDAR information into continuous values. As depicted in Figure 3, the creation of a unique state happens when an agent selects an action, preventing the duplication of action values and facilitating a more efficient selection of the optimal action value in accordance with the equation.

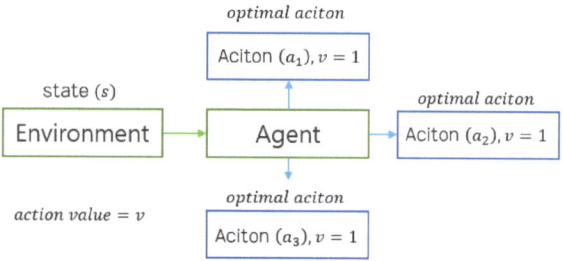

Figure 3. Overestimation in Q-learning.

For the implementation of our proposed algorithm to RL using LiDAR information, a standard procedure in autonomous vehicles, we employ ODG-based preprocessed LiDAR information. As demonstrated in Figure 4, the yellow line corresponds to the original LiDAR data, whereas the blue line symbolizes post-processed data. These data include information on obstacle location and size, derived using Equation (5) with ODG [19].

$$a = f_{rep}(\theta_i) = \sum_{k=1}^{n} A_k \exp\left(-\frac{(\theta_k - \theta_i)^2}{2\sigma_k^2}\right), \quad (5)$$

where

$$A_k = (d_{\max} - d_k) \exp(0.5), \quad (6)$$

$$Q(s_t^\Delta, a_t) = \mathbb{E}[r_t + \gamma max_a Q(s_{t+1}^\Delta, a)]. \quad (7)$$

In contrast to the overlapping LiDAR information provided by conventional methods, ODG supplies non-overlapping LiDAR data, adjusting the maximum range according to the obstacle's size and distance. This preprocessing enables the agent to make more efficient decisions related to optimal action values based on the processed information, thereby enhancing both the speed and efficiency of learning. The reward function used for training is defined in Equation (8).

$$R = R_g + R_v + R_\psi. \quad (8)$$

where R_g represents the target reward, R_v denotes the reward for speed, and R_ψ signifies the reward for steering angle.

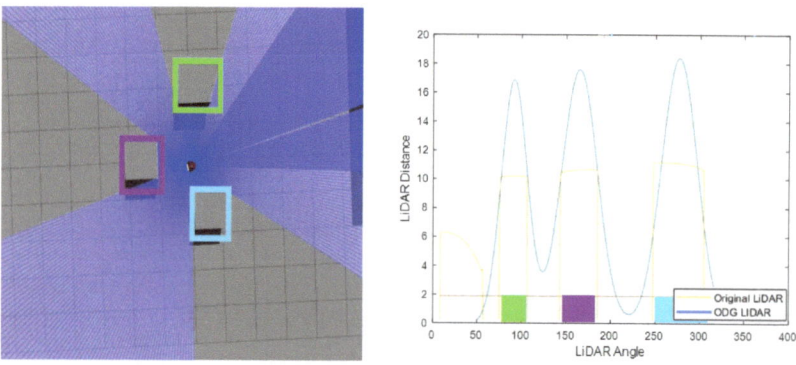

Figure 4. Difference between traditional LiDAR and ODG information.

2.2. Guide ODG DQN

The soft actor critic (SAC) method [29] is a robust approach that allows for the observation of multiple optimal values while avoiding the selection of impractical paths. This facilitates a more extensive policy exploration. The SAC employs an efficient and stable entropy framework for the continuous state and action space. As delineated in Equation (10) with SAC [29], the SAC learns the optimal Q function through updating Q-learning via the maximum entropy RL method.

$$\sum_t \mathbb{E}_{(s_t,a_t)\sim\rho_\pi}[r(s_t,a_t)], \tag{9}$$

$$J(\pi) = \sum_{t=0}^{T} \mathbb{E}_{(s_t,a_t)\sim\rho_\pi}[r(s_t,a_t) + \alpha\mathcal{H}(\pi(\cdot|s_t))]. \tag{10}$$

The algorithm initially makes the guide value sparse and, as learning progresses, gradually densifies it, employing the gamma value as outlined in Equation (12) with SAC [29]. The term min A is representative of the environmental vehicle.

$$min_\psi A < \Delta_\psi < max_\psi A, \tag{11}$$

$$v = max_\psi A - |\Delta_\psi|. \tag{12}$$

A report on hierarchical deep RL, an approach that implements RL via multiple objectives, emphasized the need to solve sparse reward problems as environments become increasingly diverse and complex. Normally, in problems tackled by RL, rewards are generated for each state, like survival time or score. Every state is linked to an action, receives a reward, and identifies the Q-value so as to maximize the sum of the rewards. However, there are instances where a reward may not be received for each state. These scenarios are referred to as sparse rewards.

$$Q(s_t,a_t) = \mathbb{E}[r_t + \alpha\gamma\mathcal{G}max_a Q(s_{t+1},a) + (1-\alpha)\gamma max_a Q(s_{t+1},a)], \tag{13}$$

where

$$\mathcal{G}max_a f(a) := Guide_{action}(S_{t+1}^\Delta). \tag{14}$$

Our proposed solution to these issues is the guide-ODG-DNQ model that integrates SAC with ODG-DQN. This proposed guide-ODG-DQN algorithm transforms the initial Q-value from the state value. This value is extracted from the environment, and it is connected with the ODG formula, which is our prior knowledge, and the LiDAR value extracted with ODG, as depicted in Figure 5. The algorithm extracts a guide action that minimizes the cases where a reward is not received for every state.

The guide-ODG-DQN is designed to store high-quality information values in the replay memory from the outset based on prior knowledge. The agent then continues learning based on this prior knowledge, facilitating easier adaptation to various environments and enabling faster and more stable convergence. Moreover, to prevent over-reliance on prior knowledge that could compromise the effectiveness of RL, the agent learns from its own experiences during the learning process, which are represented by the gamma value. The agent also contrasts this newly learned information with the values derived from the existing prior knowledge. Consequently, our proposed guide-ODG-DQN mitigates the sparse reward phenomenon, thereby enhancing both the stability and efficiency of the learning process.

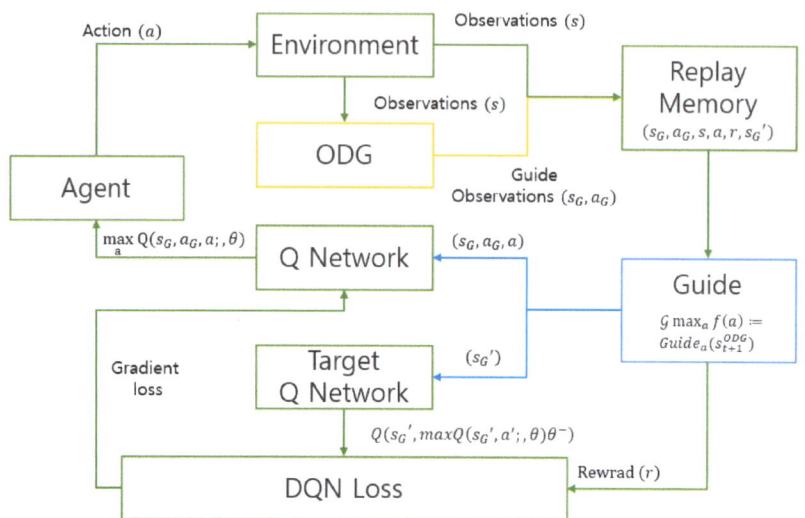

Figure 5. Structure of guide-ODG-DQN.

2.3. Meta-Learning-Based Guide ODG DDQN

RL is fundamentally a process of learning through trial and error. The RL agent must experience a diverse set of situations, making decisions in each scenario to understand which actions yield the highest rewards. Striking a balance between experimentation, to ensure no high-reward actions are overlooked, and leveraging acquired knowledge to maximize rewards is crucial. However, achieving this balance typically necessitates numerous trials and, consequently, large volumes of data. Training an RL agent with excessive data might result in overfitting, wherein the agent conforms too closely to the training data and fails to generalize well to new circumstances.

To overcome these limitations, we introduce a novel method known as meta-learning-based guide-ODG-DDQN. This approach involves storing rewards for each step an integral part of RL in the replay memory, with the stored rewards divided according to the number of targets to be learned as shown in Figure 6. This model facilitates few-shot learning within RL by training the model to recognize similarities and differences, thus preparing it to perform proficiently in unfamiliar environments with minimal data. The training is guided by two main objectives. The first is to train the target model using the initial reward, while the second is to continue learning by reducing the weight assigned to the initial reward and increasing the weight of the reward for the subsequent target, as depicted in Equation (15).

$$R_\Lambda = \gamma R_{J_1} + (1-\gamma) R_{J_2}, \gamma \in [0,1]. \tag{15}$$

By applying our meta-learning-based ODG RL, the model achieves multiple significant outcomes. It allows for the training of a universal model that can operate reliably across various environments. The model's efficiency of learning is boosted due to its ability to identify similarities and differences. Furthermore, learning can proceed using a common target while preserving the existing target. In essence, the proposed algorithms augment the efficiency and stability of traditional RL methods, safely accelerating the learning speed within a virtual environment, which ultimately improves efficiency when the model is implemented in real-world environments.

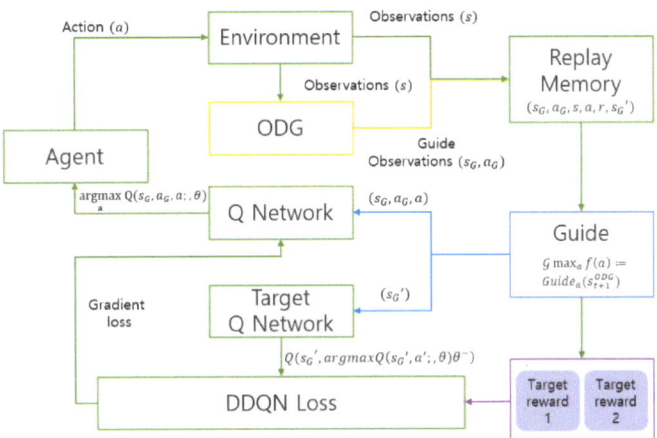

Figure 6. Structure of meta-learning-based guide-ODG-DDQN.

3. Experiment

In the process of validating our proposed algorithm, we conducted an experiment evaluating key aspects such as learning efficiency, stability, strength, and adaptability to complex environments. Learning efficiency was determined by examining the highest reward achieved as learning started to converge, in relation to the number of frames experienced in the virtual environment. The DQN algorithm was used as the basis to analyze the rate of convergence and the magnitude of the reward. For the evaluation of learning stability, we assessed the consistency between the path plan generated through RL (P_{RL}) and the target path produced by ODG (P_{ODG}). Here, P_k represents the set of paths. This assessment involved the use of the root mean square error (RMSE), where P_{RL} and P_i represent the path plans formed through RL and ODG, respectively. The route yielding the highest reward was considered optimal. Finally, we evaluated the algorithm's performance in complex environments. This part of the evaluation was focused on the vehicle's ability to effectively navigate through real world maps, leveraging learning strength. We also tested the resilience and adaptability of the algorithm when faced with unfamiliar scenarios without further training. Metrics such as entry and exit speed, as well as racing track lap time, were used to measure performance. The evaluation environments were chosen with care for distinct aspects of the study: the Gazebo map was used to evaluate learning efficiency and stability, the Sochi map for learning strength, and the Silverstone map to test adaptability to complex conditions, as shown in Figure 7. The experiment setup was designed to reflect real world dimensions, such that each unit length in the simulation corresponded to one meter in reality [30,31].

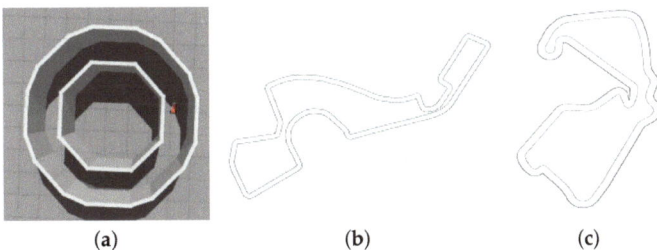

Figure 7. Map environment. (**a**) Gazebo map; (**b**) Sochi map; and (**c**) SILVERSTONE map.

First, the index for learning efficiency is determined as follows. As learning begins to converge, the learning efficiency corresponding to the highest reward for the number of frames (in millions) experienced in the virtual environment is considered. Based on the DQN algorithm, we evaluate how fast convergence occurs and how high the reward is.

Second, the evaluation metric for learning stability assesses how well the path plan generated through RL matches the target path pursued. The path plan created by RL in the virtual environment, P_{RL}, and the path plan created with the ODG, P_{ODG}, are represented in terms of the $RMSE$. Both P_{ODG} and P_{RL} are individually compared with the reference path, and their respective errors are calculated using Equation (16).

$$RMSE = \sqrt{\sum_{i=1}^{n} \frac{(\hat{y}_i - y_i)^2}{n}}, \tag{16}$$

where $\hat{y}_i$ represents the path generated by ODG in P_{ODG}, which is known to exhibit high real-time performance and stability, and y_i corresponds to P_{RL}, which is the path plan generated through RL. The optimal route with the highest reward is considered. n is the number of steps the agent operates in the simulation environment, corresponding to the episodic steps in RL. A smaller $RMSE$ corresponds to a more stable.

Finally, we evaluate the performance in complex environments, as depicted in Figure 7. The assessment metrics focus on how effectively the vehicle navigates through intricate obstacles while ensuring safety and speed. We showcase the learning strength in the Sochi Circuit and the learning diversity in the Silverstone Circuit. For this evaluation, we utilized real maps and employed the metrics of "Enter and Exit Speed" and "Racing Track Lap Time" to assess the agent's performance. In summary, our results demonstrate the learning strength and diversity of the proposed algorithm in handling complex environments and showcase its robustness when encountering new scenarios without further training.

3.1. Learning Performance and Efficiency Evaluation

The hyperparameters used in set up are listed in Table 1. The set up is aimed at verifying the efficiency of the algorithm to be applied in a real environment. Therefore, reducing the learning time is the priority. To evaluate whether learning efficiency and stability are ensure, a basic circular map is selected, and a performance comparison experiment is conducted for each RL algorithm: DQN, ODG-DQN, DDQN, and guide-ODG-DQN. The agent model and environment used in the experiment are shown in Figure 8.

Table 1. Hyperparameters in set up.

	Hyper Parameters
v	car speed $\in [0, 0.7]$ m/s
a	action (steering angle) $\in [-1/3, 1/3]°$
ψ	angular speed = $\in [0, 0.1]$ m/s
τ	update target network = 10,000
α	learning Rate = 0.00025
M_{size}	minibatch Size = 64
γ	discount = 0.99
Eps	exploration Rete = 1
R_v	$v - a * v$
R_ψ	$5 = argmax_\theta d_L$, $0 = otherwise$
R_g	crash = -200, finish = 300, checkpoint = 100

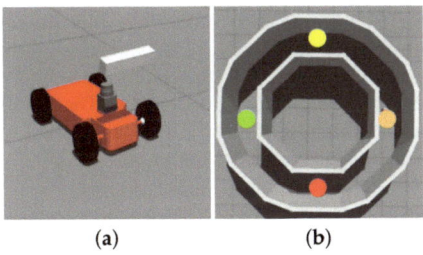

(a)　　　　　　　　(b)

Figure 8. Set up check point and arrival point. End point (red), point1 (orange), point2 (yellow), and point3 (green). (**a**) Agent; (**b**) Check point.

The reward function used for training is defined in Table 1. First, to compare the DQN and ODG-DQN algorithms for the Gazebo map, we determine the number of steps in which the checkpoint is reached during training, as indicated in Table 2. In DQN, over 50% of untrained failure cases are overestimated, whereas in ODG-DQN, 10% of untrained failure cases occur, corresponding to overestimation occurrence reduced by 80%.

Table 2. Epochs of algorithm passing checkpoints the first time. *Fail: Overestimation.*

Experiment	Algorithm (Step)							
	DQN				ODG-DQN			
	P.1	P.2	P.3	P.4	P.1	P.2	P.3	P.4
No. 1	5	10	15	20	4	7	12	18
No. 2	6	14	Fail	Fail	4	9	13	17
No. 3	7	11	16	20	4	7	12	16
No. 4	Fail	Fail	Fail	Fail	4	8	12	17
No. 5	Fail	Fail	Fail	Fail	5	8	12	18
No. 6	6	12	16	20	5	8	12	17
No. 7	5	10	16	19	4	8	13	17
No. 8	5	13	15	19	4	9	12	17
No. 9	Fail	Fail	Fail	Fail	4	8	Fail	Fail
No. 10	Fail	Fail	Fail	Fail	5	9	12	17
Average	5.75	13.3	15.6	19.6	4.3	8.9	12.2	17.1

Guide-ODG-DQN and DDQN are compared under the same conditions. Figure 9a shows the results of learning in terms of the epoch values of the safe convergence section for each algorithm implemented 10 times. As indicated in Table 3, the learning convergence rate increases by 51.7%, 89%, and 16.8%, respectively, compared with the other algorithm. Figure 9b shows that the learning is inappropriate due to overestimation in the case of DQN. In the cases of ODG-DQN, DDQN, and guide-ODG-DQN, learning converges at approximately 500, 300, and 200 epochs, respectively the results are summarized in Table 4.

Table 3. Decrease in the epochs of ODG-DQN.

Algorithm	Decrease in the Epochs
DQN → ODG-DQN	51.7%
DQN → guide-ODG-DQN	89%
DDQN → guide-ODG-DQN	16.8%

Next, to evaluate the stability of the RL results, the center line corresponding to the Gazebo map is applied as a reference. The path generated by each algorithm is shown in Figure 9a. Moreover, Table 5 shows the results obtained by comparing the algorithms in terms of the RMSE, as defined in Equation (16). The RMSE for guide-ODG-DQN is 0.04, corresponding to the highest stability. The guide-ODG-DQN achieves the lowest RMSE, corresponding to the highest stability, as shown in Figure 9c.

Table 4. Summary of normalized performance up to 10 cycles of play on track. *Fail: Overestimation.*

Experiment	Algorithm (Epoch)			
	DQN	ODG DQN	DDQN	Guide ODG DQN
No. 1	1342	587	181	134
No. 2	Fail	621	175	175
No. 3	1416	576	177	121
No. 4	Fail	572	201	143
No. 5	Fail	610	182	172
No. 6	1321	593	177	144
No. 7	1422	631	188	155
No. 8	1452	579	192	177
No. 9	Fail	Fail	181	165
No. 10	Fail	668	185	143
Average Value	1391	672	184	153

Table 5. RL RMSE.

Algorithm	RMSE
DQN	0.0745
ODG-DQN	0.1142
DDQN	0.1082
Guide-ODG-DQN	0.0395

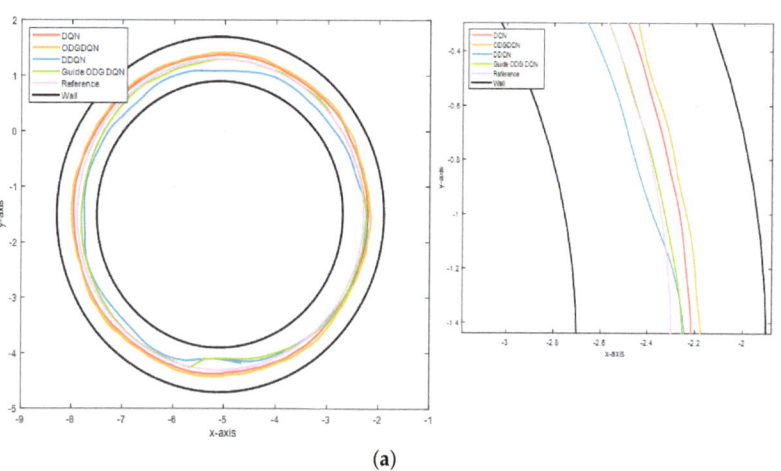

(a)

Figure 9. *Cont.*

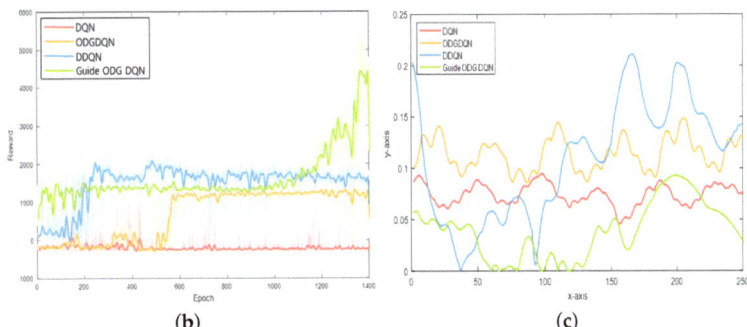

(b) (c)

Figure 9. Experiment set up result. (**a**) RL algorithm path comparison; (**b**) RL reward graph; and (**c**) RL RMS.

3.2. Results through Simulation that Mimics the Real Environment

The hyperparameters values used in circuit are listed in Table 6. As the evaluation metric for a complex environment, shown in Figure 10a, the method of learning the speed is considered instead of that for learning angles. Therefore, the angle is set to that associated with the ODG to ensure stability. The reward function used for all RL frameworks is the same as that defined in Table 6. Figure 10b shows the official competition map provided by F1TENTH. Using the control point specified in the actual Sochi Autodrom map, we compare the path in the winding road and hairpin curve.

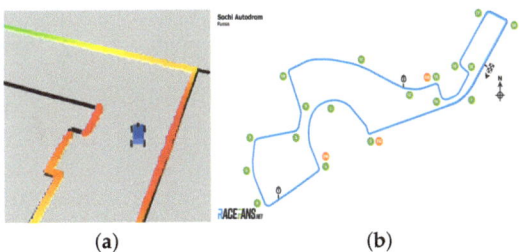

(a) (b)

Figure 10. Actual existing Sochi Autodrom map information, officially provided by F1TENTH. (**a**) Agent; (**b**) control point.

Table 6. Hyperparameters for the F1TENTH.

	Hyperparameters
a	action (car speed) $\in [0, 20]$ m/s
Δ_ψ	ODG steering angle $\in [-12, 12]°$
max_v	max car speed = 20 m/s
τ	update target network = 10,000
α	learning rate = 0.00001
M_{size}	minibatch size = 128
γ	discount = 0.99
Eps	exploration rate = 1
R_Λ	$a - max_v - |\Delta_\psi|$
R_ψ	$100 = argmax_\theta d_L$, $0 =$ otherwise
R_g	crash = -100, finish = 200, and episode step = $episode_\Lambda$

The agent starts at the wall of control point 1. Linear velocity graphs for ODG, Gap Follower, DDQN, and meta ODG DDQN are shown in Figure 13. In this case, 100 points on the x-axis are used as control points, and 100-step linear velocity values are output on both sides based on these values.

3.2.1. Sochi International Street Circuit

The Sochi Autodrom, previously known as the Sochi International Street Circuit and the Sochi Olympic Park Circuit, is a 5.848 km permanent race track in the settlement of Sirius next to the Black Sea resort town of Sochi in Krasnodar Krai, Russia, as shown in Figure 11. Here, the learning strength is demonstrated, in the Sochi Circuit.

(a) (b)

Figure 11. Circuit. (a) Sochi International Street Circuit; (b) Silverstone Circuit.

Table 7 lists the average speed for each control point for each algorithm. Table 7 shows that the ODG algorithm that prioritizes stability achieves the lowest value of 7.66, and the meta ODG DDQN achieves the highest value of 8.58. In other words, the meta ODG DDQN completes the Sochi Autodrom with a speed 12.01% higher than that of the ODG.

Table 7. Average speed control point.

Method	Algorithm			
	ODG	Gap Follower	DDQN	Meta ODG DDQN
No. 1	8.98	7.98	8.23	8.48
No. 2	8.10	7.79	7.93	8.69
No. 3	8.04	8.02	7.78	**8.86**
No. 4	7.74	7.75	8.26	8.60
No. 5	7.84	7.79	7.94	8.49
No. 6	8.41	7.95	8.59	8.66
No. 7	7.58	7.76	8.35	8.59
No. 8	7.71	7.72	8.24	**8.25**
No. 9	7.41	7.67	7.81	8.34
No. 10	7.82	7.72	8.17	8.38
No. 11	**9.15**	8.03	**8.66**	8.82
No. 12	9.08	**8.04**	8.23	8.48
No. 13	7.40	7.80	8.53	8.51
No. 14	**5.87**	7.45	8.08	8.73
No. 15	6.89	7.64	8.05	8.70
No. 16	5.44	**7.30**	7.88	8.30
No. 17	7.99	7.69	8.36	8.86
No. 18	6.34	7.42	8.12	8.61
Average speed	**7.66**	7.75	8.17	**8.58**

As shown in Figure 12a, to examine the speeds of entry and exit at the control point, which are of significance in a racing game, the entry and exit speed for each algorithm are presented in Table 8. In the case of ODG, which is an algorithm that prioritizes stability, as shown in Figure 12b, understeer or oversteer does not occur [32,33]. A report on racing high-performance tires [34] indicates that in this driving method, the vehicle enters at a high speed and exits at a low speed.

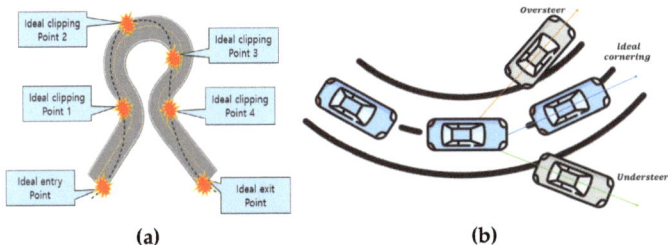

Figure 12. Corner driving: (**a**) clipping point; and (**b**) understeer and oversteer.

As shown in Table 9, ODG selects a drive with a 13.9% speed reduction. The racing algorithm, Gap Follower, uses an out-in-out driving method with a 3.41% deceleration. However, the DDQN and meta ODG DDQN algorithms lead to oversteer to achieve maximum speed based on the angle extracted from the ODG, which pursues stability, causing the vehicle to spin inward compared to the expected route. So, DDQN and meta ODG DDQN show a driving method without deceleration at control points of 1.33% and 0.46%, respectively, by drawing a path.

Table 8. Control point enter and exit speed.

	Enter and Exit Speed (m/s)							
Method	ODG		GAP Follower		DDQN		Meta ODG DDQN	
Control Point	Enter	Exit	Enter	Exit	Enter	Exit	Enter	Exit
No.1	9.46	8.59	7.99	8.04	8.07	8.46	8.42	8.63
No.2	**9.28**	**6.98**	8.07	7.58	8.02	7.91	8.86	8.61
No.3	8.08	8.08	8.05	8.06	7.63	8.00	8.83	8.97
No.4	8.69	6.86	**8.07**	**7.49**	8.16	8.44	8.75	8.54
No.5	8.83	6.92	7.98	7.66	8.21	7.74	**8.54**	**8.51**
No.6	8.59	8.32	7.95	8.03	**8.61**	**8.65**	8.77	8.64
No.7	8.42	6.81	8.05	7.54	8.26	8.51	**8.83**	**8.45**
No.8	8.35	7.15	7.88	7.62	**8.63**	**7.91**	8.25	8.34
No.9	7.11	7.77	7.56	7.86	8.01	7.68	8.24	8.54
No.10	8.97	6.74	8.03	7.49	8.38	8.03	8.34	8.52
No.11	**9.14**	**9.25**	8.06	8.07	8.56	8.84	8.96	8.77
No.12	9.23	9.02	**8.07**	**8.07**	8.35	8.18	8.64	8.41
No.13	8.51	6.37	8.07	7.60	8.70	8.43	8.39	8.72
No.14	6.33	5.48	7.61	7.36	8.43	7.80	8.71	8.85
No.15	7.63	6.22	7.89	7.47	8.13	8.04	8.85	8.65
No.16	5.84	5.07	7.48	7.17	8.05	7.78	8.58	8.10
No.17	8.96	7.09	8.00	7.44	8.42	8.38	9.02	8.79
No.18	7.36	5.39	7.67	7.23	8.18	8.12	8.59	8.72
Average speed	8.27	7.12	7.92	7.65	8.27	8.16	8.64	8.60

Moreover, the lap time is compared for the map shown in Figure 10b by considering two laps (based on the F1TENTH formula). Table 10 indicates that meta ODG DDQN achieves the highest speed.

Linear velocity graphs for ODG, Gap Follower, DDQN, and meta ODG DDQN are shown in Figure 13; using the control point specified in the actual Sochi Circuit, we compare the path in the winding road and hairpin curve, as shown in Figure 14.

Table 9. Enter and exit speed.

Algorithm	Speed Reduction
ODG	13.9%
Gap Follower	3.41%
DDQN	1.33 %
Meta ODG DDQN	0.46%

Table 10. Racing track lap time.

Algorithm	Racing Track 2 Lap Time (s)
ODG	117.09
Gap Follower	115.68
DDQN	115.41
Meta ODG DDQN(ours3)	109.85

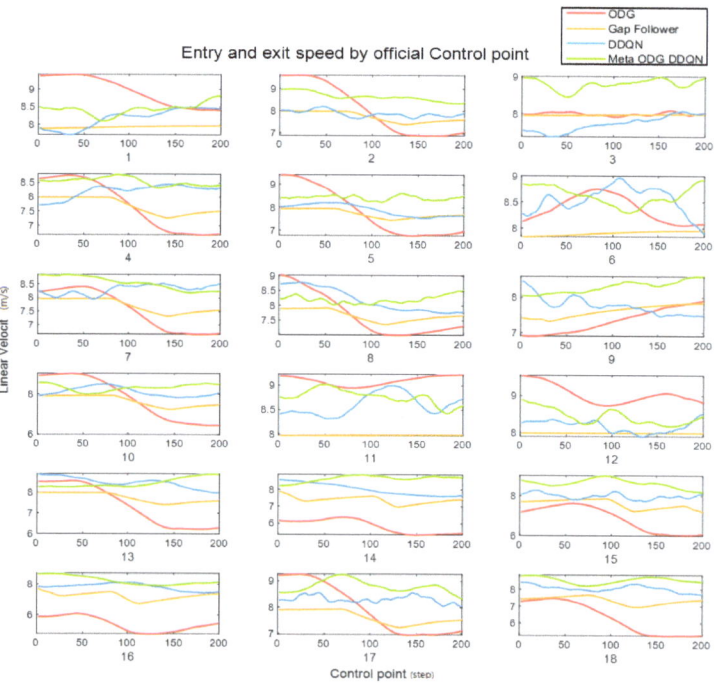

Figure 13. Control point speed.

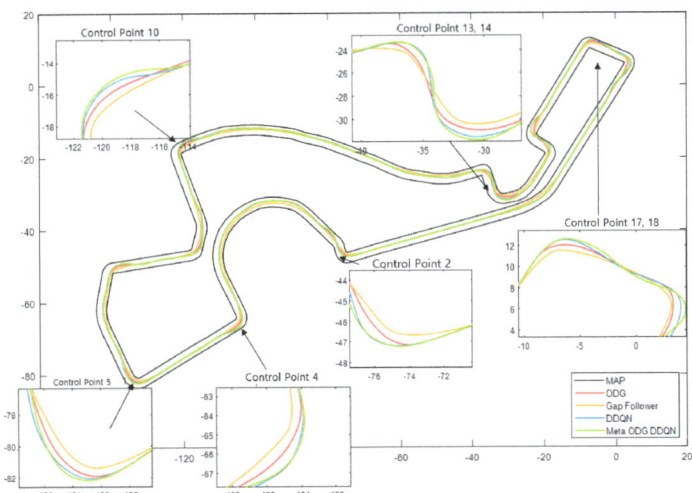

Figure 14. Map of the Sochi path.

3.2.2. Silverstone Circuit

Silverstone Circuit is a motor racing circuit in England, near the Northamptonshire villages of Towcester, Silverstone, and Whittlebury, as shown in Figure 11. In this result, the learning diversity in the Silverstone Circuit is demonstrated.

Using the RL model trained in Map Sochi, we conduct an experiment to determine the degree of robustness to unfamiliar and complex environments. Therefore, we use the algorithms ODG, Gap Follower, DDQN, and meta ODG DDQN. In addition, the meta ODG DDQN algorithm is trained in a new environment. In other words, the robustness of the new environment (c) was compared based on the driving style learned in (b) shown in Figure 7.

Table 11 presents the results for a new environment. DDQN fails; however, meta ODG DDQN exhibits high performance with the lowest lap time, as shown in Figure 15. In this result, the learning diversity in the Silverstone Circuit is demonstrated.

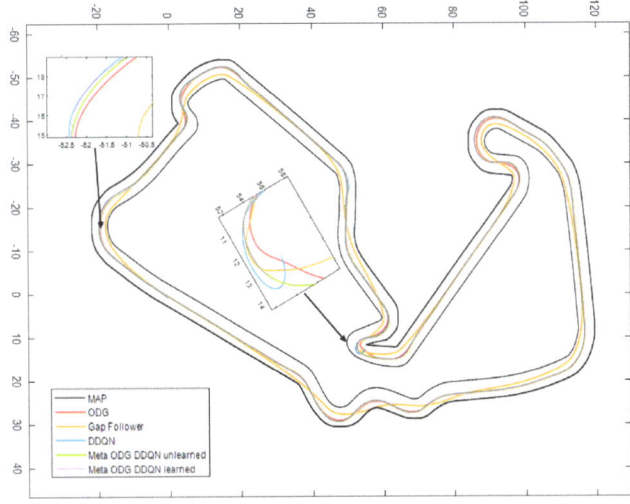

Figure 15. Map (b) SILVERSTONE path.

Table 11. Map (b) SILVERSTONE racing track lap time (two laps). *Fail* = Crash.

Algorithm	Lap Time (s)
ODG	117.39
Gap follower	110.99
DDQN	Fail
Meta ODG DDQN unlearned	108.60
Meta ODG DDQN learned	108.43

4. Conclusions

This paper introduces a novel RL-based autonomous driving system technology that implements ODG, SAC, and meta-learning algorithms. In autonomous driving technology, perception, decision-making, and control processes intertwine and interact. This work addresses the issues of the overestimation phenomenon and sparse rewards problems by applying the concept of prior knowledge. Furthermore, the fusion of meta-learning-based RL yields robust results in previously untrained environments.

The proposed algorithm was tested on official F1 circuits, a racing simulation with complex dynamics. The results of these simulations emphasize the exceptional performance of our method, which exhibits a learning speed up to 89% faster than existing algorithms in these environments. Within the racing context, the disparity between entry and exit speeds is a mere 0.46%, indicating the smallest reduction ratio. Moreover, the average driving speed was found to be up to 12.01% higher.

The primary contributions of this paper comprise a unique combination addressing the challenges of overestimation phenomenon and sparse rewards problems effectively in RL. Another major contribution is the demonstrated robust performance of the integrated meta-learning-based RL in previously untrained environments, thereby showcasing its adaptability and stability. Furthermore, we validated the performance of our proposed method via complex racing simulations, particularly on official F1 circuits. The results highlighted its superior performance in terms of learning efficiency, speed, stability, and adaptability.

In essence, this paper tackles the significant challenges encountered during the reinforcement learning process by introducing an algorithm that bolsters the efficiency and stability of RL. The high-fidelity simulations used in this study offer a realistic testing environment closely mirroring real-world conditions. Given these advancements, our proposed algorithm demonstrates significant potential for real-world applications, particularly in autonomous vehicles where learning efficiency and operational stability are of the utmost importance.

As for future research, we suggest adding various multi-tasks to verify stable and efficient learning in more complex environments. Based on this, we aim to study efficient RLs in real environments through meta-learning, with as few iterations as possible.

Author Contributions: Conceptualization, S.-H.J. and M.-T.L.; formal analysis, S.-H.J., W.-J.A. and M.-T.L.; methodology, S.-H.J., Y.-J.K., M.-T.L. and D.-S.P.; software, S.-H.J., H.-G.H. and D.-S.P.; validation, M.-T.L. and D.-S.P.; writing—original draft, S.-H.J. and M.-T.L.; and writing—review and editing, M.-T.L. and D.-S.P. All authors have read and agreed to the published version of the manuscript.

Funding: This research was supported by the Basic Science Research Program through the National Research Foundation of Korea (NRF) (grant no. NRF-2022R1F1A1073543).

Data Availability Statement: The code used in this paper is attached to the following Github address: https://github.com/jang1229/Gazebo-ODG-DQN; https://github.com/jang1229/F1Thenth-ODGPF.

Conflicts of Interest: The authors declare no conflict of interest.

References

1. Berecz, C.E.; Gabor, K. Dangers in autonomous vehicles. In Proceedings of the 2018 IEEE 18th International Symposium on Computational Intelligence and Informatics (CINTI), Budapest, Hungary, 21–22 November 2018.
2. Hoel, C.J.; Wolff, K.; Laine, L. Automated speed and lane change decision making using deep reinforcement learning. In Proceedings of the 2018 21st International Conference on Intelligent Transportation Systems (ITSC), Maui, HI, USA, 4–7 November 2018; pp. 2148–2155.
3. Qiao, Z.; Muelling, K.; Dolan, J.M.; Palanisamy, P.; Mudalige, P. Automatically generated curriculum based reinforcement learning for autonomous vehicles in urban environment. In Proceedings of the 2018 IEEE Intelligent Vehicles Symposium (IV), Changshu, China, 26–30 June 2018; pp. 1233–1238.
4. Barreto, A.; Hou, S.; Borsa, D.; Silver, D.; Precup, D. Fast reinforcement learning with generalized policy updates. *Proc. Natl. Acad. Sci. USA* **2020**, *117*, 30079–30087. [CrossRef] [PubMed]
5. Bellman, R. A Markovian decision process. *J. Math. Mech.* **1957**, *6*, 679–684. [CrossRef]
6. Lecun, Y.; Bengio, Y.; Hinton, G. Deep learning. *Nature* **2015**, *521*, 436–444. [CrossRef] [PubMed]
7. Peng, B.; Sun, Q.; Li, S.E.; Kum, D.; Yin, Y.; Wei, J.; Gu, T. End-to-end autonomous driving through dueling double deep Q-network. *Automot. Innov.* **2021**, *4*, 328–337. [CrossRef]
8. Yang, Y.; Pan, Y.; Xu, C.; Wunsch Donald, C. Hamiltonian-driven adaptive dynamic programming with efficient experience replay. *IEEE Trans. Neural Netw. Learn. Syst.* **2022**, 1–13. [CrossRef]
9. Sutton, R.S.; Barto Andrew, G. *Reinforcement Learning: An Introduction*; MIT Press: Cambridge, MA, USA, 2018.
10. Gangopadhyay, B.; Soora, H.; Dasgupta, P. Hierarchical program-triggered reinforcement learning agents for automated driving. *IEEE Trans. Intell. Transp. Syst.* **2021**, *23*, 10902–10911. [CrossRef]
11. Dayal, A.; Cenkeramaddi, L.R.; Jha, A. Reward criteria impact on the performance of reinforcement learning agent for autonomous navigation. *Appl. Soft Comput.* **2022**, *126*, 109241. [CrossRef]
12. Watkins, C.; Dayan, P. Q-learning. *Mach. Learn.* **1992**, *8*, 279–292. [CrossRef]
13. Van Hasselt, H.; Guez, A.; Silver, D. Deep reinforcement learning with double q-learning. *Proc. Aaai Conf. Artif. Intell.* **2016**, *30*. [CrossRef]
14. Mnih, V.; Kavukcuoglu, K.; Silver, D.; Rusu, A.A.; Veness, J.; Bellemare, M.G.; Graves, A.; Riedmiller, M.; Fidjeland, A.K.; Ostrovski, G.; et al. Human-level control through deep reinforcement learning. *Nature* **2015**, *518*, 529–533. [CrossRef]
15. Wang, Z.; Schaul, T.; Hessel, M.; Hasselt, H.; Lanctot, M.; Freitas, N. Dueling network architectures for deep reinforcement learning. *Int. Conf. Mach. Learn.* **2016**, *48*, 1995–2003.
16. Burrell, J. How the machine 'thinks': Understanding opacity in machine learning algorithms. *Big Data Soc.* **2016**, *3*, 2053951715622512. [CrossRef]
17. Bai, C.; Wang, L.; Wang, Y.; Wang, Z.; Zhao, R.; Bai, C.; Liu, P. Addressing hindsight bias in multigoal reinforcement learning. *IEEE Trans. Cybern.* **2021**, *53*, 392–405. [CrossRef] [PubMed]
18. Kulkarni, T.D.; Narasimhan, K.; Saeedi, A.; Tenenbaum, J. Hierarchical deep reinforcement learning: Integrating temporal abstraction and intrinsic motivation. *Adv. Neural Inf. Process. Syst.* **2016**, *29*, 3675–3683.
19. Cho, J.H.; Pae, D.S.; Lim, M.T.; Kang, T.K. A real-time obstacle avoidance method for autonomous vehicles using an obstacle dependent Gaussian potential field. *J. Adv. Transp.* **2018**, *2018*, 5041401. [CrossRef]
20. Pae, D.S.; Kin, G.H.; Kang, T.K.; Lim, M.T. Path Planning Based on Obstacle-Dependent Gaussian Model Predictive Control for Autonomous Driving. *Appl. Sci.* **2021**, *11*, 3703. [CrossRef]
21. Kim, J.C.; Pae, D.S.; Lim, M.T. Obstacle Avoidance Path Planning based on Output Constrained Model Predictive Control. *Int. J. Control. Autom. Syst.* **2019**, *17*, 2850–2861. [CrossRef]
22. Botvinick, M.; Ritter, S.; Wang, J.X.; Kurth-Nelson, Z.; Blundell, C.; Hassabis, D. Reinforcement learning, fast and slow. *Trends Cogn. Sci.* **2019**, *23*, 408–422. [CrossRef]
23. Sallab, A.; Abdou, M.; Perot, E.; Yogamani, S. Deep reinforcement learning framework for autonomous driving. *Electron. Imaging* **2017**, *2017*, 70–76. [CrossRef]
24. Korah, T.; Medasani, S.; Owechko, Y. Strip histogram grid for efficient lidar segmentation from urban environments. In Proceedings of the Computer Vision and Pattern Recognition 2011 Workshops, Colorado Springs, CO, USA, 20–25 June 2011; pp. 74–81.
25. Ramachandran, D.; Amir, E. Bayesian Inverse Reinforcement Learning. *Int. Jt. Conf. Artif. Intell.* **2007**, *7*, 2586–2591.
26. Cetin, E.; Oya, C. Learning Pessimism for Reinforcement Learning. *Proc. Aaai Conf. Artif. Intell.* **2023**, *37*, 6971–6979. [CrossRef]
27. Menache, I.; Shie, M.; Nahum, S. Basis function adaptation in temporal difference reinforcement learning. *Ann. Oper. Res.* **2005**, *134*, 215–238. [CrossRef]
28. Meng, L.; Rob, G.; Dana, K. The effect of multi-step methods on overestimation in deep reinforcement learning. In Proceedings of the 2020 25th International Conference on Pattern Recognition (ICPR), Milan, Italy, 10–15 January 2021.
29. Haarnoja, T.; Zhou, A.; Abbeel, P.; Levine, S. Soft actor-critic: Off-policy maximum entropy deep reinforcement learning with a stochastic actor. *Int. Conf. Mach. Learn.* **2018**, *80*, 1861–1870.
30. Ueter, N.; Chen, K.; Chen, J. TProject-based CPS education: A case study of an autonomous driving student project. *IEEE Des. Test* **2020**, *37*, 39–46. [CrossRef]

31. Betz, J.; Zheng, H.; Liniger, A.; Rosolia, U.; Karle, P.; Behl, M.; Krovi, V.; Mangharam, R. Autonomous vehicles on the edge: A survey on autonomous vehicle racing. *IEEE Open J. Intell. Transp. Syst.* **2022**, *3*, 458–488. [CrossRef]
32. Hosseinian, A.A.; Melzi, S. Numerical analysis of the influence of an actively controlled spoiler on the handling of a sports car. *J. Vib. Control* **2018**, *24*, 5437–5448. [CrossRef]
33. Nguyen, T.A. Establishing the Dynamics Model of the Vehicle Using the 4-Wheels Steering Systems. *Math. Model. Eng. Probl.* **2020**, *7*, 436–440. [CrossRef]
34. Paul, H. *The Racing High-Performance Tire: Using Tires to Tune for Grip Balance (R-351)*; Society of Automotive Engineers Inc.: Warrendale, PA, USA, 2003; pp. 60–61.

Disclaimer/Publisher's Note: The statements, opinions and data contained in all publications are solely those of the individual author(s) and contributor(s) and not of MDPI and/or the editor(s). MDPI and/or the editor(s) disclaim responsibility for any injury to people or property resulting from any ideas, methods, instructions or products referred to in the content.

Article

A Two-Stage Image Inpainting Technique for Old Photographs Based on Transfer Learning

Mingju Chen [1,2], Zhengxu Duan [1,2,*], Lan Li [3,*], Sihang Yi [1,2] and Anle Cui [1,2]

1. School of Automation and Information Engineering, Sichuan University of Science & Engineering, Yibin 644002, China
2. Artificial Intelligence Key Laboratory of Sichuan Province, Sichuan University of Science & Engineering, Yibin 644002, China
3. Sinograin Chengdu Grain Reserve, Chengdu 610000, China
* Correspondence: 321085404416@stu.suse.edu.cn (Z.D.); lilansinograin@163.com (L.L.)

Abstract: To address the challenge of sparse old photo datasets, we apply transfer learning to image inpainting tasks. Specifically, we improve a two-stage image inpainting network that focuses on collaborative subtasks. We also design a transform module based on the cross-aggregation of windows to improve long-distance contextual information acquisition in image inpainting and enhance the integrity of images in terms of structure and texture. Our improved two-stage network has a significantly better repair performance compared to that of the current common inpainting methods. We further apply transfer learning techniques by utilizing the improved two-stage image inpainting network as the base network and decoupling the generator into a feature extractor and classifier, which consist of an encoder and a decoder, respectively. We obtain a domain-invariant feature extractor through minimax game training using source and target domain data. This feature extractor can be combined with the original encoder to restore old photo images. To verify the effectiveness of our approach, we conducted comparative experiments. Our results show that the PSNR, SSIM, and FID indexes of the model using transfer learning are 11.8%, 2.96%, and 44.4% higher than those without transfer learning, respectively. These findings suggest that applying transfer learning techniques can be an effective solution to address the challenge of sparse old photo datasets in image inpainting tasks.

Keywords: deep learning; transfer learning; old photos images inpainting; generative adversarial network

Citation: Chen, M.; Duan, Z.; Li, L.; Yi, S.; Cui, A. A Two-Stage Image Inpainting Technique for Old Photographs Based on Transfer Learning. *Electronics* **2023**, *12*, 3221. https://doi.org/10.3390/electronics12153221

Academic Editors: Vladimir Laslo Tadić and Peter Odry

Received: 4 July 2023
Revised: 22 July 2023
Accepted: 24 July 2023
Published: 25 July 2023

Copyright: © 2023 by the authors. Licensee MDPI, Basel, Switzerland. This article is an open access article distributed under the terms and conditions of the Creative Commons Attribution (CC BY) license (https://creativecommons.org/licenses/by/4.0/).

1. Introduction

Photographs serve as important records of specific times and are a crucial tool for documenting historical development and family changes in modern times. However, early paper photographs were prone to damage due to the use of poor technology and preservation practices. To address the challenges of preserving paper photographs, digital image inpainting technology can be used to restore old and damaged photographs to their original appearance as much as possible [1,2]. Traditional image inpainting algorithms mainly include partial differential algorithms [3–5] and texture synthesis algorithms [6,7], which have obvious limitations due to the use of only the peripheral information surviving in the original image. When repairing complex and non-repetitive structures, these algorithms may produce unsatisfactory results.

In recent years, there has been significant progress in the use of deep learning techniques in computer vision and image processing, and the use of large numbers of images to train networks has enabled trained models to have a significant amount of prior knowledge, providing a new approach to image inpainting [8]. In particular, Generative Adversarial Networks [9] have been proposed and achieved promising results in image inpainting tasks [10]. Pathak et al. [11] designed and applied GANs based on traditional Convolutional

Neural Networks and proposed Context Encoders to send the output of the network to a discriminator to detect the truth, which greatly improved the plausibility of the results. However, the performance of neural networks typically depends on a large amount of training data, which makes them unsuitable for areas with minimal training data, changing scenarios, and changing tasks. To address the challenge posed by sparse samples of old photos, this paper introduces transfer learning to transfer the trained model on open-source datasets to the small dataset collected by us, so that the final model can have a generalization performance using standard datasets. Specifically, the portability of deep features [12] is used to map images with intermediate- or high-level features using pre-trained models and train target-specific classifiers from them [13], which is a process commonly referred to as feature selection. Fine-tuning the source model for the target data is also feasible, and it usually is more effective as it optimizes the entire network for the target task. Therefore, fine tuning has become the rule of thumb for deep transfer learning with limited domain data [14,15]. During the fine-tuning process, the source model needs to be moderately tuned to avoid overfitting, as deep networks are over-parameterized for small-scale target tasks. Unlike traditional machine learning and deep learning, which require labeled data for model training, transfer learning can use previously accumulated knowledge to discover commonalities in problems and apply generic knowledge learned in certain tasks to similar tasks, enabling the model to learn in a more generalized manner.

As there have been only a few studies on the application of transfer learning in the field of image inpainting, this paper aims to address this gap by introducing transfer learning into the two-stage inpainting network for training. Due to the limited number of self-collected old photo data samples, overfitting and other issues are likely to occur during the training of deep neural networks. Therefore, this paper proposes a transfer learning-based approach for inpainting damaged old photos, which allows the effective training of a better model using only a small number of old photo samples. The main contributions of this paper are as follows:

- In this paper, a two-stage image inpainting network is constructed, which embeds images into two collaborative subtasks, which are structure generation and texture synthesis under structure constraints, and embeds the window cross aggregation-based transform module into the generator, which can effectively acquire the image long-range dependencies, thereby solving the problem that convolutional operations are limited to local feature extraction and enhancing the long-range contextual information acquisition capability of the model in image inpainting.
- Transfer learning is applied to image inpainting technology. The improved two-stage image inpainting network in this paper is used as the basic network, and the generator is decoupled into a feature extractor and classifier, which are an encoder and a decoder, respectively. A domain-invariant feature extractor is obtained through the training of the minimax game using source domain data and target domain data. The feature extractor can be combined with the original encoder to repair the old photo image, and the restoration of small sample old photo image dataset is realized.
- The experiments demonstrate that the two-stage network constructed in this paper has a better inpainting performance, and the inpainting of old photos using the transfer learning technique is better than that without the use of transfer learning, which proves the effectiveness of the method.

2. Related Work

2.1. Image Inpainting Technique

Deep learning's ability to map deep features perfectly fits the requirements of image inpainting and shows the direction for new image inpainting methods. Recently, Nazeri et al. [16] proposed a two-stage GAN model named "EC". The model combines the two stages of edge information prediction and image inpainting. It first generates the edge map of the missing region, and then sends it into the inpainting network as the guiding information for image inpainting, obtaining a relatively good restoration effect.

Xiong et al. [17] demonstrated a similar model that, unlike EC, uses foreground object contours as a structural prior instead of edges for information. Ren et al. [18] pointed out that edge-preserving, smoothed images provide a better global structure due to them capturing more semantics, but these methods require a higher accuracy for structures, for instance, edges and contours. Some researchers have utilized the correlation between texture and structure to solve this problem. Li et al. [19] designed a progressive visual structure reconstruction network to progressively reconstruct structures and their associated visual features. They entangle the reconstruction of visual structures and visual features to benefit each other by sharing the parameters. Yang et al. [20] introduced a multitasking framework to generate sharp edges by adding structural constraints. Liu et al. [21] proposed a mutual coding decoding to simultaneously learn about convolutional features that correspond to different layers of structure and texture. However, a single shared framework is difficult for modeling textures and structures. Therefore, in order to effectively realize the restoration of image structure and texture information, Guo [22] et al. divided image inpainting into two subtasks, texture synthesis and structure reconstruction. They proposed a new dual-stream network for image inpainting to further improve the performance of image inpainting. Since existing image inpainting techniques are outputting only one restoration result for a broken image, but the nature of image inpainting is an uncertain task, and its output should not be limited. Based on this idea, Liu [23] et al. proposed a probabilistic diverse GAN algorithm. The closer to the center of the image hole that the area studied is, the higher its diversity is, and the more diverse it is, and thus, good results are obtained.

2.2. Transfer Learning Method

Deep learning-based transfer learning methods, that is, deep transfer learning aiming to reduce the time and cost of the training process, have become a popular research direction at present. In some domains (e.g., medical images, etc.) [24], there is the problem of difficulty in obtaining large datasets. Transfer learning provides a better solution for these domains. In addition, pre-trained models for specific jobs can be applied on simple edge devices with a limited processing power and training time, and the development of deep transfer learning opens the door to more intuitive and sophisticated artificial intelligence. Ge et al. [25] developed a method for fine-tuning by using additional data obtained from a large-scale dataset. Cui et al. [26] successfully applied the knowledge learned from large-scale datasets to domain-specific small-scale data through fine-tuning and won first place in the 2017 iNaturalist large-scale species classification challenge. As a result, their research provides new ideas for subsequent deep transfer learning. For example, Long et al. [27] proposed a new Deep Adaptation Network based on this, which generalizes deep Convolutional Neural Networks to new domain-adapted scenarios where Deep Adaptation Networks can learn transferable features with statistical guarantees and scale linearly using the unbiased estimation of kernel embeddings. Tzeng et al. [28] developed a method based on using GANs to train encoders for target samples. They use an adaptation layer to compute the Maximum Mean Difference between the source and target domain features [29]. Haeusser et al. [30] proposed the utilization of the association between source and target features in the training process. They aim to maximize the invariance of the learned feature domain, while minimizing the error in the source samples. In the field of image inpainting, the combination of deep neural networks and transfer learning technology has been successfully carried out in a preliminary exploration and has been applied to the image inpainting problem under the condition of large mask areas. Chen et al. [31] designed a transfer learning network that, for the first time, accomplished large mask image inpainting guided by a high-level understanding of abstract neuronal representation images. Zhao et al. [32] proposed a small-sample unsupervised joint transfer learning approach that combines fine-tuning with direct transfer training to enable the network to learn knowledge about the target domain.

3. Two-Stage Image Inpainting of Old Photos Based on Transfer Learning

The two-stage image inpainting network constructed in this paper adopts the BIFPN feature fusion network proposed by Li et al. [33], which effectively strengthens the fusion and interaction of information. The original network generator is a two-stream generator. In this paper, a two-stage network is adopted. By embedding the transform module into the generator network in the form of residuals, the distant image dependence relationship can be effectively obtained. This solves the problem that convolution operation is limited to local feature extraction and enhances the model's capability to obtain long-distance contextual information in image restoration. The repair performance of the network has been improved. By applying transfer learning to train the image inpainting network, the large public dataset, CelebA, is used as the source domain, and old photo images are used as the target domain. A domain-invariant feature extractor is obtained, which can cope well with the restoration task of old photo images.

3.1. Two-Stage Image Inpainting Network

The image inpainting network is implemented as a Generative Adversarial Network, where two generators generate texture and structure information, respectively, modeled by a U-Net variant. As shown in Figure 1, both texture and structure generators are encoded–decoded structures, and a structure discriminator and texture discriminator are designed to distinguish the real image from the generated image by estimating the texture and structure features, respectively. The image generated by the generator is sent to the discriminator, together with the real image. The discriminator outputs "True" if the image is real and "False" if the image is generated, prompting the generator to generate images that are similar to the real ones. The structure of the two-stage inpainting network is shown in Figure 1.

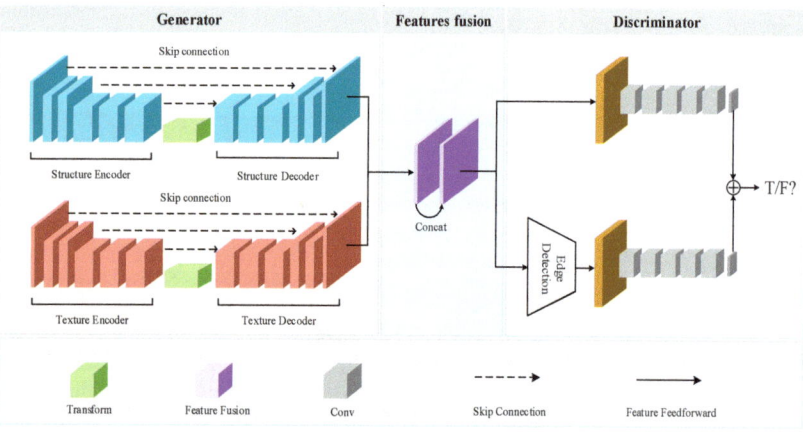

Figure 1. Structure of two-stage image inpainting network.

A transform module based on cross-aggregation of windows is embedded to improve the information aggregation between the windows, without increasing the computational complexity. This improves the aggregation of information between the windows, allowing the effective acquisition of distant image dependencies. This solves the problem that the convolution operation is limited by local feature extraction. The two parallel coupled streams are modeled separately and combined to complement each other, further improving the structural and textural integrity of the generated images.

The two-stage network is described in detail below:

3.1.1. Generator Network

The two-stage image inpainting network uses dual generators, which are a structure generator and a texture generator. In this paper, the inpainting algorithm has different tasks depending on the mask area. In general, it can be seen to complement high-frequency information (structure) and low-frequency information (texture) modeled by a U-Net variant with an encoded–decoded form. This paper uses a dilated convolutional kernel instead of a partially normal convolutional kernel, with the kernel proposed in [34]. This choice simultaneously alleviates the problems of gradient dispersion and gradient explosion, while generating more complex predictions by combining low-level and high-level features at multiple scales through jump connections. The details of the generator structure are shown in Figure 2.

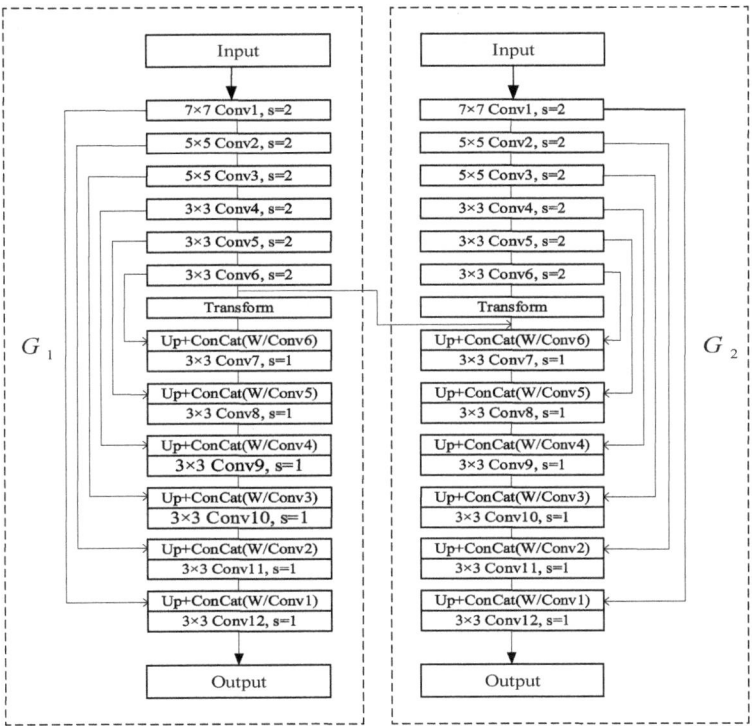

Figure 2. Generator structure detail diagram.

3.1.2. Dual Discriminators

Both the structure discriminator D_1 and the texture discriminator D_2 are selected as spectrally normalized Markov discriminators. The structural parameters are shown in Table 1.

Table 1. Details of the structure of the discriminator network.

Layers Names	Convolution Kernel Size	Step Size	Activation Function	Output Feature Maps
Convolutional layer 1	4 × 4	2	LeakyReLU	64 × 128 × 128
Convolutional layer 2	4 × 4	2	LeakyReLU	128 × 64 × 64
Convolutional layer 3	4 × 4	2	LeakyReLU	256 × 32 × 32
Convolutional layer 4	4 × 4	1	LeakyReLU	512 × 16 × 16
Convolutional layer 5	4 × 4	1	LeakyReLU	512 × 4 × 4
Fully connected layer	-	-	Sigmoid	512 × 1 × 1

However, the structure discriminator and the texture discriminator also differ significantly. The former takes into account the enhancement of its own adversarial loss, which is achieved by inputting pairs of data. In terms of the input data, there are two main points: firstly, the edge map of the fused image derived using the edge detection algorithm, and secondly, the grayed-out image. After the above optimization steps, the structure discriminator is able to steadily improve the similarity between the restored image and the original image, and at the same time, it is able to discriminate whether the structured texture of the restored image is real or not.

The image inpainting algorithm of the two-stage network is divided into three steps to complete the inpainting:

(1) Pre-processing (edge detection). The edge information of the broken image is the prerequisite for the inpainting algorithm. The discovered excellent edge detection algorithm [35] is fused into our proposed two-stage image inpainting algorithm to make it perform the high-precision edge detection of the input broken image before inpainting.

(2) Structure and texture repair. The detected broken edge image, grayscale image, and mask are inputted into the structure encoding generator together to generate a preliminary complete structure image. The complete edge image is inputted into the texture repair generator network together with the broken image to generate a preliminary complete texture image.

(3) The initial structural and textural image information are fused to obtain the complete image, which is then discriminated by the structural discriminator D_1 and textural discriminator D_2. If the generated image is determined as being false, the information is fed back to the generator, and the generator is prompted to adjust the network parameters to generate an image that is more similar to the real image. This iterative process ends when both D_1 and D_2 are unable to distinguish between true and false images.

3.1.3. Aggregation Transform

The transformer [36] omits recursion and convolution and follows an encoder–decoder structure, where the encoder consists of six identical layers, the structure of which is shown in Figure 3, with two sub-layers each. The first layer is a multi-headed self-attentive mechanism, and the second layer is a simple multilayer perceptron. Residual connectivity [37] was used around each of the two sub-layers, followed by layer normalization [38]. The decoder is similar in structure to the encoder in that it also contains six identical layers, with each decoder layer having three sub-layers. The difference is that the attention mechanism layer is embedded in the decoder, ensuring that the prediction of position i depends only on the known output with positions less than i.

The structure of the multi-head self-attentive mechanism and the self-attentive mechanism are shown in Figure 3b,c. For the self-attentive mechanism, the three matrices Q (Queries), K (Keys) and V (Values) all come from the same input, and the calculation formula is shown in (1).

$$\text{Attention}(Q, K, V) = \text{SoftMax}(\frac{QK^T}{\sqrt{d_k}})V \quad (1)$$

where $\frac{QK^T}{\sqrt{d_k}}$ counts the raw score of attention (which is actually the similarity score derived from the dot product of Q and K). $\sqrt{d_k}$ is a scaling factor that keeps the result from being too large or too small and avoids it being either 0 or 1 after softmax.

In the transformer, the self-attentive layer is further refined by adding a multi-headed attention mechanism by first mapping the Queries, Keys, and Values by h different linear transformations. Then, the different attentions are stitched together. Finally, a linear transformation is performed. Each set of attention is used to map the input them into a different sub-representation space, which allows the network model to jointly pay attention to the subspace feature information under different representatives of Queries, Keys, and Values at the same location, while acquiring more detailed features; the computational process can be expressed as:

$$\text{MultiHead}(Q, K, V) = \text{Concat}(head_1, \ldots, head_i)W^o \quad (2)$$

$$head_n = \text{Attention}(QW_n^Q, KW_n^K, VW_n^V) \quad (3)$$

where $W_n^Q \in R^{d_{model} \times d_q}$, $W_n^K \in R^{d_{model} \times d_K}$, and $W_n^V \in R^{d_{model} \times d_V}$ are the Queries, Keys, and Values of the projection matrix with head number k. All the heads ($head_1, \ldots, head_i$) are connected for linear projection to obtain the final result.

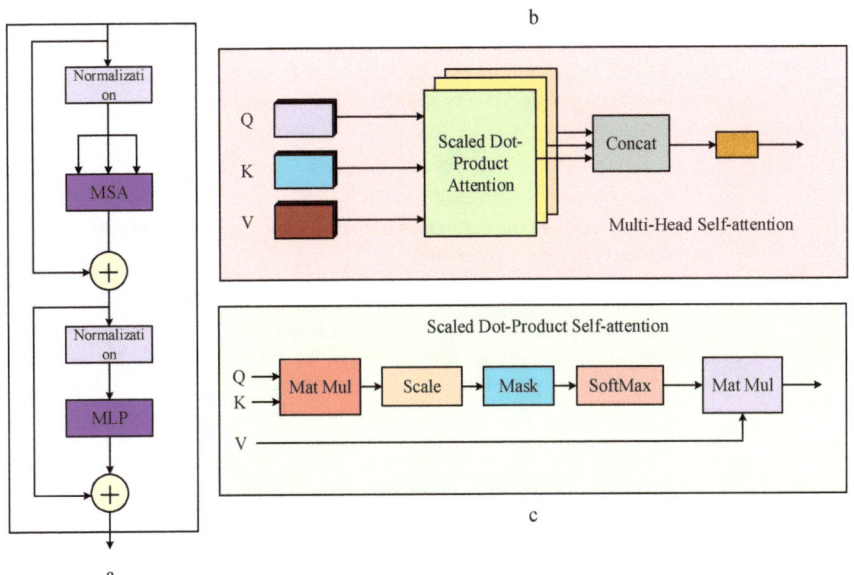

Figure 3. The framework structure of transformer. (**a**) Aggregation Transformer; (**b**) Multi-Head Self-attention; (**c**) Scaled Dot-Product Self-attention.

3.1.4. The Joint Loss Function

The two-stage inpainting network employs semantic-based joint loss training, including feature content loss, reconstruction loss, perceptual loss, style loss, and adversarial loss. By combining the above various loss functions, a complementary effect is achieved, which ultimately enables the restored images generated by the inpainting network to meet not only the visual match with the original image, but also the high accuracy requirements when the hard evaluation of metrics is performed.

(1) Feature content loss

The feature content loss L_f stabilizes the training process by comparing the activation mappings in the middle layer of the discriminator D to constrain the generator G to produce results that are more similar to the true structure map.

$$L_f = E\left[\sum_{i=1}^{n} \frac{1}{N_i} \|D_i(E_{in}) - D_i(E_{out})\|_1\right] \quad (4)$$

where n denotes the total number of convolutional layers of discriminator D, N_i is the number of elements of the i-th layer, and D_i denotes the activation function output of the i-th layer of discriminator D.

(2) Reconstruction loss

The normalized L_1 distance is generally used as the reconstruction loss; however, in this paper, we use the distance L_1 between I_{out} and I_{gt} as the reconstruction loss, with the following equation:

$$L_{rec} = \left\| I_{out} - I_{gt} \right\|_1 \tag{5}$$

(3) Perceptual loss [39]

In order to preserve the structural information of the global image and ensure the similarity of the high-level structure, image restoration requires a feature representation similar to that of the real image, rather than just pixel matching between images. The perceptual loss is calculated using a VGG-16 feature extractor [40] pre-trained on the ImageNet dataset [41] to extract the feature maps of the generated and real images separately and based on the L_1 distance between them; it is defined as follows:

$$L_{perc} = \mathrm{E}\left[\sum_i \left\| \phi_i(I_{out}) - \phi_i(I_{gt}) \right\|_1 \right] \tag{6}$$

where $\phi_i(\cdot)$ denotes the activation mapping obtained for a given input image I^* through the i-th pooling layer of VGG-16.

(4) Style loss

The perceptual loss helps to obtain a higher-level structure and avoid the generated image from deviating from the real image. In order to maintain the style consistency, this paper adds style loss to the joint loss function. The style loss calculates the L_1 distance of the Gram matrix of the feature map generated by the image after VGG-16. The perceptual loss defined as follows:

$$L_{style} = \mathrm{E}\left\{ \sum_i \left\| Gram[\varphi_i(I_{out})] - Gram[\varphi_i(I_{gt})] \right\|_1 \right\} \tag{7}$$

where **Gram** denotes the Clem matrix, $Gram[\varphi_i(\cdot)] = \phi_i(\cdot)^T \phi_i(\cdot)$.

(5) Adversarial loss [42]

Adversarial loss is used to enhance the gaming process of the generative and discriminative networks, aiming to make the data distribution of the generated image more similar to the real image, making the result more realistic. The objective function of the discriminative network is used here, which is defined in Equation (8) is shown as follows:

$$L_{adv} = \min_G \max_D \mathrm{E}_{I_{gt}, E_{gt}}\left[\log D(I_{gt}, E_{gt}) \right] \\ + \mathrm{E}_{I_{out}, E_{out}} \log[1 - G(I_{out}, E_{out})] \tag{8}$$

In summary, the joint loss function is as follows:

$$L_{joint} = \lambda_1 L_f + \lambda_2 L_{rec} + \lambda_3 L_{perc} \\ + \lambda_4 L_{style} + \lambda_5 L_{adv} \tag{9}$$

where $\lambda_1 = 10, \lambda_2 = 10, \lambda_3 = 0.1, \lambda_4 = 250, \lambda_5 = 0.1$.

3.2. Training of the Model

A large public dataset is used as the source domain, and the old photo dataset is used as the target domain, and the training process is made smoother by adding data to the source domain. The goal of this transfer learning is to train a domain-invariant feature extractor, and the training is divided into three main steps, as shown in Figure 4. The solid line indicates that the modules are being trained, and the dashed line indicates the trained models.

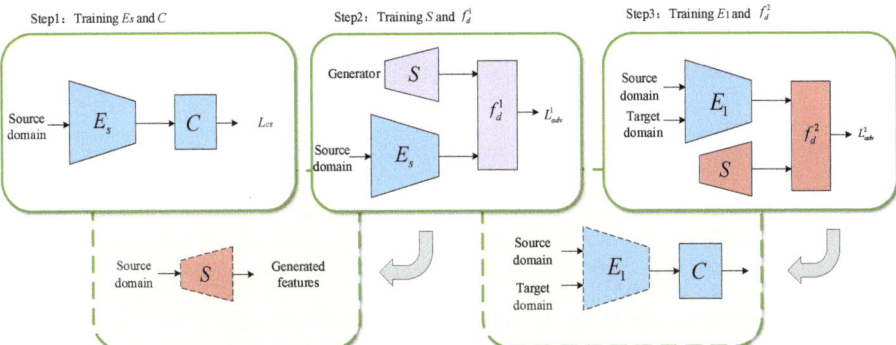

Figure 4. Training procedure.

In the first step, this model is decoupled into a feature extractor E and a classifier C, which are an encoder and a decoder, respectively. During training E_S, one performs feature extraction on the source domain samples, and C denotes the fully connected Softmax layer. Minimized cross-entropy loss is used.

$$L_{CE} = \min_{\theta E_s, \theta C} E_{(x_i) \sim (X_s)} H(C \circ E_s(x_i)) \qquad (10)$$

where θE_s and θC denote the parameters of E_S and C, respectively, X_s denotes the distribution of samples in the source domain, and H denotes the softmax cross-entropy function.

In the second step, the model S is trained to generate feature generators similar to the source domain features, and then training is performed using adversarial loss, as exemplified by the structural generation:

$$L_{adv}^1 = \min_{\theta S} \max_{\theta f_d^1} E_{(z,e_i) \sim (p_z(z),E_i)} \left\| f_d^1(S(z \parallel e_i) \parallel e_i) - 1 \right\|^2 \\ + E_{(e_i,x_i) \sim (E_i,X_i)} \left\| f_d^1(E_s(x_i) \parallel e_i) \right\|^2 \qquad (11)$$

where θS and θf_d denote the parameters of S and f_d, respectively, $p_z(z)$ is the sample distribution extracted from e, and e is the edge feature vector. In order to generate an arbitrary number of new feature samples, it is only necessary for S to take a cascade of noise vectors and an edge feature as an input and to output the desired generated feature vector:

$$F(z|e) = S(z \parallel e) \qquad (12)$$

where $z \sim p_z(z)$ and F are feature vectors belonging to e.

In the third step, after initialization using the weights optimized in step one, the following maximum minimum training domain-invariant encoder E_1 is obtained to achieve optimal convergence.

$$L_{adv}^2 = \min_{\theta E_1} \max_{\theta f_d^2} E_{x_i \sim X_s \cup X_t} \left\| f_d^2(E_1(x_i)) - 1 \right\|^2 \\ + E_{(z,e_i) \sim (p_z(z),E_i)} \left\| f_d^2(S(z \parallel e_i)) \right\|^2 \qquad (13)$$

where θE_1 and θf_d^2 denote the parameters of E_1 and f_d^2, respectively. Since the model E_1 is trained using source and target domains, the results of the feature extractor are domain-invariant. It maps source and target samples in a common feature space, where features are indistinguishable from those generated using S. Since the latter is trained to produce features indistinguishable from the source samples, the feature extractor can be combined with the encoder of step one for image structure feature generation, and the texture generator is consistent with the above steps.

4. Experimental Analysis

4.1. Analysis of Experimental Results of Inpainting Model

We used the CelebA and Places datasets, which are widely used in the literature, to evaluate the proposed approach. We selected 10 categories from Places, each with 5000 training images, 900 test images, and 100 validation images. We used 30,000 images for training and 10,000 images for testing. The mask datasets for the experiments all used irregular masks obtained from [43], classified according to their hole size relative to the whole image in 10% increments; all images and corresponding masks were adjusted to 256 × 256 pixels, the batch size processed was 16 sheets, and 300,000, training iterations were used, optimized using the Adam optimizer [44] with the parameters set to $\beta_1 = 0.001$ and $\beta_2 = 0.9$. The model was first initially trained using a learning rate of 2×10^{-4}, and then fine-tuned with a learning rate of 5×10^{-5}, and the BN layer of the generator was frozen, and the discriminator was trained with a learning rate of $1/10$ of the generator. The deep learning framework used for the experiments was Pytorch, the computer operating system was Windows 10, and the graphics card model was NVIDIA TITAN XP with 12G of video memory.

4.1.1. Qualitative Analysis

To verify the effectiveness of the two-stage image inpainting network proposed in this paper, test sets of the CelebA dataset and the Places dataset were used to compare the subjective as well as numerical results of this paper's method with the MED [21], CTSDG, and BIFPN algorithms. Figure 5 shows the inpainting results of the method in this paper on the CelebA datasets.

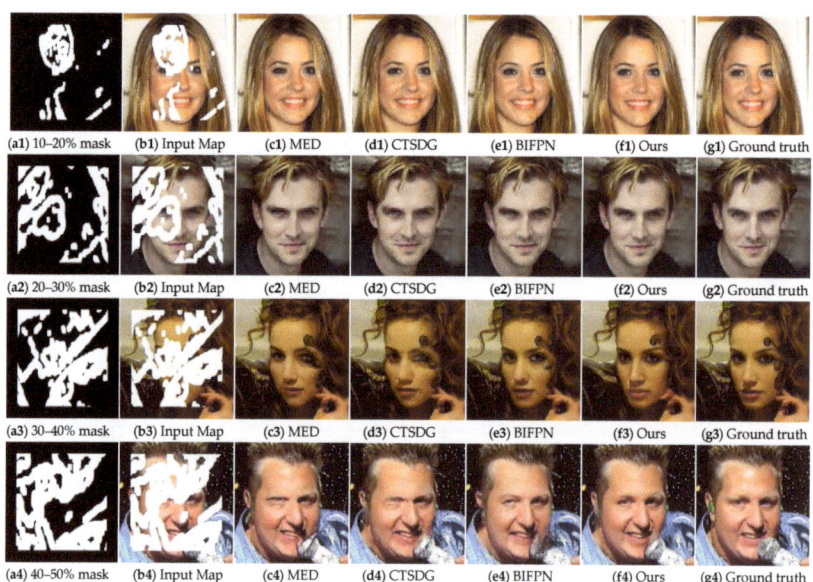

Figure 5. Comparison of qualitative analysis results on CelebA.

Figure 5 shows the inpainting results of MED, CTSDG, BIFPN, and the methods proposed in this paper for different mask rates on the CelebA dataset. It can be observed that all the inpainting methods show a good performance when the mask area is small, specifically when the mask area is 10–20% of the original size, with only minor differences between the original and inpainted result maps. The MED and CTSDG methods (subfigure c2 and subfigure d2, respectively) exhibit varying degrees of blurring at 20–30% of the masked area, whereas the proposed methods maintain good inpainting, with sharper textural and structural properties. At a mask area of 30–40%, the MED, CTSDG, and BIFPN methods (subfigure c3, subfigure d3, and subfigure e3, respectively) all exhibit artifacts and even facial distortions, with some facial features being lost. Although the proposed algorithm also exhibits blurring and distortion, it still yields better inpainting results compared with those of the other three methods. At 40–50% of the masked area, it becomes clear that the restored image from the inpainting other algorithms is significantly distorted and no longer conveys the texture information that the original image should. In contrast, the proposed algorithm maintains a large amount of texture detail, with only a few differences with the ground truth.

Figure 6 shows the inpainting results of MED, CTSDG, BIFPN, and the proposed methods for different mask rates on the Places dataset. It can be observed that most of the inpainting methods show a good performance when the mask area is between 10–20% of the original size, with only MED exhibiting significant distortion. At a mask area of 20–30%, the image itself shows good inpainting due to its characteristics (e.g., the structure information is not obvious), but a detailed comparison reveals that the proposed method yields a clearer texture and structure inpainting performance. At a mask area of 30–40%, the MED, CTSDG, and BIFPN methods (subfigure c3, subfigure d3, and subfigure e3, respectively) exhibit artifacts and even facial distortions, with some image features being lost. At a mask area of 40–50%, it is evident that the remaining three algorithms have lost too many landscape details, with a significant portion of the area lacking texture details, which is significantly different from the results obtained by the proposed algorithm.

Figure 6. Comparison of qualitative analysis results on Places.

4.1.2. Quantitative Analysis

We refer to all the current studies in the field related to image inpainting and decide to adopt the three types of metrics, PSNR, SSIM, and FID, which were all used in quantitative evaluation to evaluate our restored images. At the same time, we designed the comparison experiments with other algorithms, and all algorithms used mask rates in inpainting based on 10–20% with 10% increments. Ultimately, the comparison of the quantitative analysis results clearly shows that the inpainting performance of our proposed algorithm model is much better than that of the other algorithms. The quantitative results of the three metrics for each specific algorithm are shown in Tables 2 and 3.

Table 2. Comparison of quantitative analysis results on CelebA.

	Mask Rate	MED	CTSDG	BIFPN	Ours
PSNR↑	10–20%	28.75	**32.67**	32.11	32.03
	20–30%	26.97	28.13	**28.67**	28.44
	30–40%	23.67	25.32	25.81	**26.43**
	40–50%	22.07	23.46	23.56	**24.79**
SSIM↑	10–20%	0.922	0.958	**0.960**	0.953
	20–30%	0.904	0.917	0.924	**0.931**
	30–40%	0.837	0.852	0.863	**0.882**
	40–50%	0.811	0.826	0.833	**0.841**
FID↓	10–20%	5.63	**2.61**	2.67	2.95
	20–30%	6.79	3.74	3.24	**3.11**
	30–40%	8.64	5.35	5.02	**4.78**
	40–50%	9.11	7.69	7.63	**7.11**

Table 3. Comparison of quantitative analysis results on Places.

	Mask Rate	MED	CTSDG	BIFPN	Ours
PSNR↑	10–20%	28.05	30.54	31.09	**31.86**
	20–30%	25.44	26.55	26.61	**27.14**
	30–40%	22.89	23.73	24.17	**25.71**
	40–50%	21.76	22.54	22.78	**23.64**
SSIM↑	10–20%	0.924	0.929	**0.934**	0.926
	20–30%	0.874	0.897	0.906	**0.907**
	30–40%	0.846	0.856	0.862	**0.873**
	40–50%	0.811	0.826	0.834	**0.842**
FID↓	10–20%	5.71	4.11	3.88	**3.16**
	20–30%	6.59	5.21	4.16	**4.07**
	30–40%	9.14	7.68	7.11	**6.89**
	40–50%	11.54	9.13	8.75	**8.18**

From Table 2, it can be seen that the MED algorithm is clearly at a disadvantage when it needs to deal with the task of CelebA image inpainting at different mask rates. While our proposed algorithm model has its own advantages over the remaining two algorithms when facing different mask rates, it can be found that the model in this paper still significantly outperforms the rest of the algorithms, and this phenomenon can be clearly seen when targeting the image inpainting task of CelebA with high mask rates.

As for the Places dataset in natural scenes, Table 3 shows that the SSIM metrics of our proposed image inpainting model are slightly lower than those of the BIFPN model only at the mask rate interval of 10–20%. When restoration is performed at the rest of the mask rates, the restoration performance of our proposed inpainting model outperforms the rest of the algorithms, and the effect is especially prominent at high mask rates.

In summary, our algorithm outperforms current state-of-the-art image inpainting models.

4.2. Analysis of Old Photo Inpainting Results with Transfer Learning

In this paper, a modified two-stage image inpainting network is used as the base network by employing a model initialized using pre-trained source domain data in the initialization phase of the model. The pre-trained source domain model is trained on the CelebA dataset to obtain the weights. For training, the learning rate of all the fine-tuning layer parameters was 0.1 times the learning rate of the training layer parameters, using an Adam optimizer with momentum set to 0.95. The domain discriminators all use three fully connected layers and the ReLU activation layer. L2 regularization was also used for all the parameters with a factor of 0.1. In order to obtain a more stable representation of the data distribution, the data batch size is set to six for each iteration, and the number of model training iterations is based on the number of traversals of the small dataset, with the maximum number of traversals being 100. The mask dataset used in transfer learning training adopts the irregular mask obtained from [43]. In order to restore the old photo image more realistically, the mask used in the test experiment is extracted from the damaged old photo.

4.2.1. Experimental Content

In order to verify the practicality of the feasibility and effectiveness of transfer learning on old photo image inpainting tasks, we have prepared corresponding comparative experiments. Both sets of experiments used a two-stage inpainting network as the base network, and both sets of experiments were as follows:

Group 1 (without transfer learning): The hybrid dataset was used as the training data for the model, and the model was trained directly without transfer learning, when all the parameters in the model were initialized. (The hybrid dataset is the sum of the CelebA training set and the old photo training set).

Group 2 (using transfer learning): This group was training using transfer learning, and the steps are shown in Figure 4.

4.2.2. Dataset Acquisition and Pre-Processing

In the experiments and results analysis in this paper, it can be concluded that our proposed image inpainting model can obtain a good image inpainting performance; however, when the trained model is applied to the old photo inpainting task, it was found that the model does not restore the old photos well. After analysis, the main reason for the poor robustness of the model is that the open-source dataset is not exactly in the same style as the old photo dataset. Old photographs are subject to fading and blurring due to the limitations of past filming equipment and preservation conditions, and there are significant differences between them and the images obtained from the open-source dataset.

Due to the sparse sample of old photo image dataset, a transfer learning approach is used to implement the task of inpainting of old photos. A total of 316 images of complete old photo faces were collected from the internet, and 91 images of broken or blurred old photos were obtained after screening. The complete old photo images were divided into a training set, a validation set, and a test set in a ratio of approximately 8:1:1, and the results are shown in Table 4:

Table 4. Old photo images segmentation dataset.

	Train Set	Validation Set	Test Set
Old photos	252	32	32

We use the random mask in this paper for training, and in order to make the broken old photos more realistic, the test mask for old photo inpainting uses the broken mask detected from the real broken old photo images as the test mask.

4.2.3. Analysis of Experimental Results

As the core work in this subsection is the task of old photo images inpainting, a subjective comparison was carried out with a focus on the overall inpainting of old photos.

1. Subjective evaluation

An example plot of the comparison results for the first and second groups, respectively, on the old photo dataset is shown below, as shown in Figure 7.

As can be seen in Figure 7, the inpainting results for the first group have significant pixel inconsistencies, as seen in the third row where the shoulders appear to be colored, and in the second row where inconsistent facial colors are observed for the faces. On the other hand, the second group of inpainting results have better consistency, and it can be seen that the inpainted images are largely visually unobstructed.

(a) Mask. (b) Damage map. (c) Group 1. (d) Group 2. (e) Ground truth.

Figure 7. Comparison of qualitative analysis results on old photo datasets.

In summary, the use of transfer learning methods in old photo image inpainting tasks gives more stability and accuracy in the results in terms of structural and texture features. It can produce more realistic results with more natural facial features for face images.

2. Objective evaluation

In order to more objectively evaluate the strengths and weaknesses of the algorithms used in this paper, quantitative analysis experiments were set up. The inpainting results of the two groups of methods were quantitatively analyzed, and the experimental mask used the broken mask detected from the real broken old photo images as the test mask, and the test masks were consistent in both groups, and the quantitative results are shown in Table 5.

Table 5. Objective quantitative comparison on old photos of human faces.

Methods	PSNR	SSIM	FID
Group 1	32.42	0.943	3.62
Group 2	**36.25**	**0.971**	**2.01**

From Table 5, it can be concluded that the use of transfer learning can make the inpainting of old photos more natural, and both PSNR and SSIM are far better than those without the use of transfer learning, which is basically consistent with the results of the qualitative analysis, thus proving the effectiveness of using the method of transfer learning in the inpainting of old photos images.

5. Discussion

At the early stage of the COVID-19 outbreak, it was not possible to conduct relevant research using neural networks because of the sparse dataset samples and the need for neural networks to rely on a large number of datasets for training. Due to this, in this paper, the authors applied transfer learning to the field of image inpainting for the first time. Specifically, the authors took the inpainting of old photo images as the research object, constructed a two-stage image inpainting model, and embedding Transform into the generator in the form of residual blocks, which solves the problem of long-distance feature acquisition that cannot be achieved by convolution. The generator was decoupled into a feature extractor and a classifier, and a domain-invariant feature extractor was trained with a large public dataset as the source domain and an old photo image as the target domain. Experimentally, the application of transfer learning to image inpainting in this paper has achieved initial success and proved the effectiveness of the method. And this work in this paper also provides new ideas for the subsequent research of image inpainting techniques for small sample datasets, so that it can be satisfied with more application scenarios.

6. Conclusions

In this paper, we introduce transfer learning techniques to address the problem of sparse samples of old photo datasets. In order to build an inpainting network more suitable for transfer learning, a two-stream network is decoupled into two parallel streams to form a two-stage network based on the original two-stream structure of the image inpainting model. A dual discriminator is designed to give the model a better inpainting performance by estimating texture and structure separately. Secondly, using a two-stage image inpainting network as the base model, the generator is decoupled into a feature extractor and a classifier, which are an encoder and a decoder, respectively, and a domain-invariant feature extractor is obtained by training the source and target domain data, which can be combined with the original encoder for the inpainting task of old photo images. The experiments show that the inpainting of old photos using transfer learning is better than that without transfer learning, maintaining pixel consistency and reasonableness. In the qualitative experimental analysis, the PSNR, SSIM, and FID indexes of the model using transfer learning are 11.8%, 2.96%, and 44.4% higher than those without transfer learning, respectively.

Author Contributions: M.C. designed the two-stage inpainting network and verified the feasibility of the model by verification; Z.D. proposed the idea of transfer learning inpainting of old photos and conducted transfer learning experiments using the model; S.Y. derived the results of the comparison algorithms and compared them with the method in this paper; A.C. wrote the overall article; L.L. translated and checked the full article and provided the server required for the experiments, etc. All authors have read and agreed to the published version of the manuscript.

Funding: This research was funded by Natural Science Foundation of Sichuan, China (2023NSFSC1987, 2022ZHCG0035); The Opening Fund of Artificial Intelligence Key Laboratory of Sichuan Province (2020RZY03); The Key Laboratory of Internet Information Retrieval of Hainan Province Research Found (2022KY03); The Opening Project of International Joint Research Center for Robotics and Intelligence System of Sichuan Province (JQZN2022-005); Sichuan University of Science & Engineering Postgraduate Innovation Fund Project (Y2022132).

Institutional Review Board Statement: Not applicable.

Informed Consent Statement: Not applicable.

Data Availability Statement: Data are contained within the article.

Conflicts of Interest: The authors declare no conflict of interest.

Abbreviations

GAN (Generative Adversarial Network); EC (EdgeConnect); MED (Mutual Encoder-Decoder); CTSDG (Conditional Texture and Structure Dual Generation); BIFPN (Bi-directional Feature Pyramid Network); PSNR (Peak Signal-to-Noise Ratio); SSIM (Structural Similarity Index Measure); FID (Frechet Inception Distance score).

References

1. Criminisi, A.B.; Perez, P.; Toyama, K. Region Filling and Object Removal by Exemplar-Based Image Inpainting. *IEEE Trans. Image Process.* **2004**, *13*, 200–1212. [CrossRef]
2. Li, L.; Chen, M.J.; Shi, H.D.; Duan, Z.X.; Xiong, X.Z. Multiscale Structure and Texture Feature Fusion for Image Inpainting. *IEEE Access* **2022**, *10*, 82668–82679. [CrossRef]
3. Bertalmio, M.; Sapiro, G.; Caselles, V.; Ballester, C. Image Inpainting. In Proceedings of the 27th Annual Conference on Computer Graphics and Interactive Techniques, New Orleans, LA, USA, 23–28 July 2000; pp. 417–424.
4. Levin, A.; Zomet, A.; Weiss, Y. Learning how to inpaint from global image statistics. In Proceedings of the ICCV, Nice, France, 13–16 October 2003; pp. 305–312.
5. Li, L.; Chen, M.J.; Xiong, X.Z.; Yang, Z.W.; Zhang, J.S. A Continuous Nonlocal Total Variation Image Restoration Model. *Radio Eng.* **2021**, *51*, 864–869.
6. Darabis, S.; Shechtman, E.; Barnes, C.; Goldman, D.B.; Sen, P. Image melding: Combining inconsistent images using patch-based synthesis. *ACM Trans. Graph.* **2021**, *31*, 4. [CrossRef]
7. Efrosa, A.; Freemanw, T. Image quilting for texture synthesis and transfer. In Proceedings of the 28th Annual Conference on Computer Graphics and Interactive Techniques, New York, NY, USA, 12–17 August 2001; pp. 341–346.
8. Yeh, R.A.; Chen, C.; Lim, T.Y.; Schwing, A.G.; Hasegawa-Johnson, M.; Do, M.N. Semantic image inpainting with deep generative models. In Proceedings of the ICCV, Venice, Italy, 22–29 October 2017; pp. 6882–6890.
9. Goodfellow, I.J.; Pouget-Abadie, J.; Mirza, M.; Xu, B.; Warde-Farley, D.; Ozair, S.; Courville, A.; Bengio, Y. Generative adversarial nets. In Proceedings of the NIPS, Montreal, BC, Canada, 8–13 December 2014; pp. 2672–2680.
10. Yu, X. Research on Face Image Inpainting Method Based on Generative Adversarial Network. Master's Thesis, Southwest University of Science and Technology, Mianyang, China, 2022. [CrossRef]
11. Deepak, P.; Philipp, K.; Jeff, D.; Darrell, T.; Efros, A.A. Context encoder: Feature Learning by Inpainting. In Proceedings of the CVPR, Las Vegas, NV, USA, 26 June–1 July 2016; pp. 2536–2544.
12. Jason, Y.; Jeff, C.; Yoshua, B.; Lipson, H. How transferable are features in deep neural networks? In Proceedings of the NIPS, Montreal, BC, Canada, 8–13 December 2014. [CrossRef]
13. Zeiler, M.D.; Rob, F. Visualizing and under-standing convolutional networks. In Proceedings of the ECCV, Zurich, Switzerland, 6–12 September 2014.
14. Azizpour, H.; Razavian, A.S.; Sullivan, J.; Maki, A.; Carlsson, S. Factors of transferability for a generic convnet representation. *IEEE Trans. Pattern Anal. Mach. Intell.* **2016**, *38*, 1790–1802. [CrossRef] [PubMed]
15. Zhao, M.; Kang, M.; Tang, B.; Pecht, M. Deep residual networks with dynamically weighted wavelet coefficients for fault diagnosis of planetary gearboxes. *IEEE Trans. Ind. Electron.* **2017**, *65*, 4290–4300. [CrossRef]
16. Nazeri, K.; Ng, E.; Joseph, T.; Qureshi, F.; Ebrahimi, M. Edgeconnect: Structure guided image inpainting using edge prediction. In Proceedings of the 2019 IEEE/CVF International Conference on Computer Vision Workshop (ICCVW), Seoul, Republic of Korea, 27–28 October 2019.
17. Xiong, W.; Yu, J.; Lin, Z.; Yang, J.; Lu, X.; Barnes, C.; Luo, J. Foreground-aware image inpainting. In Proceedings of the 2019 IEEE Conference on Computer Vision and Pattern Recognition (CVPR), Long Beach, CA, USA, 15–20 June 2019.
18. Ren, Y.; Yu, X.; Zhang, R.; Li, T.H.; Liu, S.; Li, G. Structureflow: Image inpainting via structure-aware appearance flow. In Proceedings of the 2019 IEEE/CVF International Conference on Computer Vision (ICCV), Seoul, Republic of Korea, 27 October–2 November 2019.
19. Li, J.; He, F.; Zhang, L.; Du, B.; Tao, D. Progressive reconstruction of visual structure for image inpainting. In Proceedings of the 2019 IEEE/CVF International Conference on Computer Vision (ICCV), Seoul, Republic of Korea, 27 October–2 November 2019.
20. Yang, J.; Qi, Z.Q.; Shi, Y. Learning to incorporate structure knowledge for image inpainting. In Proceedings of the AAAI Conference on Artificial Intelligence, New York, NY, USA, 7–12 February 2020.
21. Liu, H.; Jiang, B.; Song, Y.; Huang, W.; Yang, C. Rethinking image inpainting via a mutual encoder-decoder with feature equalizations. In Proceedings of the 16th European Conference on Computer Vision (ECCV), Glasgow, UK, 23–28 August 2020.
22. Guo, X.; Yang, H.; Huang, D. Image Inpainting via Conditional Texture and Structure Dual Generation. In Proceedings of the 2021 IEEE/CVF International Conference on Computer Vision (ICCV), Montreal, BC, Canada, 11–17 October 2021; pp. 14114–14123.
23. Liu, H.; Wan, Z.; Huang, W.; Song, Y.; Han, X.; Liao, J. PD-GAN: Probabilistic diverse GAN for image inpainting. In Proceedings of the 2021 IEEE/CVF Conference on Computer Vision and Pattern Recognition (CVPR), Nashville, TN, USA, 20–25 June 2021; pp. 9367–9376.
24. Tan, C.; Sun, F.; Kong, T.; Zhang, W.; Yang, C.; Liu, C. A survey on deep transfer learning. In Proceedings of the International Conference on Artificial Neural Networks, Barcelona, Spain, 5–7 October 2018; pp. 270–279.
25. Ge, W.F.; Yu, Y.Z. Borrowing treasures from the wealthy: Deep transfer learning through selective joint fine-tuning. In Proceedings of the ICCV, Venice, Italy, 22–29 October 2017; pp. 1086–1095.
26. Cui, Y.; Song, Y.; Sun, C.; Howard, A.; Belongie, S. Large scale fine-grained categorization and domain-specific transfer learning. In Proceedings of the CVPR, Salt Lake City, UT, USA, 18–23 June 2018; pp. 4109–4118.
27. Long, M.; Cao, Y.; Wang, J.; Jordan, M. Learning transferable features with deep adaptation networks. In Proceedings of the International Conference on Machine Learning, Lille, France, 7–9 July 2015; pp. 97–105.
28. Tzeng, E.; Hoffman, J.; Zhang, N.; Saenko, K.; Darrell, T. Deep domain confusion: Maximizing for domain invariance. *arXiv* **2014**, arXiv:1412.3474. [CrossRef]

29. Gretton, A.; Borgwardt, K.M.; Rasch, M.J.; Schölkopf, B.; Smola, A. A kernel two-sample test. *J. Mach. Learn. Res.* **2012**, *13*, 723–773.
30. Haeusser, P.; Frerix, T.; Mordvintsev, A.; Cremers, D. Associative domain adaptation. In Proceedings of the ICCV, Venice, Italy, 22–29 October 2017.
31. Chen, H.; Zhang, Z.; Deng, J.; Yin, X. A Novel Transfer-Learning Network for Image Inpainting. In Proceedings of the ICONIP, Sanur, Bali, Indonesia, 8–12 December 2021; pp. 20–27.
32. Zhao, Y.M.; Zhang, Y.X.; Sun, Z.S. Unsupervised Transfer Learning for Generative Image Inpainting with Adversarial Edge Learning. In Proceedings of the 2022 5th International Conference on Sensors, Signal and Image Processing, Birmingham, UK, 28–30 October 2022; pp. 17–22.
33. Li, L.; Chen, M.J.; Shi, H.D.; Liu, T.T.; Deng, Y.S. Research on Image Inpainting Algorithm Based on BIFPN-GAN Feature Fusion. *Radio Eng.* **2022**, *52*, 2141–2148.
34. Yu, F.; Koltun, V. Multi-scale Context Aggregation by Dilated Convolutions. *arXiv* **2015**, arXiv:1511.07122.
35. Lou, L.; Zang, S. Research on Edge Detection Method Based on Improved HED Network. *J. Phys. Conf. Ser.* **2020**, *1607*, 012068. [CrossRef]
36. Vaswani, A.; Shazeer, N.; Parmar, N.; Uszkoreit, J.; Jones, L.; Gomez, A.N.; Kaiser, Ł.; Polosukhin, I. Attention is all you need. In Proceedings of the NIPS, Long Beach, CA, USA, 4–9 December 2017; pp. 5998–6008.
37. He, K.; Zhang, X.; Ren, S.; Sun, J. Deep residual learning for image recognition. In Proceedings of the CVPR, Las Vegas, NV, USA, 27–30 July 2016; pp. 770–778.
38. Jimmy, L.B.; Jamie, R.K.; Geoffrey, E.H. Layer normalization. *arXiv* **2016**, arXiv:1607.06450. [CrossRef]
39. Johnson, J.; Alahi, A.; Fei-Fei, L. Perceptual losses for real-time style transfer and super-resolution. In Proceedings of the ECCV, Amsterdam, The Netherlands, 11–14 October 2016.
40. Jia, D.; Wei, D.; Socher, R.; Li, L.J.; Li, K.; Fei-Fei, L. ImageNet: A large-scale hierar-chical image database. In Proceedings of the CVPR, Miami, FL, USA, 20–25 June 2009; pp. 248–255.
41. Simonyan, K.; Zisserman, A. Very deep convolutional net-works for large-scale image recognition. *arXiv* **2014**, arXiv:1409.1556. [CrossRef]
42. Jolicoeur-Martineau, A. The relativistic discriminator: A key element missing from standard GAN. In Proceedings of the ICLR, Vancouver, BC, Canada, 30 April–3 May 2018.
43. Liu, G.; Reda, F.A.; Shih, K.J.; Wang, T.C.; Tao, A.; Catanzaro, B. Image Inpainting for Irregular Holes Using Partial Convolutions. In Proceedings of the ECCV, Munich, Germany, 8–14 September 2018; pp. 85–100.
44. Kingma, D.; Ba, J. Adam: A Method for Stochastic Optimization. *arXiv* **2014**, arXiv:1412.6980. [CrossRef]

Disclaimer/Publisher's Note: The statements, opinions and data contained in all publications are solely those of the individual author(s) and contributor(s) and not of MDPI and/or the editor(s). MDPI and/or the editor(s) disclaim responsibility for any injury to people or property resulting from any ideas, methods, instructions or products referred to in the content.

Article

Physiological Signal-Based Real-Time Emotion Recognition Based on Exploiting Mutual Information with Physiologically Common Features

Ean-Gyu Han [1], Tae-Koo Kang [2,*] and Myo-Taeg Lim [1,*]

1 School of Electrical Engineering, Korea University, Seoul 02841, Republic of Korea; wlrdmlrja@korea.ac.kr
2 Department of Human Intelligence and Robot Engineering, Sangmyung University, Cheonan 31066, Republic of Korea
* Correspondence: tkkang@smu.ac.kr (T.-K.K.); mlim@korea.ac.kr (M.-T.L.)

Abstract: This paper proposes a real-time emotion recognition system that utilizes photoplethysmography (PPG) and electromyography (EMG) physiological signals. The proposed approach employs a complex-valued neural network to extract common features from the physiological signals, enabling successful emotion recognition without interference. The system comprises three stages: single-pulse extraction, a physiological coherence feature module, and a physiological common feature module. The experimental results demonstrate that the proposed method surpasses alternative approaches in terms of accuracy and the recognition interval. By extracting common features of the PPG and EMG signals, this approach achieves effective emotion recognition without mutual interference. The findings provide a significant advancement in real-time emotion analysis and offer a clear and concise framework for understanding individuals' emotional states using physiological signals.

Keywords: emotion recognition; physiological signal; PPG; EMG; multimodal network; convolutional autoencoder; short-time Fourier transform (STFT); complex-valued convolutional neural network (CVCNN)

Citation: Han, E.-G.; Kang, T.-K.; Lim, M.-T. Physiological Signal-Based Real-Time Emotion Recognition Based on Exploiting Mutual Information with Physiologically Common Features. *Electronics* **2023**, *12*, 2933. https://doi.org/10.3390/electronics12132933

Academic Editors: Vladimir Laslo Tadić and Peter Odry

Received: 23 May 2023
Revised: 27 June 2023
Accepted: 30 June 2023
Published: 3 July 2023

Copyright: © 2023 by the authors. Licensee MDPI, Basel, Switzerland. This article is an open access article distributed under the terms and conditions of the Creative Commons Attribution (CC BY) license (https://creativecommons.org/licenses/by/4.0/).

1. Introduction

There is increasing importance in ergonomics, supporting designs based on scientific and engineering analyses of human physical, cognitive, social, and emotional characteristics. Ergonomics encompasses human engineering, biomechanics, cognitive engineering, human–computer interactions (HCI), emotional engineering, and user experiences (UX). Sophisticated technologies continue to be developed for measurement, experimentation, analysis, design, and evaluation. In particular, HCI has become an important field that has attracted extensive research, resulting in significant advances and expansion in a variety of fields, including recognizing and using emotions in computers.

Emotion recognition plays an important role in HCI, facilitating interactions between humans and intelligent devices (such as computers, smartphones, and the IoT). There are many ways to express emotions, including facial expressions, voice, gestures, text, and physiological signals, and each method has several advantages [1]. Facial expressions appear as facial images, and these image data can be acquired easily in various ways. Voice signals are good to find useful reference information as they are widely used in various fields. Gestures can express people's emotions clearly, and text can be acquired easily through crawling or scraping. However, the characteristics of voice and text are different for each country. Moreover, gestures have limitations because it is difficult to obtain a dataset, as this requires complex processes, such as recognizing a person's physical appearance. Furthermore, with regard to the emotion of facial expressions, voice, gestures, and text, they can be intentionally controlled, meaning the reliability of a person's actual emotions in terms of recognition is low. In contrast, since physiological signals are related to the central nervous system, emotions cannot be deliberately controlled. Accordingly, the reliability of physiological signals when recognizing emotions is guaranteed [2–4]. Therefore, psychological studies focusing on the relationship between physiological signals (including electroencephalography (EEG), photoplethysmography (PPG), and electromyography (EMG) signals) and emotions have been conducted and applied in various fields. The reason for this research interest is that physiological reactions can reflect dynamic changes in the central nervous system, which are difficult to hide compared to emotions expressed through words or facial expressions.

Among the physiological signals, EEG signals are the most commonly used for emotion recognition [5–7] because they are directly related to the central nervous system and contain exceptional emotional features. Significant recent research using EEG signals has focused on extracting EEG features using deep-learning-based methods. Wen et al. [8] proposed a deep convolutional neural network (CNN) and an autoencoder to extract relevant emotion-specific features from EEG signals. Alhagry et al. [9] proposed a long short-term memory (LSTM) approach to classify emotions using EEG signals, and Xing et al. [10] proposed a framework for emotion recognition using multi-channel EEG signals. Transitions in emotional states are usually accompanied by changes in the power spectrum of the EEG. Previous studies have also reported that spectral differences in EEG signals in the anterior brain region of the alpha band can generally capture different emotional states. Moreover, different spectral changes between different brain regions are also associated with emotional responses, such as theta and gamma-band power changes at the right parietal lobe, theta-band power changes at the frontal midline, and asymmetry of the beta-band power at the parietal region. Moreover, different spectral changes between different brain regions are also related to emotional responses. Examples here include changes in theta and gamma band power in the right parietal lobe, changes in the theta band power in the frontal midline, and asymmetry in the beta band power in the parietal region.

Soleymani et al. [11] proposed a multimodal dataset termed MAHNOB-HCI for emotion recognition and implicate tagging research. Based on this dataset, they obtained an EEG spectral output and the valence score of the electrodes and calculated a correlation between them. They also revealed that higher frequency components on the frontal, parietal, and occipital lobes had a higher correlation with self-assessment-based valence responses. Furthermore, they improved the classification performance for continuous emotion recognition by fusing the power spectral density (PSD) and facial features. Koelstra et al. [12] presented a multimodal dataset for the analysis of human affective states termed DEAP and extracted the spectral power features of five frequency bands from 32 participants. In another study, Zheng et al. [13] presented a dataset termed SEED for analyzing stable patterns across sessions. Lin et al. [14] evaluated features specialized for emotions based on the power spectral changes of EEG signals and assessed the relationship between EEG dynamics and music-induced emotional states. They revealed that emotion-specific features from the frontal and parietal lobes could provide discriminative information related to emotion processing. Finally, Chanel et al. [15] employed the naive Bayes classifier to categorize three arousal-assessment-based emotion classes from specific frequency bands at particular electrode locations.

Despite the previously mentioned advantages, there are some limitations when using EEG signals. First, EEG can cause simple partial seizures, or rarely, complex partial seizures (particularly with frontal onset). This means that interpreting EEG signals can become difficult or impossible due to body movements that generate excessive artifacts. Therefore, knowledge of relevant clinical seizures that can accompany EEG changes is required. Moreover, EEG signals have a high dimensionality, requiring diverse and difficult processing, rendering subsequent analyses difficult. Finally, signal processing requires complicated algorithms to analyze brainwave signals, and multiple EEG electrodes must be attached to subjects to collect reliable brainwave data. For these reasons, it is very difficult to gather practical EEG data applicable to real life, even if good classification can be achieved with follow-up analyses. To avoid this limitation, we selected PPG and EMG signals to recognize emotions rather than EEG, as they contain extensive emotion-specific information and can be incorporated into wearable devices practically [16–18]. Thus, they are easily measurable and somewhat less complex to analyze compared to EEG signals. Therefore, in this study, we paid attention to emotion recognition using a deep learning model based on PPG and EMG signals.

Psychologists and engineers have attempted to analyze these data to explain and categorize emotions. Although there are strong relationships between physiological signals and human emotional states, traditional manual feature extraction suffers from fundamental limitations to describe emotion-related characteristics from physiological signals.

1. Hand-crafted feature performance largely depends on the signal type and level of experience. Hence, poor domain knowledge can result in inappropriate features that are unable to capture some signal characteristics.
2. There is no guarantee that any given feature selection algorithm will extract the optimal feature set.
3. Moreover, most manual features are statistical and cannot incorporate signal details, which results in information loss.

In contrast, deep learning can automatically derive features from raw signals, allowing automatic feature selection and the bypassing of feature selection computational costs, and is applied to many industrial fields [19,20]. Similarly, deep learning methods have been recently applied to processing physiological signals (such as EEG or skin resistance), achieving comparable results with conventional methods. Martinez et al. [21] were the first to propose CNNs models to establish physiological models for emotion, resulting in many subsequent deep emotion recognition studies. While deep learning has these advantages, features with conflicting information can disturb the process of recognizing emotions.

Following the above-mentioned research and limitations, the research problem is described as follows. First, there are many problems in using EEG data in real-time emotion recognition. Second, traditional manual feature extraction does not guarantee an optimal feature set, leading to data loss. Finally, if there is a feature with conflicting information, it can interfere with emotion recognition [22]. Therefore, in this work, we select PPG and EMG signals and propose a deep learning model that prevents feature interference by extracting the common features of both signals.

This study is structured as follows. Section 2 describes the overall structure of the proposed system, including the method of splitting the PPG and EMG signals into a single pulse. In Section 3, the experimental environment regarding the dataset and experimental settings and the experimental results are presented, and the performance of the proposed emotion recognition model is compared with other studies. Finally, Section 4 contains a summary of the paper and presents the conclusions.

2. Proposed Real-Time Emotion Recognition System

2.1. Overview of the Proposed Real-Time Emotion Recognition System

An overview of the proposed real-time emotion recognition system developed in this study is presented in Figure 1. To extract the emotional features of a person based on PPG and EMG signals, a convolutional autoencoder (CAE) and a CNN-based architecture are combined. Emotional recognition is possible with these features only, but they contain conflicting information, which can confuse recognition. Therefore, in order to mediate the confusion, shared emotional features are extracted from the complex-valued convolutional neural network (CVCNN), in which the inputs are the results of a short-time Fourier transform (STFT). By using the CVCNN, efficient features are acquired from the complex-valued results of the STFT. Then, those features are concatenated and used to recognize emotions.

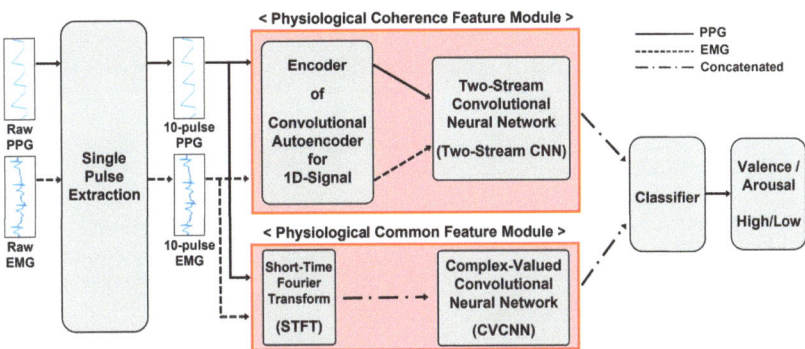

Figure 1. Overview of the proposed system.

As shown in Figure 1, the proposed system mainly comprises two modules. The physiological coherence feature module extracts features that exhibit a correlation between the PPG and EMG signals using a convolutional autoencoder and a two-stream CNN. Furthermore, the physiological common feature module extracts features that share both frequency information and overall details over time using a short-time Fourier transform (STFT) and a CVCNN. This module can contribute to successful emotion recognition by preventing feature interference that may occur in the physiological coherence feature module.

2.2. Single-Pulse Extraction Using Peak-to-Peak Segmentation for PPG and EMG Signals

By including the time or frequency domain and a geometric analysis, there is a variety of different physiological signal analysis techniques. The most commonly used method is a time domain analysis, which is divided by the average cycle rate and the difference between the longest and shortest signal values. However, preprocessing at an average cycle rate is inefficient because the aim is to capture changing trends immediately. Here, the difference between the longest and shortest signals is irrelevant, because the data fundamentally differ between participants. Therefore, the captured signal was split into short periods based on the peak value to extract the maximum amount of information within the raw signal while minimizing any losses. These short periods of signals are often directly associated with underlying physiological properties. Introducing even small variations in these short periods could potentially distort the underlying properties. As a result, in order to preserve the integrity of the signals and avoid any potential distortion of the underlying properties, we chose not to apply any signal augmentation techniques.

Figure 2 indicates that the PPG high peaks and EMG low peaks were clearly distinguishable from the characteristic waveforms. However, full-length signals were difficult to correlate with specific emotions, since emotional expressions weaken or deteriorate with increasing measurement time. Therefore, we segmented the signals into short signals to reflect emotion trends and eliminated any signals that differed from this trend. Regular periodicity signals were divided into single-pulse sections. Comparing the PPG and EMG data, we set the single-pulse data length to 86 sample points, although segmenting this length differed depending on the particular signal characteristics.

$$\text{Segmentation criteria} = \begin{cases} \text{PPG}_{\text{single-pulse}} = [x^*_{Hp} - c_L, \; x^*_{Hp} + c_R] \\ \text{EMG}_{\text{single-pulse}} = [x^*_{Lp} - c_L, \; x^*_{Lp} + c_R] \end{cases} \quad (1)$$

where x^* denotes the partial (single-pulse) signal length extracted from the entire signal; H_p and L_p are high and low peak locations, respectively; and c_L and c_R are the left and right constants, respectively, which were assigned to the relative to the peak points. Figure 3 displays typical resulting extracted signals.

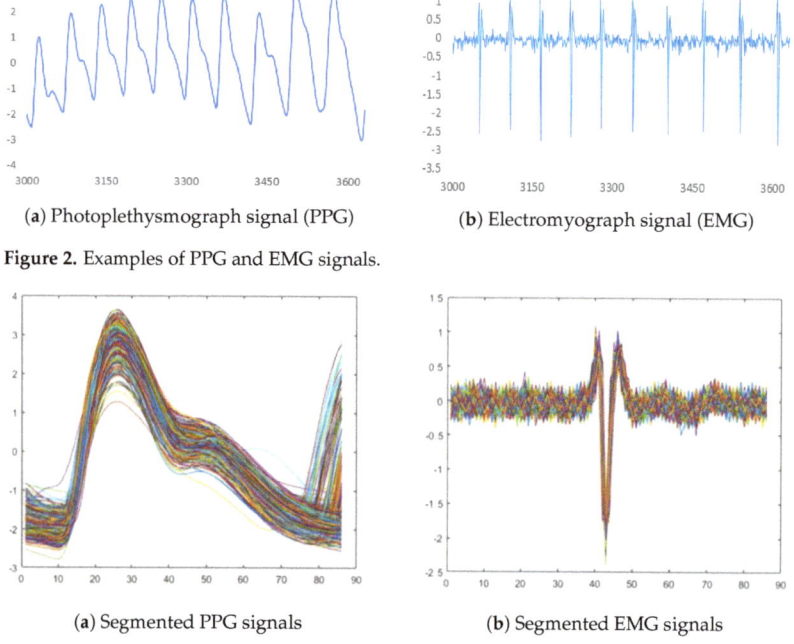

Figure 2. Examples of PPG and EMG signals.

(a) Segmented PPG signals (b) Segmented EMG signals

Figure 3. Results of single-pulse segmentation for PPG and EMG signals.

Using the entire signal does not always help in recognizing emotions. Rather, the signals typically contain artifact noise which distorts the signal waveform and complicates the fitting task. Using the entire signal is also rather complicated because we have to consider the possibility of each emotion starting in an arbitrary time frame [23–25]. In order to efficiently recognize emotions, it was necessary to determine the appropriate length to input to the deep learning model after properly segmenting the signal. Therefore, as a result of exploring the appropriate input signal length through experiments, we found that the appropriate input signal length is between 10 and 15 pulses. Furthermore, normalization is essential when processing data that vary from person to person, such as biosignals.

The maximum or minimum value of the signal (the amplitude) is different for each person. Therefore, to find appropriate peak values, appropriate threshold values must be determined. For this purpose, a quartile analysis was applied to all peak values.

A quartile analysis is a statistical method used to divide a set of data into four equal parts (quartiles). The data are sorted in ascending order, and then three equally sized cut points are selected that divide the data into four groups, with each group containing an equal number of observations. These cut points are known as quartiles and are often denoted as Q1, Q2, (median), and Q3. A quartile analysis is useful for understanding the distribution of a set of data, particularly when the data contain outliers or are not normally distributed. Moreover, it can provide information on the spread, skewness, and central tendency of the data.

Using this method, the threshold value that can obtain the maximum information without losses was 0.15 for PPG and 1.2 for EMG. Figure 4 shows the single-pulse appearance of PPG and EMG when various thresholds (including appropriate threshold values) are applied.

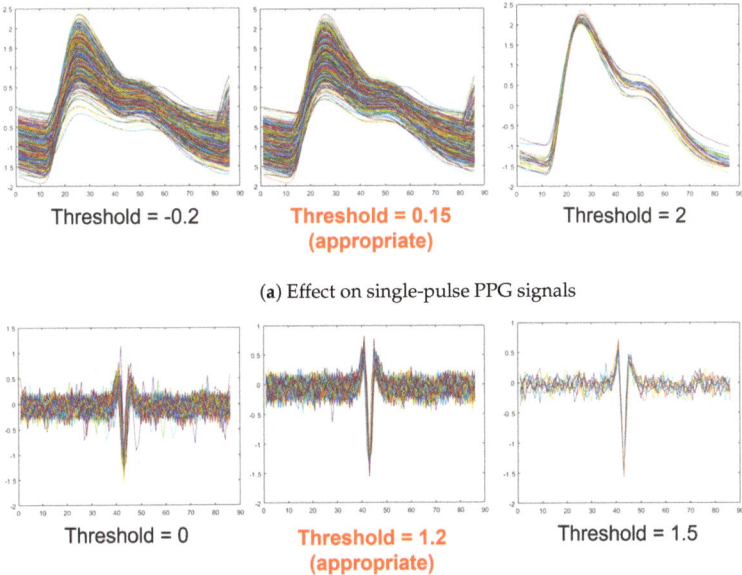

(a) Effect on single-pulse PPG signals

(b) Effect on single-pulse EMG signals

Figure 4. Effect on single-pulse signals with different thresholds.

2.3. Physiological Coherence Feature Module

2.3.1. Convolutional Autoencoder for 1D Signals

The CAE extends the basic structure of the simple autoencoder by changing the fully connected layers to convolution layers [26–28]. Identical to the simple autoencoder, the size of the input layer is also the same as the output layers, although the network of the encoder changes to convolution layers and the network of the decoder change to transposed convolutional layers.

As illustrated in Figure 5, an autoencoder consists of two parts: an encoder and a decoder. The encoder converts the input x to a hidden representation y (feature code) using a deterministic mapping function. Typically, this is an affine mapping function followed by a nonlinearity, where W is the weight between the input x and the hidden representation y and b is the bias.

$$y = f(Wx + b) \tag{2}$$

$$z = f'(W'y + b') \tag{3}$$

The CAE combines the local convolution connection with the autoencoder, which is a simple step that adds a convolution operation to inputs. Correspondingly, a CAE consists of a convolutional encoder and a convolutional decoder. The convolutional encoder realizes the process of convolutional conversion from the input to the feature maps, while the convolutional decoder implements the convolutional conversion from the feature maps to the output. In a CAE, the extracted features and the reconstructed output are calculated through the CNN. Thus, (2) and (3) can be rewritten as follows:

$$y = ReLU(wx + b) \tag{4}$$

$$z = ReLU(w'y + b') \tag{5}$$

where, ω represents the convolutional kernel between the input and the code y and ω' represents the convolutional kernel between the code y and the output. Terms b and b' are the bias. Moreover, the parameters of the encoding and decoding operations can be computed using unsupervised greedy training. The proposed architecture of a CAE for 1D signals is shown in Figure 6.

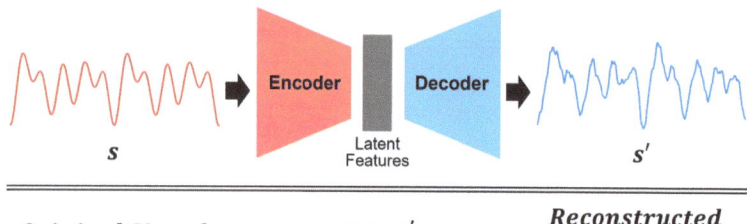

Figure 5. General structure of an autoencoder in which the encoder and decoder are neural networks.

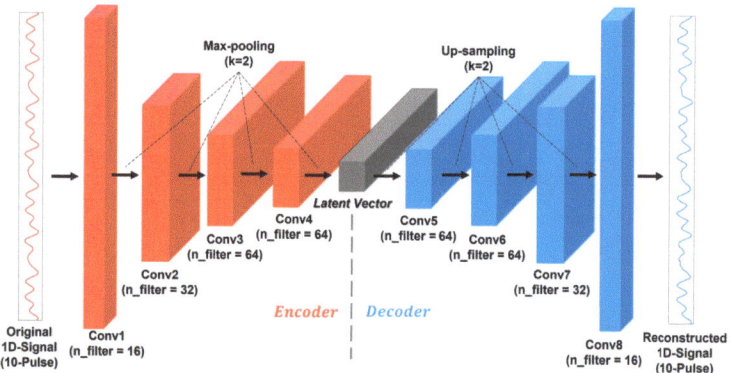

Figure 6. Architecture of a convolutional autoencoder for 1D signals.

2.3.2. Feature Extraction of Physiological Coherence Features for PPG and EMG Signals

In the previous section, each latent vector of the PPG and EMG signals was extracted through the CAE. Data compression of the signal was achieved through a dimensionality reduction, which is the main role of the autoencoder, allowing essential information about the signals to be extracted. To extract the physiological coherence features through this latent vector, a feature extraction module was constructed, as depicted in Figure 7. In the physiological coherence feature module, starting with latent vectors for each PPG and EMG signal, emotion-related features were extracted using the following process. Moreover, the features extracted in this way are complementary to PPG and EMG and contain information about the overall details over time.

First, effective features related to emotions were obtained through a 1D convolutional layer in each latent vector of the PPG and EMG signals. Complementary features of the PPG and EMG signals were then extracted by concatenating each feature and passing through the 1D convolutional layer again. When extracting features from the PPG and EMG signals, after the first 1D convolutional layer of each process, batch normalization and max pooling were performed to solve the problem of internal covariate shift and to transfer strong features with emotional characteristics to the next layer. However, while performing max pooling and passing strong features with emotional characteristics to the next layer, delicate representations may be discarded which can capture sophisticated emotional information. Therefore, only batch normalization was performed at the second convolutional layer. In a situation where features are fused through concatenation, this could be performed after arranging features in a row through flattening, as shown in Figure 8a. However, we did not employ flattening to preserve the overall details over time (also known as temporal information). Instead, temporal-wise concatenation was performed to ensure that it could be fused by time steps, as shown in Figure 8b.

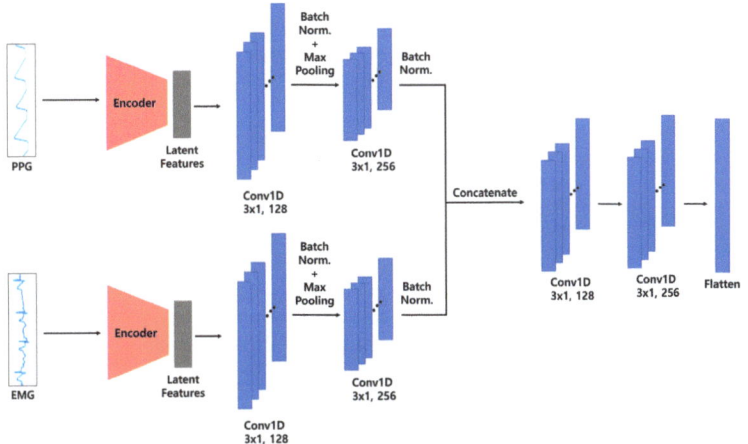

Figure 7. Architecture of the physiological coherence feature module.

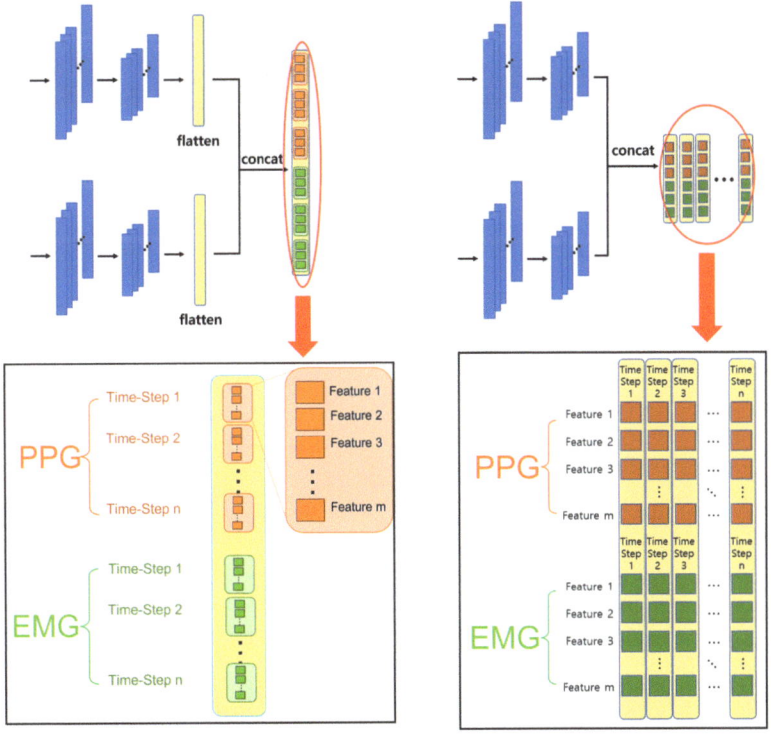

(**a**) Feature fusion using flattening (**b**) Feature fusion without flattening

Figure 8. Effects of flattening on feature fusion.

2.4. Physiological Common Feature Module

Basically, there are two main methods of extracting features from physiological signals in emotion recognition. One is the statistical feature extraction method, which extracts statistical features based on statistical facts. The other is deep-learning-based feature extraction, which extracts features through a deep learning model.

Statistical features (also known as hand-crafted features) are less reliable because people judge necessary features. People judge the statistical features related to the task that they want to perform and select them, although it is unclear whether the features are actually related to the task that they want to perform. Therefore, the deep-learning-based feature extraction method is currently being used extensively. Although it has the advantage of being able to extract features related to emotion recognition by automatically extracting extensive amounts of important information from the signal, it has the disadvantage of not being able to obtain information about the frequency band.

In order to compensate for the disadvantages of each method, the results of the STFT were applied to a deep learning model to extract features that also included the information of the frequency band in addition to information about overall details over time.

2.4.1. Signal Conversion from Time Domain to Time-Frequency Domain Using the Short-Time Fourier Transform

The STFT is a Fourier-related transform used to determine the sinusoidal frequency and phase content of local sections of a signal as it changes over time [29]. Although the fast Fourier transform (FFT) can clearly indicate the frequency of a signal, it has the disadvantage of having difficulty determining how much the frequency has changed over time. In contrast, the STFT can easily determine the frequency over time because it performs a Fourier transform by dividing the section over time.

The process of the STFT is depicted in Figure 9. Here, the hop length is the length that the window jumps from the current section to the next section, and the overlap length is the overlapping length between the current window and the next window. The resulting value of the STFT comprises a complex number that contains information on both the magnitude and phase. Therefore, the use of complex numbers is inevitable when using both the magnitude and phase information of the STFT as shown in Figure 10.

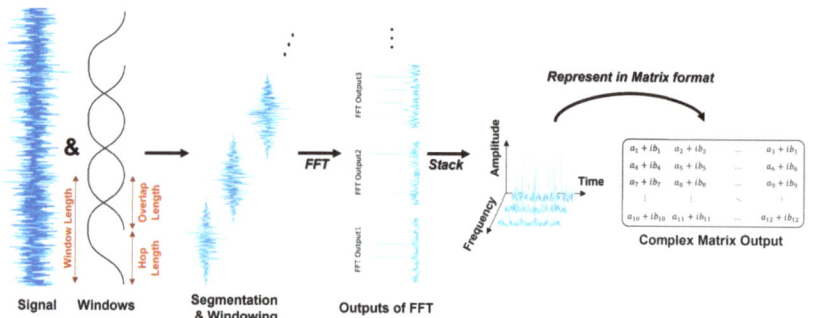

Figure 9. Process of the STFT.

2.4.2. Complex-Valued Convolutional Neural Network (CVCNN)

In general neural networks, neurons have weights, inputs, and outputs in the real domain, and these neural networks are called real-valued neural networks (RVNNs). Moreover, each neuron constituting an RVNN is called a real-valued neuron (RVN). The complex number resulting value of the STFT mentioned in Section 2.4.1 cannot be treated with RVNs. Therefore, to treat the complex number value from deep learning, the complex-valued neuron (CVN) and complex-valued neural network (CVNN) are necessary.

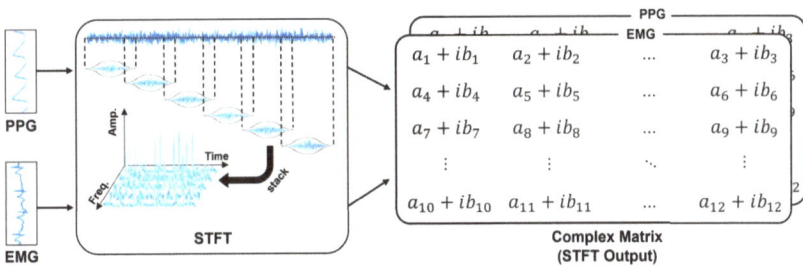

Figure 10. STFT process for the physiological common feature module.

The CVN has the same structure as an RVN, as depicted in Figure 11. However, the weights, inputs, and outputs of CVNs all exist in the complex domain. Therefore, they can be applied to various fields that use a complex system [30,31].

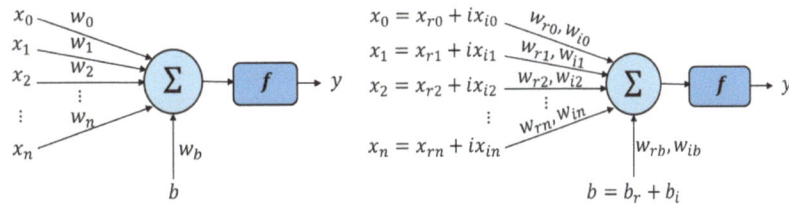

(a) Real-valued neuron (RVN)   (b) Complex-valued neuron (CVN)

Figure 11. Structure of an RVN and a CVN.

A real-valued convolution operation takes a matrix and a kernel (a smaller matrix) and outputs a matrix. The matrix elements are computed using a sliding window with the same dimensions as the kernel and each element is the sum of the point-wise multiplication of the kernel and matrix patch at the corresponding window.

Herein, we use the dot product to represent the sum of a point-wise multiplication between two matrices

$$X \cdot A = \sum_{ij} X_{ij} A_{ij} \qquad (6)$$

In the complex generalization, both the kernel and input patch are complex values. The only difference stems from the nature of multiplying complex numbers. When convolving a complex matrix with the kernel $W = A + iB$, the output corresponding to the input patch $Z = X + iY$ is given by

$$Z \cdot W = (X \cdot A - Y \cdot B) + i(X \cdot B + Y \cdot A) \qquad (7)$$

To implement the same functionality with a real-valued convolution, the input and output should be equivalent. Each complex matrix is represented by two real matrices stacked together in a three-dimensional array. Denoting this array $[X, Y]$, it is equivalent to $X + iY$. X and Y are the array's channels (Figure 12).

2.4.3. Feature Extraction of Physiological Common Features for PPG and EMG Signals

As mentioned at the beginning of this chapter, there are shortcomings in the method of extracting each feature. Therefore, in this section, to address these shortcomings, features were extracted while preserving the general details over time of the signals and the information of the frequency band by applying the STFT and CVNN, as explained previously. Figure 13 shows the structure of the proposed physiological common feature module.

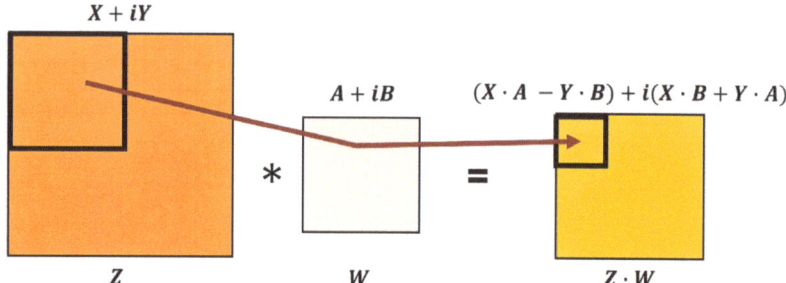

Figure 12. Process of complex-valued convolution.

As shown in Figure 13, the common features of the two biosignals (PPG and EMG) were extracted in this study, because extracting the features of PPG and EMG separately is an inherently inefficient method. In other words, selecting individual features provides too much input data in single-task learning and creates the possibility that each feature would adversely affect other features and interfere with the task to be performed. In addition, the resultant value of the STFT is composed of complex numbers and includes information on both magnitude and phase. Therefore, to use both the intensity and phase information of the STFT, the use of complex numbers is inevitable. Accordingly, a CVNN was used to extract the features.

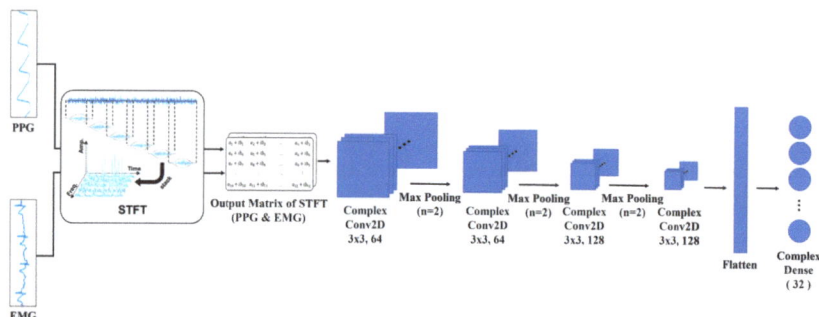

Figure 13. Structure of the physiological common feature module.

For the following reasons, we propose to extract the common features of the PPG and EMG signals through a CVNN instead of extracting the features for each PPG and EMG signal.

Therefore, the total structure of our proposed real-time emotion recognition system can be represented as shown in Figure 14.

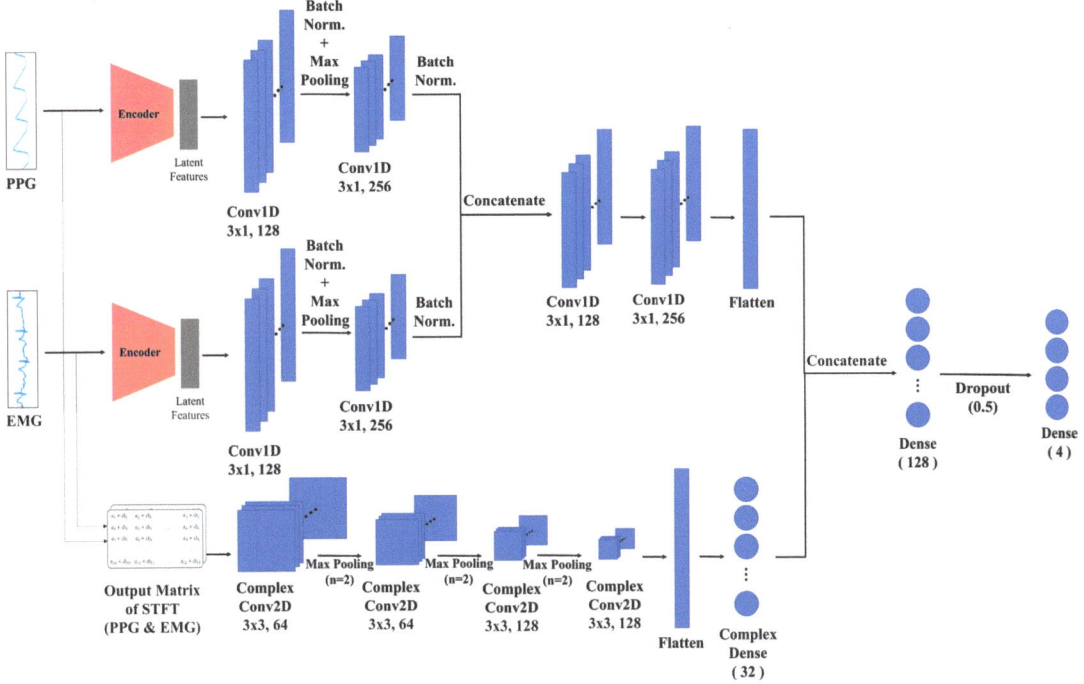

Figure 14. Total structure of the proposed emotion recognition system.

3. Experimental Results

3.1. Datasets

It is important to decide which dataset to use for a study since the type and characteristics of a dataset have a significant influence on the results. In particular, datasets containing only physiological signals (not image-generated datasets) are required for emotion recognition through physiological signals. We required a dataset containing PPG and EMG signals; thus, among the available datasets, we chose the DEAP dataset [12]. Moreover, we created a dataset, EDPE, for more granular emotions (as used in a previous study [32]).

Emotions can be affected by many factors, and each emotion has fuzzy boundaries. Therefore, it is ambiguous to quantify emotions or define them using objective criteria. Various models that define emotion have been developed, although most emotion recognition studies use Russell's circumplex theory [33], which assumes emotions are distributed in a two-dimensional circular space with arousal and valence dimensions. Generally, arousal is considered as the vertical axis and valence the horizontal, with the origin (circle center) representing neutral valence and medium arousal level.

As shown in Figure 15, emotional states can be represented at any valence and arousal level. For example, "Excited" has high arousal and high valence, whereas "Depressed" has low arousal and low valence. Emotions can manifest in various ways, and current emotion recognition systems are generally based on facial expressions, voice, gestures, and text.

3.1.1. Database for Emotion Analysis Using Physiological Signals (DEAP)

The DEAP dataset contains 32-channel EEG and peripheral physiological signals (including PPG and EMG). Furthermore, these signals were measured from a total of 32 participants (16 male and 16 female) who watched 40 music videos and self-assessed on five criteria (including arousal and valence). Each participant's age was within the range of 19–37 years (average of 26.9 years), and self-evaluation was on a continuous scale from 1 to

9, except for familiarity (which was a discrete scale from 1 to 5). Thirty-two participants first put on a device that can collect the signals and started the device three seconds before watching the video to measure the signals when they were in a calm state. After that, they watched the videos and started the self-assessment after the video was finished. This step was repeated to collect the signals. The signals were measured at 512 Hz and also the data were downsampled to 128 Hz. Furthermore, the dataset is summarized in Table 1.

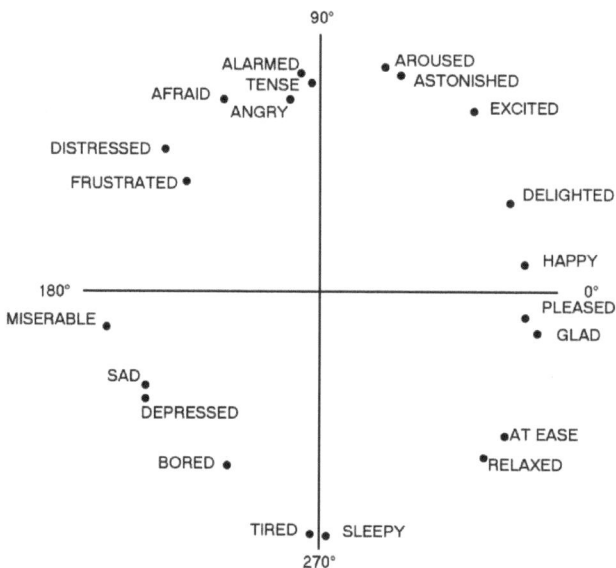

Figure 15. Russell's circumplex model [33].

Table 1. DEAP dataset summary.

DEAP Dataset Experiment	
Participants	32 (male: 16, female: 16)
Videos	40 music videos
Age	Between 19 and 37
Rating categories	Arousal, Valence, Dominance, Liking, Familiarity
Rating values	Familiarity: discrete scale of 1–5 Others: continuous scale of 1–9
Recorded signals	32-channel EEG Peripheral physiological signals Face video (only for 22 participants)
Sampling rate	512 Hz (or downsampled to 128 Hz)

3.1.2. Emotion Dataset Using PPG and EMG Signals (EDPE)

The EDPE dataset has a total of 40 participants (30 males and 10 females) who watched 32 videos that evoked specific emotions and then self-evaluated their arousal and valence. Each video lasted 3–5 min and the total duration of the experiment was 2.5–3.0 h. Each participant's age was within the range of 20–28 years and the self-assessment proceeded with a four discrete step evaluation of −2, −1, +1, +2 in Arousal and Valence. Through these four-step self-assessments, emotions are classified into 16 areas expressed in Figure 16, not four areas. This makes it more efficient to recognize emotions at the level of emotions defined by adjectives. The overall experimental process is as follows. First, participants attach a sensor and wait in a normal state for 10 min without measuring the signals. After that, they watch videos corresponding to the four quadrants of Russell's model while the signals are measured. After each videos finishes, they start a self-assessment. The measured signals are PPG and EMG, which are sampled and measured at 100 Hz, as summarized in Table 2.

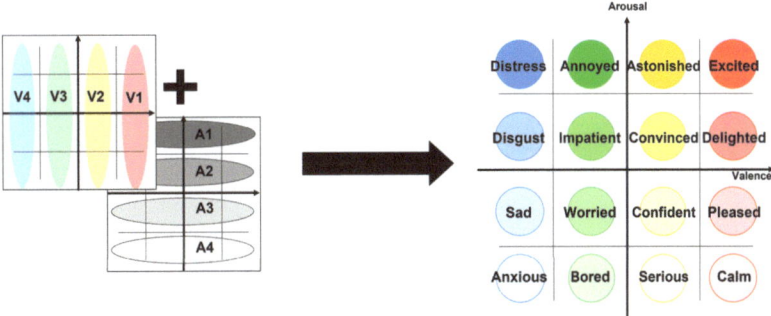

Figure 16. Proposed emotion plane (valence–arousal plane).

Table 2. EDPE dataset summary.

EDPE Dataset Experiment	
Participants	40 (male: 30, female: 10)
Videos	32 videos
Age	Between 20 and 28
Rating categories	Arousal, Valence
Rating values	Discrete scale of −2, −1, +1, +2
Proposed emotion states	16 emotions depicted in Figure 16
Recorded signals	PPG, EMG
Sampling rate	100 Hz

3.2. Experimental Setup

The experiment was conducted by setting the single-pulse lengths to 86 and 140 data points for the DEAP and EDPE datasets, respectively. Each sample was preprocessed through MATLAB (R2020b), and learning was conducted using Tensorflow (2.6.0) and Keras (2.6.0). In the fields of cognitive engineering, HCI (emotion engineering and medicine) and BCI (perception of an individual's emotional state) are very important. Hence, the experiment in this study was not conducted in a subject-independent way. Therefore, 80% randomly-selected samples from the DEAP dataset were used for training and 20% for testing. Similarly, a randomly selected 80% of samples from the entire EDPE dataset was used for training and 20% of the samples was used for testing.

In addition, the accuracy of each pulse number was measured to confirm how many pulses from each dataset were suitable for recognizing emotions. Based on the appropriate number of pulses (confirmed from the experiment), the performances of the algorithm proposed in this study and other algorithms were compared. Finally, by learning each of the 16 emotions classified by arousal and valence, an experiment was conducted to determine how well they could be measured in the emotion class.

3.3. Classification Results on Deap Dataset

Figure 17 shows the average accuracies of valence and arousal according to the number of pulses in the DEAP dataset. When the DEAP dataset contained only a single pulse, the accuracy was very low (47%). However, as the number of pulses increased from 1 to 10, the accuracy increased rapidly, although, beyond 10 pulses, the accuracy remained the same. In regard to the DEAP dataset, although the accuracy increased rapidly up to 10 pulses, the ideal number of pulses in the DEAP dataset was set to 15, because this produced the optimum performance (75%).

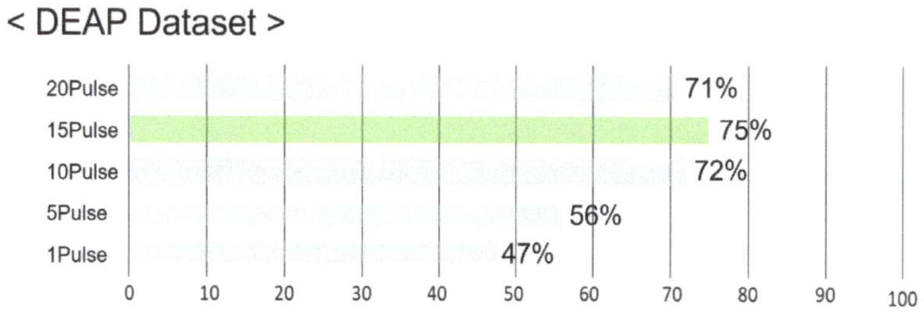

< DEAP Dataset >

Pulses	Accuracy
20Pulse	71%
15Pulse	75%
10Pulse	72%
5Pulse	56%
1Pulse	47%

Figure 17. Classification accuracy of DEAP dataset according to pulse length.

Table 3 shows a comparison of the results of the emotion recognition using the DEAP dataset. The proposed method exhibited an accuracy of 75.76% and 74.32% in arousal and valence. Except for studies [10,34,35], it can be seen that the proposed method shows the best performance and is also superior in terms of the recognition interval. Compared to the proposed method, the study [34] performs poorly in valence, but outperforms in arousal. Conversely, study [10] performs well in valence, but does not perform well in arousal. In the case of study [35], it can be seen that both valence and arousal perform better than the proposed method. However, it is difficult to make an appropriate comparison because the three studies have a longer recognition interval than the proposed method.

Table 3. Comparison with other studies using the DEAP dataset.

Method	Recognition Interval	Signals	Accuracy	
			Arousal	Valence
Naïve Bayes with Statistical Features (Koelstra, 2011) [12]	63 s	GSR, RSP, SKT, PPG, EMG, EOG	57%	62.7%
CNN (Martinez, 2013) [21]	30 s	BVP, SC	69.1%	63.3%
DBN (Xu, 2016) [36]	60 s	EEG	69.8%	66.9%
Deep Sparse AE (Zhang, 2017) [34]	20 s	RSP	80.78%	73.06%
MEMD (Mert, 2018) [37]	60 s	EEG	75%	72.87%
SAE-LSTM (Xing, 2019) [10]	60 s	EEG	74.38%	81.1%
HOLO-FM (Topic, 2021) [35]	60 s	EEG	77.72%	76.61%
Proposed Method	**15 s**	PPG, EMG	75.76%	74.32%

Therefore, as shown in Table 4, the performance was compared again by matching the recognition interval to the same 15 s as the proposed method. Study [10] used LSTM to construct the model according to relatively long-term signals; thus, it seems that the performance has decreased significantly compared to studies [34,35]. Therefore, when comparing the proposed method and research [10,34,35] under the same conditions, the proposed method shows the best performance.

Table 4. Re-comparison with the top-3 studies in Table 3 (with the recognition interval set to 15 s).

Method	Recognition Interval	Signals	Accuracy	
			Arousal	Valence
Deep Sparse AE (Zhang, 2017) [34]	15 s	RSP	69.8%	70.67%
SAE-LSTM (Xing, 2019) [10]	15 s	EEG	54.46%	50.98%
HOLO-FM (Topic, 2021) [35]	15 s	EEG	70.54%	72.32%
Proposed Method	15 s	PPG, EMG	75.76%	74.32%

3.4. Classification Results on the EDPE Dataset

Figure 18 shows the average accuracies of valence and arousal according to the number of pulses in the EDPE dataset. When the EDPE dataset contained only a single pulse, the accuracy was very low (46%). However, as the number of pulses increased from 1 to 10, the accuracy increased rapidly, although, beyond that number, the accuracy decreased. Therefore, for the EDPE dataset, the performance was optimum (85%) when it contained 10 pulses. Accordingly, the ideal number of pulses in the EDPE dataset was set to 10.

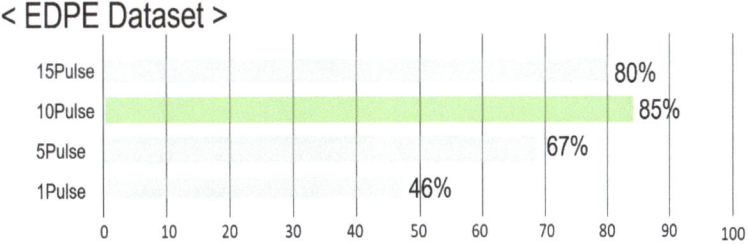

Figure 18. Classification accuracy of the EDPE dataset according to pulse length.

Figure 19 shows the confusion matrix of the arousal and valence results when the ideal number of pulses in the EDPE dataset was set to 10. Figure 19 exhibits that many numbers were on the descending right diagonal where the predictions and answers matched, indicating that the learning was successful. Items with relatively high numbers (except for numbers on the diagonal) were <Very High–High> and <Very Low–Low>, and Very High became High, High became Very High, or Very Low became Low and Low (which refers to the case of confusion with Very Low). Even though there were cases of confusion, the overwhelming majority of correctly predicted cases proved the excellent classification performance of the method proposed in this study.

Experiments were also conducted with various deep learning models based on a CNN and LSTM (commonly used in deep learning models) using the same EDPE dataset. Although CNNs are one of the most-used deep neural networks for analyzing visual images, they have frequently been employed in recent emotion recognition research by analyzing patterns of adjacent physiological signals. Therefore, we compared the performance of CNNs and models that combined a stacked autoencoder and a CNN or LSTM. Finally, the performance of the bimodal stacked sparse autoencoder [32] was compared. Table 5 summarizes the experimental results of emotion recognition.

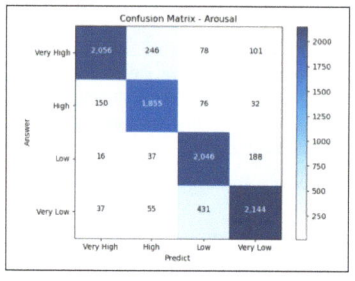
(a) Confusion matrix—arousal

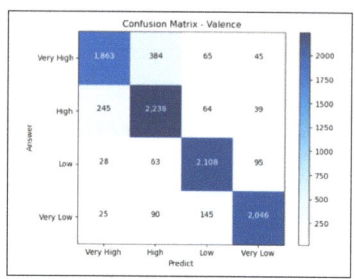
(b) Confusion matrix—valence

Figure 19. Confusion Matrix of classification result—EDPE dataset.

As shown in Table 5, the performance was low when recognizing emotions using LSTM. This result indicated that the data were not just time dependent but also more complex. Therefore, this suggested that improved results could be obtained by analyzing data patterns using a fully connected layer and a convolutional layer. As a result, our proposed model outperformed the other deep learning models.

Table 5. Comparison with various deep learning models.

Model	Dataset	Recognition Interval	Accuracy	
			Arousal	Valence
CNN	EDPE dataset	10 s	70.24%	74.34%
Stacked Auto-encoder + CNN			71.47%	72.01%
Stacked Auto-encoder + LSTM			61.03%	59.25%
Bimodal-Stacked Auto-encoder [32]			75.86%	80.18%
Proposed Model			**84.84%**	**86.50%**

Recognizing the highs and lows of arousal and valence has a very different meaning from recognizing emotion itself. Being able to recognize arousal well does not necessarily mean that valence can also be recognized well, and vice versa. In other words, recognizing emotions is a more complicated and difficult problem than recognizing high and low levels of arousal or valence, in which both arousal and valence standards are applied simultaneously, as shown in Figure 16. Therefore, to recognize emotions, we reconstructed the EDPE dataset with data and labels for each of the 16 emotions in Figure 16, and training and testing were conducted by dividing the sample into 80% for training and 20% for testing.

Table 6 presents the recognition results for the 16 emotions, which displayed an average recognition accuracy of 82.52%. Although this result was slightly lower than the recognition accuracy for arousal and valence, it was sufficiently accurate to be applied successfully in real-life scenarios, considering the difficulty of recognizing 16 emotions compared to each recognition task for arousal and valence.

Table 6. Results of emotion recognition for sixteen emotions by the proposed model.

Quadrant	Emotions			
Quadrant I (HVHA)	Astonished	Convinced	Excited	Delighted
	85.37%	87.09%	81.34%	80.20%

Table 6. *Cont.*

Quadrant	Emotions			
Quadrant II (LVHA)	Distress	Disgust	Annoyed	Impatient
	78.35%	80.97%	75.26%	82.97%
Quadrant III (LVLA)	Sad	Anxious	Worried	Bored
	79.61%	82.89%	77.49%	90.04%
Quadrant IV (HVLA)	Confident	Serious	Pleased	Calm
	85.08%	83.24%	86.87%	83.40%

HVHA: High Valence High Arousal, LVLA: Low Valence Low Arousal, LVHA: Low Valence High Arousal, HVLA: High Valence Low Arousal.

4. Conclusions

This paper proposed a novel approach for real-time emotion recognition using physiological signals (PPG and EMG) through the extraction of physiologically common features via a CVCNN. The results indicated that the proposed approach achieved an accuracy of 81.78%, which is competitive with existing methods. Furthermore, we confirmed that the recognition interval was significantly shorter than in other studies, rendering the proposed method suitable for real-time emotion recognition.

The findings of this study suggest that the proposed approach has the potential to be applied in various fields, such as healthcare, human–computer interactions, and affective computing. Moreover, this study provides insights into the relationship between physiological signals and emotions, which can further advance our understanding of the human affective system.

While the proposed approach shows promise in real-time emotion recognition using physiological signals, there are some limitations. Firstly, the concept of cross-subject analysis, which involves analyzing data from multiple subjects, is not incorporated in this study. This limits the generalizability of the findings to a broader population. Next, the experiments were conducted in a controlled laboratory setting, which may not fully capture the range of emotions experienced in real-life situations. Therefore, there is a need for future research to address these limitations.

In light of these limitations, future research should consider conducting experiments in wild environments to better understand the applicability of the proposed approach in real-world scenarios. This would provide a more comprehensive understanding of how emotions manifest in different contexts. In addition, by understanding the properties of the matrix, which is the result of a STFT, it is possible to derive novel approaches such as spectrograms [38] or graph transformer models [39,40]. Furthermore, it is important to expand the scope of the investigation beyond short-term emotion recognition. Long-term emotion recognition should be explored to gain insights into how emotions evolve and fluctuate over extended periods of time.

Moreover, future research could focus on defining and recognizing personality traits based on changes in emotions. By studying the relationship between emotions and personality, we can gain a deeper understanding of the human affective system. This would not only contribute to the field of affective computing, but also have practical implications in various domains, such as healthcare and human–computer interactions.

In summary, by addressing the limitations related to cross-subject analysis and conducting experiments in real-life settings, future research can enhance the applicability and generalizability of the proposed approach. Additionally, exploring long-term emotion recognition and its connection to personality traits would provide valuable insights into the complex nature of human emotions.

Author Contributions: Conceptualization, E.-G.H., T.-K.K. and M.-T.L.; data curation, E.-G.H.; formal analysis, E.-G.H., T.-K.K. and M.-T.L.; methodology, E.-G.H., T.-K.K. and M.-T.L.; software, E.-G.H. and T.-K.K.; validation, M.-T.L. and T.-K.K.; writing—original draft, E.-G.H. and T.-K.K.; writing—review and editing, M.-T.L. and T.-K.K. All authors have read and agreed to the published version of the manuscript.

Funding: This research was supported by the Basic Science Research Program through the National Research Foundation of Korea (NRF) (grant no. NRF-2022R1F1A1073543).

Data Availability Statement: Not applicable.

Conflicts of Interest: The authors declare no conflict of interest.

References

1. Ali, M.; Mosa, A.H.; Al Machot, F.; Kyamakya, K. Emotion recognition involving physiological and speech signals: A comprehensive review. In *Recent Advances in Nonlinear Dynamics and Synchronization*; Springer: Berlin/Heidelberg, Germany, 2018; pp. 287–302.
2. Sim, H.; Lee, W.H.; Kim, J.Y. A Study on Emotion Classification utilizing Bio-Signal (PPG, GSR, RESP). *Adv. Sci. Technol. Lett.* **2015**, *87*, 73–77.
3. Chen, J.; Hu, B.; Moore, P.; Zhang, X.; Ma, X. Electroencephalogram-based emotion assessment system using ontology and data mining techniques. *Appl. Soft Comput.* **2015**, *30*, 663–674. [CrossRef]
4. Shu, L.; Xie, J.; Yang, M.; Li, Z.; Li, Z.; Liao, D.; Xu, X.; Yang, X. A review of emotion recognition using physiological signals. *Sensors* **2018**, *18*, 2074. [CrossRef] [PubMed]
5. Houssein, E.H.; Hammad, A.; Ali, A.A. Human emotion recognition from EEG-based brain–computer interface using machine learning: A comprehensive review. *Neural Comput. Appl.* **2022**, *34*, 12527–12557. [CrossRef]
6. Al-Qazzaz, N.K.; Alyasseri, Z.A.A.; Abdulkareem, K.H.; Ali, N.S.; Al-Mhiqani, M.N.; Guger, C. EEG feature fusion for motor imagery: A new robust framework towards stroke patients rehabilitation. *Comput. Biol. Med.* **2021**, *137*, 104799. [CrossRef] [PubMed]
7. Sung, W.T.; Chen, J.H.; Chang, K.W. Study on a real-time BEAM system for diagnosis assistance based on a system on chips design. *Sensors* **2013**, *13*, 6552–6577. [CrossRef]
8. Wen, T.; Zhang, Z. Deep convolution neural network and autoencoders-based unsupervised feature learning of EEG signals. *IEEE Access* **2018**, *6*, 25399–25410. [CrossRef]
9. Alhagry, S.; Fahmy, A.A.; El-Khoribi, R.A. Emotion recognition based on EEG using LSTM recurrent neural network. *Int. J. Adv. Comput. Sci. Appl.* **2017**, *8*, 355–358. [CrossRef]
10. Xing, X.; Li, Z.; Xu, T.; Shu, L.; Hu, B.; Xu, X. SAE + LSTM: A New framework for emotion recognition from multi-channel EEG. *Front. Neurorobot.* **2019**, *13*, 37. [CrossRef]
11. Soleymani, M.; Lichtenauer, J.; Pun, T.; Pantic, M. A multimodal database for affect recognition and implicit tagging. *IEEE Trans. Affect. Comput.* **2011**, *3*, 42–55. [CrossRef]
12. Koelstra, S.; Muhl, C.; Soleymani, M.; Lee, J.S.; Yazdani, A.; Ebrahimi, T.; Pun, T.; Nijholt, A.; Patras, I. Deap: A database for emotion analysis; using physiological signals. *IEEE Trans. Affect. Comput.* **2011**, *3*, 18–31. [CrossRef]
13. Zheng, W.L.; Zhu, J.Y.; Lu, B.L. Identifying stable patterns over time for emotion recognition from EEG. *IEEE Trans. Affect. Comput.* **2017**, *10*, 417–429. [CrossRef]
14. Lin, Y.P.; Wang, C.H.; Jung, T.P.; Wu, T.L.; Jeng, S.K.; Duann, J.R.; Chen, J.H. EEG-based emotion recognition in music listening. *IEEE Trans. Biomed. Eng.* **2010**, *57*, 1798–1806. [PubMed]
15. Chanel, G.; Kronegg, J.; Grandjean, D.; Pun, T. Emotion assessment: Arousal evaluation using EEG's and peripheral physiological signals. In Proceedings of the Multimedia Content Representation, Classification and Security: International Workshop, MRCS 2006, Istanbul, Turkey, 11–13 September 2006; Proceedings; Springer: Berlin/Heidelberg, Germany, 2006; pp. 530–537.
16. Udovičić, G.; Đerek, J.; Russo, M.; Sikora, M. Wearable emotion recognition system based on GSR and PPG signals. In Proceedings of the 2nd International Workshop on Multimedia for Personal Health and Health Care, Mountain View, CA, USA, 23 October 2017; pp. 53–59.
17. Li, C.; Xu, C.; Feng, Z. Analysis of physiological for emotion recognition with the IRS model. *Neurocomputing* **2016**, *178*, 103–111. [CrossRef]
18. Lee, Y.K.; Kwon, O.W.; Shin, H.S.; Jo, J.; Lee, Y. Noise reduction of PPG signals using a particle filter for robust emotion recognition. In Proceedings of the 2011 IEEE International Conference on Consumer Electronics—Berlin (ICCE—Berlin), Berlin, Germany, 3–6 September 2011; pp. 202–205.
19. Noroznia, H.; Gandomkar, M.; Nikoukar, J.; Aranizadeh, A.; Mirmozaffari, M. A Novel Pipeline Age Evaluation: Considering Overall Condition Index and Neural Network Based on Measured Data. *Mach. Learn. Knowl. Extr.* **2023**, *5*, 252–268. [CrossRef]
20. Mirmozaffari, M.; Yazdani, M.; Boskabadi, A.; Ahady Dolatsara, H.; Kabirifar, K.; Amiri Golilarz, N. A novel machine learning approach combined with optimization models for eco-efficiency evaluation. *Appl. Sci.* **2020**, *10*, 5210. [CrossRef]
21. Martinez, H.P.; Bengio, Y.; Yannakakis, G.N. Learning deep physiological models of affect. *IEEE Comput. Intell. Mag.* **2013**, *8*, 20–33. [CrossRef]

22. Ozbulak, U.; Gasparyan, M.; Rao, S.; De Neve, W.; Van Messem, A. Exact Feature Collisions in Neural Networks. *arXiv* **2022**, arXiv:2205.15763.
23. Wu, C.K.; Chung, P.C.; Wang, C.J. Representative segment-based emotion analysis and classification with automatic respiration signal segmentation. *IEEE Trans. Affect. Comput.* **2012**, *3*, 482–495. [CrossRef]
24. Picard, R.W.; Vyzas, E.; Healey, J. Toward machine emotional intelligence: Analysis of affective physiological state. *IEEE Trans. Pattern Anal. Mach. Intell.* **2001**, *23*, 1175–1191. [CrossRef]
25. Zeng, Z.; Pantic, M.; Roisman, G.I.; Huang, T.S. A survey of affect recognition methods: Audio, visual and spontaneous expressions. In Proceedings of the 9th International Conference on Multimodal Interfaces, Aichi, Japan, 12–15 April 2007; pp. 126–133.
26. Masci, J.; Meier, U.; Cireşan, D.; Schmidhuber, J. Stacked convolutional auto-encoders for hierarchical feature extraction. In Proceedings of the Artificial Neural Networks and Machine Learning—ICANN 2011: 21st International Conference on Artificial Neural Networks, Espoo, Finland, 14–17 June 2011; Proceedings, Part I 21; Springer: Berlin/Heidelberg, Germany, 2011; pp. 52–59.
27. Wang, Y.; Xie, Z.; Xu, K.; Dou, Y.; Lei, Y. An efficient and effective convolutional auto-encoder extreme learning machine network for 3d feature learning. *Neurocomputing* **2016**, *174*, 988–998. [CrossRef]
28. Huang, H.; Hu, X.; Zhao, Y.; Makkie, M.; Dong, Q.; Zhao, S.; Guo, L.; Liu, T. Modeling task fMRI data via deep convolutional autoencoder. *IEEE Trans. Med. Imaging* **2017**, *37*, 1551–1561. [CrossRef] [PubMed]
29. Sejdic, E.; Djurovic, I.; Jiang, J. Time–frequency feature representation using energy concentration: An overview of recent advances. *Digit. Signal Process.* **2009**, *19*, 153–183. [CrossRef]
30. Amin, M.F.; Murase, K. Single-layered complex-valued neural network for real-valued classification problems. *Neurocomputing* **2009**, *72*, 945–955. [CrossRef]
31. Zimmermann, H.G.; Minin, A.; Kusherbaeva, V.; Germany, M. Comparison of the complex valued and real valued neural networks trained with gradient descent and random search algorithms. In Proceedings of the of ESANN 2011, Bruges, Belgium, 27–29 April 2011.
32. Lee, Y.K.; Pae, D.S.; Hong, D.K.; Lim, M.T.; Kang, T.K. Emotion Recognition with Short-Period Physiological Signals Using Bimodal Sparse Autoencoders. *Intell. Autom. Soft Comput.* **2022**, *32*, 657–673. [CrossRef]
33. Russell, J.A. A circumplex model of affect. *J. Personal. Soc. Psychol.* **1980**, *39*, 1161. [CrossRef]
34. Zhang, Q.; Chen, X.; Zhan, Q.; Yang, T.; Xia, S. Respiration-based emotion recognition with deep learning. *Comput. Ind.* **2017**, *92*, 84–90. [CrossRef]
35. Topic, A.; Russo, M. Emotion recognition based on EEG feature maps through deep learning network. *Eng. Sci. Technol. Int. J.* **2021**, *24*, 1442–1454. [CrossRef]
36. Xu, H.; Plataniotis, K.N. EEG-based affect states classification using deep belief networks. In Proceedings of the IEEE 2016 Digital Media Industry & Academic Forum (DMIAF), Santorini, Greece, 4–6 July 2016; pp. 148–153.
37. Mert, A.; Akan, A. Emotion recognition from EEG signals by using multivariate empirical mode decomposition. *Pattern Anal. Appl.* **2018**, *21*, 81–89. [CrossRef]
38. Pusarla, N.; Singh, A.; Tripathi, S. Learning DenseNet features from EEG based spectrograms for subject independent emotion recognition. *Biomed. Signal Process. Control.* **2022**, *74*, 103485. [CrossRef]
39. Yun, S.; Jeong, M.; Kim, R.; Kang, J.; Kim, H.J. Graph transformer networks. *Adv. Neural Inf. Process. Syst.* **2019**, *32*. Available online: https://proceedings.neurips.cc/paper_files/paper/2019/file/9d63484abb477c97640154d40595a3bb-Paper.pdf (accessed on 22 May 2023).
40. Dwivedi, V.P.; Bresson, X. A generalization of transformer networks to graphs. *arXiv* **2020**, arXiv:2012.09699.

Disclaimer/Publisher's Note: The statements, opinions and data contained in all publications are solely those of the individual author(s) and contributor(s) and not of MDPI and/or the editor(s). MDPI and/or the editor(s) disclaim responsibility for any injury to people or property resulting from any ideas, methods, instructions or products referred to in the content.

Article

A Transformer-Based Cross-Window Aggregated Attentional Image Inpainting Model

Mingju Chen [1,2], Tingting Liu [1,2,*], Xingzhong Xiong [1,2], Zhengxu Duan [1,2] and Anle Cui [1,2]

[1] Sichuan Key Laboratory of Artificial Intelligence, Sichuan University of Science and Engineering, Yibin 644002, China; chenmingju@suse.edu.cn (M.C.); xzxiong@suse.edu.cn (X.X.); 321085404416@stu.suse.edu.cn (Z.D.); cccall@126.com (A.C.)
[2] School of Automation and Information, Sichuan University of Science and Engineering, Yibin 644002, China
* Correspondence: 321085404414@stu.suse.edu.cn

Abstract: To overcome the fault of convolutional networks, which can be over-smooth, blurred, or discontinuous, a novel transformer network with cross-window aggregated attention is proposed. Our network as a whole is constructed as a generative adversarial network model, and by embedding the Window Aggregation Transformer (WAT) module, we improve the information aggregation between windows without increasing the computational complexity and effectively obtain the image long-range dependencies to solve the problem that convolutional operations are limited by local feature extraction. First, the encoder extracts the multi-scale features of the image with convolution kernels of different scales; second, the feature maps of different scales are input into a WAT module to realize the aggregation between feature information and finally, these features are reconstructed by the decoder, and then, the generated image is input into the global discriminator, in which the discrimination between real and fake images is completed. It is experimentally verified that our designed Transformer window attention network is able to make the structured texture of the restored images richer and more natural when performing the restoration task of large broken or structurally complex images.

Keywords: cross-window aggregated attention; detail feedforward networks; transformer

1. Introduction

Image inpainting is the process of filling the missing areas of an image with reasonable content so that the inpainted image is semantically reasonable and visually realistic. It is widely used in many practical scenarios, such as removing objects, restoring old photographs, image editing [1–3], etc. For image inpainting, it is crucial to be able to give reasonable content to fill the target area based on the observed area and make the whole image consistent. Traditional image inpainting methods usually match and copy background patches to the missing areas or by propagating information from the boundaries around the missing areas. These methods are very effective for images with only a small portion of damage or repetitive patterns, but for images with large damaged areas or complex structures, it is often difficult to generate semantically reasonable images because of the lack of semantic understanding of the image.

Generative Adversarial Network (GAN) can improve the visual effect of network generated images. Pathak et al. [4] applied GAN and designed a contextual compiler (CE) as a repair method, which improved on the traditional convolutional neural network and achieved significant repair results. However, this network has the limitation that it can only repair masked images with fixed shapes, and its repair results are not satisfactory when performing image repair tasks with random masks. For this reason, Iizuka et al. [5] achieved image inpainting of arbitrary region breakage by reducing the number of downsamples and used a null convolution layer instead of a fully connected layer [6]. Moreover, the method uses global and local discriminators to ensure the overall consistency of the global

Citation: Chen, M.; Liu, T.; Xiong, X.; Duan, Z.; Cui, A. A Transformer-Based Cross-Window Aggregated Attentional Image Inpainting Model. *Electronics* **2023**, *12*, 2726. https://doi.org/10.3390/electronics12122726

Academic Editors: Peter Odry and Vladimir Laslo Tadić

Received: 27 May 2023
Revised: 14 June 2023
Accepted: 14 June 2023
Published: 19 June 2023

Copyright: © 2023 by the authors. Licensee MDPI, Basel, Switzerland. This article is an open access article distributed under the terms and conditions of the Creative Commons Attribution (CC BY) license (https://creativecommons.org/licenses/by/4.0/).

discriminator, and the local discriminator achieves better restoration results by judging the local consistency of small central regions. However, due to the limited neural telepresence field output from the convolution operation, the feature information at a distance cannot be utilized, which results in semantic connectivity inconsistencies in the generated information. To cope with this problem, Yu et al. [7] proposed a feedforward generative network model for image inpainting, which was solved using an attention mechanism [8–10]. The model consists of two stages. First, an expanded convolutional network trained with reconstruction loss is used for rough restoration. Second, a context-aware layer with a spatial propagation layer is built using convolution to match the generated patches with known context patches, which enhances the spatial consistency and achieves fine repair. Song et al. [11] adopted a similar approach by introducing a "patch swapping layer" to replace the patches in the region to be filled with the most pixel consistent patches on the boundary.

In addition, Nazeri et al. [12] proposed a two-stage GAN model called "EC", which combines two stages of edge information prediction and image inpainting and first generates the edge map of the missing region as image inpainting guidance information to be sent to the restoration network for restoration, and it achieves better restoration results. Xiong et al. [13] showed a similar model that uses foreground object contours as a structural prior, unlike EC that uses edges as information as a prior. Ren et al. [14] pointed out that edge-preserving smoothed images provide better global structure due to capturing more semantics, but these methods require higher accuracy for the structure (e.g., edges and contours). To overcome this weakness, some researchers have addressed this problem by exploiting the correlation between texture and structure. Li et al. [15] designed a progressive visual structure reconstruction network (PRVS) to progressively reconstruct the structure and associated visual features. The reconstruction of visual structures and visual features are entangled together to benefit each other by sharing parameters. Yang et al. [16] introduced a multitasking framework to generate sharp edges by adding structural constraints. Liu et al. [17] proposed a mutual encoding–decoding to simultaneously learn features of convolution that correspond to different layers of structure and texture. However, a single shared framework is difficult for modeling texture and structure. Therefore, to effectively implement image structure and texture information restoration, Guo [18] et al. proposed a new dual-stream network for image inpainting (CTSDG) to further enhance the performance of image inpainting by dividing it into two subtasks, texture synthesis and structure reconstruction. Since existing image inpainting techniques are outputting only one restoration result for a broken image, but image inpainting is by nature an uncertain task and its output should not be limited, Liu [19] et al. proposed a PD-GAN algorithm based on this idea (that is, the closer to the center of the hole, the higher its diversity and the stronger the diversity) and obtained good results.

When convolution is used to process image features, each convolutional layer shares convolutional kernel parameters spatially. For a single image with both broken and normal regions, the operation of assigning the same kernel to features that are valid, invalid, or located on broken boundaries can easily lead to problems, such as structural distortion, texture blurring, or artifacts. In addition, neural networks operating only within a local window are inefficient in modeling images over long distances while in the processing of image inpainting, appropriate information within the entire image needs to be utilized, and sometimes information far from the damaged area needs to be acquired to repair the broken area. Therefore, a Transformer-based cross-window aggregation attention image inpainting method is proposed, and a rectangular window cross aggregation Transformer module (WAT) is constructed to combine the respective advantages of the attention module and convolution to complete the extraction of image features, which solves the restrictive problem that convolutional operations can only extract local features. It is experimentally verified that the Transformer window aggregation attention network designed in this paper can make the structural texture of the restored images richer and more natural when performing the restoration task of large broken or structurally complex images. The innovative work of this paper is as follows:

1. We propose a novel Transformer-based cross-window aggregated attentional image restoration network, which improves the information aggregation between windows by embedding WAT modules.
2. We effectively obtain the long-range dependence of images without increasing the computational complexity and solve the problem that convolutional operations are limited by local feature extraction.
3. Experiments on several datasets demonstrate the effectiveness of the proposed method and outperform the current restoration methods.

2. Overall Model Design

In this paper, we proposed a Transformer-based window aggregation attention image network. The overall design of the network model is shown in Figure 1, and the restoration model consisted of three parts, including the generator, discriminator and window aggregation attention. The encoder was a stack of convolutional layers with multiple different convolutional kernels and was responsible for extracting multi-scale features from the input image. In the encoder's backbone of the generator, partial convolution layers were employed to replace all the normal convolution in order to better capture information from irregular boundaries since partial convolution [20] was conditioned only on uncorrupted pixels, and in addition, jump connections produced more complex predictions by combining low and high level features at multiple scales. The decoder was similar in structure to the encoder and was used to reconstruct the features into images. The discriminator used a Markov global discriminator, which ensured the consistency of the regional structure with the overall structure. The WAT module was introduced into the partial convolution of the encoder to aggregate the multi-scale information extracted by the encoder, and the powerful remote modeling capability of attention was exploited to fully exploit the contextual information in the hierarchical features. In particular, the WAT module could effectively obtain the image long-range dependencies and solve the problem that the convolution operation was limited by local feature extraction. Figure 1A–C represent the generator and discriminator structure diagram, the generator internal detail diagram and the discriminator workflow diagram, respectively.

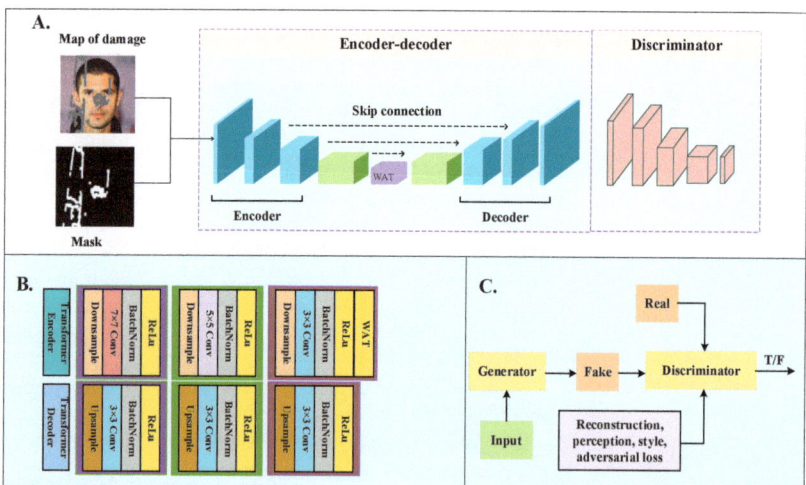

Figure 1. Overall network model. (**A**) represents the generator and discriminator structure diagram, (**B**) shows the internal details of the generator, and (**C**) shows the discriminator workflow diagram.

3. Transformer-Based Window Aggregation Attention Image Inpainting Network

3.1. WAT Module

We improved a window aggregation module (R-MSA) based on the literature [21] to replace the common multi-headed self-attention module and form a cross-window aggregation Transformer (WAT) module. Our WAT used local window self-attention to limit computational complexity and aggregated features across different windows to extend the perceptual field and improve the aggregation of window information. The first layer was a window aggregation module (R-MSA), and the second layer was a simple multilayer perceptron (MLP). Around each of the two sublayers, an in-residual connection [22] was used, followed by layer normalization [23]. This is presented in Figure 2.

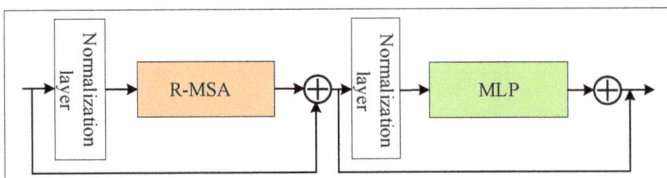

Figure 2. Structure of the WAT module.

The window aggregation module R-MSA, a key part of the WAT module, employed a new attention mechanism and contained two novel designs: the rectangular window self-attention mechanism (Rwin-MSA) and the local complementary module (LCM).

3.1.1. Construction of Rwin-MSA

The Rectangular window multi-head self-attention mechanism (Rwin-MSA), which performs self-attention in a non-overlapping local window, significantly reduced the computational cost and computational complexity from $O(H^2W^2C)$ to $O(M^2HWC)$, as depicted in Figure 3.

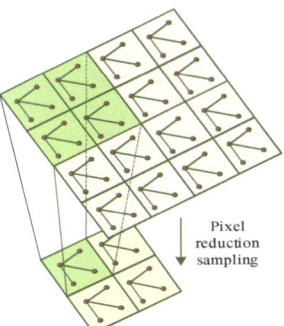

Figure 3. Change in computational complexity.

Given a two-dimensional feature mapping $X \in R^{C \times H \times W}$, where H and W were the height and width of the mapping and C was the depth, X was decomposed into non-overlapping windows of window size $M \times M$ and then, features and transposed features $X^i \in R^{M^2 \times C}$ were obtained from each window. Then, the features of each window were self-attended. Suppose the size of the head number k was $d_k = C/k$; then, the kth head self-attention in the non-overlapping window could be defined as:

$$X = \left\{X^1, X^2, \ldots, X^N\right\}, N = HM/M^2, \qquad (1)$$

$$Y_k^i = Attention(X^i W_k^Q, X^i W_k^K, X^i W_k^V), i = 1, \ldots, N, \quad (2)$$

$$X_k' = \{Y_k^1, Y2, \ldots, Y_k^M\}. \quad (3)$$

where $W_k^Q, W_k^K, W_k^V \in R^{C \times d_k}$ were the queries, keys and values of the projection matrix of the head number k, respectively. X_k' was the output of the kth head, and then, all heads $\{1, 2, \ldots, k\}$ were connected for linear projection to obtain the final result. Inspired by [24,25], the relative position encoding was applied to the attention module, so the attention calculation formula could be reduced to the following:

$$Attention(Q, K, V) = Softmax(\frac{QK^T}{\sqrt{d_k}} + B)V. \quad (4)$$

where B was the relative position deviation. Compared with the global self-attention mechanism, the window-based attention mechanism could significantly reduce the computational cost. The computational complexity decreased from $O(H^2W^2C)$ to $O(M^2HWC)$ for a given feature mapping $X \in R^{C \times H \times W}$.

3.1.2. Construction of LCM

Transformer could efficiently capture global information and model long-term dependencies between pixels. However, CNNs can aggregate local features and extract the underlying structure of an image (e.g., corners and edges) due to their translation invariance and localization that occupy an indispensable position in image inpainting tasks. To complement the local nature of the Transformer and to achieve global and local coupling, we therefore added a separate convolution operation, the Local Complementary Module (LCM), when computing the self-attentive mechanism using the Rwin-MSA module. The LCM could complement the Rwin-MSA with local information, which operated on the value (V) in parallel with the Rwin-MSA module, as demonstrated in Figure 4.

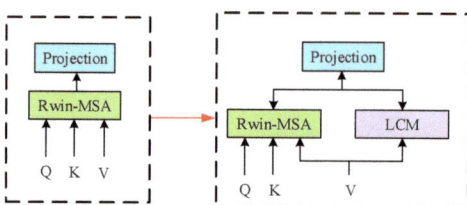

Figure 4. Partial complementary module.

Using the LCM module, the convolution operation was performed directly on the value (V) with the following formula:

$$Rwin - MSA(X) = (Concat(Y_k^1, Y_k^2, \ldots, Y_k^M) + Conv(V)W^P \quad (5)$$

where $Y_k^1, Y_k^2, \ldots, Y_k^M$ was the same as Equation (3), $V \in R^{C \times H \times W}$ was the value projected directly from X without window aggregation, $W^P \in R^{C \times C}$ denoted the projection matrix for feature aggregation and Conv(.) was the convolution operation with a convolution kernel of 3. Compared to performing convolution sequentially or using convolution directly on X, the operation in this paper had two features: (1) using convolution as a parallel module enabled the Transformer module to adaptively choose whether to employ attention or convolution operations, which was more flexible than sequential convolution execution. (2) From Equation (4), we can see that self-attention can be considered a content-dependent dynamic weight, and the convolution operation is equivalent to a static weight that can be learned. Therefore, the convolution operation on V was performed in the same feature domain as the attention operation.

3.2. Discriminator Network

In the repair network of this paper, the discriminator was Markov discriminator [26] (Patch-GAN), which mainly consisted of four convolutional layers and one fully connected layer. Unlike other discriminator networks, the Markov discriminator first output an $N \times N$ matrix and then calculated the mean of the $N \times N$ matrix as the final discriminator output, which was fundamentally different from the traditional discriminator output of only one true/false vector. Each position in the Markov discriminator output matrix could represent a receptive field of the generated image, and each receptive field corresponded to a part of the region in the generated image. Therefore, the Markov discriminator was used to more accurately distinguish the differences between the images generated by the generator and the real images and thus better adjust the network gradient.

To ensure that the discriminator focused on the structure of the whole image as much as possible and to evaluate whether the generated image was consistent with the real image, only the global discriminator was used as the discriminator for the whole network in this paper. This was because the local discriminator woul only focus on the region after network restoration when identifying the difference between the generated image and the real image, which satisfied the consistency of the restored region but ignored the global structure of the overall image, and the global discriminator could better ensure the consistency between the regional structure and the overall structure so that the generator could generate more realistic and vivid face images. Finally, to prevent a gradient explosion in the training process of the generative network, Spectral Normalization [27] (SN) was introduced in the discriminator to enable a stable training process as a way to improve the training quality of the GAN network. Table 1 shows the discriminator parameters.

Table 1. Discriminator parameters.

Layers	Convolution Kernels	Step Lengths	Activation Functions
1	4	2	LeakyReLu
2	4	2	LeakyReLu
3	4	2	LeakyReLu
4	4	1	LeakyReLu
Full Connection	-	-	Sigmoid

3.3. Loss Function

In order to minimize the loss in the training session, the algorithm in this paper used a semantic-based joint loss function, which consisted of four terms, including reconstruction loss, perceptual loss, style loss and adversarial loss, to obtain a repair network that made the repair network visually realistic and semantically reasonable.

(1) Reconstruction loss

L_{re} reconstruction loss was the value of the L_1 parametric number that compensated for the difference between the image I_{out} and the actual image I_g:

$$L_{re} = ||I_{out} - I_g||_1. \tag{6}$$

(2) Perceptual loss [28]

Since the reconstruction loss was difficult to capture the high-level semantics, the perceptual loss L_{pere} was introduced to evaluate the global structure of the image. The perceptual loss measured the feature mapping between the real image I_g and the output image I_{out}, with L_1 being the distance between the feature space I_{out} and I_g, and it was calculated as follows:

$$L_{pere} = E[\sum_i \frac{1}{N} ||\phi_i(I_{out}) - \phi_i(I_g)||_1]. \tag{7}$$

where $\phi_i(\cdot)$ denoted the activation mapping obtained for a given input image I through the i-th pooling layer of VGG-16.

(3) Style loss

The style loss was further designed in order to ensure style consistency. Similarly, the style loss calculated the L_1 distance between feature maps, which was calculated as:

$$L_{style} = E[\sum_i ||\Phi_i(I_{out}) - \Phi_i(I_{gt})||_1]. \tag{8}$$

where, $\Phi_i(.) = \Phi_j^T(.)\Phi_j(.)$ denoted the Gram matrix from the activation mapping Φ_i.

(4) Adversarial loss [29]

The adversarial loss guaranteed the visual realism of the reconstructed image and the consistency of texture and structure, where D was the discriminator. The adversarial loss was introduced into the Markov discriminator to add a new regularization to the network for discriminating the true and false images, which was calculated as:

$$L_{adv} = \min_G \max_D E_{I_{gt},g_{gt}}[\log D(I_{gt}, E_{gt})] + E_{I_{out},E_{out}} \log[1 - D(I_{out}, E_{out})]. \tag{9}$$

In summary, the joint loss function is:

$$L_{all} = \alpha L_{re} + \beta L_{pere} + \gamma L_{style} + \lambda L_{adv}, \tag{10}$$

where α, β, γ and λ were hyper-parameters. In the experimental procedure of this paper, we set $\alpha = 10$, $\beta = 0.1$, $\gamma = 250$ and $\lambda = 0.1$.

4. Experimental Environment and Evaluation Index

The deep learning framework used for the experiments was pytorch, the computer operating system was Windows 10, and the graphics card model was NVIDIA TITAN XP with 12G of video memory.

Distortion metrics and perceptual quality metrics were used to quantitatively evaluate model performance. Distortion metrics are used to measure the degree of distortion of the results, including Peak Signal to Noise Ratio (PSNR) and Structural Similarity Index (SSIM). Among them, PSNR was used to evaluate the error between the corresponding pixel points in two images, and a larger value indicated less distortion. SSIM was used to evaluate the overall similarity between two images in three aspects: brightness, structure and contrast, and a result closer to 1 indicated a higher similarity. The perceptual quality metric was used to represent the perceptual quality of the result, representing the subjective perceptual quality of an image. Here, it was represented by Fréchet inception distance (FID), and its lower value indicated better subjective perceptual quality.

4.1. Experimental Dataset and Pre-Processing

To verify and evaluate the robustness and generalization ability of the algorithmic network, the CelebA [30] and Places datasets [31] were used to evaluate the method in this paper, where the CelebA dataset used contains 165,000 face images in the training set, 19,500 face images in the test set and 19,400 face images in the validation set. We selected six categories from the Places dataset, each with 5000 training images, 900 test images and 100 validation images, and we used 30,000 images for training and 5400 images for testing. Classification was performed in 10% increments for the size of the broken area of the image. The model took about 7 days to train on CelebA and about 11 days to train on

Places, and the fine-tuning was done in one day. Our method was compared with three popular methods, which were CTSDG, BIFPN and DF-Net.

The mask datasets for the experiments all used irregular masks obtained from [20], classified according to their hole size relative to the whole image in 10% increments, all images and corresponding masks adjusted to 256 × 256 pixels, batch size processed to 16 sheets, training iterations 300,000 and optimized using the Adam optimizer [32] with parameters set to $\beta_1 = 0.001$, $\beta_2 = 0.9$.

4.2. Qualitative Analysis

Our Transformer cross-window aggregated attention mechanism image restoration model was visually compared with a representative model as illustrated in Figure 5. CTSDG was basically able to repair the structure of the original image when the broken area was small, but artifacts appeared when the broken area was large; for example, artifacts appeared in the right eye of the female in the third row of the second column. The face of the male in the second column of the last row showed a confusing structure and blurred texture. BIFPN was able to repair the structure and texture of the broken image better, but both showed masking artifacts. DF-Net performed better in small broken areas and also showed structure confusion and texture blurring in large broken areas. DF-Net performed better in small breaks and also showed structural confusion and texture blurring in large breaks, such as in the fourth, fifth and sixth rows of the fourth column. In contrast, our proposed method performed very well in both large-area and small-area breakage, and the restored image had clear texture and continuous structure, generating an image that was closer to the original image and more consistent with the visual effect of the human eye.

Figure 5. Qualitative comparison of experimental results of restoration on the CelebA dataset (zoom in for a better view): (**a**) Damage map, (**b**) CTSDG, (**c**) BIFPN, (**d**) DF-Net, (**e**) Ours, (**f**) Real Images.

A visual comparison of the restoration model we used with the representative model is presented in Figure 6. BIFPN was basically able to repair the structure of the original image when the broken area was small, but artifacts appeared when the broken area was large; for instance, the windows of the house in the third row of the second column appeared distorted and deformed. CTSDG was able to repair the structure of the broken image better, but both showed masking artifacts and blurred textures in the second row of the girl's head in the third column and in the windows of the house in the third row. DF-Net performed well in small areas of breakage and showed a lack of clear structure and blurred texture in large areas of breakage, such as the three and four rows of the fourth column. Our proposed method performed well in both large and small areas of breakage, and the restored images had clear textures and continuous structures that were more consistent with the human eye's vision.

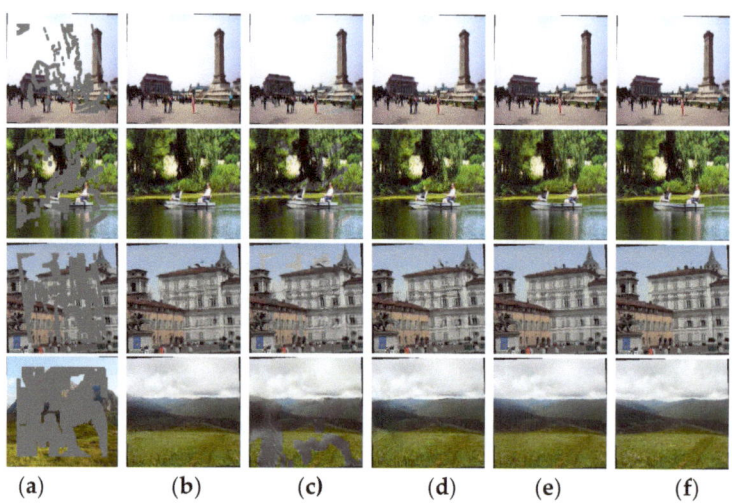

Figure 6. Qualitative comparison of experimental results of restoration on the Places dataset (zoom in for a better view): (**a**) Damage map, (**b**) CTSDG, (**c**) BIFPN, (**d**) DF-Net, (**e**) Ours, (**f**) Real Images.

4.3. Quantitative Analysis

In addition to the qualitative comparison test, three objective evaluation indexes were used for quantitative analysis in this paper, namely PSNR, SSIM and FID, and it can be seen from Table 2 that this paper outperformed other methods in all indexes. The test results of our method improved 1.42, 5.17 and 1.29 in PSNR metrics; 0.74%, 0.56% and 0.30% in SSIM and 2.75, 3.16 and 1.12 in FID metrics over CTSDG, BIFPN and DF-Net algorithms, respectively (the above contrasting values are calculated from the average values).

Table 2. Comparison of quantitative analysis results on CelebA.

Evaluation Metrics	Mask Category	BIFPN	CTSDG	DF-Net	Ours
PSNR	10–20%	32.34	38.78	38.56	**38.61**
	20–30%	31.82	37.75	38.63	**38.71**
	30–40%	29.28	31.76	31.79	**34.34**
	40–50%	26.13	29.30	29.12	**31.25**
	50–60%	23.73	24.37	25.50	**26.15**
SSIM	10–20%	0.968	0.967	0.969	**0.973**
	20–30%	0.963	0.962	0.965	**0.967**
	30–40%	0.929	0.927	0.929	**0.940**
	40–50%	0.858	0.855	0.861	**0.865**
	50–60%	0.734	0.729	0.737	**0.741**
FID	10–20%	6.31	5.48	4.98	**4.86**
	20–30%	8.51	7.69	7.80	**7.67**
	30–40%	18.96	20.77	16.04	**15.24**
	40–50%	22.36	21.18	18.98	**17.74**
	50–60%	25.26	23.74	22.91	**19.58**

As can be seen from Table 3, this paper outperformed other methods in all indicators. The test results in this paper showed improvements of 3.40, 2.27 and 1.08 in PSNR; 1.62%, 1.02% and 0.65% in SSIM and 1.90, 4.42 and 0.76 in FID, respectively, compared with CTSDG, BIFPN and DF-Net algorithms (the above comparison values are calculated from the average values).

Table 3. Comparison of quantitative analysis results on Places.

Evaluation Metrics	Mask Category	BIFPN	CTSDG	DF-Net	Ours
PSNR	20–30%	31.34	30.21	32.08	33.32
	30–40%	29.85	28.53	30.97	32.79
	40–50%	28.69	27.53	30.06	31.20
	50–60%	28.20	27.29	29.68	29.76
SSIM	20–30%	0.954	0.958	0.957	0.961
	30–40%	0.864	0.850	0.861	0.872
	40–50%	0.847	0.835	0.849	0.854
	50–60%	0.812	0.809	0.826	0.831
FID	20–30%	11.23	10.98	10.40	10.34
	30–40%	19.61	20.70	15.26	15.13
	40–50%	24.36	18.18	17.98	17.58
	50–60%	26.27	21.74	21.30	19.92

4.4. Ablation Experiments

In order to analyze the contribution of the WAT module to the performance of the image inpainting network, ablation experiments were therefore designed for this module. Experiments were conducted with 300 randomly selected test sets from the CelebA and Places datasets species, and similarly, 300 random masks with the different mask rate were used for the ablation experiments. Ten randomly selected results from the test result plots were analyzed for qualitative and quantitative comparisons, and the experimental results are in Figures 7 and 8.

(a)   (b)   (c)   (d)

Figure 7. Ablation experiments on CelebA (zoom in for a better view): (**a**) Broken graph, (**b**) No WAT module, (**c**) Ours, (**d**) Real Images.

In Figure 7, the facial information of the experimental results without the WAT module in the first row could be basically kept intact, but when the broken area increased, blurring and structural confusion appeared. The eyes and nose of the third row appeared to be significantly blurred. The shape of the eyes in the fourth row appeared distorted, and the eyes and mouth in the fifth row appeared structurally disorganized. The details of the mouth and eyes in the third, fourth and fifth rows can be seen to be better restored by the method in this paper. Especially for the repair of the human eyes in the third, fourth and fifth rows, it can be seen that the method in this paper has a consistent color and better detail repair of the eyes due to the introduction of the WAT module, which enhances the ability of the repair network to capture long-distance dependent information. Therefore, it can be visually seen that the WAT module helps to improve the restoration results.

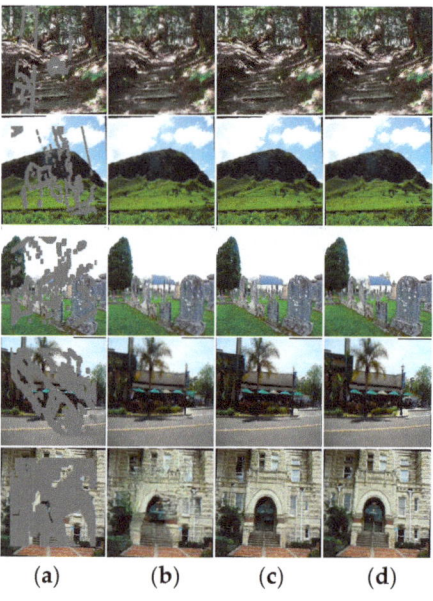

Figure 8. Ablation experiments on Places (zoom in for a better view): (**a**) Broken graph, (**b**) No WAT module, (**c**) Ours, (**d**) Real Images.

In Figure 8, the overall information of the experimental results without WAT module could be basically kept intact when the damage area was small, but when the damage area increased, blurring and structural confusion appeared. The details of the trees in the fourth row were not clear enough, and the structure of the house in the fifth row appeared confused and blurred in terms of the details of the trees and houses in the fourth and fifth rows. Looking at the details of the trees and houses in the fourth and fifth rows, we can see that our method restores better. Therefore, the WAT module helped to improve the restoration effect.

As indicated in Tables 4 and 5, the WAT model outperformed the no-WAT module in all three evaluation metrics, indicating that the WAT module helped to improve the repair performance, which was consistent with the results of the qualitative analysis.

Table 4. CelebA ablation experiments.

Evaluation Metrics	Mask Category	No/WAT	Ours
PSNR	10–20%	37.34	38.61
	20–30%	36.82	38.21
	30–40%	30.28	34.34
	40–50%	26.13	31.25
	50–60%	19.73	26.15
SSIM	10–20%	0.968	0.973
	20–30%	0.961	0.967
	30–40%	0.921	0.930
	40–50%	0.848	0.865
	50–60%	0.714	0.741
FID	10–20%	5.10	4.86
	20–30%	8.72	7.67
	30–40%	18.56	15.24
	40–50%	22.10	17.74
	50–60%	25.12	19.58

Table 5. Places ablation experiments.

Evaluation Metrics	Mask Category	No/WAT	Ours
PSNR	10–20%	34.15	34.21
	20–30%	32.72	33.21
	30–40%	30.89	32.57
	40–50%	28.13	30.39
	50–60%	24.73	28.46
SSIM	10–20%	0.968	0.971
	20–30%	0.956	0.963
	30–40%	0.856	0.867
	40–50%	0.839	0.850
	50–60%	0.794	0.834
FID	10–20%	7.53	6.78
	20–30%	11.02	10.29
	30–40%	16.76	15.56
	40–50%	20.10	17.51
	50–60%	24.19	19.91

5. Discussion

The limitations of this study were that, similar to other restoration models, our model still has difficulty in handling images with very high breakage rates, especially in images with very high breakage rates and complex patterns. Future research directions can start from large broken area restoration using known features and training experience to reconstruct images that are reasonable and not limited to the original image.

6. Conclusions

In this paper, we propose a Transformer-based cross-window aggregated attention model for image restoration, which improves the information aggregation between windows and effectively reduces the complexity of the network by embedding the cross-window aggregated attention module (WAT) in the generator based on the generative adversarial network image restoration. First, multi-scale features are extracted from the input by the encoder, and the WAT module is introduced into the partial convolution of the encoder to aggregate the extracted multi-scale information, and the powerful remote modeling capability of attention is utilized to fully exploit the contextual information in the layered features, which solves the restrictive problem that the convolution operation can only extract local features and which enhances the network's access to contextual information in image restoration capability. Second, the global discriminator is used to better ensure the consistency between the regional structure and the overall structure so that the generator can generate more realistic and vivid restored images. Finally, the experimental results show that the restoration network proposed in this paper is better able to perform the task of restoring images with blurred and large broken areas.

Author Contributions: T.L. conceived the algorithm model of this paper and conducted comparison experiments with representative algorithms and performed data analysis. M.C. conducted the ablation experiments and analyzed them. X.X. determined the research direction and wrote some of the content. Z.D. wrote some chapters and made the final revisions. A.C. created the diagrams and performed the document search. All authors have read and agreed to the published version of the manuscript.

Funding: This research was funded by Natural Science Foundation of Sichuan, China (2023NSFSC1987, 2022ZHCG0035); The Key Laboratory of Internet Information Retrieval of Hainan Province Research Found (2022KY03); the Opening Project of International Joint Research Center for Robotics and Intelligence System of Sichuan Province (JQZN2022-005); Sichuan University of Science & Engineering Postgraduate Innovation Fund Project, grant number Y2022130.

Institutional Review Board Statement: Not applicable.

Informed Consent Statement: Not applicable.

Data Availability Statement: We use publicly available datasets for our research. The CelebA face dataset we use is an open source large-scale face detection benchmark dataset from the Chinese University of Hong Kong, and the official download URL for the dataset; CelebA Dataset (cuhk.edu.hk), and the Places dataset is an open source dataset released by the Massachusetts Institute of Technology. Official download URL: Places: A 10 million Image Database for Scene Recognition (mit.edu). Both datasets can be used for academic research.

Conflicts of Interest: The authors declare no conflict of interest.

References

1. Barnes, C.; Shechtman, E.; Finkelstein, A.; Goldman, D.B. PatchMatch: A randomized correspondence algorithm for structural image editing. *ACM Trans. Graph.* 2009, 28, 24. [CrossRef]
2. Patwardhan, K.A.; Sapiro, G.; Bertalmio, M. Video inpainting of occluding and occluded objects. In Proceedings of the IEEE International Conference on Image Processing, Genoa, Italy, 11–14 September 2005; Volume 2, pp. 69–72.
3. Kumar, S.; Biswas, M.; Belongie, S.; Nguyen, T.Q. Spatio-temporal texture synthesis and image inpainting for video applications. In Proceedings of the IEEE International Conference on Image Processing, Genoa, Italy, 11–14 September 2005; Volume 2, pp. 85–88.
4. Pathak, D.; Krahenbuhl, P.; Donahue, J.; Darrell, T.; Efros, A.A. Context encoder: Feature Learning by Inpainting. In Proceedings of the IEEE Conference on Computer Vision and Pattern Recognition (CVPR), Las Vegas, NV, USA, 27–30 June 2016; pp. 2536–2544.
5. Iizuka, S.; Simo-Serra, E.; Ishikawa, H. Globally and Locally Consistent Image Completion. *ACM Trans. Graph. (TOG)* 2017, 36, 107. [CrossRef]
6. Yu, F.; Koltun, V. Multi-scale context aggregation by dilated convolutions. In Proceedings of the International Conference on Learning Representations (ICLR), San Juan, Puerto Rico, 2–4 May 2016.
7. Yu, J.; Lin, Z.; Yang, J.; Shen, X.; Lu, X.; Huang, T.S. Generative image inpainting with contextual attention. In Proceedings of the IEEE Conference on Computer Vision and Pattern Recognition, Salt Lake City, UT, USA, 18–23 June 2018; pp. 5505–5514.
8. Jaderberg, M.; Simonyan, K.; Zisserman, A.; Kavukcuoglu, K. Spatial transformer networks. In Proceedings of the Proceedings of the Advances in Neural Information Processing Systems, Montreal, QC, Canada, 7–12 December 2015; pp. 2017–2025.
9. Jeon, Y.; Kim, J. Active convolution: Learning the shape of convolution for image classification. In Proceedings of the IEEE Conference on Computer Vision and Pattern Recognition, Honolulu, HI, USA, 21–26 July 2017; pp. 1846–1854.
10. Dai, J.; Qi, H.; Xiong, Y.; Li, Y.; Zhang, G.; Hu, H.; Wei, Y. Deformable convolutional networks. In Proceedings of the IEEE International Conference on Computer Vision, Venice, Italy, 22–29 October 2017; pp. 764–773.
11. Song, Y.; Yang, C.; Lin, Z.; Liu, X.; Huang, Q.; Li, H.; Jay Kuo, C.-C. Contextual-based image inpainting: Infer, match, and translate. In Proceedings of the European Conference on Computer Vision (ECCV), Munich, Germany, 8–14 September 2018; pp. 3–19.
12. Nazeri, K.; Ng, E.; Joseph, T.; Qureshi, F.Z.; Ebrahimi, M. Edgeconnect: Structure guided image inpainting using edge prediction. In Proceedings of the IEEE International Conference on Computer Vision Workshop (ICCVW), Seoul, Republic of Korea, 27 October–2 November 2019.
13. Xiong, W.; Yu, J.; Lin, Z.; Yang, J.; Lu, X.; Barnes, C.; Luo, J. Foreground-aware image inpainting. In Proceedings of the IEEE Conference on Computer Vision and Pattern Recognition (CVPR), Long Beach, CA, USA, 16–20 June 2019.

14. Yurui, R.; Xiaoming, Y.; Ruonan, Z.; Li, T.H.; Liu, S.; Li, G. Structureflow: Image inpainting via structure-aware appearance flow. In Proceedings of the IEEE/CVF International Conference on Computer Vision (ICCV), Seoul, Republic of Korea, 27 October–2 November 2019; IEEE: Piscataway, NJ, USA, 2019.
15. Li, J.; He, F.; Zhang, L.; Du, B.; Tao, D. Progressive reconstruction of visual structure for image inpainting. In Proceedings of the IEEE/CVF International Conference on Computer Vision (ICCV), Seoul, Republic of Korea, 27 October–2 November 2019; IEEE: Piscataway, NJ, USA, 2019.
16. Yang, J.; Qi, Z.Q.; Shi, Y. Learning to incorporate structure knowledge for image inpainting. In Proceedings of the AAAI Conference on Artificial Intelligence, New York, NY, USA, 7–12 February 2020.
17. Liu, H.; Jiang, B.; Song, Y.; Huang, W.; Yang, C. Rethinking image inpainting via a mutual encoder-decoder with feature equalizations. In Proceedings of the European Conference on Computer Vision (ECCV), Glasgow, UK, 23–28 August 2020.
18. Guo, X.; Yang, H.; Huang, D. Image Inpainting via Conditional Texture and Structure Dual Generation. In Proceedings of the IEEE/CVF International Conference on Computer Vision (ICCV), Montreal, QC, Canada, 10–17 October 2021; pp. 14114–14123.
19. Liu, H.; Wan, Z.; Huang, W.; Song, Y.; Han, X.; Liao, J. PD-GAN: Probabilistic diverse GAN for image inpainting. In Proceedings of the IEEE/CVF Conference on Computer Vision and Pattern Recognition (CVPR), Nashville, TN, USA, 20–25 June 2021; pp. 9367–9376.
20. Liu, G.; Reda, F.A.; Shih, K.J.; Wang, T.-C.; Tao, A.; Catanzaro, B. *Image Inpainting for Irregular Holes using Partial Convolutions*; Springer: Cham, Switzerland, 2018.
21. Zheng, C.; Zhang, Y.; Gu, J.; Zhang, Y.; Kong, L.; Yuan, X. Cross aggregation transformer for image inpainting. In Proceedings of the Conference on Neural Information Processing Systems (NeurIPS), New Orleans, LA, USA, 28 November–9 December 2022.
22. He, K.; Zhang, X.; Ren, S.; Sun, J. Deep residual learning for image recognition. In Proceedings of the IEEE Conference on Computer Vision and Pattern Recognition, Las Vegas, NV, USA, 27–30 June 2016; pp. 770–778.
23. Ba, J.L.; Kiros, J.R.; Hinton, G.E. Layer normalization. *arXiv* 2016, arXiv:1607.06450.
24. Dosovitskiy, A.; Beyer, L.; Kolesnikov, A.; Weissenborn, D.; Zhai, X.; Unterthiner, T.; Dehghani, M.; Minderer, M.; Heigold, G.; Gelly, S.; et al. An image is worth 16 × 16 words: Transformers for image recognition at scale. In Proceedings of the International Conference on Learning Representations (ICLR), Vienna, Austria, 3–7 May 2021.
25. Shaw, P.; Uszkoreit, J.; Vaswani, A. Self-attention with relative position repre-sentations. *arXiv* 2018, arXiv:1803.02155.
26. Isola, P.; Zhu, J.Y.; Zhou, T.H.; Efros, A.A. Image-to-image translation with conditional adversarial networks. In Proceedings of the IEEE Conference on Computer Vision and Pattern Recognition, Honolulu, HI, USA, 21–26 July 2017; IEEE: Piscataway, NJ, USA, 2017; pp. 1125–1134.
27. Miyato, T.; Kataoka, T.; Koyama, M.; Yoshida, Y. Spectral normalization for generative adversarial networks. In Proceedings of the 6th International Conference on Learning Representations, Vancouver, BC, Canada, 30 April–3 May 2018; Available online: OpenReview.net (accessed on 5 October 2021).
28. Johnson, J.; Alahi, A.; Fei-Fei, L. Perceptual losses for real-time style transfer and super-resolution. In Proceedings of the European Conference on Computer Vision (ECCV), Amsterdam, The Netherlands, 11–14 October 2016; p. 80.
29. Jolicoeur-Martineau, A. The relativistic discriminator: A key element missing from standard GAN. In Proceedings of the International Conference on Learning Representations, Vancouver, BC, Canada, 30 April–3 May 2018.
30. Liu, Z.; Luo, P.; Wang, X.; Tang, X. Deep learning face attributes in the wild. In Proceedings of the IEEE International Conference on Computer Vision, Santiago, Chile, 11–18 December 2015; pp. 3730–3738.
31. Zhou, B.; Lapedriza, A.; Khosla, A.; Oliva, A.; Torralba, A. Places: A 10 million image database for scene recognition. *IEEE Trans. Pattern Anal. Mach. Intell.* 2017, 40, 1452–1464. [CrossRef] [PubMed]
32. Kingma, D.; Ba, J. Adam: A method for stochastic optimization. In Proceedings of the International Conference on Learning Representations (ICLR), San Diego, CA, USA, 7–9 May 2015; Ithaca: New York, NY, USA, 2015.

Disclaimer/Publisher's Note: The statements, opinions and data contained in all publications are solely those of the individual author(s) and contributor(s) and not of MDPI and/or the editor(s). MDPI and/or the editor(s) disclaim responsibility for any injury to people or property resulting from any ideas, methods, instructions or products referred to in the content.

Article

Analysis of the Security Challenges Facing the DS-Lite IPv6 Transition Technology

Ameen Al-Azzawi * and Gábor Lencse

Department of Networked Systems and Services, Faculty of Electrical Engineering and Informatics, Budapest University of Technology and Economics, Műegyetem rkp. 3., H-1111 Budapest, Hungary; lencse@hit.bme.hu
* Correspondence: alazzawi@hit.bme.hu

Abstract: This paper focuses on one of the most prominent IPv6 transition technologies named DS-Lite (Dual-Stack Lite). The aim was to analyze the security threats to which this technology might be vulnerable. The analysis is based on the STRIDE method, which stands for Spoofing, Tampering, Repudiation, Information Disclosure, and Elevation of Privilege. A testbed was built for the DS-Lite topology using several virtual machines, which were created using CentOS Linux images. The testbed was used to perform several types of attacks against the infrastructure of DS-Lite, especially against the B4 (Basic Bridging Broadband) and the AFTR (Address Family Transition Router) elements, where it was shown that the pool of source ports can be exhausted in 14 s. Eventually, the most common attacks that DS-Lite is susceptible to were summarized, and methods for mitigating such attacks were proposed.

Keywords: DS-Lite; 464XLAT; DNS; IPv4aaS; STRIDE; translation; encapsulation; spoofing; thc-ipv6 toolkit; port number exhaustion

Citation: Al-Azzawi, A.; Lencse, G. Analysis of the Security Challenges Facing the DS-Lite IPv6 Transition Technology. *Electronics* **2023**, *12*, 2335. https://doi.org/10.3390/electronics12102335

Academic Editors: Vladimir Laslo Tadić and Peter Odry

Received: 21 April 2023
Revised: 16 May 2023
Accepted: 19 May 2023
Published: 22 May 2023

Copyright: © 2023 by the authors. Licensee MDPI, Basel, Switzerland. This article is an open access article distributed under the terms and conditions of the Creative Commons Attribution (CC BY) license (https:// creativecommons.org/licenses/by/ 4.0/).

1. Introduction

With the depletion of the public IPv4 address pool in 2011 [1], the integration of IPv4 and IPv6 has become a pressing issue in the field of networking. Various transition technologies have been proposed to address this challenge, but each comes with its own set of drawbacks and vulnerabilities. In previous research work, a survey of the most prominent IPv6 transition technologies was conducted [2], in which it was pointed out that the combination of DNS64 [3] and NAT64 [4] could be a working solution for the communication of IPv6 clients with IPv4 servers.

However, this technology still faces challenges in terms of IPv4 literals communications and establishing connections from the IPv4 host side. To address these challenges, the 464XLAT technology has been developed to tackle some of the DNS64 + NAT64 issues [5]. 464XLAT uses a double translation mechanism by deploying two separate translators: CLAT (client-side translator) and PLAT (provider-side translator).

Several papers have been published regarding the 464XLAT transition technology. In [6], a security analysis for 464XLAT using the STRIDE method was presented, which highlighted the vulnerabilities and potential security threats of the technology. In [7], a testbed of 464XLAT was built using Debian-based virtual machines to evaluate the performance of the PLAT under a DoS (Denial of Service) attack, specifically testing the CPU performance and the pool of source port numbers. In a subsequent paper [8], the previous work was extended using a more powerful computer, allowing for an increase in the number of attacking clients (virtual machines) from 1 to 8. The PLAT performance was then tested after an attack using the hping3 command, ultimately demonstrating the susceptibility of the PLAT to DoS attacks. These studies underscore the importance of further investigating the potential security threats and vulnerabilities of 464XLAT and other IPv6 transition technologies.

On the other hand, DS-Lite (Dual-Stack Lite) has its own unique topology and application. It is a promising technology that enables the ISPs (Internet service providers) to use only IPv6 in their access and core network, while providing the users with fully functional IPv4 Internet access, too. DS-Lite has the highest deployment rate among the five important IPv4aaS (IPv4-as-a-Service) technologies (464XLAT, DS-Lite, Lw4o6, MAP-E, MAP-T) [9]. The literature is very scarce when it comes to security threat analysis for DS-Lite, which is why the security analysis of DS-Lite was chosen as the topic of the current research.

The main target of this paper is to analyze the security threats that the DS-Lite IPv6 transition technology might face and to come up with mitigation methods for such attacks. The goals of the research are intended to be accomplished through the following steps:

- Applying the STRIDE threat modeling technique to DS-Lite, where some of its potential security threats were examined at every inbound and outbound gateway within the infrastructure;
- Building a testbed for the DS-Lite topology;
- Testing the real capabilities of DS-Lite under several kinds of attack scenarios;
- Coming up with potential mitigations of the tested attacks.

In Section 2, the related work is discussed. In Section 3, the operation of DS-Lite and its structure is explained, while Section 4 is devoted to tunneling in general and its security concerns. Section 5 discusses the operation of the STRIDE method, its elements, and how it works. In Section 6, the STRIDE method is applied to the DS-Lite topology. In Section 7, the testbed is built and its infrastructure, topology elements, attacking scenarios, and possible mitigation methods are explained. In addition, Section 7 also points out the importance of the research and narrows down potential areas for further research. In Section 8, the results of the study are summarized and concluded. In the same section, the efficiency of DS-Lite and its flexibility to deal with all connection scenarios are proven, especially when a private IPv4 address client wants to communicate with a public IPv4 address server while there is an IPv6 address island in the middle. Finally, the security analysis of DS-Lite and its vulnerabilities and their mitigation methods are summarized.

2. Related Work

Very few experiments have been published regarding DS-lite and its security analysis. Therefore, we seized the opportunity to take the lead in this uncharted territory. A survey of the most prominent IPv6 transition technologies and their security analysis was carried out in [9], where DS-Lite was mentioned, and its security analysis has been classified as important but replaceable due to several issues mentioned by [10], such as the following:

- The need for two separate physical interfaces at the AFTR;
- The need for high scalability at the AFTR side due to the fact that many B4 routers may be connected to the same AFTR [10];
- The location of deploying AFTR router within the ISP network and the trade-off it creates between the high operation cost and installing an extremely powerful AFTR [10]. The trade-off can be explained by dividing the issue at hand into two options:
  - o Deploying AFTR at the edge of the network to cover a small area serves few B4s and requires less-powerful AFTR;
  - o Deploying AFTR at the core of the network to cover a big area covers more B4s and requires extremely powerful AFTR (or even more than one AFTR);
- The complexity of deploying a proxy DNS resolver, which will proxy every DNS query stemming from all IPv4 clients heading towards a DNS server that resides in an IPv6 network [10].

Another work [11] conducted a security analysis for DS-Lite in terms of its MIB (Management Information Base), and it consists of several objects. MIB is a module that can be used to monitor the AFTR router within the DS-Lite infrastructure by leveraging SNMP (Simple Network Management Protocol). According to [11], the most vulnerable objects that are susceptible to attacks are:

- Notification threshold objects: an attacker manipulating a threshold's value to a very low level, which will lead to a flood of useless alarms and thus disrupt the AFTR and its monitoring mechanism, or the attacker sets it to a very high level that makes the idea of setting the alarm literally useless:
    o DsliteAFTRAlarmConnectNumber: The alarm is sent when the number of current DS-Lite tunnels reaches the threshold, which means for every B4 router, the AFTR has to have a separate tunnel for it;
    o DsliteAFTRAlarmSessionNumber: An alarm will be sent when the threshold of sessions per IPv4 user is reached. This metric goes hand in hand with RFC-6333 [12], where AFTR has to be able to log softwire-ID, IP, ports, and protocol (see Table 1) in order to keep track of user sessions;
    o DsliteAFTRAlarmPortNumber: An alarm is to be sent when the threshold for the number of ports used by a user is reached or even crossed;
- Table entry objects: An attacker can alter the content of such entries causing the drop of legitimate entries or adding harmful and faulty ones:
    o DsliteTunnelTable: Consists of mapping entries of B4 address to AFTR address;
    o DsliteNATBindTable: Contains entries about the current active bindings within the NAT table of the AFTR (see Table 1).

Table 1. Dual-Stack Lite Carrier-Grade NAT translation table [12].

Softwire-ID/IPv4/Protocol/Port	IPv4/Protocol/Port
2001:db8:0:1::2/10.0.0.1/TCP/10000	192.0.2.1/TCP/5000

What makes these table entries a potential security threat is the possibility of an attacker assessing the number of hosts being served by a single AFTR router, which reveals sensitive information about the whole topology of DS-Lite [11]. A chance of an inside job is also possible, where an internal employee can access the list of hosts that are in active sessions, which will be a violation of the subscriber's privacy [11]. Moreover, RFC-6334 [13] referred to DS-Lite security briefly and recommended that an IP firewall be implemented in order to avoid MitM (Man-in-the-Middle) attacks along the softwire connection of DS-Lite.

RFC-8513 [14] proposed another method to implement DS-Lite using the YANG module, which is a schema that facilitates data assessment mechanisms through network management protocols such as NETCONF and RESTCONF. This module allows the administrator to add some features and add-ons to the B4 and AFTR interfaces such as "b4-address-change-limit", "Tunnel-MTU (Maximum Transmission Unit)", etc.

Moreover, RFC-8513 [14] suggested a solution for the DoS attack by raising the "b4-address-change-limit". This value specifies the minimum time between two consecutive changes in the IPv6 address of the B4 device. Setting it to a low value would enable the attacker to send a higher number of attacking packets with different source addresses. The recommended mitigation is to set its value to 30 min.

In RFC-8513 [14], the authors presented the security analysis of their DS-Lite architecture, which emphasized that the main vulnerability is an attacker having access to either B4 or AFTR router and undertaking several kinds of malicious activities:

- Manipulating the AFTR IPv6 address on the B4 tunnel endpoint, which will deceive the B4 router and force it to forward the 4in6 traffic to the wrong recipient;
- Altering the value of the "b4-address-change-limit", which gives the B4 more flexibility in configuring the softwire. An attacker lowering this value will boost the possibility of a DoS attack against the B4 router.

Similar research was conducted on vehicular network security, where the author investigated the possibility of preventing a selfish or malicious user from occupying limited resources in a mobile edge network and proposed a trusted deep reinforcement learning (DRL) cybersecurity approach [15]. The author also presented the idea of a reputation record table, which contains a list of untrusted interference vehicle devices [15]. Furthermore, another research work proposed a Truth Detection-based Task Assignment (TDTA) scheme to assign micro-tasks to reliable workers and establish a credible task execution environment for crowdsourced industrial Internet of Things (IoT) [16].

3. The Operation of DS-Lite

The general purpose of DS-Lite is to provide the home network with IPv4 connectivity across an IPv6-only access network. DS-Lite was presented in RFC 6333 [12], where it consists of two main parts (B4 and AFTR). Figure 1 illustrates the infrastructure of DS-Lite and how it functions (with some simplification, please refer to the operation of the AFTR below).

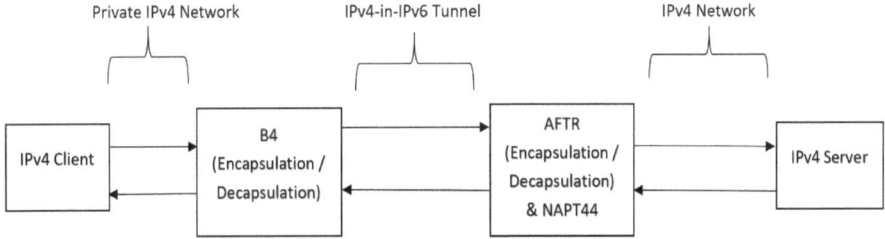

Figure 1. Overview of the DS-Lite architecture [17].

3.1. B4 (Basic Bridging Broadband)

This router is responsible for encapsulating IPv4 packets into IPv6 ones and then sending them over the IPv6 network until they reach the AFTR router. It also has another vital role when it processes the returning packets from the AFTR toward the B4, where it decapsulates the IPv6 packet and extracts the original IPv4 packet from the payload [12]. The tunnel that is created by the CPE (customer-provided equipment), which is the B4, is called the softwire tunnel that connects the B4 with the AFTR.

Some facts about the B4 router that were mentioned by RFC-6333 [12]:

- B4 announces itself as the default IPv4 router, and this route is applicable for all IPv4 clients sitting behind this B4 router;
- The B4 router should also announce itself as a DNS server in the DHCP (Dynamic Host Configuration Protocol) option 6 [12];
- As for the operation side, it acts as a DNS proxy for all IPv4 clients who are willing to connect with it and beyond, it forwards those requests to the DNS server of the ISP (Internet Service Provider) [12];
- B4 also forwards native IPv6 packets to the AFTR without any intervention;
- The default structure of DS-Lite is as explained above (client → CPE → ISP). However, some devices (IPv4 clients) are connected directly to the ISP without the home gateway. The reason behind this is that those devices have the ability to act as CPEs themselves [12].

3.2. AFTR (Address Family Transition Router)

The AFTR decapsulates the 4in6 traffic that comes from the B4 router; then, it translates the IPv4 packet into public IPv4, which is a function similar to the well-known stateful NAT44 [12]. However, it is a more complex function than stateful NAT44, because here the translation table contains also the Softwire-ID, which is the IPv6 address of the CE device, as shown in Table 1. Of course, it also performs the reverse functions for the returning packets.

The technology in general has two types of topologies (Gateway-based and Host-based architecture), and each one has its own applications:

- Gateway-based: Mostly based in residential broadband infrastructure, where the client and the CPE are based in different but directly connected machines [12];
- Host-based: Designed for large-scale deployments and especially when the client is directly connected to the service provider network, which means the IPv4 client and the CPE are both mounted on the same device [12].

In this paper, the focus is on the Gateway-based architecture topology because this topology is easier to build for testing purposes and a virtual environment. It is the most represented topology in residential households; for example, IPv4 client >> router >> ISP.

The AFTR has two main interfaces (softwire interface and network interface), and each one of them faces one end of the device:

- Softwire interface: Its main function is connecting B4 with AFTR and translating the datagram of (softwire identifier + IPv4 + source port) to another source IPv4 and source port. So, it decapsulates the IPv4 in the IPv6 datagram (for the packets coming from B4 side), and performs the reverse by encapsulating IPv4 in the IPv6 datagram (for the packets heading towards the B4 side);
- Network interface: Resides on the other side of the AFTR—the WAN (wide-area network) side—and translates the decapsulated source IPv4 and source port into the interface IP (192.0.2.1) and source port 5000 (for example purposes only). The interface is also in charge of the translation in the reverse direction (IPv4 server → AFTR → B4), where it translates the original packet's destination IP and destination port (according to AFTR's Carrier-Grade NAT translation table) to the destination IP and destination port of the softwire.

Figure 2 shows the outbound communication between B4 and AFTR. The NAT table in this example is configured in a way that translates any incoming packet with the source IP address 10.0.0.1 and source port number 10,000 to IP/port pair of 192.0.2.1:5000.

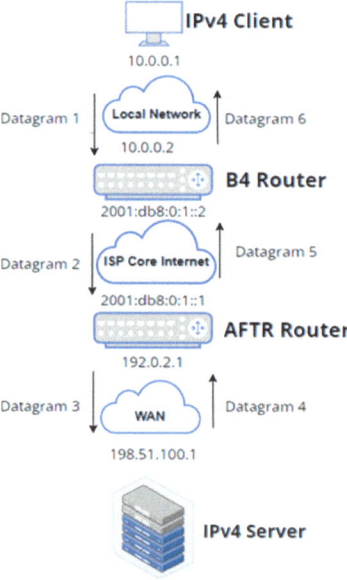

Figure 2. Overview of the DS-Lite datagram path.

- Once Datagram 1 reaches the B4 router, it will be encapsulated into Datagram 2, which is an IPv4 in IPv6 datagram, and then forwarded to the AFTR through the softwire tunnel;

- When the AFTR receives Datagram 2, it decapsulates it, extracts the IPv4 datagram from it, and forwards it to the stateful NAT function, which performs the following (according to its NAT table);
- The received datagram with source IP and port pair of 10.0.0.1:10000 should be translated to Datagram 3 with the following specifications:
    o Source IP and port pair: 192.0.2.1:5000.

How does the AFTR translation table function?

The IPv6 address for the B4 router is called the softwire-ID. This ID is being shared by every client that wants to connect with the B4 router and triggers the DS-Lite communication process. Every single client of those is equipped (by the B4 router) with a source IPv4 address [RFC 1918] such as 10.0.0.1, and it is unique within its network.

When an embedded packet (source IP address: 10.0.0.1, source port number: 10,000) is forwarded from B4 to AFTR through the softwire tunnel, AFTR combines the softwire-ID with this packet's details as one entry: softwire-id/IPv4/TCP/10000. In fact, this is only half of the entry. The other half will be the IP address of the AFTR network interface, the protocol identifier (e.g., TCP or UDP), and the source port number (192.0.2.1/TCP/5000), as shown in Table 1. The reverse direction of the packet (IPv4 server > AFTR > B4 > IPv4 client) functions in a similar manner:

- AFTR receives Datagram 4 through the network interface with a public IPv4 address, then processes it by checking the internal NAT table and looking for matching entries. In this case, Datagram 4 has the following details:
    o IPv4 destination address: 192.0.2.1;
    o Destination port: 5000;
    o Protocol is TCP;
- The corresponding entry does exist in the NAT table (see Table 1); AFTR, therefore, translates the IPv4 packet of Datagram 4 to IPv4 destination address 10.0.0.1 and TCP destination port 10,000;
- AFTR then encapsulates the translated IPv4 packet into an IPv6 packet and sends Datagram 5 over to the B4 router at 2001:db8:0:1::2 IPv6 address (which the AFTR knows from the table entry itself as softwire-ID);
- B4 receives Datagram 5, decapsulates the embedded packet, extracts the original IPv4 packet from the 4in6 Packet, and forwards it accordingly to the IPv4 client (10.0.0.1:10000) as Datagram 6.

Table 2 lists all IP addresses and port numbers for the DS-Lite packet route for Datagrams 1–6.

Table 2. DS-Lite datagrams.

Datagram	Header Details
IPv4 Datagram 1	IPv4 Src: 10.0.0.1 IPv4 Dst: 198.51.100.1 TCP Src: 10000 TCP Dst: 80
IPv6 Datagram 2	IPv6 Src: 2001:db8:0:1::2 IPv6 Dst: 2001:db8:0:1::1 IPv4 Src: 10.0.0.1 IPv4 Dst: 198.51.100.1 TCP Src: 10000 TCP Dst: 80
IPv4 Datagram 3	IPv4 Src: 192.0.2.1 IPv4 Dst: 198.51.100.1 TCP Src: 5000 TCP Dst: 80

Table 2. *Cont.*

Datagram	Header Details
IPv4 Datagram 4	IPv4 Src: 198.51.100.1 IPv4 Dst: 192.0.2.1 TCP Src: 80 TCP Dst: 5000
IPv6 Datagram 5	IPv6 Src: 2001:db8:0:1::1 IPv6 Dst: 2001:db8:0:1::2 IPv4 Src: 198.51.100.1 IPv4 Dst: 10.0.0.1 TCP Src: 80 TCP Dst: 10000
IPv4 Datagram 6	IPv4 Src: 198.51.100.1 IPv4 Dst: 10.0.0.1 TCP Src: 80 TCP Dst: 10000

To understand the functionality of AFTR translation even more, please refer to RFC 6333 [12], where further details about the translation steps are explained.

4. Tunneling

4.1. Tunneling History

Tunneling goes back to the 1990s when PPTP (point-to-point tunneling protocol) was presented by Microsoft engineers and some other vendors, where the original purpose was to support Windows users with data encryption, which gained huge popularity among small and medium-sized corporations later on and is in fact still being used to some extent [18]. Since then, it has consistently faced scrutiny from critics. It was even presented as an RFC [19] in 1999. PPTP functions at Data Layer 2 and uses general routing encapsulation (GRE) as a packet creation system, where GRE encapsulates the original packet inside another packet. Some vulnerabilities were discovered by Schneier [20]; he showed that PPTP has several weak points such as its Challenge/Response authentication protocol (CHAP), and he also presented the fact that PPTP uses a very low-security aware hashing algorithm, where eavesdropping was also quite easy to implement. Schneier [20] also emphasized that PPTP uses a low-security encryption standard called MPPE, which has a key that could be easily broken.

Later, Microsoft presented another solution called MS-CHAPv1 [21] and then MS-CHAPv2 [22], which is used as one authentication option in Microsoft's implementation of the PPTP protocol for virtual private networks [21].

The most secure tunneling is OpenVPN and it has proven to be very hard to crack [18]. In conclusion, there are alternatives to the regular PPTP such as the IKEv2 and a combination of IPsec and L2TP, which is used in the Microsoft VPN (virtual private network), and it is safer and quicker than regular PPTP [18]. Tunneling in general can come in so many forms such as MAP-E, 6over4, 6to4, Teredo, 6rd, DS-Lite, etc. [9]. It makes the connection between two devices possible despite having a different IP version island in the middle, as is the case in the DS-Lite tunnel example, though it brings some security threats with it.

4.2. Tunneling Issues and Solutions

The most serious issue with tunneling is that tunneled IP traffic does not go through the same inspection process that the normal traffic (non-encapsulated packets) will be liable to unless extra dedicated devices are installed on the premise to double-check the traffic as deep packet inspection [23]. For instance, in the Teredo tunnel, the router will check the IP and UDP layer normally. However, it cannot find out that there is actually another IP layer encapsulated within the UDP payload.

Another issue with tunneling is when the already encapsulated packet is targeting a host that lies further beyond the tunnel endpoint. In this case, the machine will normally forward the packet simply to the built-in next hop [23].

The tunneled data endpoints are aware of the tunneled data and the encapsulated packets. The network devices in the middle are not, and that could be an issue [23].

A solution is proposed in [23], where in case IPv6 transition is required, native IPv6 is the way forward in terms of connecting two sides with tunneling solutions, such as ISATAP, 6over4, etc. [24], in order to encapsulate traffic between a device and the router on the other side that resides in the same network. The difficulties that come with inspecting the inner content of the encapsulated packet make it a quite complicated process.

NAT process also presents another challenge when it comes to tunneling, opening more doors for attacking possibilities on the incoming NAT interface. Therefore, it is recommended that the NAT interface should not be configured by default and only used when it is the last resort [23]. Another recommendation is to deactivate the interface itself after its usage [23].

Furthermore, IP address guessing emerged as a potential risk to the tunnel endpoint, where some protocols use a regular or a well-known IP address or range of IP addresses. For instance, Teredo uses a specific IP address range in its infrastructure, which makes the tunnel liable to IP address guessing attacks. Furthermore, sometimes guessing the IP address gives an indication about which kind of OS is being used. For instance, Teredo implies that the machine is most probably running Microsoft Windows. The solution is to avoid those well-known IP address ranges and use random ones [23].

On the other hand, an adversary can have the ability to alter the tunnel's server settings on the client side while the client itself has no idea about it. One way to avoid such a breach is to use authentication for tunnel endpoints such as https [23]. A second mitigation method can be the use of secure ND (neighbor discovery) [24] whenever a client receives a router advertisement packet. Tunnels, in general, are less secure than normal conventional links due to the fact that an attacker can send an already encapsulated packet to the tunnel end-node where it is supposed to be decapsulated [23]. This action might cause an injection of the faulty packet into the decapsulator side. This threat might be avoided by turning on a decapsulation check, which will drop such malicious packets [25]; it is also highly discouraged to set the tunnel interface to reply by acknowledging the existence of a tunnel, such as an "ICMP error message", representing another valuable recommendation.

In general, [26] has mentioned two important general tunnel security points:

- There is no correlation between the amount of security regulations and procedures on the tunnel packets and the level of security measures applied to the original packet inside the tunnel (the payload) [26];
- The security header authentication (HA) or encryption security payload (ESP) parameters are the deciding factors for the three security pillars (integrity, authentication, and confidentiality) of any tunnel endpoint [26].

4.3. Attack Scenarios

In [27], the attack possibilities were categorized into three types:

- Denial of Service (DoS): The act of sending too many requests to a specific device to overwhelm its computation and processing power or bandwidth in order to force the targeted machine to drop or not serve the useful requests;
- Reflecting DoS: Where the attacker will reflect the traffic from normal (innocent) machines toward the targeted machine to inflict harm;
- Service theft: Gaining unauthorized access.

One of the most used types of tunnels is the well-known 6in4 [28], which has several attacking scenarios. Each element within the IPv6 network sends an RA message to declare that it is there and to allow other routers to update their table of existing IPv6 addresses. An attacker might take advantage of this process especially when all routers are sitting on the same network, which gives the possibility to attack the 6to4 router with a route advertisement (RA) message, by sending spoofed packets to the victim [27]. The second type is spoofing, as explained by [28], where an attacker can take advantage of an existing tunnel and spoof one side of the tunnel endpoint and attack the other side, as shown in Figure 3. The reason for executing such an attack is that tunnels are not aware of what is behind the requester due to the absence of authentication, so a specific tunnel endpoint does not know which other endpoints reside in the same tunnel. The tunnel endpoint only assumes that packets come from the other tunnel endpoint [29]. This lack of knowledge has drawn the attention of attackers to exploit it, especially if the attacker's packet is difficult to trace. That means the attacker is able to conduct sniffing, spoofing, and DoS attacks by leveraging this vulnerability.

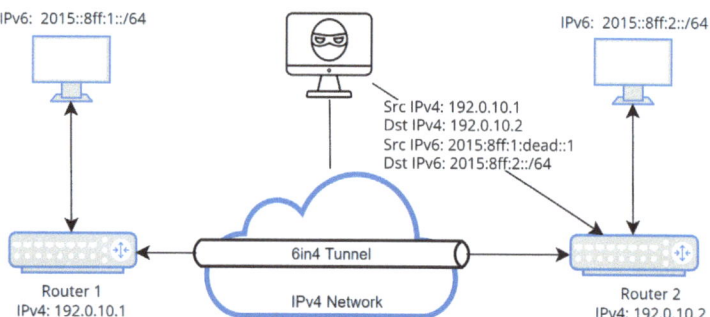

Figure 3. 6in4 tunnel attacking scenario [28].

IPv6 tunnels have some other weaknesses, being liable to password and "internet key exchange" attacks [30]. The golden rule according to [31] is that the security of the tunnel comes from the security of the tunnel endpoints themselves and the inner packets of the tunnel. If they are secured, then the tunnel in general is secured. So, the attacks to which tunnels are generally susceptible are as follows:

- Sniffing;
- Spoofing;
- DoS;
- Password and Internet key exchange.

4.4. Mitigation Methods

End-to-end secure communication systems such as IPsec [32] can help to protect the tunnel endpoint nodes. Packet filters such as firewalls can also be helpful [32]. The only drawback with this solution is the inability to see the content of the packet at the edge firewall when applying the filtering method, which means the authentication and host validation steps must be implemented.

Furthermore, some research works suggest the usage of separate firewall filters, one for IPv4 packets and another for IPv6 packets, in order to make sure that every packet is being filtered and examined [28]. Another method is to deny the IPv6 tunnel by blocking a specific protocol and its associated ports [28]. In the case of a 6in4 tunnel, an attacker might inject an already encapsulated packet within the tunnel, which is why firewalls should be enabled to inspect tunneled packets and the firewall should also permit any 6in4 traffic which is generated from the same segment or from outside it, to be able to filter traffic behind the segment as well [28]. Finally, IPsec has the ability to block any traffic that did not pass the authentication phase [28].

Another proposal was made by [33], which is based on the validation of the real source IP address by using the IP trace-back method; by doing so, the tunnel endpoint can drop any incoming spoofed IP packet. However, this technique comes also with its limitations: it cannot trace the packet source IP address until the tunnel endpoint node due to the stateless IP routing, where a router can only see the next hop IP address, in which the tunnel end-node cannot trace the incoming packet to its original sender, which means a full end-to-end route knowledge is unachievable [33].

One more spoofing mitigation trial has been introduced by [34], which focuses on preventing the spoofed packet at the network edge. The principle is based on using an authentication algorithm by the sender, where every packet has a uniquely generated signature attached to its extension header.

Finally, Lee [35] has presented his own spoofing mitigation method, where he tackles sneaky packets that are trying to avoid filters by presenting a packet-filtering mechanism using the well-known Linux Netfilter framework [36].

4.5. DS-Lite Tunnel Challenges

The literature is rich with attack scenarios regarding 6in4 tunnels. However, little is known about the 4in6 tunnel in terms of security vulnerabilities. The concept might seem the same, but the implementation might differ a bit, leading us to focus in this paper on DS-Lite and its security analysis.

DS-Lite uses 4in6 tunneling. This type of tunneling was first presented in RFC 2473 [26], where IPv6 tunneling basically creates a link (virtual one) between the two ends of the tunnel. The IPv4 original packet will be sent as a payload encapsulated in the IPv6 tunnel packet, as shown in Figure 4.

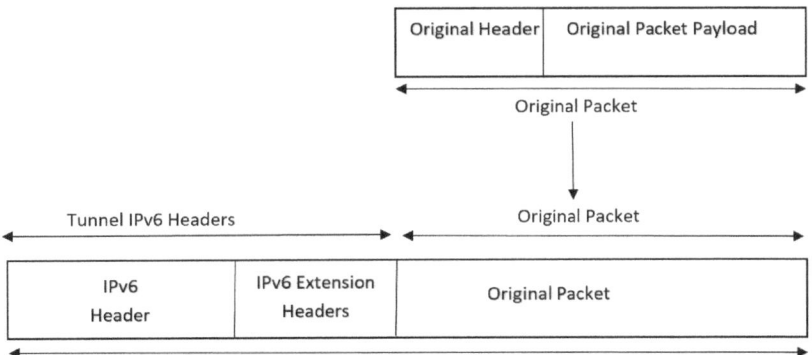

Figure 4. 4in6 tunnel encapsulation overview [26].

The process begins by grabbing the original IPv4 packet and prepending it to another IPv6 header (tunnel header) and sometimes the extension header, as it is an optional feature, and then sending this encapsulated packet through the softwire tunnel to the other tunnel end-point node, where the packet will be decapsulated and the original packet will be extracted and forwarded according to its destination and routing table.

For a better understanding of 4in6 tunnel components, the below tunnel terminologies are clarified [26]:

- Virtual link: Refers to the IPv6 tunnel itself;
- Original packet: The IPv4 packet that is supposed to be sent over the link, which consists of two components: packet header and payload;
- Tunnel IPv6 header: Refers to the IPv6 tunnel header without the payload;
- Tunnel IPv6 packet: Refers to the whole IPv6 tunnel packet (tunnel IPv6 header + original packet);
- Tunnel entry-point node: The node responsible for initiating the encapsulation process, also called the "encapsulator node". It is the source of the IPv6 tunnel packet;
- Tunnel exit-point node: The node responsible for receiving the encapsulated packet and then decapsulating it, extracting the original IPv4 packet components (header + payload)

and then forwarding the IPv4 packet to its destination, also called the "decapsulator node". It is the destination of the IPv6 tunnel packet;
- TTL (Time to Live) behavior: During the packet-forwarding process of the tunnel IPv6 packet, the IPv4 header's (the original packet header) TTL value decreases by 1.

Note: Both end-nodes are capable of encapsulation/decapsulation; the naming refers only to the function of the process initiators. DS-Lite has an advantage when it comes to DoS attacks from random public IPv4 addresses. This is due to the following process:
- AFTR receives an encapsulated packet, then decapsulates it;
- If the extracted packet payload has a source IPv4 address that is not private RFC 1918, it will be immediately dropped;
- This built-in security feature gives DS-Lite the ability to stop DoS attacks stemming from unauthorized IPv4 addresses [12].

DS-Lite, however, has a drawback because it uses stateful translation on the AFTR side, which makes the machine liable to DoS attacks and limits its scalability in case of expansion or the need in bigger projects, especially when there are numerous amounts of B4s routers within the infrastructure [17].

5. STRIDE Methodology

STRIDE stands for Spoofing, Tampering, Repudiation, Information Disclosure, and Elevation of Privilege. The method was explained in detail in [37], which summarized the general attacks that any network system may be vulnerable to. Below is a brief description of each attack:
- Spoofing: The claim to be someone you are not or the act of some malicious user who pretends to be, e.g., a trusted website [37];
- Tampering: The changing in the actual data flow between two nodes [37];
- Repudiation: The ability of the sender to deny the fact that he did send a specific packet or sign a specific document [37];
- Information Disclosure: The access to confidential information that one should not have, such as the TTL value of a packet, or confidential data such as online banking credentials or any other login credentials [37];
- Denial of Service: The process of overwhelming a specific server or network connection with a huge number of useless queries or data in order to block the legitimate ones from receiving a reply or even being processed [37]. In other words, DoS makes the targeted machine unavailable for its original purpose;
- Elevation of Privileges: The access of a specific user to a certain level of sensitive data which might be a strictly confidential file that is meant to be for upper management or the root user, for instance [37].

According to [37], the best method to test the system's vulnerabilities is to build a DFD (data flow diagram) for the system and apply the STRIDE method to it. Table 3 shows the different potential security threats for each DFD element.

Table 3. Vulnerability of different DFD elements to different threats [1].

Element	Spoofing	Tampering	Repudiation	Information Disclosure	Denial of Service	Elevation of Privilege
Data Flow		✓		✓	✓	
Data Stores		✓		✓	✓	
Processes	✓	✓	✓	✓	✓	✓
Interactors	✓		✓			

6. Applying STRIDE to DS-Lite

The first step in applying the STRIDE method is to build the DFD of the examined system and specify the potential attacking points at each element. Therefore, the DFD for

DS-Lite was built as shown in Figure 5, which shows the spots (1–11). The security analysis is divided into several groups such as the traffic between the client and B4, then between B4 and the AFTR, etc.

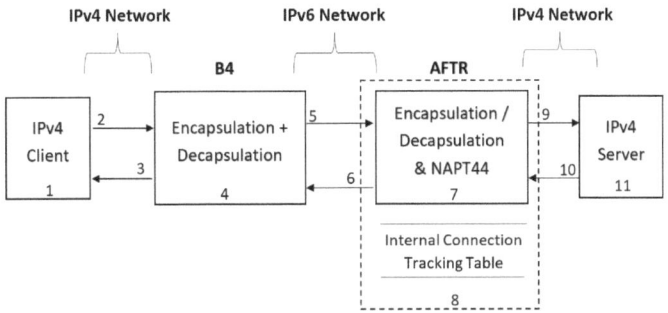

Figure 5. Data flow diagram of DS-Lite.

6.1. IPv4 Client

1. Spoofing: A malicious user might spoof the IP address of the client and attack the B4 router by sending many useless requests to the B4 and fully utilizing its computation power;
2. Repudiation: The request initiator might deny the fact that he made the request in the first place. By doing so, a malicious user might attack the B4 router and then deny the fact that he was the one who sent this specific request such as an echo request, DNS resolution request, etc.

6.2. Data Flow from the Client to the B4 Router

1. Tampering: An adversary might tamper (change or modify) the content of the flowing packets such as IP address, source port number, etc. The attacker might also diverge the packet toward a fraudulent server which might cause an FoS (failure of service) attack, which is the prevention of the legitimate requester from receiving a response [1];
2. Information Disclosure: An attacker might get hold of confidential information such as the TTL value of a packet, e.g., some sensitive information sent by the client as plain text or the browsing habits of the client [1];
3. Denial of Service: An attacker sends too many useless requests to the B4 router and blocks the legitimate requester from having his query processed.

6.3. Data Flow from B4 Router to IPv4 Client

1. Tampering: In this case, the potential victim is the client, who is vulnerable to an attack at the application level, such as sending a TCP RST signal that will end the already established TCP connection [6] and also a de-authentication attack [38] that results in disconnecting the device from the router's Wi-Fi, in addition to a plain-text injection attack [38] that allows the B4 router to send misleading information to the client, such as false routing details;
2. Information Disclosure: An attacker gaining access to sensitive information in a malicious way, such as an important text sent back by the IPv4 server behind AFTR;
3. Denial of Service: Sending a high number of forged replies to overwhelm the client and prevent the client from sending more requests to the B4.

6.4. B4 Router

1. Spoofing: Another machine presents itself as the legitimate B4 router and starts communicating with the rest of the DS-Lite network elements, which puts everyone that deals with this machine at high risk, such as a malicious device initiating a

communication with the AFTR router and presenting itself as the B4 router, which leads to whole traffic (from AFTR side) pouring in the wrong direction by changing the destination IP address of the packet, which results in the original sender not receiving a response to his request. Another consequence could be when the malicious server starts recording the data passing through and using it for illegal activities such as blackmailing;
2. Tampering: Modifying the current source and destination address of the 4in6 traffic that is being processed within the B4 router in order to shift the traffic and prevent it from being sent to the real AFTR, forwarding it to a malicious server. Another possibility could be tampering with the IP address/port pair of the sender, which eventually results in a different entry in the AFTR translation table, and therefore, the packet reply will not return to the original sender;
3. Repudiation: In this case, when the B4 is spoofed, the malicious user will deny the fact that he sent a specific packet even though he did. The obvious solution to this issue is proper logging [6];
4. Information Disclosure: Attacker gaining access to sensitive data within the router such as the client's source IP address, TTL value, browsing data, etc.;
5. Denial of Service: Flooding the AFTR router with unnecessary requests in order to overwhelm the AFTR and stop it from processing any further incoming packets (see Section 6.2, item 3);
6. Elevation of Privileges: The attacker gains access to high-level (privileged) data, which mainly occurs due to an inside job [1], when an employee is implicit in the act.

6.5. Data Flow from B4 to AFTR

1. Tampering: 4in6 traffic might be altered and the source IP address or port number is liable to be modified by the attacker;
2. Information Disclosure: The access to confidential information in many ways (see Section 6.2, item 2);
3. Denial of Service: The flood of useless queries exhausts the resources of the AFTR and hinders its main job (see Section 6.2, item 3).

6.6. Data Flow from AFTR to B4

1. Tampering: Modifying the traffic details before it reaches the B4 router, such as the source IP address or port number of the 4in6 flowing traffic;
2. Information Disclosure: The unauthorized access to sensitive data (see Section 6.2, item 2);
3. Denial of Service: Flooding the B4 router with useless traffic (see Section 6.2, item 3).

6.7. AFTR Router

1. Spoofing: Attacker impersonates the AFTR and starts communicating with the rest of the machines around him, such as the B4 router and IPv4 server, which might lead to exchanging sensitive data with the wrong person (see Section 6.4, item 1);
2. Tampering: Changing the content of the 4in6 packet payload (see Section 6.4, item 2);
3. Repudiation: Hiding the packet sender identity (see Section 6.4, item 3);
4. Information Disclosure: The possibility of an attacker gaining access to confidential data (see Section 6.4, item 4);
5. Denial of Service: Various types of attacks can be described in this section, such as exhausting the AFTR with too many useless requests and hindering the process of encapsulating the desired packet;
6. Elevation of Privileges: The act of unauthorized access to a very confidential data center of a specific folder in a malicious way (see Section 6.4, item 6).

6.8. Internal Connection Tracking Table of the AFTR

1. Tampering: An attacker can manipulate the connection tracking table of the AFTR router that saves the incoming 4in6 traffic packet with its source address and port number and maps it with a destination IPv4 device according to the stateful NAT rule within the router (see Table 1). So, the manipulation can cause a faulty destination address and disturb the encapsulation process and result in a packet loss;
2. Denial of Service: Flooding the connection tracking table with too many unnecessary entries (false connections) might overwhelm the table beyond its capabilities and cause it to flush its data or saturate the AFTR itself, which means the AFTR will no longer be able to process any incoming packet, or it will at least lose some legitimate connections.

6.9. Data Flow from AFTR to IPv4 Server

1. Tampering: The destination IP of the traffic might be altered and redirected to a malicious server instead of being directed to the legitimate IPv4 server;
2. Information Disclosure: Unauthorized access to sensitive data of the IPv4 traffic;
3. Denial of Service: Overwhelming the host with too many requests (see Section 6.3, item 3).

6.10. Data Flow from IPv4 Server to AFTR

1. Tampering: The IPv4 packets might be altered in terms of the IP source address or port number, which will definitely change the corresponding 4in6 traffic details;
2. Information Disclosure: Unauthorized access to IPv4 traffic before it reaches the AFTR router, which might leak the confidential browsing habits of the client;
3. Denial of Service: Exhausting the AFTR and its main encapsulation function (see Section 6.2, item 3).

6.11. IPv4 Server

1. Spoofing: An attacker impersonates the IPv4 server and initiates communication with AFTR and the rest of DS-Lite topology;
2. Repudiation: The host (IPv4 sever) might hide his identity, perform all sorts of malicious acts, and then deny any responsibility for them. For example, in the previous point of spoofing, the attacker might spoof the IPv4 server, perform an attack against AFTR, and then deny the fact that he initiated the communication in the first place.

7. DS-Lite Testbed

7.1. Testbed Topology and Specifications

As shown in Figure 6, the testbed consisted of five machines (IPv4 client, B4, AFTR, IPv4 server, and the attacker). They were all based on VMware workstation VMs and built upon CentOS-7 images. Every machine had the following specifications:

- RAM: 3 GB;
- Hard disk: 20 GB;
- CPU: 1 core.

The host PC that hosted the whole testbed had the following specifications:

- OS: Windows 10 Pro;
- RAM: 16 GB;
- Hard disk: 1 TB;
- CPU: Intel-Core i7, 4 physical cores.

The IPIP6 tunnel was built between B4 and AFTR, which took care of encapsulating the IPv4 packet inside the IPv6 packet and then decapsulating it. For the NAT process on the AFTR side, the `iptables` rule was configured to masquerade the source IP address to the AFTR's network interface (ens35). As for the tunnel between B4 and AFTR, a shell script was executed on the B4 machine, which consists of the following commands:

```
ip link add name ipip6 type ip6tnl local 2001:db8:0:1::2\
remote 2001:db8:0:1::1 mode any dev ens39
ip link set dev ipip6 up
ip route add 198.51.100.0/24 dev ipip6
```

It is noted that an important simplification is contained in the above setup compared to Table 1: the Softwire-ID is missing from the connection tracking table. It was observed that the experiments were not influenced by this change, but rather the set-up of the testbed was simplified: `iptables` could be used instead of a real AFTR implementation.

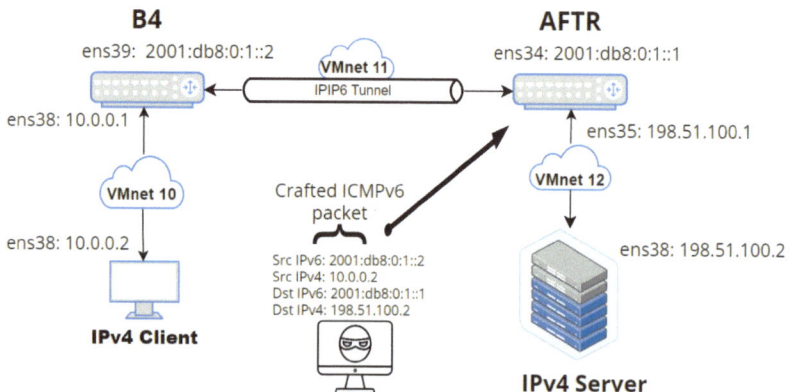

Figure 6. DS-Lite testbed (attack Scenario 1).

7.2. Attack Scenarios

7.2.1. Spoofing Attack from within VMnet-11 (an Inside Job)

The proposed attack shown in Figure 6 is spoofing the ingress tunnel endpoint (ens39), which is the softwire tunnel interface of the B4 router, and then sniffing/logging traffic or performing MitM attack against the egress tunnel endpoint (AFTR).

The attack was based on the "thc-ipv6" toolkit [39], which has several tools within it. One powerful tool was chosen to perform the attack (four2six). It manually creates a crafted packet of IPv4 inside IPv6 (encapsulated packet) and sends it over the channel to the victim (AFTR).

This crafted packet is actually a spoofed one, imitating that it was sent by the B4 router, having the same specifications as a genuine B4-originated packet:

- IPv6 Src: 2001:db8:0:1::2;
- IPv6 Dst: 2001:db8:0:1::1;
- IPv4 Src: 10.0.0.2;
- IPv4 Dst: 198.51.100.2.

In fact, the spoofed attack went through AFTR and then to the end receiver (IPv4 server), and a series of ICMP echo requests and replies had been exchanged between the attacker and victim. In more detail, what happened is:

- The AFTR received the malicious packet;
- The AFTR saw the packet as a 4in6 packet, and therefore decapsulated the packet;
- The AFTR then forwarded the extracted IPv4 packet with the source address of 198.51.100.1 towards the IPv4 server (198.51.100.2);
- IPv4 server sent ICMPv4 echo reply back;
- The AFTR saw the later packet and encapsulated it in an IPv6 packet;
- The echo reply from the AFTR, which is an IPv6 packet with an IPv4 packet in its payload, was sent back to its destination IPv6 of address 2001:db8:0:1::2;

- Figure 7 shows three different terminals: the top one is the incoming packets at the attacker interface, the one in the middle is the B4 incoming traffic from the AFTR side, and at the bottom is the incoming traffic at the IPv4 client;
- B4 received the IPv6 packet carrying an IPv4 packet with ICMP echo reply because it is the legitimate owner of the 2001:db8:0:1::1 IPv6 destination address;
- The attacker saw the same reply because its NIC runs in promiscuous mode;
- The interesting thing here is illustrated by the IPv4 client receiving an ICMP4 echo reply for a request that he did not request in the first place, which was issued by the attacker initially;
- Echo replies in Figure 7 are circled in red.

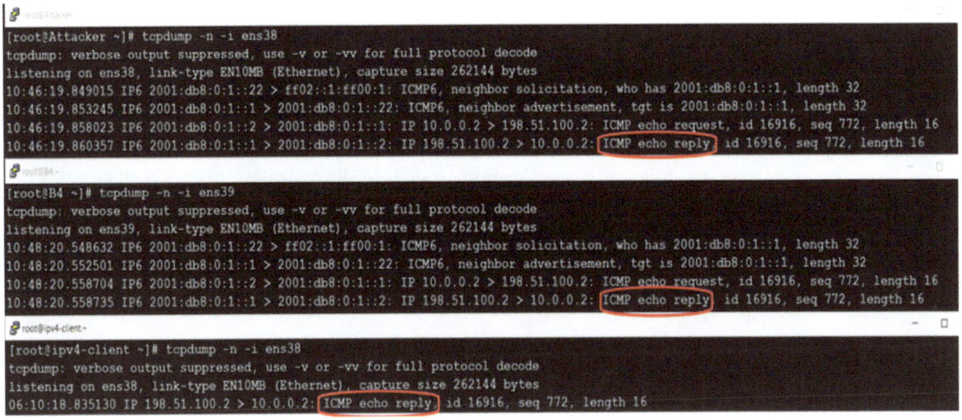

Figure 7. Spoofed packet echo reply.

7.2.2. Attack from within VMnet-10 (Compromised B4 Network)

It is also worth mentioning that B4 by design is also capable of routing native IPv6 packets, which takes us to Figure 8, where the IPv6 address was added to interface ens38 at the B4 machine in order to process and forward incoming IPv6 packets.

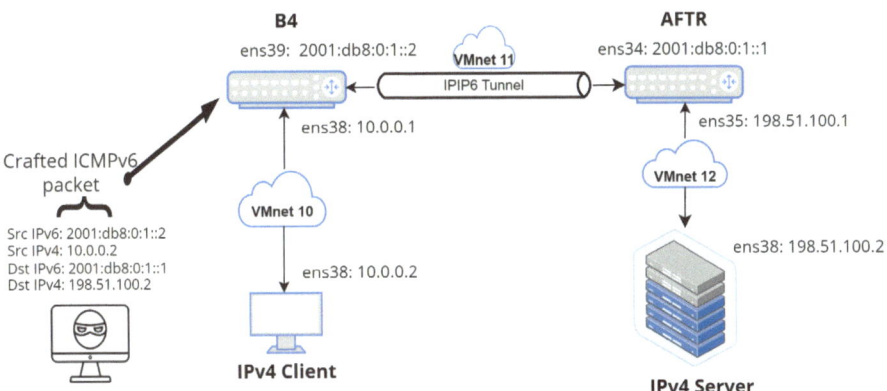

Figure 8. DS-Lite testbed (attack Scenario 2).

A real-life spoofing scenario could also be stopped before reaching the internal network of AFTR (VMnet-11 in the current example). Therefore, another attacking scenario was proposed in Figure 8, where the attacker is not sitting directly in the AFTR network, but outside it. The idea behind such an attack is that an attacker has access to the home router network, which gives him direct contact with the CPE. This access allows the attacker to send a crafted packet with a spoofed IPv6 address of a B4 router or any other IPv6 address from the internal network of AFTR (VMnet-11 in the current example).

Fortunately for the user, the attack did not go through—the B4 router was always dropping any incoming packet from the attacker-2 machine that has an IP address (a spoofed one) from the pool of (VMnet-11). The reason for that is simple: there was no route configured on the B4 router to forward the crafted IPv6 packet to the AFTR router. The tunnel was hardcoded in the B4 machine by creating an ipip6 tunnel interface to forward any IPv4 packet (heading towards 198.51.100.0/24 network) to the ipip6 tunnel interface which has been configured. However, the attacker packet has no route to the tunnel interface, and that is why it was dropped.

7.2.3. Source Port Exhaustion Attack from within VMnet-10

At first, the attack was conducted using the same platform, a regular specs Windows-based computer; however, the results were not stable and not reproducible due to limited cores on the host PC. Therefore, the decision was made to use the resources of NICT StarBED, Japan. A "P" series node [40] was used, which is a Dell PowerEdge 430 server with the following specifications: two Intel(R) Xeon(R) CPU E5-2683 v4 @ 2.1 GHz CPUs having 16 cores each and 348 GB 2400 MHz DDR4 SDRAM.

Windows 10 Pro operating system was installed, and the same process was repeated by building the testbed using VMware workstation player and CentOS-7-based virtual machines. The specifications for each machine were as follows:

- RAM: 4 GB;
- Cores: 4 cores, except for AFTR having 6 cores;
- Disk: 20 GB.

Before disclosing the attack details, it is important to explain the mathematical sense behind it.

In the networking world, ports are counted based on a 16-bit standard. The 16 bits were chosen when the TCP and UDP standards were designed [41]. As a result, the maximum number of ports equals 2^{16} = 65,536. This number applies to TCP and UDP ports. In this experiment, the focus was on the UDP ports and how to exhaust them by sending too many queries (UDP requests) in a short period of time. However, not all ports in the range are usable for establishing new connections, because ports between 1 and 1024 are called well-known ports and they are reserved for specific functions such as FTP, HTTP, DNS, etc.

Therefore, the total range of ports that the NAPT (Network Address and Port Translation) device can use as UDP source port numbers equal 65,536 − 1024 = 64,512 ports.

Figure 9 shows the attacking Scenario 3 of sending too many AAAA queries from "IPv4 Client-1" and "IPv4 Client-2" machines. In order for the attack to function, a few files must be correctly configured:

- /sys/module/nf_conntrack/parameters/hashsize: The hash size is actually the size of the hash table storing the lists of conntrack entries [42], which is better as a base of 2, which means that hash size could be 2^{14} = 16,384;
- /proc/sys/net/netfilter/nf_conntrack_max: It represents the maximum number of allowed conntrack entries that netfilter can keep running simultaneously. It was set to hashsize × 8 = 16,384 × 8 = 131,072. This number will have a significant impact when the attack is run later so that the NAT table does not get full easily;
- /proc/sys/net/netfilter/nf_conntrack_udp_timeout: This timeout means that after 30 s, the already used UDP ports are ready to be re-assigned by the kernel, and the default value of 30 s was left as it is;
- /etc/security/limits.conf: This file controls the number of maximum open files at the same time, where the below line was added: root hard nofile 1000000.

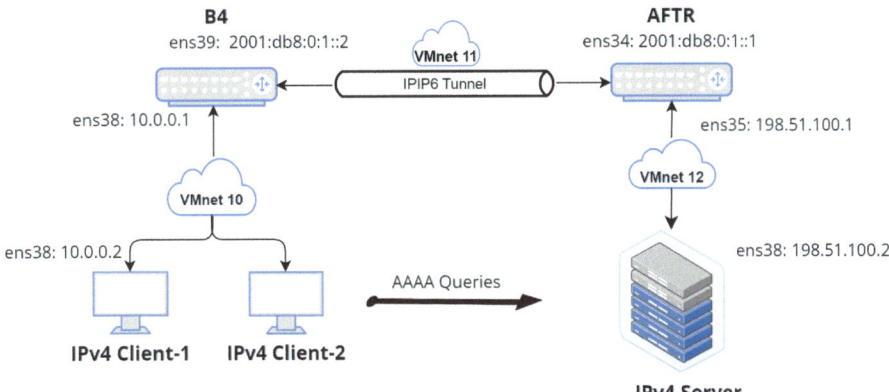

Figure 9. Attacking Scenario 3 (AAAA queries).

To perform this kind of attack, another tool can be used, where a huge number of DNS queries can be sent to the target machine (AFTR), which is called "dns64perf++" [43] (described in [44]). When all parameters (on the attacking machine side) are set correctly (number of requests, the delay between requests, etc.), the AFTR pool of source ports will be exhausted, and the machine will not be able to process incoming packets anymore until the UDP timeout (port allocation timeout in AFTR machine) is up. The below command was used on each of the attacking clients:

/dns64perf++v4 198.51.100.2 53 0.0.0.0/5 60000 1 1 60000 400000 0.1

This command sends 60,000 queries from each client. For two clients, this number reaches 120,000 queries, which is still under 131,072 (nf_conntrack_max). As a result, the NAT table will not be overfilled with packets that exceed its capacity. Another interesting fact in the command is the delay of 400,000 nanoseconds between queries, resulting in 2500 queries per second, which means that for two clients, a total of 5000 queries per second can be sent.

The attack was executed by an automated script from client 1, carrying out the following:

- Accesses AFTR remotely (via ssh) and runs tshark (traffic monitoring software) and captures the traffic at the ens35 interface;
- Runs the attack from IPv4-client-1 (the same machine);
- Accesses IPv4 client-2 remotely (via ssh) and runs the same attack with the same parameters;
- Waits until attacks are finished on both clients;
- Accesses AFTR remotely (via ssh) and stops tshark;
- Sends the tshark results as a pcap file to the host machine, so it can be read in the Wireshark software.

Figure 10 shows the exhaustion of the source ports clearly to prove that a total of 64,512 sent queries must be visible, which comes from subtracting the well-known 1024 ports from the total of 65,536 ports. Figure 10 shows that AFTR processed only 64,536 packets at the ens35 interface. After digging deeper, more packets embedded within Wireshark results were found, such as 20 ICMP and 4 ARP packets. As a result, the remaining packets are 64,536 − 20 − 4 = 64,512, which is exactly the anticipated number.

No.	Time	Src. IP	Dst. IP	Protocol	Src. port	Dst. port	Info.
64534	14.336138714	198.51.100.1	198.51.100.2	DNS	38628	53	Standard query 0x8131 AAAA 000-000-129-049
64535	14.339424635	198.51.100.1	198.51.100.2	DNS	38624	53	Standard query 0x8139 AAAA 000-000-129-057
64536	14.386624374	198.51.100.1	198.51.100.2	DNS	38625	53	Standard query 0x81b0 AAAA 000-000-129-176

Figure 10. Last lines for Wireshark capture at ens35 on AFTR.

In principle, 60,000 queries were sent from each client (120,000 in total), and AFTR was able to process no more than 64,512 packets and ran out of ports in around 14 s. This failure of service is supposed to last until the UDP session timeout at AFTR is over and new source ports are available to be reallocated. Moreover, Figure 11 shows the interaction between all nodes of DS-Lite topology, where the port exhaustion process at AFTR is clearly illustrated with a sequence of packets and when exactly the pool of ports is exhausted.

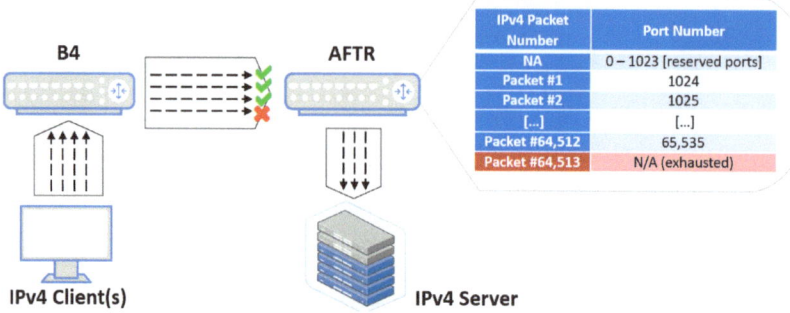

Figure 11. Illustration of port exhaustion at the AFTR.

7.3. Mitigation Method

Several IDS and IPS (intrusion detection and prevention systems) were tested in order to identify and drop the spoofed packet from the legitimate one. The process proved to be quite hard to implement, especially when the attacker machine is located inside the access network of the ISP (VMnet-11). Therefore, a workaround had been put in place and iptables rules were emplaced to perform the job.

7.3.1. First Attack Mitigation

An ip6tables rule was configured at AFTR in order to allow the incoming traffic at the ens34 interface of the AFTR only under the condition that the incoming packet's source MAC address belongs to the B4 ens39 interface (see Figure 6).

    ip6tables -A INPUT -i ens34 -s 2001:db8:0:1::2 -m mac ! -mac-source 00:0c:29:67:14:14 -j DROP

On the other hand, such a mitigation method will not be effective if the attacker clones the "00:0c:29:67:14:14" MAC address to bypass the iptables filtering rule.

7.3.2. Second Attack Mitigation

Despite the fact that this attack did not go through and the spoofed packet had been dropped, a proposed solution is presented here in case of building the topology using another machine (different Linux distribution for instance), where such an attack could be prevented at the B4 router side with the following rules:

    iptables -A FORWARD -i ens38 -s 10.0.0.0/24 -j ACCEPT
    iptables -A FORWARD -i ens38 -j DROP

The first rule accepts packets with source addresses from the private IPv4 address network (10.0.0.0/24), while the second one drops every packet that approaches the ens38 interface and needs to be forwarded. These two rules take care of a malicious packet as it reaches the B4 side and before it heads toward the AFTR (see Figure 8).

However, restricting access to the private IP address network of VMnet-10 (10.0.0.0/24) will not fully protect from DoS attack, because the attack might be originated from a machine that resides within the network of the IPv4 client (an inside job).

7.3.3. Third Attack Mitigation Method

One of the ways to mitigate this attack or at least reduce its impact is by adding two (or more) IP addresses to the AFTR ens35 interface (see Figure 9), where the whole calculation will be double (or triple, depending on how many IP addresses were added) due to the fact that extended NAT works by binding the IP/port pair together. The fact that ens35 has two IP addresses now gives the AFTR more flexibility by having one additional pool of exactly the same port numbers of 64,512 ports, but they will be coupled with another source IP address. In case two IP addresses were not enough to mitigate the attack, the system administrator can easily add a third, fourth, or more as needed. On the practical side, two extra IP addresses were added to the ens35 interface on AFTR. As a result, the AFTR was able to process all incoming 120,000 packets, unlike last time, when it stopped after 64,512 packets.

Another mitigation method is possible through the rate-limiting process, which limits the number of packets per second that can be sent and received by the NIC (network interface card) [45]; it also enables the administrator to assign bandwidth restrictions to specific traffic such as ICMP, UDP, etc. Some research works [46,47] have proposed the rate-limiting mitigation mechanism after noticing the difference and the asymmetry between incoming and outgoing traffic in the designated network.

7.4. Summary

As the testbed for DS-Lite investigated in a topic that has rarely been discussed and analyzed, valuable results were collected based on the attacking scenarios, which can be used to enhance the security around DS-Lite infrastructure's vulnerable spots and, therefore, provide a more secure network infrastructure. Therefore, researchers are encouraged to invest more effort in analyzing the potential security threats that face IPv6 transition technologies, especially DS-Lite. It is recommended that the focus be placed on DoS attacks and source IP address spoofing, as it was found through analysis that these attacks are the most common. As for mitigation methods, a sophisticated IDS and IPS tool is highly recommended, such as SNORT [48] or Suricata [49].

8. Conclusions

In this paper, we have demonstrated the significance of transition technologies, specifically through the tunneling method, and how practical they can be. Our testbed effectively simulated a DS-Lite topology and uncovered its security vulnerabilities. The findings show that the IPv4 client did not need a public IPv4 address to communicate with an IPv4 server. On the other hand, every element within the DS-Lite topology is vulnerable to various types of attacks, including DoS, tampering, and spoofing. As such, further analyses and addressing vulnerabilities are crucial for the successful implementation of IPv6 transition technologies that use tunneling. Our work has benefited from the "thc-ipv6" toolkit, which provided us with a range of tools and attacking possibilities. These tools can be used in future research to better understand the weaknesses and threats associated with DS-Lite and other transition technologies.

Overall, our study highlights the importance of thorough analysis and vulnerability testing when implementing IPv6 transition technologies that use tunneling. Our findings can benefit network administrators, policy makers, and researchers who seek to enhance the security of their networks and prevent attacks.

Author Contributions: All authors contributed to the study's conception and design. Material preparation and testbed building by A.A.-A., with valuable support from G.L. The first draft of the manuscript was written by A.A.-A., and all authors commented on previous versions of the manuscript. Conceptualization: G.L.; methodology: A.A.-A.; formal analysis and investigation: A.A.-A.; writing—original draft preparation: A.A.-A.; writing—review and editing: G.L. and A.A.-A.; resources: A.A.-A. and G.L.; supervision: G.L. All authors have read and agreed to the published version of the manuscript.

Funding: This research received no external funding.

Data Availability Statement: The Public GitHub repository of the first author contains several automation scripts to build every machine that was used to build the topology: https://github.com/ameen-mcmxc/DS-Lite_Test_Bed (accessed on 16 March 2021). The "pcap" file generated by Wireshark software captures the traffic at the ens35 interface of the AFTR machine in case of attack scenario 3. The results of the attack were published in the same public GitHub repository file directory: https://github.com/ameen-mcmxc/DS-Lite_Test_Bed/blob/main/DNS_Perf_Results.pcap (accessed on 12 June 2022).

Acknowledgments: In part, the resources of NICT StarBED, Japan, were used for conducting the experiment. The authors thank Shuuhei Takimoto for the opportunity to use these resources. The authors thank Sándor Répás, András Gerendás, and Omar D'yab for their reading and commenting on the manuscript. The authors also would like to acknowledge the preprint version of this work, which is available at [50]. This paper is based on material previously published in the preprint, and we thank the previous reviewers for their valuable feedback.

Conflicts of Interest: The authors declare no conflict of interest.

References

1. Lencse, G.; Kadobayashi, Y. Methodology for the identification of potential security issues of different IPv6 transition technologies: Threat analysis of DNS64 and stateful NAT64. *Comput. Secur.* **2018**, *77*, 397–411. [CrossRef]
2. Al-Azzawi, A. Towards the Security Analysis of the Five Most Prominent IPv4aaS Technologies. *Acta Tech. Jaurinensis* **2020**, *13*, 85–98. [CrossRef]
3. Bagnulo, M.; Sullivan, A.; Matthews, P.; Beijnum, I. DNS64: DNS Extensions for Network Address Translation from IPv6 Clients to IPv4 Servers. IETF RFC 6147. 2011. Available online: https://www.rfc-editor.org/info/rfc6147 (accessed on 18 May 2023).
4. Bagnulo, M.; Matthews, P.; Beijnum, I. Stateful NAT64: Network Address and Protocol Translation from IPv6 Clients to IPv4 Servers. IETF RFC 6146. 2011. Available online: https://www.rfc-editor.org/info/rfc6146 (accessed on 12 January 2021).
5. Mawatari, M.; Kawashima, M.; Byrne, C. 464XLAT: Combination of stateful and stateless translation. IETF RFC 6877. 2013. Available online: https://www.rfc-editor.org/info/rfc6877 (accessed on 16 January 2021).
6. Al-Azzawi, A.; Lencse, G. Towards the Identification of the Possible Security Issues of the 464XLAT IPv6 Transition Technology. In Proceedings of the 2020 43rd International Conference on Telecommunications and Signal Processing (TSP), Milan, Italy, 7–9 July 2020. [CrossRef]
7. Al-Azzawi, A.; Lencse, G. Testbed for the Security Analysis of the 464XLAT IPv6 Transition Technology in a Virtual Environment. In Proceedings of the 2021 44th International Conference on Telecommunications and Signal Processing (TSP), Brno, Czech, 26–28 July 2021. [CrossRef]
8. Al-Azzawi, A.; Lencse, G. Identification of the Possible Security Issues of the 464XLAT IPv6 Transition Technology. *Infocommun. J.* **2021**, *13*, 10–18. [CrossRef]
9. Lencse, G.; Kadobayashi, Y. Comprehensive survey of IPv6 transition technologies: A subjective classification for security analysis. *IEICE Trans. Commun.* **2019**, *102*, 2021–2035. [CrossRef]
10. Lee, Y.; Maglione, R.; Williams, C.; Jacquenet, C.; Boucadair, M. Deployment Considerations for Dual-Stack Lite. IETF RFC 6908. 2013. Available online: https://www.rfc-editor.org/info/rfc6908 (accessed on 9 March 2021).
11. Fu, Y.; Jiang, S.; Dong, J.; Chen, Y. Dual-Stack Lite (DS-Lite) Management Information Base (MIB) for Address Family Transition Routers (AFTRs). IETF RFC 7870. 2016. Available online: https://www.rfc-editor.org/info/rfc7870 (accessed on 11 March 2021).
12. Durand, A.; Droms, R.; Woodyatt, J.; Lee, Y. Dual-Stack Lite Broadband Deployments following IPv4 Exhaustion. IETF RFC 6333. 2011. Available online: https://www.rfc-editor.org/info/rfc6333 (accessed on 19 March 2021).
13. Hankins, D.; Mrugalski, T. Dynamic Host Configuration Protocol for IPv6 (DHCPv6) Option for Dual-Stack Lite. IETF RFC 6334. 2011. Available online: https://www.rfc-editor.org/info/rfc6334 (accessed on 12 March 2021).
14. Boucadair, M.; Jacquenet, C.; Sivakumar, S. A YANG Data Model for Dual-Stack Lite (DS-Lite). IETF RFC 8513. 2019. Available online: https://www.rfc-editor.org/info/rfc8513 (accessed on 18 May 2023).
15. Chen, M.; Yi, M.; Huang, M.; Huang, G.; Ren, Y.; Liu, A. A novel deep policy gradient action quantization for trusted collaborative computation in intelligent vehicle networks. *Expert Syst. Appl.* **2023**, *221*, 119743. [CrossRef]
16. Zhang, R.; Li, Z.; Xiong, N.N.; Zhang, S.; Liu, A. TDTA: A truth detection based task assignment scheme for mobile crowdsourced Industrial Internet of Things. *Inf. Sci.* **2022**, *610*, 246–265. [CrossRef]
17. Lencse, G.; Palet Martinez, J.; Howard, L.; Patterson, R.; Farrer, I. Pros and cons of IPv6 transition technologies for IPv4aaS. Internet Draft. 2022. Available online: https://datatracker.ietf.org/doc/html/draft-ietf-v6ops-transition-comparison-04 (accessed on 18 May 2023).
18. Scott, O. The PPTP VPN Protocol: Is It Safe? Infosec Resources. 2019. Available online: https://resources.infosecinstitute.com/topic/the-pptp-vpn-protocol-is-it-safe (accessed on 11 April 2021).

19. Hamzeh, K.; Pall, G.; Verthein, W.; Taarud, J.; Little, W.; Zorn, G. Point-to-Point Tunneling Protocol (PPTP). IETF RFC 2637. 2019. Available online: https://www.rfc-editor.org/info/rfc2637 (accessed on 5 April 2021).
20. Schneier, B. Cryptanalysis of Microsoft's point-to-point tunneling protocol (PPTP). In Proceedings of the 5th ACM Conference on Computer and Communications Security, San Francisco, CA, USA, 2–5 November 1998; pp. 132–141.
21. Zorn, G.; Cobb, S. Microsoft PPP CHAP Extensions. IETF RFC 2433. 1998. Available online: https://www.rfc-editor.org/info/rfc2433 (accessed on 9 April 2021).
22. Zorn, G. Microsoft PPP CHAP Extensions, version 2. IETF RFC 2759. 2000. Available online: https://www.rfc-editor.org/info/rfc2759 (accessed on 1 March 2021).
23. Krishnan, S.; Thaler, D.; Hoagland, J. Security Concerns with IP Tunneling. IETF RFC 6169. 2011. Available online: https://www.rfc-editor.org/info/rfc6169 (accessed on 18 May 2023).
24. Carpenter, B.; Jung, C. Transmission of IPv6 over IPv4 Domains without Explicit Tunnels. IETF RFC 2529. 1999. Available online: https://www.rfc-editor.org/info/rfc2529 (accessed on 9 March 2021).
25. Nordmark, E.; Inc, R.G. Basic Transition Mechanisms for IPv6 Hosts and Routers. IETF RFC 4213. 2005. Available online: https://www.rfc-editor.org/info/rfc4213 (accessed on 4 May 2021).
26. Conta, A.; Deering, S. Generic Packet Tunneling in IPv6 Specification. IETF RFC 2473. 1998. Available online: https://www.rfc-editor.org/info/rfc2473 (accessed on 21 April 2021).
27. Savola, P.; Patel, C. Security Considerations for 6to4. IETF RFC 3964. 2004. Available online: https://www.rfc-editor.org/info/rfc3964 (accessed on 6 January 2021).
28. Abdulla, S.A. Survey of security issues in IPv4 to IPv6 tunnel transition mechanisms. *Int. J. Secur. Netw.* **2017**, *12*, 83–102. [CrossRef]
29. Hogg, S. IPv6: Dual Stack Where You Can; Tunnel Where You Must. Networkworld. 2017. Available online: https://www.networkworld.com/article/2285078/ipv6-dual-stack-where-you-can-tunnel-where-you-must.html (accessed on 8 April 2021).
30. Yang, D.; Song, X.; Guo, Q. Security on IPv6. In Proceedings of the 2nd IEEE International Conference on Advanced Computer Control, Shenyang, China, 27–29 March 2010; pp. 323–326.
31. Mi, W. The Applicability and Security Analysis of IPv6 Tunnel Transition Mechanisms. In Proceedings of the International Conference on Algorithms and Architectures for Parallel Processing, Dalian, China, 24–27 August 2014; pp. 560–570.
32. Hei, Y.; Katsuno, S.; Ano, S. An implementation and evaluation of IPv6 end-to-end secure communication system for closed members. In Proceedings of the International Symposium on Applications and the Internet Workshops (SAINTW'06), Phoenix, AZ, USA, 27 January 2006.
33. Amin, S.A.; Choong, S.H. On IPv6 Traceback. In Proceedings of the International Conference on Advanced Communication Technology (ICACT2006), Phoenix Park, Republic of Korea, 20–22 February 2006.
34. Xie, L.; Bi, J.; Wu, J. An authentication based source address spoofing prevention method deployed in IPv6 edge network. In Proceedings of the International Conference on Computational Science, Kuala Lumpur, Malaysia, 26–29 August 2007; pp. 801–808.
35. Lee, W.J.; Heo, S.Y.; Byun, T.Y.; Sohn, Y.H.; Han, K.J. A secure packet filtering mechanism for tunneling over Internet. In Proceedings of the International Conference on Embedded Software and Systems, Daegu, Republic of Korea, 14–16 May 2007; pp. 641–652.
36. Engelhardt, J.; Bouliane, N. Writing Netfilter Modules. July 2012. Available online: http://inai.de/documents/Netfilter_Modules.pdf (accessed on 7 March 2021).
37. Shostack, A. *Threat Modeling: Designing for Security*; John Wiley & Sons, Inc.: Indianapolis, IN, USA, 2014.
38. Kristiyanto, Y.; Ernastuti, E. Analysis of Deauthentication Attack on IEEE 802.11 Connectivity Based on IoT Technology Using External Penetration Test. *CommIT (Commun. Inf. Technol.) J.* **2020**, *14*, 45–51. [CrossRef]
39. van Hauser Heuse, M. thc-ipv6 (Version 3.8) [Computer Software]. 2020. Available online: https://github.com/vanhauser-thc/thc-ipv6 (accessed on 9 April 2021).
40. Making a synthesis emulation in IOT ERA possible Starbed5 Project Website. StarBED5 Project website /StarBED Equipment/. (n.d.). Available online: https://starbed.nict.go.jp/en/equipment/ (accessed on 20 March 2021).
41. Reed, D.P. User Datagram Protocol. IETF RFC 768. 1980. Available online: https://www.rfc-editor.org/info/rfc768 (accessed on 16 April 2021).
42. Netfilter Conntrack Performance Tweaking v0.8. Available online: https://wiki.khnet.info/index.php/Conntrack_tuning (accessed on 11 January 2021).
43. Bakai, D. DNS64perf++ Program. Available online: https://github.com/bakaid/dns64perfpp (accessed on 14 March 2021).
44. Lencse, G.; Bakai, D. Design and implementation of a test program for benchmarking DNS64 servers. *IEICE Trans. Commun.* **2017**, *100*, 948–954. [CrossRef]
45. Noormohammadpour, M.; Raghavendra, C.S. Datacenter traffic control: Understanding techniques and tradeoffs. *IEEE Commun. Surv. Tutor.* **2017**, *20*, 1492–1525. [CrossRef]
46. Gil, T.M.; Poletto, M. MULTOPS: A Data-Structure for Bandwidth Attack Detection. In Proceedings of the 10th USENIX Security Symposium (USENIX Security 01), Washington, DC, USA, 13–17 August 2001.
47. Mahajan, R.; Bellovin, S.M.; Floyd, S.; Ioannidis, J.; Paxson, V.; Shenker, S. Controlling high bandwidth aggregates in the network. *ACM SIGCOMM Comput. Commun. Rev.* **2002**, *32*, 62–73. [CrossRef]
48. Caswell, B.; Beale, J. *Snort 2.1 Intrusion Detection*; Elsevier Inc.: Amsterdam, The Netherlands, 2004.

49. OISF, Open Source Network Analysis and Threat Detection Software. 2020. Available online: https://suricata.io/ (accessed on 7 May 2021).
50. Al-Azzawi, A.; Lencse, G. The Possible Security Issues of the DS-Lite IPv6 Transition Technology, 26 August 2022, PREPRINT (Version 1). Available online: https://doi.org/10.21203/rs.3.rs-1972342/v1 (accessed on 9 May 2021).

Disclaimer/Publisher's Note: The statements, opinions and data contained in all publications are solely those of the individual author(s) and contributor(s) and not of MDPI and/or the editor(s). MDPI and/or the editor(s) disclaim responsibility for any injury to people or property resulting from any ideas, methods, instructions or products referred to in the content.

Perspective

Study on Automatic Electric Vehicle Charging Socket Detection Using ZED 2i Depth Sensor

Vladimir Tadic [1,2]

[1] Institute of Information Technology, University of Dunaujvaros, Tancsics Mihaly u. 1/A Pf.: 152, 2401 Dunaujvaros, Hungary; tadityv@uniduna.hu or laslo.tadic@gmail.com
[2] John von Neumann Faculty of Informatics, University of Obuda, Becsi ut 96/B., 1034 Budapest, Hungary

Abstract: This article introduces the utilization of the ZED 2i depth sensor in a robot-based automatic electric vehicle charging application. The employment of a stereo depth sensor is a significant aspect in robotic applications, since it is both the initial and the fundamental step in a series of robotic operations, where the intent is to detect and extract the charging socket on the vehicle's body surface. The ZED 2i depth sensor was utilized for scene recording with artificial illumination. Later, the socket detection and extraction were accomplished using both simple image processing and morphological operations in an object extraction algorithm with tilt angles and centroid coordinates determination of the charging socket itself. The aim was to use well-known, simple, and proven image processing techniques in the proposed method to ensure both reliable and smooth functioning of the robot's vision system in an industrial environment. The experiments demonstrated that the deployed algorithm both extracts the charging socket and determines the slope angles and socket coordinates successfully under various depth assessment conditions, with a detection rate of 94%.

Keywords: robotic applications; automotive applications; CCS2 electric vehicle charging socket; image processing; object detection; ZED 2i; depth map

Citation: Tadic, V. Study on Automatic Electric Vehicle Charging Socket Detection Using ZED 2i Depth Sensor. *Electronics* **2023**, *12*, 912. https://doi.org/10.3390/electronics12040912

Academic Editors: Sara Deilami and Byung Cheol Song

Received: 17 January 2023
Revised: 4 February 2023
Accepted: 9 February 2023
Published: 10 February 2023

Copyright: © 2023 by the author. Licensee MDPI, Basel, Switzerland. This article is an open access article distributed under the terms and conditions of the Creative Commons Attribution (CC BY) license (https://creativecommons.org/licenses/by/4.0/).

1. Introduction

The recent spread of electric vehicles is an ongoing trend that can be observed all over the world. According to current analyses, electric vehicles will appear in larger numbers on the roads in the near future. A main limitation considered for the greater propagation of electric vehicles is their battery, since there has not yet been a fundamental breakthrough in their development, given that the capacity and the lifetime of currently used batteries are very limited, and it results in a short driving range of the electric vehicles themselves. In order to overcome these limitations, the development of specific fast chargers is in progress, as well as the development of new charging methods of electric vehicles. Today, automotive consumers expect products tailored to their mobile information and entertainment needs, and these products should be tightly integrated in novel automotive applications such as autonomous electric car charging applications, automatic vehicle washing applications, etc. [1–4].

Expedited development of electric vehicles will increase the need for applications related to them in the future [4–6]. Certainly, one of the basic and most momentous operations is charging the batteries of electric vehicles and why there is a need for applications related to this purpose. Since the charging of electric vehicles takes a certain amount of time, there is a need on the part of users and operators to automate this process in order to meet the needs of customers. Thus, after parking the vehicle at the charging station, the user would have no further work on charging, except for opening the charging door, as the process would be fully automated by robots and the user would be free to perform various tasks during the charging time [7,8]. Hence, the concept of comfort electric vehicle charging, where no human intervention is required, is very interesting to customers, and many companies have started research related to this topic. Further, automated charging will become even more pertinent in the future due to progress in autonomous car driving and driverless parking applications. In these situations, a robot will take over the whole charging process when the vehicle is parked autonomously without any human intervention. Using automation technology will indicate that the manual charging process as we currently know it will no longer be required. Naturally, the specific problems related to this application should be analyzed and solved, such as the requirement of precise parking, robot movement around the parked vehicle, the illumination conditions demanded for cameras used for charging socket detection, urgent interruption of the charging process and disconnection of the plug, etc.

This paper represents initial research within an industrial project whose goal is to develop a robotic application for the automatic charging of electric vehicles using image processing techniques. As a result, a new approach for automatic electric vehicle charging socket detection using the ZED 2i depth sensor will be proposed.

The main research task of this industrial project is the deployment of a simple image processing method supported by information from a depth sensor, and the investigation of the capabilities of the ZED 2i depth camera in the application of the automated position and tilt detection of the Combined Charging System 2 (CCS2) socket of electric vehicles. The socket extraction procedure is based on intensity transformations, simple image processing operations, and a series of morphological operations. This project is part of the 2020-1.1.2-PIACI-KFI-2020-00173 industrial project related to the development of robot-based applications for autonomous electric vehicle charging. The main demand of the project is to use well-known, already proven, and reliable image processing operations and methods to provide the smooth and dependable operation of the robot [9–12]. The generated depth map and the recorded point cloud of the scene model serve as resources for the robot to determine the exact position and the slope angles of the charging socket on electric vehicles. It should be noted that later the Universal Robot 10e (UR10e) with an included force torque sensor will be used as a robotic arm during the deployment of an autonomous charging application [1–3].

The specific requirement of the project client was the deployment of a vision system that records the image from one position and, later, the socket region must be extracted with a much simplified, but reliable, image processing technique [13,14]. The ZED 2i depth sensor was embedded in the Robotic Operating System (ROS) framework via its ROS wrapper. This wrapper ensures the obtainment of real-time measurements on multiple ROS topics. A detailed description of the robot and its work is outside the scope of this paper; it will be fully depicted in a future research paper.

In the end, using the strict instructions about the simplicity and reliability of the project, a novel image processing procedure was developed for the automatic electric vehicle charging CCS2 socket detection and extraction. Thus, this initial research entirely fulfilled the aim of the project, and in the near future the testing will be extended on real electric vehicles with a camera mounted on the robot's arm.

The contribution of this study in terms of an industrial research project is the development of a simplified and reliable image processing algorithm for the detection of a CCS2 charging socket position and its tilt angles with a depth sensor for the automated electric vehicle charging application. The utilization of well-known and common image processing operations for charging socket detection purposes is not yet published in the scientific literature, as well as in papers related to industrial research with the aim of the charging socket detection. Thus, this is a novel and, at the same time, a proven approach for solving the problem of the electric vehicle charging socket detection for a future industrial application.

The paper can be summarized as follows. The first section is the Introduction, the second section is the literature overview, and the third section introduces the ZED 2i sensor in brief. Section four describes the proposed method, section five shows the experiments and results, and section six provides the conclusion followed by suggested future works.

2. Related Work

Object detection and extraction are general problems in robotic vision systems [15–26]. This operation can be determined in specific applications where it is necessary to both distinguish and extract some shapes from the background scene. There are various procedures to execute this separation task. Notably, there is a small volume of research and solutions for electric vehicle charging socket detection in the literature, and this section will give a brief overview of the related works in this field.

Pan et al. [27] proposed a charging socket detection method with three steps: recognition, localization, and inlay. For the charging socket localization, a convolutional neural network-based (CNN) method is used. The MER-125-30UM/C industrial camera was utilized for recording. In the socket localization process, an adopted pose solving method was used based on circle features. In the insertion step, an AUBO-i3 robotic arm was employed. The authors reported an accuracy rate of 98.9%. Zhang and Jin [28] introduced a new procedure built on machine vision for electric vehicle charging socket detection and localization, with a goal to solve the low efficacy and space restrictions in the artificial charging operation for electric vehicles. A special image segmentation method is proposed based on the Hue Saturation Intensity (HSI) color model to extract the properties of the charging socket targeting the subpixel precision. Moreover, the image segmentation procedure involves thresholding in the Hue component of the input image, morphological operations, and edge detection using the Canny edge operator. The HALCON computer vision platform is used for development. The authors claim that experiments show that their algorithm can successfully detect and locate the charging socket position with a 100% accuracy rate. Mišeikis et al. [29] presented an automatic robot-based car charging application using 3D computer vision. The system is based on a 3D vision system, an UR10 robot, and a charging station. A shape-based matching process is used for identification and exact pose determination of the charging socket. A similar approach is utilized for camera–robot system calibration. Finally, a three-step robot motion planning process is used for charger plug-in. Based on experiments, the proposed method works in laboratory conditions under indoor lighting with a custom-made charging socket holder. Quan et al. [30] proposed an automatic system for the recognition and positioning of charging sockets of electric vehicles. The system is split into two parts: the coarse and the precise positioning. The coarse positioning is based on the Hough circle and Hough line transformations, and it locates the position information of the charging socket itself. The precise positioning step uses the Canny edge operator to determine the contour information of the input and gradient images, respectively. In the end, the Perspective-n-Point (PNP) algorithm is used to find the pose information of the charging socket. The AUBO-i10 6-DOF (degree of freedom) articulated robot is utilized to test the recognition and inlay accuracies in different conditions and environments. The authors reported that the average detection rate of the coarse positioning is 97.9%, while the average success rate is 94.8%. Quan et al. [31] introduced a set of effective and accurate procedures for determining the pose of an electric vehicle charging connector. The method is divided into two steps: the search stage and the aiming stage. In the search stage, the feature circle procedure is used to fit the ellipse information to acquire the pixel coordinates of the feature point. In the aiming stage, the contour matching and logarithmic assessment indicators are used in the cluster template matching algorithm introduced in their research to determine the matching position of the socket itself. Finally, the efficient Perspective-n-Point algorithm is employed to obtain the pose information of the charging socket. The reported plug-in success rate is 95%. Lou and Di [32] presented a 4-DOF cable-guided automatic-charging robot consisting of a 3-DOF cable-guided serial manipulator with a moving platform. In their design, the 3-DOF cable-guided serial manipulator is actuated by six cables being routed alongside five disks fixed to the manipulator's rigid links. The end-effector of the robot is an elastic plug that has the capability to resist negligible elastic deformation. The control algorithm and the plugging–unplugging strategy were developed to answer various parking situations, with or without yaw fault. The pose detection method measured the pose of the charging port. In their experiments, the authors demonstrated the achievability and the effectiveness of using the cable-guided automatic-charging robot to realize an automated charging application for electric vehicles. Lin et al. [33] proposed a model-independent collision detection and classification algorithm for cable-guided serial manipulators. Firstly, relying on the dynamic features of the manipulator, datasets of terminal collision were realized. Later, the collected datasets were enforced to build and train a collision localization and classification model, which consisted of a double layer CNN and a Support Vector Machine (SVM). The authors claim that, compared to preceding works, the developed procedure can extract properties without manual intervention and can deal with collisions when the contact superficies is irregular. The simulated experiments and results showed the validity of their method with promising prediction accuracy. Li et al. [34] proposed a low-cost, high-precision procedure to detect and localize the charging connectors based on Scale-Invariant Feature Transform (SIFT) and Semi-Global Block Matching (SGBM) algorithms. The feature extraction procedure based on SIFT was adjusted to yield the Difference of Gaussians (DOG) algorithm for scale space construction, and the feature matching algorithm with nearest-neighbor search was employed to yield the set of matching points. The disparity determination has been conducted with a semi-global matching (SGM) algorithm to obtain high-precision positioning results for the charging socket position. The feasibility of the method was verified using OpenCV and MATLAB platforms. Chablat et al. [35] proposed a robot with parallel structure for automatic electric vehicle charging, where the charging socket of the vehicle is at its front side. Kinematic models are deployed to design the robot for a given workspace that matches the car's plug placements. They employed a QR code stuck next to the plug-in order to locate the port on the vehicle. When the robot moves, the QR code seen by the vision sensor is utilized to tune the trajectory before starting the inlay of the socket. A prototype of the robot was successfully realized as a concept related with the patent demand. The authors reported that the development of the robotic charging system will be continued. The robust overview of the previously presented and cited references, with their possible issues, are summarized in Table 1.

Table 1. Summary of related works, with an emphasis on proposed methods and their possible issues.

References	Proposed Methods	Possible Issues
Pan et al. [27]	Adopted pose solving method based on circle features	Problems with the positioning accuracy caused by the pixel extraction process error
Zhang and Jin [28]	HSI model-based segmentation and edge detection	Inappropriate illumination
Mišeikis et al. [29]	3D shape-based matching	Poor illumination in template matching process and positional error due to the calibration
Quan et al. [30]	Hough circle and Hough line transform followed by PNP algorithm	Low recognition accuracy due to the uneven illumination
Quan et al. [31]	Cluster template matching algorithm	Recognition errors caused by weather conditions (overcast, sunlight)
Lou and Di [32]	Pose measurement	Positioning error caused by the used vision sensor
Lin et al. [33]	CNN and SVMA-based algorithm	Signal variation and parking offset
Li et al. [34]	SIFT and SGBM-based algorithm	Distance measurement error caused by the illumination conditions and binocular camera properties
Chablat et al. [35]	QR code-based localization	Error caused by the camera during the trajectory adjustment of the plug

In the end, it should be mentioned that there are several demonstration videos on the Internet with robots developed for autonomous electric vehicle charging presented by companies and personal developers, however, without any published official and appropriate scientific and technical documentation related to the proposed solutions. Therefore, these demonstrations will not be cited in this paper.

3. ZED 2i Depth Sensor

The following section will introduce the technology and some of the most significant properties of the ZED 2i depth sensor, along with its working principle in brief.

Fundamentally, the ZED 2i depth camera is a passive stereo camera without an active ranging appliance. This stereo device utilizes a binocular camera to generate 3D scene data, retrieves the disparity of the object and scene using a stereo matching algorithm, and in the end determinates the depth map according to the sensor parameters in millimeters (mm) [36–40].

The new ZED 2i depth camera shown in Figure 1 shares some features with other Stereolabs ZED depth cameras; nevertheless, the new ZED 2i sensor owns several important improvements [36].

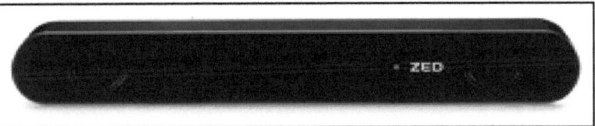

Figure 1. ZED 2i depth sensor (courtesy of Stereolabs) [36].

ZED 2i is the first stereo depth sensor that employs artificial neural networks (ANN) to reproduce and imitate human vision, taking stereo image perception to a new level [36]. It has a neural network mechanism that notably enhances the recorded depth map, or depth video stream. This ANN is linked with the image digital signal processor (DSP), and jointly they yield to creating the best possible depth information [36]. Furthermore, the ZED 2i sensor possesses an embedded shape detection framework. This framework detects both objects and shapes with spatial context. It integrates artificial intelligence (AI) with 3D localization to create spatial cognizance in the image [36]. Moreover, the embedded skeleton tracking option is included in ZED 2i, which employs 18× body principal points for tracking applications. This method detects and tracks human body skeletons in real-time. The tracking outcome is represented via a bounding box and according to the documentation, the algorithm works up to a 10 m range.

Furthermore, the ZED 2i depth sensor possesses an improved positional tracking algorithm that is a pertinent improvement convenient for robotic applications [12,36]. This benefit comes from a wide 120° angle field of view (FOV), advanced sensor stack, and thermal calibration for considerably enhanced positional tracking precision and accuracy [36]. The ZED 2i depth sensor also has an embedded inertial measurement unit (IMU), barometer, temperature sensor, and magnetometer. All these sensors supply extraordinary potentials of simple and precise multi-sensor recording. These sensors are factory calibrated on 9-axis with robots [36]. All these sensors with its characteristics designate that the ZED 2i depth sensor is convenient for the deployment of autonomous and industrial robotic applications [20–25].

Figure 2 presents the accuracy graph of the ZED 2i depth sensor depending on the distance of an object from the depth sensor. As can be seen in the diagram, the depth resolution, i.e., the depth precision, decreases with the increasing distance [36].

One of the most significant attributes of the ZED 2i is the ultra-sharp 8-element all glass lenses capable of grabbing video and depth with up to 120° field of view (FoV), with optically compensated distortion and a wider $f/1.8$ aperture which permits the capture of 40% more light [36]. Further, the ZED 2i optionally can use a polarizer. The embedded polarizing filter contributes to the highest-possible image quality in various applications outdoors. This special polarized lens helps decrease glare and reflections and also augments color depth and quality of the recorded images [36]. Moreover, the ZED 2i stereo sensor offers two lens options: the 2.1 mm focal length lens for a wide field of view or a 4 mm focal length lens for enhanced depth and image quality at long range [36]. These are the major characteristics related to stereo cameras since the lens, aperture, and light notably affect the image quality of any camera, not only the stereo depth camera. These properties enable the obtaining of a high-quality depth map [36]. Further, the ZED 2i can be cloud linked, and this option provides a possibility to monitor and control the depth camera remotely. Using a particular cloud platform, depth map recording and analyzing the 3D data is possible from anywhere in the world [36,37].

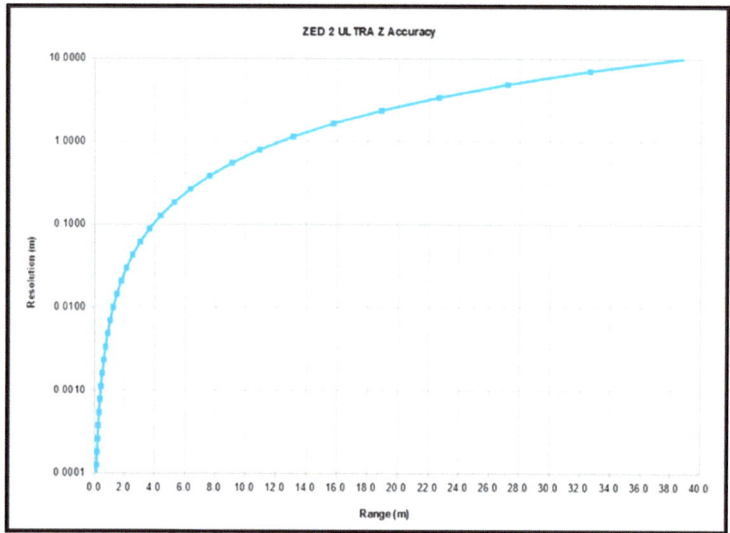

Figure 2. The accuracy graph of the ZED 2i depth sensor (courtesy of Stereolabs) [36].

Finally, based on the features of the ZED 2i sensor and its availability, the project's management decided to acquire this sensor and use it in the initial research study of this industrial project.

The essential properties of the ZED 2i depth sensor are summarized in Table 2 [36].

Table 2. Features of ZED 2i depth sensor (courtesy of Stereolabs) [36].

Features	ZED 2i
Size and weight	Dimensions: 175 × 30 × 33 mm Weight: 166 g
Depth	Baseline: 120 mm Format: 32 bits Range: 0.3–20 m
Image sensors	Size: 1/3″ Pixel Size: 2 µ pixels Format: 16:9
Lens	Field of View: 120° f/1.8 aperture Wide-angle 8-element all-glass dual lens with optically corrected distortion

Table 2. *Cont.*

Features	ZED 2i
Individual image and depth resolution in pixels	HD2K: 2208 × 1242 (15 fps) HD1080: 1920 × 1080 (30, 15 fps) HD720: 1280 × 720 (60, 30, 15 fps) WVGA: 672 × 376 (100, 60, 30, 15 fps)
Connectivity and working temperature	USB 3.0 (5 V/380 mA) −10 °C to +45 °C
SDK system minimal requirements	Windows or Linux Dual-core 2.3 GHz CPU 4 GB RAM Nvidia GPU with compute capability > 3.0
Additional sensors	Gyroscope Barometer Magnetometer Accelerometer Temperature sensor
Software enhancements	Built-in object detection Depth perception with neural engine

4. Proposed Method

In the following section, the proposed algorithm will be described with the corresponding digital image processing operations.

The block diagram of the proposed method is given in Figure 3. The system has two inputs, the Red–Blue–Green (RGB) color image and the original depth image with 32-bit depth resolution. Since the image with 32-bit resolution cannot be visibly displayed, only a dark image can be seen [36]. The main operation in this vision system is the application of the intensity transformation using the Gamma function and contrast stretching on the grayscaled input image [13]. This is a crucial action in the algorithm because it will remove most of the unwanted surrounding image components around the CCS2 connector region. This step is followed by the median filtering in order to remove the noise from the remained surrounding elements around and inside the charging socket itself [14]. Further, a series of morphological operations are implemented in order to obtain the binary mask of the socket area and the centroid coordinates of the socket itself [13]. After the binary mask is formed, the CCS2 socket region is detected combining logical image operations on the thresholded and binarized RGB images with the previously obtained binary mask. Next, using the detected socket from the RGB image, the CCS2 socket area is extracted from the original depth map using logical operations [14]. Finally, based on the detected CCS2 socket from the depth image with the corresponding depth information, and using the binary mask of the socket, the tilt angles of the socket in all three planes (XY, XZ, and YZ) were determined. Later, the obtained information would be forwarded to the UR robot's control system in order to automatically, without human interaction, plug-in the charging plug [9–12].

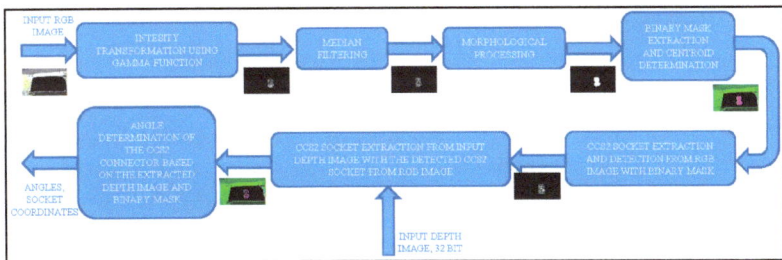

Figure 3. Block diagram of the proposed algorithm.

A detailed explanation of the robot and control system is not within the scope of this article and is not possible at this time. The robot's construction and the control system will be entirely described in a future research paper.

Further, the digital image processing algorithm will be described in detail through image processing examples. The recording environment and the illumination conditions will be explained later in the experiments section. It should be noted that, for the research and testing purposes, a vehicle body model was used with a built-in CCS2 socket. In the presented example, the car body model was covered with aluminum foil in order to increase the illumination reflection and artefacts appearance, which in reality would certainly appear on all vehicles due to the paintwork and environment illumination. In this way, the developed algorithm will have certain robustness to various disturbances and noise to the captured input images [9–11].

In the beginning, it should be noted that the dimensions of the input images are 2208×1242 pixels [36]. After the RGB and depth images are captured with the ZED 2i depth sensor, the second step is the conversion of the color image to a grayscale image. The reason for this conversion lies in the fact that the grayscaled image is the most suitable for processing using most image processing operations [13]. Figure 4a shows the captured RGB image. It is highly noised and contains artefacts and illumination reflection. The CCS2 connector is very poorly visible since its surrounding is very dark, as well the socket also. It is obvious from the shown RGB image that the socket detection is not a trivial task, because its textures are not visible and the surrounding regions are highly reflective and shadowed. Figure 4b shows the grayscale version of the original input depth map converted to 8-bit resolution in order to make visible the image itself, since the original depth map in 32-bit resolution is not visible on common monitors, because only a completely black image without any details would be seen [36]. As can be seen, the measured and generated depth map contains measured depth values in the socket region; however, due to the small difference between the depth values in the socket area, the socket is displayed in white shades and melted into its surrounding white area. Obviously, due to the impossibility of discerning the socket from its environment, the CCS2 socket cannot be distinguished and detected based only on the depth map itself [11,12,36]. Thus, the socket extraction algorithm uses both the RGB and depth images for the socket detection and tilt angles determination, as it is presented with the block diagram in Figure 3 and explained later in the paper.

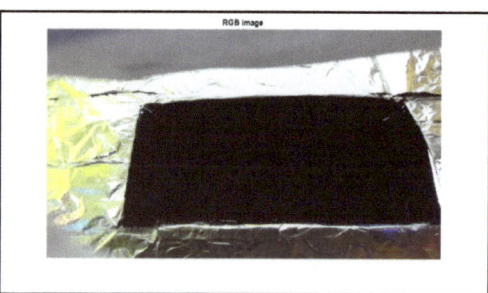 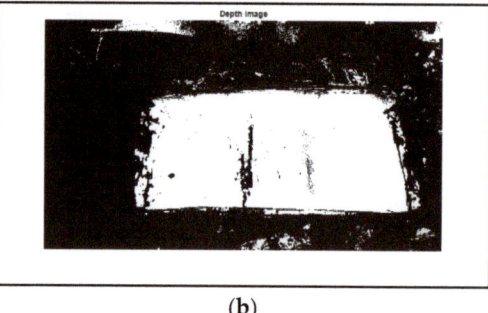

(a) (b)

Figure 4. (a) RGB image and (b) original input depth map converted to 8-bit depth resolution.

In order to enhance the contours of the connector, the input RGB image has been converted to grayscale image, and next the grayscale dilation operation is performed on the grayscaled input image [13]. Basically, the grayscale dilation is a local-maximum operation, where the maximum is taken over a set of pixel neighbors defined by the spatial shape of the elements with value 1 in the domain of the structuring element (SE) [14].

The grayscale dilation of a grayscale image f by SE B, denoted by $f \oplus B$, is defined as:

$$(f \oplus B)(x,y) = max\{f(x - x', y - y') + B(x', y') \mid (x', y') \in D_B\}, \quad (1)$$

where D_B is the domain of SE B and $f(x,y)$ is assumed to be $-\infty$ outside the domain of f [13]. Basically, this expression executes a process similar to spatial convolution [14]. An important difference between convolution and grayscale dilation is that, in the latter, D_B is a binary matrix that determines which locations in the neighborhood are included in the maximum operation. In convolution, the corresponding matrix is not binary [13]. Hence, this local-maximum calculation via grayscale dilation yields in stronger textures in the resulting image, as shown in Figure 5a. The grayscale dilation was performed using a disk-shaped structuring element. It should be noted that the sizes of SEs in all morphological operations depend on the image size, and in this algorithm, the dimensions of all the SEs are determined empirically [14]. In the resulting image, the contours of the socket are more visible and the surrounding area is slightly blurred.

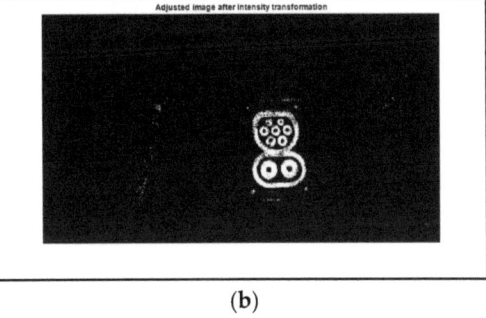

(a) (b)

Figure 5. (a) Grayscale dilation result and (b) intensity transformation result.

In the next step, the main operation of the algorithm is performed: the intensity transformation. The transformation is executed jointly with an application of the Gamma function, followed by contrast stretching [14]. The use of the Gamma function in the literature is commonly named as gamma correction, gamma encoding, or power-law gamma transformation [13]. To explain this operation in the spatial domain, a simple expression is introduced:

$$g(x,y) = T[f(x,y)], \quad (2)$$

where $f(x,y)$ is the input image, $g(x,y)$ is the output image, and the T is an operator on f determined over a defined neighborhood around point (x,y) [14]. The simplest version of the transform T is when the neighborhood in image is a single pixel of size 1×1. Thus, the value of g output at point (x,y) relies only on the intensity of f input image at that point and T becomes an intensity transformation function [14]. Since the output of the intensity transformation function relies only on the intensity value at a point and not on a neighborhood of points, the expression is frequently simplified as:

$$s = T(r), \quad (3)$$

where r denotes the intensity of f and s the intensity of g, both at the same coordinates (x,y) in the input and output images [13].

The power-law gamma transformations are defined as follows:

$$s = cr^\gamma, \quad (4)$$

where γ and c are positive constants [14]. This gamma correction-based intensity transformation with fractional values of γ maps a straight range of dark input values into a wider range of output values, with the opposite mapping for higher values of input intensity levels. Parameter γ defines the shape of the transformation curve that maps the intensity values from input f to output g [14]. If γ is less than 1, the mapping is weighted toward higher output values, while if γ is greater than 1, the mapping is weighted toward lower output values [13]. The intensity transformation is performed jointly with contrast stretching, where the narrow interval of input intensity values is expanded into a wider interval of output values [14]. In this algorithm, the value of γ is 0.001. This value of γ eliminates the brighter background of the CCS2 socket and retains the dark socket components and textures in the image. As shown in Figure 5b, almost the whole area around the charging socket is eliminated. The remained connector elements contain noise that will be suppressed later with additional processing.

In the next step, a noise removal operation is performed using median filtering. The median filter is a well-known noise eliminating operation, and it is a very simple and efficient procedure [14]. Basically, this is an order-statistic filter in image processing which substitutes the value of a pixel by the median of the intensity levels in a predetermined neighborhood of the corresponding pixel. The median filtering operation is defined as:

$$\hat{f}(x,y) = \underset{(r,c) \in S_{xy}}{median} \{g(r,c)\}, \quad (5)$$

where S_{xy} denotes a subimage centered on point (x,y), $\hat{f}$ is the noise-reduced image, r and c are the row and column coordinates, respectively, of the pixels in neighborhood S_{xy}, and g represents the corrupted image with noise [14]. Median filters are highly favored because, for certain types of random noise, they yield outstanding noise reduction abilities, with noticeably less blurring than linear smoothing filters with a similar size. Moreover, median filters are specifically effective in the existence of both bipolar and unipolar impulse noise [13]. In the algorithm, the empirically determined size of the employed median filter is 9×9, with the result of the median filtering shown in Figure 6a. As can be seen, the noise from the image is removed and the CCS2 socket area is sharp and clear. It should be noted that the dimensions of the median filter depend on the dimensions of the input image, and it can be easily adopted during the experiments [14]. However, there are several remaining components around the connector. These components will be removed via morphological filtering in further processing steps of the algorithm.

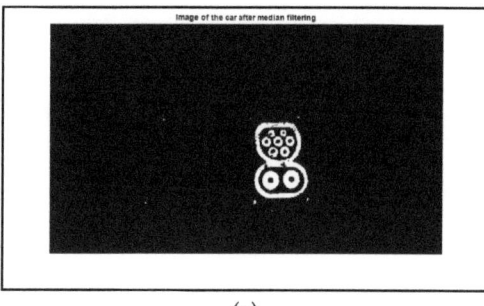
(a)

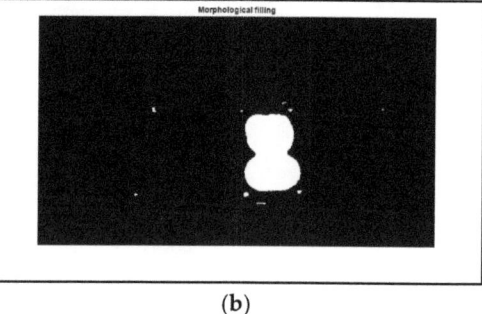
(b)

Figure 6. (a) Result of the median filtering and (b) result of the sequence of morphological processing and filling operation.

The next step in the algorithm is the binary morphological processing preceded by the simple thresholding operation. After the binarization is accomplished, a series of morphological dilations with plus-shaped structuring elements were performed in order to thicken the components in the connector area. Dilation is one of the main operations in morphology, together with erosion [13]. Basically, dilation grows, or thickens, the objects in the binary image, thus making their textures more filled without small holes. Hence, one of the primary applications of dilations is for bridging holes in the image. The method and the extent of the thickening is controlled by the shape and the size of the used SE. Basically, the result of all morphological operations depends on the utilized SEs [14]. The dilation operation of A by SE B, where A and B are sets in integer space Z^2, is determined as:

$$A \oplus B = \left\{ z \middle| [(\hat{B})_z \bigcap A] \subseteq A \right\}, \tag{6}$$

where z denotes a translation in image space and $\hat{B}$ denotes the reflection of SE B about its origin [13]. Unlike dilation, which is a thickening operation, erosion shrinks, or thins, the shapes in a binary image. The erosion of A by B is determined as:

$$A \ominus B = \{z | (B)_z \subseteq A\}, \tag{7}$$

where A is a set of foreground pixels, B is a SE, and z represents the foreground values. Simply, based on Equation (7), the erosion of A by B is a set of all points z such that B, translated by z, is contained in set A [13].

The dilation operations in the algorithm are followed by the morphological closing operation with disk-shaped SE. It should be noted that since dilation and erosion are elementary operations in morphology, all the other morphological algorithms are based on these two principal operations [14]. The closing operation tends to smooth sections of contours in the image; however, it generally fuses straight breaks and long thin gulfs, eliminates small cavities, and fills gaps in the contour of a shape in a binary image. The goal of the closing operation is to fuse small breaks of the CCS2 socket in a dilated image. The closing of A by B simply is a dilation of A by B, accompanied by erosion of the result by SE B [13]:

$$A \cdot B = (A \oplus B) \ominus B. \tag{8}$$

Next, a morphological filling operation is performed in order to fill the socket area, with a goal to form the binary mask of the CCS2 socket. The morphological hole-filling algorithm is based on dilation, complementation, and intersection operations. The following process fills all the holes with 1 s surrounded by values of 1 in a binary image:

$$X_k = (X_{k-1} \oplus B) \bigcap I^c \quad k = 1, 2, 3, \ldots, \tag{9}$$

where B is the symmetric SE, k is an iteration step, X_k is the object inside the binary image that contains all the filled holes, ^{c} denotes the complementation operation, and I is the binary image [13]. The dilation in Equation (9) would fill the complete region of the image, but the intersection at each step with I^c limits the result to inside the area of interest. This algorithm is an example presenting the possibilities of a simple morphological operation to develop an efficient procedure in order to meet a desired property and result. Figure 6b presents the result of the morphological filling operation. As can be seen, the whole CCS2 socket area is filled with binary 1 values. The small image components around the connector area will be eliminated in morphological post-processing in order to determine the binary mask of the socket.

Finally, the binary mask is obtained by the sequence of morphological closing and opening with disk-shaped SEs. The opening operation also smooths the contour of a shape; however, as opposed to closing, it breaks narrow isthmuses and eliminates thin protrusions. The opening of A by SE B is expressed as:

$$A \circ B = (A \ominus B) \oplus B, \tag{10}$$

where the equation states that the opening of A by B is the erosion of A by B, accompanied by dilation of the result by SE B [13]. Figure 7a shows the formed binary mask of the CCS2 socket, while Figure 7b displays the binary mask overlapping the original RGB image in order to present the accuracy of the detected mask. The pink surface represents the binary mask that overlaps the socket region in the input RGB image. As can be seen, the obtained binary mask is very accurate, and it completely masks the connector area.

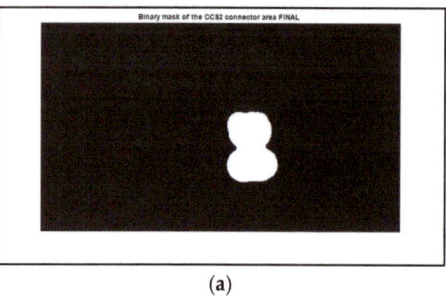 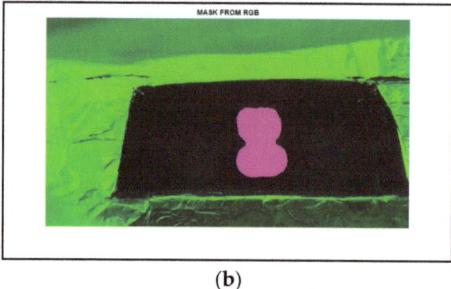

(a) (b)

Figure 7. (a) The binary mask of the CCS2 socket and (b) overlapped image of the RGB image with the binary mask of the CCS2 socket.

To this point, the upper part of the image processing procedure is explained from Figure 3. Further, the remaining steps of the algorithm will be explained. The following task is the extraction of the CCS2 socket shape from the RGB image using the extracted binary mask. This is accomplished with a simple logical image multiplication of the binary mask with the binarized image of the previously obtained result after median filtering, as shown in Figure 8a. The resulting connector contains small gaps and holes that will be post-processed again with a sequence of morphological operations. This series of operations involves dilation, closing, opening, and erosion with small-sized, plus-shaped, and disk-shaped SEs. The reason for the usage of several operations with small SEs lies in the fact that it is mandatory to keep all the vital components of the socket, without a possible cutoff in it. The obtained result of the morphological post-processing is shown in Figure 8b, with the corresponding bounding box around the CCS2 socket itself.

 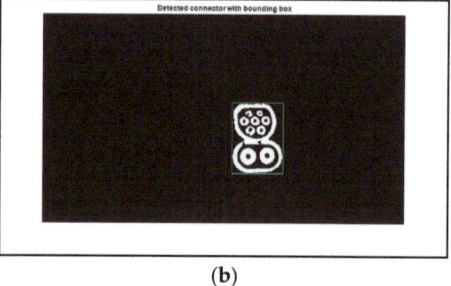

(a) (b)

Figure 8. (a) Result of the extraction with logical image multiplication and (b) result of the sequence of morphological post-processing.

Figure 9a shows the accuracy of the CCS2 socket detection, where the extracted socket from the RGB image overlaps the input RGB image. Again, the pink surface that overlaps the charging socket region represents the extracted socket. It can be seen that the obtained contours and textures of the derived charging socket area fit well on the original image. In Figure 9b, the centroid coordinate of the detected socket region is marked as a yellow cross in the input image. This coordinate will serve as crucial information for the robot's control system during the positioning of a charger plug, before its connection to the CCS2 socket [5–11].

 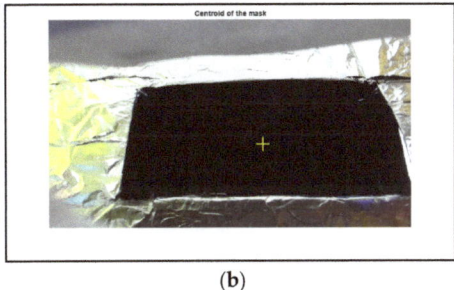

(a) (b)

Figure 9. (a) Overlapped image of the extracted CCS2 socket and (b) marked centroid coordinate of the CCS2 socket in the original input image.

After the centroid coordinate of the socket is determined, the next step is to extract the socket area from the original 32-bit depth resolution depth map in order to calculate the tilt angles of the socket relative to the ZED 2i camera position in space. Basically, the depth image is a projection of Z measured distance values on the XY plane of the image. These distance values will be used for the determination of tilt angles in the XZ and YZ planes, while the previously obtained binary mask will be used for the determination of the orientation angle in the XY plane of the image. The angle in the XZ plane represents the slope angle in the horizontal direction, while the angle in the YZ plane represents the slope in the vertical direction relative to the stereo camera position. The socket extraction is accomplished again with a simple logical image multiplication of the previously extracted and post-processed binary CCS2 socket image with the original input depth map. Thus, the resulting image contains only the original depth values that belong to the CCS2 socket. Figure 10a shows the result of the multiplication operation, where the binary image of the detected socket from the RGB image (Figure 8a) is multiplied with the original input depth map in 32-bit depth resolution. Since the binary image is multiplied with the input depth map in 32-bit depth resolution, the content of the image cannot be displayed on common displays [36]. Figure 9a is included for the generality of the presentation of the procedure. In Figure 10b, the resulting image is converted to 8-bit depth resolution in order to be visible, and the accuracy of the detected CCS2 socket from the original depth map can be observed relative to the input RGB image. The pink surface region is the extracted CCS2 socket from the original depth map, and here it overlaps the input RGB image in order to highlight the accuracy of the detection.

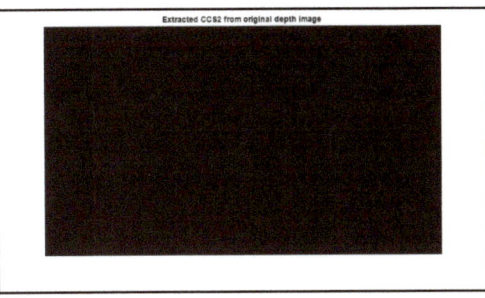 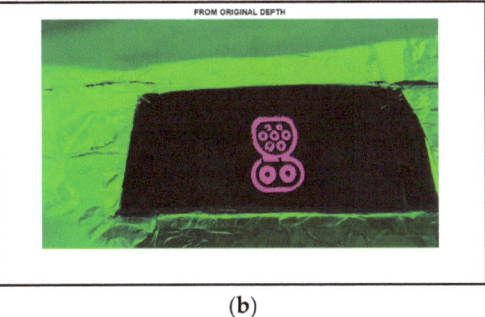

(a) (b)

Figure 10. (a) Extracted CCS2 socket in 32-bit depth resolution and (b) extracted CCS2 socket from the original depth map converted to 8-bit depth resolution.

It is desirable that the extracted socket from the depth map has the same or a similar quality as the extracted socket from the RGB image for the better tilt angle calculation of the socket; however, it also depends on the measured depth map quality. If the depth map does not contain sufficient information related to the socket region, even the appropriate socket detection from the input RGB image will not extract the socket from the depth map properly.

Finally, the determination of the tilt angles remained. First, the orientation angle in the XY plane of the input image is obtained via measuring image region properties and ellipse fitting procedure of the obtained binary mask [38]. The calculated XY plane angle in this particular example is 6.4733 degrees. The two other angles are determined using simple trigonometry [41] and using the known dimensions of the real socket itself. The first step is the cropping of the extracted CCS2 socket from the 32-bit depth resolution depth map using the previously obtained bounding box around the socket itself. Then, if the furthermost upper and furthermost lower rows with stereometry-calculated distances in the cropped socket area are averaged, the results will be the averaged farthest and nearest distances in vertical direction from the depth sensor's plane in millimeters. Thus, using the known height (H) in millimeters of the CCS2 socket, the tilt angle of YZ plane can be determined as:

$$\varphi_{YZ} = \sin^{-1} \frac{z_{upper} - z_{lower}}{H} \tag{11}$$

where z_{upper} and z_{lower} are the averaged distance values in the vertical direction.

Similarly, if the furthermost left and right columns of the determined distances in the cropped socket are averaged, the results will be the averaged farthest and nearest distances in the horizontal direction from the depth sensor's plane in millimeters, and using the known width (W) in millimeters of the CCS2 socket, the tilt angle of XZ plane can be obtained as:

$$\varphi_{XZ} = \sin^{-1} \frac{z_{left} - z_{right}}{W}, \tag{12}$$

where z_{left} and z_{right} are the averaged distance values in the horizontal direction.

Naturally, the resulting angles can have an ancestor of + or −, depending on the averaged distance values. In practice, this manifests itself as a slope of the top or bottom parts of the connector forward or backward, or as a slope of the left or right parts of the connector forward or backward. In this particular example, the angles are $\varphi_{YZ} = 9.7721$ degrees and $\varphi_{XZ} = 6.4733$ degrees. It is obvious that the determination of these angles depends on appropriate and high-quality CCS2 socket extraction from the original 32-bit depth map, as well on the generated high-quality depth map by the depth sensor.

Finally, all the determined angles and the detected centroid coordinate of the connector position will be forwarded to the UR robot's controlling system, and based on these parameters, the robot will be able to connect the charger plug to the charging CCS2 socket.

In the end it should be noted that when the UR robot arrives, the depth sensor will be installed on the robot's arm and the testing will be conducted live in real time on the vehicle body model with built-in CCS2 socket and with electric vehicles. Later, when the system is verified, the testing will be expanded to other available electric vehicles.

5. Experiments and Results

In this section, the experiments and their results are explained in detail. As it was mentioned in the Introduction, the goal and the main demand of the project is to use only proven and well-known digital image processing operations during the development of the socket detection algorithm. The algorithm was tested on artificial vehicle body models with a built-in CCS2 connector. Various backgrounds and illumination conditions were tested in order to analyze and determine the potentials and limitations of the deployed object detection algorithm based on common image processing methods.

One of the key factors in the development of the image processing algorithm is the generation of a high-quality, usable input image. In addition to the use of high-quality capturing devices, the main requirement is the formation of an appropriately illuminated environment without disturbing effects, which can ensure the repeatability of a quality image capturing. Thus, it should be noted that an artificial white lighting

Light Emitting Diode (LED) illumination is used with paper shadowing during the image capturing in experiments to ensure the needed diffuse lighting conditions for the ZED 2i camera [36]. This illumination source was proposed by Stereolabs' engineering team during the consultations. The power of LED lights separately is 1.5 W, and they are connected to a 12 V voltage source. The intensity of LED lights is controlled with a simple regulation circuit presented in Figure 11a. The LED lights are mounted in the same plane in a line with the ZED 2i, to an approximate 35 cm distance left and right from the depth sensor, and they provide directly diffuse illumination both to the car body model and to the CCS2 socket. Despite the lights' regulation possibility, almost all the measurements were conducted with the maximum light intensity, since the visibility of the charging socket area is very poor due to its darkness. Moreover, it is possible to mount more LED sources or increase the intensity of the illumination; however, it is not shown to be the best solution, since too much light can cause reflection and it will simply blind the depth sensor, and the stereo device will not be able to generate an appropriate depth map [36], while it could also spoil the RGB image. In contrast to highly intense lighting, if the lighting is insufficient, the details in the images of the left and right cameras will be insufficiently visible; thus, the stereo-matching algorithm will not have enough useful information to be able to generate a correct and accurate depth map [36]. This is a commonly known issue when passive depth sensors are used in various applications, where the light source is close to the camera [11,36]. The depth sensor is mounted on a tripod together with the LED illumination sources and shadowing elements, as shown in Figure 11b. The experiments were conducted at daylight, sunlight, shadow, under room lighting, and in a complete dark environment.

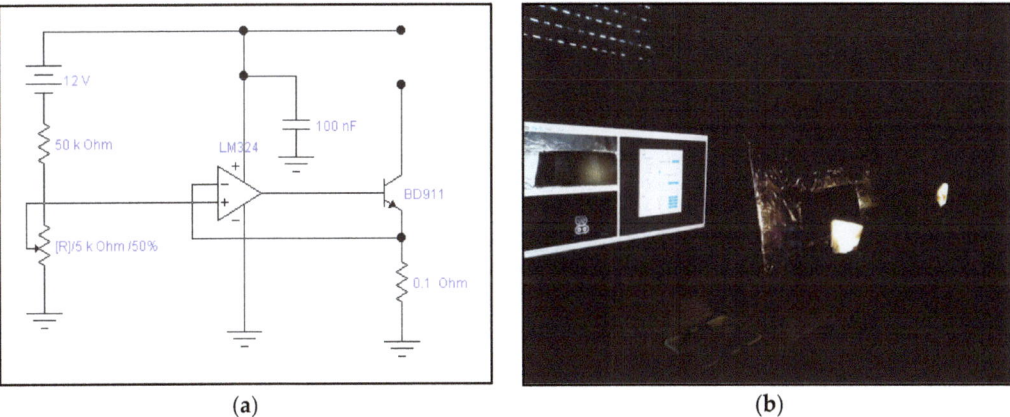

(a) (b)

Figure 11. (**a**) LED lights regulation circuit and (**b**) experiment setup.

Further, since the aim was to examine the ultimate capabilities of the developed algorithm, the colors and shades of the vehicle body model are chosen so that the glare, noise, and artefacts are as pronounced as possible, or that the complete socket surrounding will be very dark to absorb light and thus spoil the input RGB and depth images. The socket and the surrounding where it is mounted are very dark (on real vehicles also) and, thus, they absorb light and the socket looks dark in the presented examples. Additionally, it should be noted that the vehicle body model is tilted a little to reflect the real situation, because real vehicles also narrow in a truncated pyramid shape in the upward direction around the socket position, and that is the reason why the presented examples will look like they are being captured from above slightly. Hence, the socket is observed from in front with minor displacements, and that will also be the intent in the real application. The depth sensor was positioned approximately 20–22 cm from the vehicle body model; thus, the CCS2 socket was approximately 24–28 cm from the camera. It should be mentioned that the minimal working distance of ZED 2i is 20 cm, since according to Stereolabs' documentation, the dead zone of the sensor is starting from 19 cm [36]. This means that this depth sensor cannot generate a depth map below this distance. Further, the proposed capturing distances were determined empirically in consultation with Stereolabs, since this problem is very specific due to the very dark and textureless CCS2 socket that should be detected with its tilt angles. Moreover, starting with the 30 cm distance, the depth sensor cannot generate an adequate and quality depth map with sufficient details of the socket area; hence, the proposed capturing distance [36] was kept in all experiments. Later, when the UR robot will be involved in testing, a quality ultrasonic distance sensor will be utilized to bring the robotic arm with the stereo camera to the desired distance from the vehicle body. The electric vehicles will be properly positioned with physical borders and signs on a parking lot; knowing the model of the electric vehicle and the position of the charger socket on the specified vehicle, the robot will, with the help of these known parameters, position the robotic arm with the camera and distance sensor in front of the CCS2 charging socket at the proper distance and position.

Lastly, the goal of this research is to develop and examine the possibilities of the object detection algorithm with the ZED 2i depth sensor in challenging image recording situations.

Finally, since the ZED 2i device requires appropriate hardware which supports a Graphical Processing Unit (GPU), in experiments, an Intel i7-10700 2.90 GHz processor with 16 GB RAM memory and the NVidia GeForce GTX 1650 SUPER GPU is used. The proposed procedure is developed in Matlab [41]. In future, the algorithm will be connected to the UR robot's control system via ROS and Node-RED. Node-RED is a programming tool for wiring together various hardware devices inside the deployed system [42].

Next, several examples will be presented with the main emphasis on the image processing results, without serving the numerical data for angles and coordinates, because the slope angles and centroid coordinates can be easily determined based on the extracted CCS2 socket. Thus, the determination of the angles and coordinates itself is affected by the efficiency of the algorithm in addition to the quality input RGB and depth images. In all figures, the pink surface in overlapped images will represent the region of the formed binary mask and the extracted socket, respectively, in order to visibly present the obtained results. Finally, it should be noted that in all experiments, the RGB image obtained from the left image sensor of the ZED 2i is used, since the built-in software of the depth sensor automatically aligns the generated depth map with the left RGB image of the depth camera [36].

In Figure 12a, a white vehicle body model is shown, where the image recording was performed at daylight. The white nuance of the body model is slightly matted, while the socket area is very dark and poorly visible due to the shadow from the right side. This is also a common situation in the real world, since the socket area will always be very dark, almost black, and its textures will always be hardly noticeable in all images.

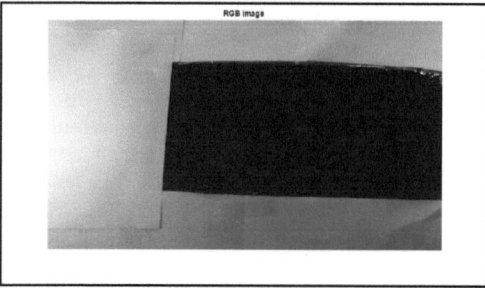
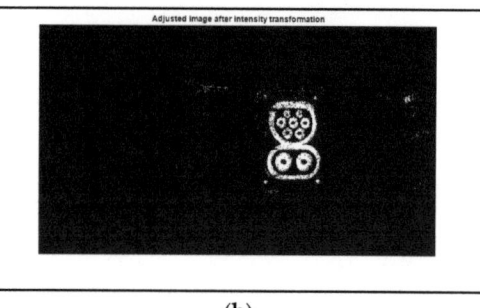

(a) (b)

Figure 12. *Cont.*

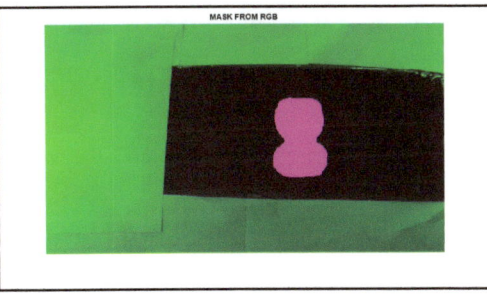

Figure 12. (**a**) Input RGB image, (**b**) result of the intensity transformation, (**c**) obtained binary mask, and (**d**) detected CCS2 connector.

The LED lights were on full power, and that is the reason for sufficient scene illumination. Figure 12b displays the result of the applied intensity transformation with gamma correction. As can be seen, the socket area is well retained in the resulting image, with a small number of surrounding components and noise. After executing the median filtering and morphological processing, as explained in the previous section, the binary mask of the socket region is obtained with high accuracy, as shown in Figure 12c. Finally, using the binary mask and the previously proposed post-processing procedure, the CCS2 socket area from the original depth image is determined, as shown in Figure 12d. The contours of the socket are slightly deficient; however, they contain sufficient information for appropriate slant calculation. Hence, the detected and extracted charging socket shape with its corresponding depth information will serve for the determination of tilt angles of the socket itself. Naturally, after the binary mask of the socket is derived, its centroid coordinate is also appropriately determined.

In the next example, a matted black vehicle body is chosen. As can be seen, the whole surrounding and the background of the socket is similarly dark. The LED lights are again fully turned on and the car body model with the socket is adequately illuminated. The image recording was conducted at daylight, with small shades visible from both sides of the socket area, as shown in Figure 13a. The second image displays the effect of the intensity transformation. As shown in Figure 13b, the CCS2 socket region is well highlighted; however, some surrounding image components remained from both sides of the socket, and there are some small black gaps inside the targeted object. Following the performed noise removal and morphological operations, the aimed binary mask of the socket is detected with high fidelity, as shown in Figure 13c. The mask completely overlaps the socket in the original input image. In the end, after the final processing is accomplished, the connector is successfully detected and derived from the input depth map. The result of this extraction is presented in Figure 13d. Due to the darkness and poor visibility of the input RGB image, the stereometric algorithm generated a low-quality depth map, and that is the reason for the damaged, torn-look socket textures in the resulting image. It is generally known that the main requirement of stereometry is the adequate visibility of all details in the left and right camera images in order to generate a depth map with adequate quality [36]. However, despite the given low-quality depth map, the detection was successful and all the desired angles and coordinates were appropriately determined.

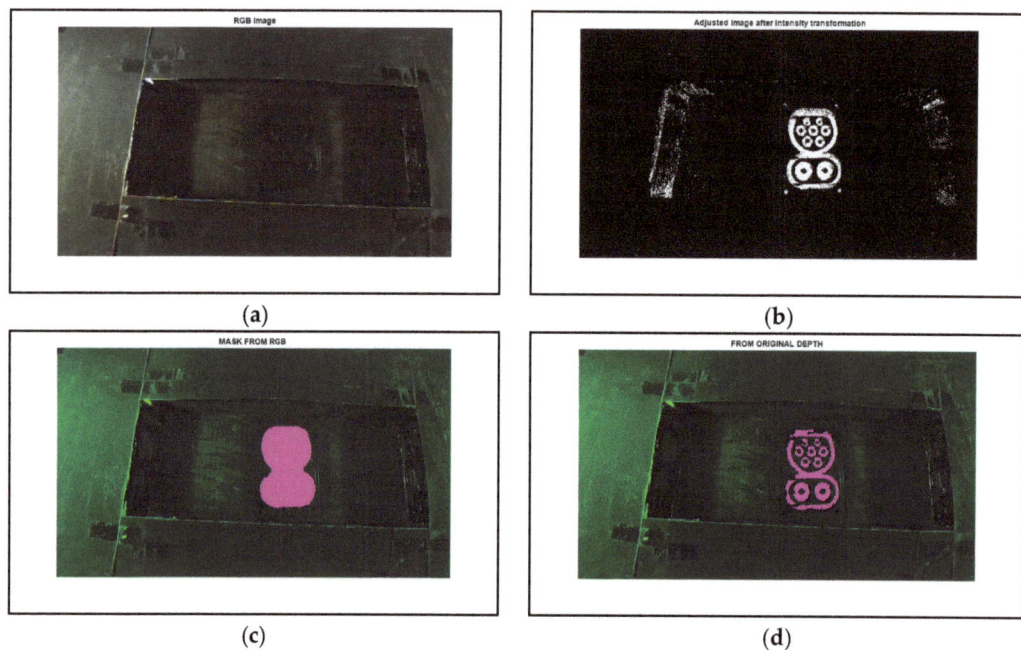

Figure 13. (**a**) Input RGB image, (**b**) result of the intensity transformation, (**c**) obtained binary mask, and (**d**) detected CCS2 connector.

In the next experiment, in Figure 14, a highly reflective yellow–gold-colored vehicle body model with bright small patterns was tested. The intensity of LED lights is maximal, and the reflection due to the illumination is very expressed near the connector region, as shown in Figure 14a. The image was captured in the evening. The second example shows the outcome of the performed intensity transformation. The socket is highly distinguishable from the background, and only a small number of surrounding components remained. All those components are successfully removed with the proposed median filter [41] and morphological filtering. As a result, in Figure 14c, the binary mask is formed with high accuracy. Finally, executing the suggested post-processing operations, the CCS2 socket is detected and extracted, as shown in Figure 14d. Again, the extracted connector contains small cracks; however, it is considered to be a satisfactory result and all the needed parameters are determined.

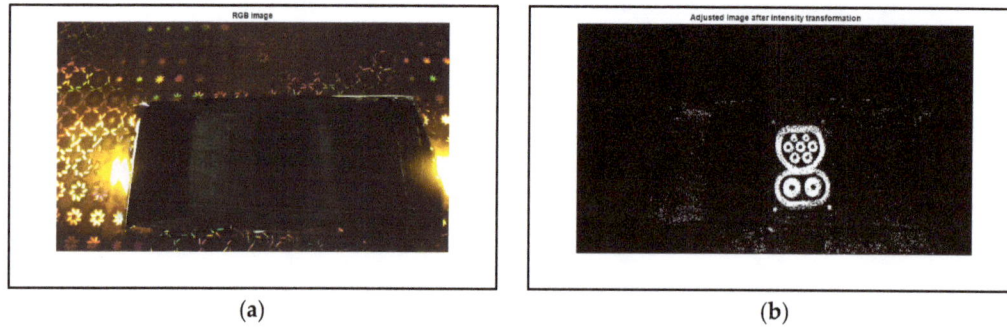

Figure 14. *Cont.*

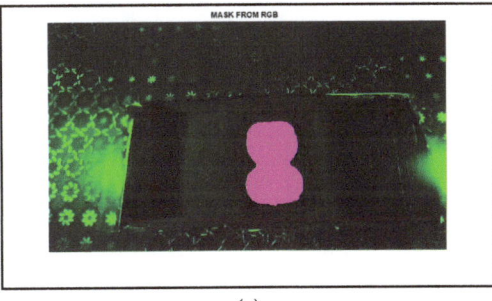
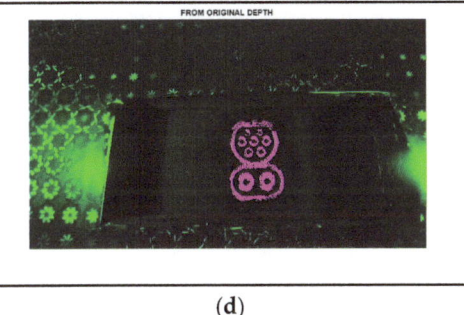

(c) (d)

Figure 14. (**a**) Input RGB image, (**b**) result of the intensity transformation, (**c**) obtained binary mask, and (**d**) detected CCS2 connector.

In the next example, a highly reflective red–gold-colored vehicle body model with bright small patterns was examined. Once more, the intensity of LED lights is maximal, and the reflection due to the illumination is very expressed close to the connector region, as shown in Figure 15a. The image was captured at night. Figure 15b shows the result of the execution of intensity transformation. The connector is highly visible and only a small number of image components remained; however, the upper left part of the socket is damaged slightly. After the noise removal and morphology operations are executed, the small image components are successfully removed, and a binary mask is obtained. The third example displays the binary mask overlapping the input image. As can be seen, the mask entirely covers the socket region with sufficient accuracy. Finally, performing the post-processing operations, the CCS2 socket is extracted, as shown in Figure 15d. Again, the obtained socket contains small holes, it is ripped, and damaged slightly; however, all the required angles and coordinates are determined properly, since the extracted socket region provided sufficient depth information.

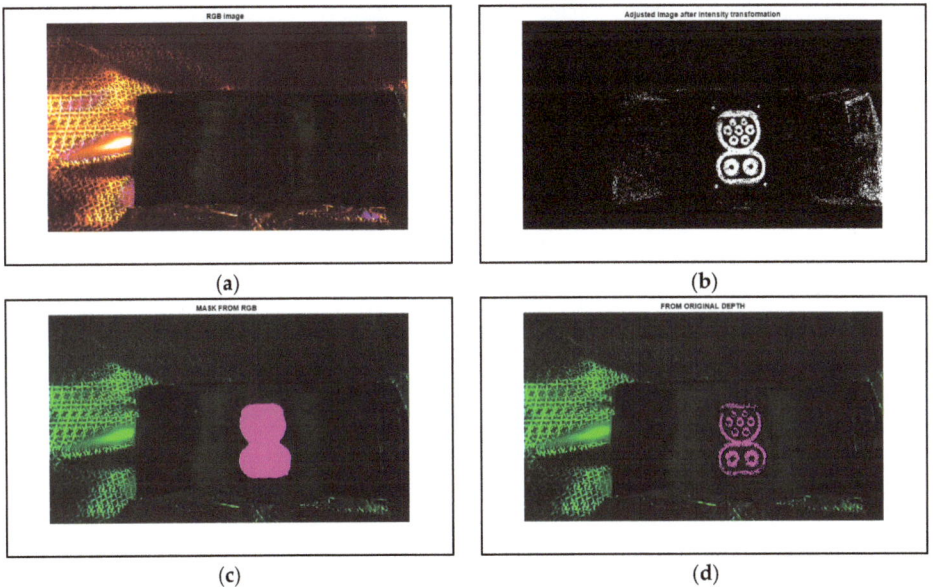

Figure 15. (**a**) Input RGB image, (**b**) result of the intensity transformation, (**c**) obtained binary mask, and (**d**) detected CCS2 connector.

The final example presents a highly reflective blue–silver-colored car body model with bright small patterns. The LED lights intensity were fully on, and the reflection due to the illumination is very high in the connector region, as shown in Figure 16a.

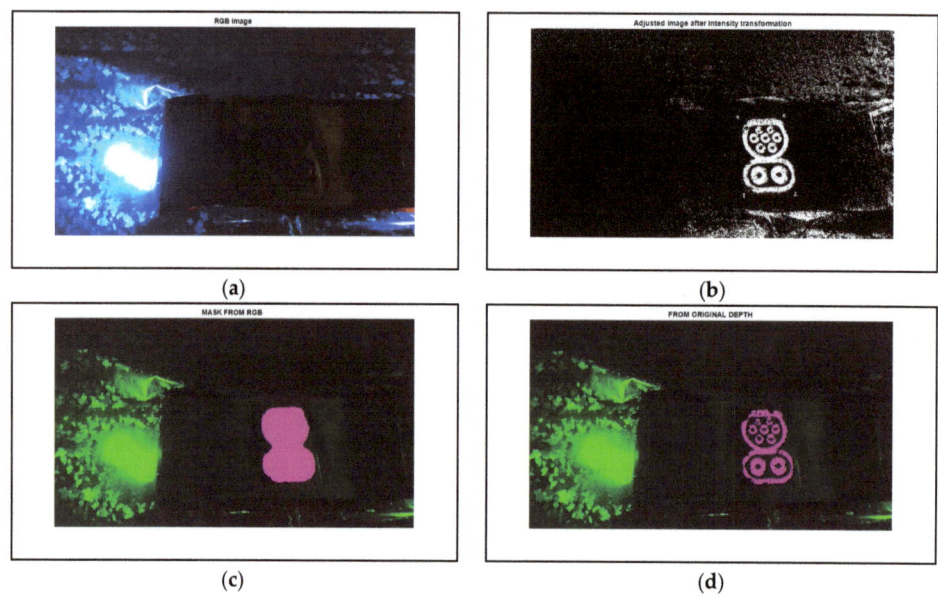

Figure 16. (**a**) Input RGB image, (**b**) result of the intensity transformation, (**c**) obtained binary mask, and (**d**) detected CCS2 connector.

The image was captured in the evening with low intensity room lights turned on. The right part of the image is highly shadowed. In Figure 16b, the outcome of the intensity transformation is shown. The connector is well noticeable, although a large number of image components remained in the right part of the image. After the median filtering and morphological processing were performed, all the remaining unwanted components were eliminated and the binary mask was formed successfully. Figure 16c presents the binary mask surface. As can be seen, the mask overlaps the socket area with notable accuracy. In the end, executing the post-processing actions, the CCS2 socket is detected, as shown in Figure 16d. Again, the extracted socket contains small gaps and its texture is slightly uneven; nevertheless, all the demanded tilt angles and centroid coordinates are calculated suitably, since it supplied adequate depth values from the extracted socket region.

In the end, it should be noted that the SEs in the morphological operations were defined empirically during the algorithm development. These SEs are size-dependent matrices, which means that they can be simply tuned depending on the size of the objects in the image, where the size of the shapes in the image depends on the model of the depth sensor, as well as on the range of the depth sensor from the object itself [12,36]. These modifications are very frequently made throughout the reproduction of this procedure. Additionally, the high-quality lens produces less dispersion when mapping the depth of the scene, and in the case of a poor-quality depth sensor with low quality lens, the socket detection and extraction cannot be successfully performed. This is because the determination of the Z distance values could be deficient, and this could result in missing the sufficient and accurate depth values in the socket surface that represents the CCS2 socket in the depth map. In this situation, the detection and extraction cannot be established.

Based on the experiments, the main limitations of the algorithm arise from inappropriate illumination conditions and artefacts caused by various influences such as shadows, light reflection, poor visibility, etc. All these issues can be solved with a proper illumination source that will provide a quality illuminated environment to the depth sensor, which will result in an adequately generated depth map.

The evaluation of the algorithm was performed on six previously presented vehicle body models with the mounted CCS2 socket under various lighting and capturing conditions. The successful detection rate was 94% based on 150 depth image measurements and the recorded corresponding RGB images. All the failed detections related exclusively to inadequate illumination conditions that deteriorated the appropriate socket detection and the proper generation of the depth map.

A comparison with other methods is very difficult, since all the proposed methods in the literature deal with the detection of Asian-type charging sockets, which have a different shape and content compared to the CCS2 socket. The CCS2 socket is a combined socket with two charging ports, with AC (Alternating Current) and DC (Direct Current) charging options. The Asian-type sockets contain only one charging port [27–35]. Further, the presented procedure in this paper is using well-known, common image processing operations, and only the methods proposed by Zhang and Jin [28] and Quan et al. [30], where the reported success rates were 100% [28] and 94.8% [30], respectively, could be compared with it in some parts; however, the number of tested images/examples is not listed in the paper by Zhang and Jin. Overall, the proposed methods in the literature deal with the qualitative analysis without numerical results, or incomplete numerical results are reported without the listed image numbers in testing sets [27–35]. However, due to the generality of the presentation, Table 3 presents a comparison of the proposed method compared to other methods from the literature. As can be seen, the procedure presented in this paper achieved similar results regardless of the fact that only common and well-known image processing techniques were used in the algorithm development. It is expected that by improving the illumination quality of the scene and working in an industrial environment, the successful detection rate will be higher, hopefully near 100%.

Table 3. Comparison with other methods.

Methods	Number of Images	Success Rate
Proposed method	150	94%
Pan et al. [27]	30	98.9%
Zhang and Jin [28]	not available	100%
Mišeikis et al. [29]	not available	90%
Quan et al. [30]	180	94.8%
Quan et al. [31]	100	95%
Lin et al. [33]	not available	94.12%

Further, the qualitative comparison of the proposed method will be presented, comparing it to the Circular Hough Transform-based method proposed by Quan et al. [30], since the testing conditions of their procedure is similar to the testing conditions in this research. A very important feature of the Asian-type socket is the regular circle-shaped frame around the electrical contacts; therefore, the Circular Hough Transform is very convenient for the detection of the Asian-type of sockets [30]. The results of this detection approach are the coordinates of the circle centers with the corresponding radiuses. Moreover, as was noted, the Asian-type of charging socket has a different shape, content, size, and only one charging option. Thus, this comparison does not fully reflect the reality, since the compared algorithms are designed for different types of sockets that are not comparable in any matter. Further, in [30], all the experiments were executed on only one dark vehicle body model (black panel) with the mounted Asian-type socket under various illumination conditions, while six differently colored vehicle body models were tested with the proposed algorithm in this study. Figure 17 shows two examples from the comparison. The Circular Hough Transform is applied in the algorithm to specifically detect the circle-shape electrical contacts inside the socket body [30], and the detection results are marked with green circles in the images. Figure 17a presents an example of correct detection of the charging socket contacts, while the second image shows the result when one electric contact of the socket is not detected. The detection rate with the Circular Hough Transform is 90.7%; however, it should be noted that the comparison would be complete and appropriate if it was performed on the Asian-type of socket, since the Circular Hough Transform-based approach is developed specifically for that socket due to its circle-shaped frame [30] around the electric contacts. Nevertheless, a meaningful comparison on the Asian-type of socket would also require an adaptation of the proposed algorithm due to the different shape of the socket, and that is outside the scope of this research.

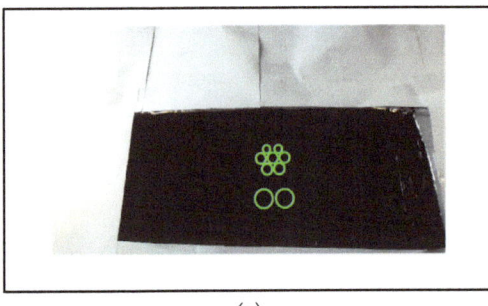
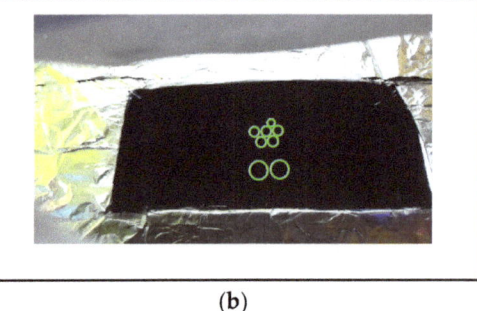

(a) (b)

Figure 17. Results of the comparison with Circular Hough Transfom: (**a**) Correct detection, (**b**) incomplete detection.

Finally, this initial study entirely fulfilled the goal of the project, and the automatic detection of the charging socket with well-known image processing operations was achieved. The practical application of the obtained results will be tested in the future, where the experiments will be conducted with a robot on electric vehicles with adequate industrial illumination equipment. The future managerial implications are the rent of a certain number of electric vehicles for testing purposes and the construction of an adequate real-world parking space for experiments with the robot in an industrial environment.

6. Conclusions

Herein, both the working concepts and the characteristics of an algorithm for the detection and extraction of the CCS2 charging socket for the automatic electric car charging application were introduced. The main steps of the charging socket extraction process were presented, i.e., intensity transformation, median filtering, binarization, and the series of morphological operations. The aim of this industrial research project was to develop a simple robot vision system with well-known and dependable image processing techniques to secure the trustiness of the robot's running process. Suitable experiments were conducted on certain vehicle body models with a built-in CCS2 socket. All experiments were accomplished successfully and the developed algorithm showed considerable accuracy, as well as an adequate robustness and resistance to adverse illumination conditions and poor capturing conditions. Based on the experiments, the main limitations of the algorithm in terms of inadequate lighting conditions were determined, and in the future, they will be avoided with a special illumination source on the constructed charging station. The inadequate illumination caused artefacts and various influences such as shadows, light reflection, poor visibility, etc., that resulted in a corrupted input RGB image and its corresponding depth map. All these problems are expected to be avoided with proper illumination equipment that will provide an adequate illumination to the depth camera. During the deployment of the image processing system, all the project requirements and instructions were accompanied. As a result, the project's aim was utterly achieved, and further development of the system will be continued with an installed UR10e robot and various electric vehicles on the appropriately constructed and illuminated parking lot.

7. Future Works

In future, a high-quality stereo camera with an industrial illumination source and a special 3D scanner mounted on a UR robot should be acquired and utilized for further research in the field of robotic vision for automotive applications related to autonomous electric vehicle charging robot development. The use of industrial illumination equipment is expected to solve the limitations of the algorithm in terms of the unsuited lighting conditions of the scene with the charging socket. Moreover, new experiments will be conducted on available electric vehicles with a UR10e cobot.

Funding: This research was funded by projects GINOP_PLUSZ-2.1.1-21-2022-00249 of the University of Obuda and 2020-1.1.2-PIACI-KFI-2020-00173 of the University of Dunaujavaros, co-financed by the Hungarian State and European Union.

Acknowledgments: The author would like to thank the editors and the anonymous reviewers for their valuable comments that significantly improved the quality of this paper.

Conflicts of Interest: The author declares no conflict of interest.

References

1. Akella, P.; Peshkin, M.; Colgate, E.; Wannasuphoprasit, W.; Nagesh, N.; Wells, J.; Holland, S.; Pearson, T.; Peacock, B. Cobots for the automobile assembly line. In Proceedings of the 1999 IEEE International Conference on Robotics and Automation (Cat. No.99CH36288C), Detroit, MI, USA, 10–15 May 1999; Volume 1, pp. 728–733. [CrossRef]
2. Asif, S.; Webb, P. Realtime Calibration of an Industrial Robot. *Appl. Syst. Innov.* **2022**, *5*, 96. [CrossRef]
3. Available online: https://www.universal-robots.com/ (accessed on 8 January 2020).
4. Cheng, K.W.E. Recent development on electric vehicles. In Proceedings of the 2009 3rd International Conference on Power Electronics Systems and Applications (PESA), Hong Kong, China, 20–22 May 2009; pp. 1–5, ISBN 978-1-4244-3845-7.
5. Zhou, X.; Zou, L.; Ma, Y.; Gao, Z.; Wu, Y.; Yin, J.; Xu, X. The current research on electric vehicle. In Proceedings of the 2016 Chinese Control and Decision Conference (CCDC), Yinchuan, China, 28–30 May 2016; pp. 5190–5194. [CrossRef]
6. Matharu, H.S.; Girase, V.; Pardeshi, D.; William, P. Design and Deployment of Hybrid Electric Vehicle. In Proceedings of the 2022 International Conference on Electronics and Renewable Systems (ICEARS), Tuticorin, India, 16–18 March 2022; pp. 331–334. [CrossRef]
7. Luo, W.; Shen, L. Design and Research of an Automatic Charging System for Electric Vehicles. In Proceedings of the 2020 15th IEEE Conference on Industrial Electronics and Applications (ICIEA), Kristiansand, Norway, 9–13 November 2020; pp. 1832–1836. [CrossRef]
8. Wang, H. A New Automatic Charging System for Electric Vehicles. In Proceedings of the 2021 2nd International Conference on Computing and Data Science (CDS), Stanford, CA, USA, 28–29 January 2021; pp. 19–26. [CrossRef]
9. Tadic, V.; Odry, A.; Burkus, E.; Kecskes, I.; Kiraly, Z.; Klincsik, M.; Sari, Z.; Vizvari, Z.; Toth, A.; Odry, P. Painting Path Planning for a Painting Robot with a RealSense Depth Sensor. *Appl. Sci.* **2021**, *11*, 1467. [CrossRef]
10. Tadic, V.; Odry, A.; Burkus, E.; Kecskes, I.; Kiraly, Z.; Odry, P. Edge-preserving Filtering and Fuzzy Image Enhancement in Depth Images Captured by Realsense Cameras in Robotic Applications. *Adv. Electr. Comput. Eng.* **2020**, *20*, 83–92. [CrossRef]
11. Tadic, V.; Odry, A.; Burkus, E.; Kecskes, I.; Kiraly, Z.; Vizvari, Z.; Toth, A.; Odry, P. Application of the ZED Depth Sensor for Painting Robot Vision System Development. *IEEE Access* **2021**, *9*, 117845–117859. [CrossRef]
12. Tadic, V.; Toth, A.; Vizvari, Z.; Klincsik, M.; Sari, Z.; Sarcevic, P.; Sarosi, J.; Biro, I. Perspectives of RealSense and ZED Depth Sensors for Robotic Vision Applications. *Machines* **2022**, *10*, 183. [CrossRef]
13. Gonzales, R.C.; Woods, R.E. *Digital Image Processing*, 4th ed.; Pearson: New York, NY, USA, 2018.
14. Gonzales, R.C.; Woods, R.; Eddins, S.L. *Digital Image Processing Using MATLAB*, 3rd ed.; Gatesmark: Knoxville, TN, USA, 2020.
15. Flacco, F.; Kroger, T.; De Luca, A.; Khatib, O. A Depth Space Approach to Human-Robot Collision Avoidance. In Proceedings of the 2012 IEEE International Conference on Robotics and Automation RiverCentre, Saint Paul, MN, USA, 14–18 May 2012.
16. Saxena, A.; Chung, S.H.; Ng, A.Y. 3-D Depth Reconstruction from a Single Still Image. *Int. J. Comput. Vis.* **2008**, *76*, 53–69. [CrossRef]
17. Sterzentsenko, V.; Karakottas, A.; Papachristou, A.; Zioulis, N.; Doumanoglou, A.; Zarpalas, D.; Daras, P. A low-cost, flexible and portable volumetric capturing system. In Proceedings of the 14th International Conference on Signal-Image Technology & Internet-Based Systems (SITIS), Las Palmas de Gran Canaria, Spain, 26–29 November 2018. [CrossRef]
18. Carey, N.; Nagpal, R.; Werfel, J. Fast, accurate, small-scale 3D scene capture using a low-cost depth sensor. In Proceedings of the 2017 IEEE Winter Conference on Applications of Computer Vision (WACV), Santa Rosa, CA, USA, 24–31 March 2017. [CrossRef]

19. Labbé, M.; Michaud, F. RTAB-Map as an open-source lidar and visual simultaneous localization and mapping library for large-scale and long-term online operation. *J. Field Robot.* **2018**, *36*, 416–446. [CrossRef]
20. Rusu, R.B.; Marton, Z.C.; Blodow, N.; Dolha, M.; Beetz, M. Towards 3D Point cloud based object maps for household environments. *Robot. Auton. Syst.* **2008**, *56*, 927941. [CrossRef]
21. Schwarze, T.; Lauer, M. Wall Estimation from StereoVision in Urban Street Canyons. In Proceedings of the 10th International Conference on Informatics in Control, Automation and Robotics, Reykjavík, Iceland, 29–31 July 2013; pp. 83–90. [CrossRef]
22. Deschaud, J.-E.; Goulette, F. A Fast and Accurate Plane Detection Algorithm for Large Noisy Point Clouds Using Filtered Normals and Voxel Growing. In Proceedings of the 3DPVT, Paris, France, 17–20 May 2010.
23. Aghi, D.; Mazzia, V.; Chiaberge, M. Local Motion Planner for Autonomous Navigation in Vineyards with a RGB-D Camera-Based Algorithm and Deep Learning Synergy. *Machines* **2020**, *8*, 27. [CrossRef]
24. Yow, K.-C.; Kim, I. General Moving Object Localization from a SingleFlying Camera. *Appl. Sci.* **2020**, *10*, 6945. [CrossRef]
25. Qi, X.; Wang, W.; Liao, Z.; Zhang, X.; Yang, D.; Wei, R. Object Semantic Grid Mapping with 2D LiDAR and RGB-D Camera for Domestic Robot Navigation. *Appl. Sci.* **2020**, *10*, 5782. [CrossRef]
26. Tadic, V.; Odry, A.; Toth, A.; Vizvari, Z.; Odry, P. Fuzzified Circular Gabor Filter for Circular and Near-Circular Object Detection. *IEEE Access* **2020**, *8*, 96706–96713. [CrossRef]
27. Pan, M.; Sun, C.; Liu, J.; Wang, Y. Automatic recognition and location system for electrlc vehicle charging port in complex environment. *IET Image Process.* **2020**, *14*, 2263–2272. [CrossRef]
28. Zhang, H.; Jin, X. A Method for New Energy Electric Vehicle Charging Hole Detection and Location Based on Machine Vision. In Proceedings of the 5th International Conference on Environment, Materials, Chemistry and Power Electronics, Zhengzhou, China, 11–12 August 2016.
29. Mišeikis, J.; Rüther, M.; Walzel, B.; Hirz, M.; Brunner, H. 3D Vision Guided Robotic Charging Station for Electric and Plug-in Hybrid Vehicles. In Proceedings of the OAGM&ARW Joint Workshop, Wien, Austria, 10–12 May 2017. [CrossRef]
30. Quan, P.; Lou, Y.; Lin, H.; Liang, Z.; Di, S. Research on Fast Identification and Location of Contour Features of Electric Vehicle Charging Port in Complex Scenes. *IEEE Access* **2022**, *10*, 26702–26714. [CrossRef]
31. Quan, P.; Lou, Y.; Lin, H.; Liang, Z.; Wei, D.; Di, S. Research on Fast Recognition and Localization of an Electric Vehicle Charging Port Based on a Cluster Template Matching Algorithm. *Sensors* **2022**, *22*, 3599. [CrossRef]
32. Lou, Y.; Di, S. Design of a Cable-Driven Auto-Charging Robot for Electric Vehicles. *IEEE Access* **2020**, *8*, 15640–15655. [CrossRef]
33. Lin, H.; Quan, P.; Liang, Z.; Lou, Y.; Wei, D.; Di, S. Collision Localization and Classification on the End-Effector of a Cable-Driven Manipulator Applied to EV Auto-Charging Based on DCNN–SVM. *Sensors* **2022**, *22*, 3439. [CrossRef]
34. Li, T.; Xia, C.; Yu, M.; Tang, P.; Wei, W.; Zhang, D. Scale-Invariant Localization of Electric Vehicle Charging Port via Semi-Global Matching of Binocular Images. *Appl. Sci.* **2022**, *12*, 5247. [CrossRef]
35. Chablat, D.; Mattacchione, R.; Ottaviano, E. Design of a robot for the automatic charging of an electric car. In *ROMANSY 24-Robot Design, Dynamics and Control*; Springer: Berlin/Heidelberg, Germany, 2022.
36. Available online: https://www.stereolabs.com (accessed on 10 November 2022).
37. Ortiz, L.E.; Cabrera, E.V.; Goncalves, L.M. Depth Data Error Modeling of the ZED 3D Vision Sensor from Stereolabs. *Electron. Lett. Comput. Vis. Image Anal.* **2018**, *17*, 1–15. [CrossRef]
38. Foster, N.J.; Sanderson, A.C. Determining Object Orientation Using Ellipse Fitting. In *Proceedings of SPIE, Intelligent Robots and Computer Vision*; Cambridge Symposium: Cambridge, MA, USA, 1985; Volume 0521. [CrossRef]
39. Odry, Á. An Open-Source Test Environment for Effective Development of MARG-Based Algorithms. *Sensors* **2021**, *21*, 1183. [CrossRef]
40. Odry, Á.; Fullér, R.; Rudas, I.J.; Odry, P. Kalman filter for mobile-robot attitude estimation: Novel optimized and adaptive solutions. *Mech. Syst. Signal Process.* **2018**, *110*, 569–589. [CrossRef]
41. Available online: https://www.mathworks.com (accessed on 20 November 2022).
42. Available online: https://www.nodered.org (accessed on 4 December 2022).

Disclaimer/Publisher's Note: The statements, opinions and data contained in all publications are solely those of the individual author(s) and contributor(s) and not of MDPI and/or the editor(s). MDPI and/or the editor(s) disclaim responsibility for any injury to people or property resulting from any ideas, methods, instructions or products referred to in the content.

MDPI AG
Grosspeteranlage 5
4052 Basel
Switzerland
Tel.: +41 61 683 77 34

Electronics Editorial Office
E-mail: electronics@mdpi.com
www.mdpi.com/journal/electronics

Disclaimer/Publisher's Note: The title and front matter of this reprint are at the discretion of the Guest Editors. The publisher is not responsible for their content or any associated concerns. The statements, opinions and data contained in all individual articles are solely those of the individual Editors and contributors and not of MDPI. MDPI disclaims responsibility for any injury to people or property resulting from any ideas, methods, instructions or products referred to in the content.